Palgrave Studies in the Enlightenment, Romanticism and Cultures of Print

General Editors: **Professor Anne K.** Mellor and **Professor Clifford Siskin**

Editorial Board: **Isobel Armstrong**, Birkbeck; **John Bender**, Stanford; **Alan Bewell**, Toronto; **Peter de Bolla**, Cambridge; **Robert Miles**, Stirling; **Claudia L.** Johnson, Princeton; **Saree Makdisi**, UCLA; **Felicity Nussbaum**, UCLA; **Mary Poovey**, NYU; **Janet Todd**, Glasgow

Palgrave Studies in the Enlightenment, Romanticism and Cultures of Print will feature work that does not fit comfortably within established boundaries—whether between periods or between disciplines. Uniquely, it will combine efforts to engage the power and materiality of print with explorations of gender, race, and class. By attending as well to intersections of literature with the visual arts, medicine, law, and science, the series will enable a large-scale rethinking of the origins of modernity.

Titles include:

Scott Black
OF ESSAYS AND READING IN EARLY MODERN BRITAIN

Claire Brock
THE FEMINIZATION OF FAME, 1750–1830

Brycchan Carey
BRITISH ABOLITIONISM AND THE RHETORIC OF SENSIBILITY
Writing, Sentiment, and Slavery, 1760–1807

E. J. Clery
THE FEMINIZATION DEBATE IN 18TH-CENTURY ENGLAND
Literature, Commerce and Luxury

Adriana Craciun
BRITISH WOMEN WRITERS AND THE FRENCH REVOLUTION
Citizens of the World

Peter de Bolla, Nigel Leask and David Simpson (*editors*)
LAND, NATION AND CULTURE, 1740–1840
Thinking the Republic of Taste

Ian Haywood
BLOODY ROMANTICISM
Spectacular Violence and the Politics of Representation, 1776–1832

Anthony S. Jarrells
BRITAIN'S BLOODLESS REVOLUTIONS
1688 and the Romantic Reform of Literature

Mary Waters
BRITISH WOMEN WRITERS AND THE PROFESSION OF LITERARY CRITICISM, 1789–1832

David Worrall
THE POLITICS OF ROMANTIC THEATRICALITY, 1787–1832
The Road to the Stage

Palgrave Studies in the Enlightenment, Romanticism and Cultures of Print
Series Standing Order ISBN 1–4039–3408–8 hardback
1–4039–3409–6 paperback *(outside North America only)*

You can receive future titles in this series as they are published by placing a standing order. Please contact your bookseller or, in case of difficulty, write to us at the address below with your name and address, the title of the series and the ISBN quoted above.

Customer Services Department, Macmillan Distribution Ltd, Houndmills, Basingstoke, Hampshire RG21 6XS, England

The Politics of Romantic Theatricality, 1787–1832

The Road to the Stage

David Worrall

First published 2007 by
PALGRAVE MACMILLAN
Houndmills, Basingstoke, Hampshire RG21 6XS and
175 Fifth Avenue, New York, N.Y. 10010
Companies and representatives throughout the world

PALGRAVE MACMILLAN is the global academic imprint of the Palgrave Macmillan division of St. Martin's Press, LLC and of Palgrave Macmillan Ltd. Macmillan® is a registered trademark in the United States, United Kingdom and other countries. Palgrave is a registered trademark in the European Union and other countries.

ISBN-13: 978–0–230–51802–5 hardback
ISBN-10: 0–230–51802–8 hardback

This book is printed on paper suitable for recycling and made from fully managed and sustained forest sources.

A catalogue record for this book is available from the British Library.

Library of Congress Cataloging-in-Publication Data
Worrall, David.
    The politics of Romantic theatricality, 1787–1832:the road to the stage/ by David Worrall.
        p.   cm. — (Palgrave studies in the Enlightenment, romanticism and the cultures of print)
    Includes bibliographical references (p.   ) and index.
    ISBN-13: 978–0–230–51802–5 (cloth)
    ISBN-10: 0–230–51802–8 (cloth)
    1. Musical theater—England—London—18th century.   2. Musical theater—England—London—19th century.   3. Music and state—England—London—History.   4. Music—Social aspects—England—London.   5. Romanticism—England—London.   I. Title.
    ML1731.3.W672007
    792.09421'033—dc22   2006052972

10   9   8   7   6   5   4   3   2   1
16   15   14   13   12   11   10   09   08   07

Printed and bound in Great Britain by
Antony Rowe Ltd, Chippenham and Eastbourne

Contents

Preface

I am grateful to the Arts and Humanities Research Council for research leave in 2001–2002 which, together with a fellowship at the Huntington Library, California, enabled me both to write *Theatric Revolution: Drama, Censorship and Romantic Period Subcultures, 1773–1832* (2006) and complete the first half of *The Politics of Romantic Theatricality, 1787–1832: The Road to the Stage*. Throughout, the British Library has been a wonderfully functioning resource. I am also grateful to Lynda Pratt for introducing me to the Hallward Library, Nottingham University, where I first chanced across Leman Thomas Rede's extraordinary *The Road to the Stage*, and to Stuart Sillars for supplying a photocopy of the *Confession of Charles French*, the misguided Canadian who went to see *Tom and Jerry*.

Nottingham Trent University and all my colleagues there provide an ever supportive and encouraging environment. Through sun at the Huntington, snow at the Houghton and spring at the Beinecke, Mei-Ying Sung continues to be my loving companion in our journey through life.

Introduction

The subtitle of this book is drawn from Leman Thomas Rede's *The Road to the Stage; or, The Performer's Preceptor* (1827). Rede's extraordinary volume was not merely an acting manual of gesture and speech but offered would-be players 'Clear and Ample Instructions for Obtaining Theatrical Engagements,' together with details of the principal Georgian touring, metropolitan and provincial companies, all supplemented with historically invaluable advice about contemporary make-up and wigging.[1] It is a remarkable work, bringing to light many forgotten performance practices from a period of drama still relatively neglected by modern scholars.

My purpose is to elucidate the structural conditions of Romantic-period drama and to argue that – despite censorship and the imposition of burletta – the playhouses managed to remain extraordinarily vital in the midst of the oppressive conditions affecting writing for the stage. Although not a primary concern, by contrast, a number of the canonical Romantic poets encountered – with amazing naivety – the legal, institutional and regulatory mechanisms which impaired or even obliterated their efforts to find theatrical production on the London stage. A principal aim of this book will be to show that drama outside of the two royal patent theatres of Covent Garden and Drury Lane developed within what had virtually become a separate public sphere of drama, an essentially popular or plebeian network of intricate intertextuality largely cut off from the heritage of English spoken drama as exemplified by Shakespeare.

Rede's *The Road to the Stage*, posthumously revised by his brother in 1836 and republished in revised New York editions of 1858, 1859, 1861, 1864 and 1868, records the repertoire, playhouses and acting practices of the early decades of the nineteenth century, all set out for the assistance of a new generation of actors and actresses on both sides of the Atlantic. The Londoners who visited and acted in the urban private theatres described in Chapter 6 were only one component in a growing-class mobility connected to theatricality. The 'little painted Trollop' the poet John Keats observed, costumed and ready to act at the Minor private theatre in 1818, was part of the upwardly mobile young population of London possessed of an active appetite for acting and theatricality. As well as being present in Catherine Street off the Strand when Keats was present, this theatrical propensity reached deep into the provinces. The comedian Thomas Meadows's compilation of new and abridged songs and sketches for amateur performance, *Thespian Gleanings* (1805), printed in Ulverston, Cumberland, where Meadows was associated with the local theatre, was sold by booksellers across the whole of the north of England but dedicated to his local 'Society of Strangers at Home, or, Theatrical Club.' In Ayr, Scotland, a theatre company that had originally opened in a soap factory attracted the great Edmund Kean to their new playhouse. Ayr theatre performances of works such as Benjamin Webster's *The Golden Farmer; or, the Last Crime: A Domestic Drama* (c.1832), a tale about a corn-chandler moonlighting as a highwayman, are good indicators not only of local anti-farming, anti-landowner sentiment but also how provincial theatres carefully selected their repertoire from the lesser metropolitan playhouses such as the Royal Coburg, Sadler's Wells and Pavilion Theatre where Webster's play had already been performed.[2]

Works such as *Thespian Gleanings* are important because they denote the new types of social configuration initiated by amateur performance in the Romantic period, creating definable theatrical followings right across the country and forming new types of sociability which some-times clearly transcended demarcations of class.[3] In 1820 a Shrewsbury correspondent wrote to R.W. Elliston, manager of the Olympic and Theatre Royal Drury Lane, recommending for employment (albeit only in 'the lower walks of the Theatre'), a 20-year-old 'poor Laborer's Son' then working as an 'out door' servant but who had 'completed a Stage Scenery & Figures & performed [John C. Cross's] Black Beard [1809] in private families.'[4] These plebeian enthusiasts, exactly the sort of theat-rical precursors of the Cockney literary vanguard reviews such as *Black-wood's Edinburgh Magazine* most feared, were almost certainly typical purchasers of Rede's manual of acting.

As a 20-year-old, Rede had made his first stage appearance in 1819 at the theatre in Stafford in the English Midlands, playing Wilford in George Colman the Younger's *The Iron Chest* (1796), a successful Drury

Lane adaptation of William Godwin's novel *Caleb Williams; or, Things as They Are* (1794), earning his living by 'perpetrating[sic] divers melodramatic characters in the provinces.'[5] By October 1821 he had travelled to London and performed in I.R. Planché's unprinted Adelphi theatre burletta, *Capers at Canterbury* (1821). Unlike earlier guides to theatrical employment, such as James Winston's *Theatric Tourist* (1805), Rede's *The Road to the Stage* was full of practical information.[6] It passed on to newcomers such professional tricks as keeping 'a greased napkin' in the iron chest so that Wilford can quickly wipe off his base make-up colour of pomatum or carmine to affect the pallor of shock upon his discovery by Sir Edward Mortimer, Colman's substitute for Godwin's Falkland.[7] Rede must also have been one of the first professional actors to have witnessed T.P. Cooke's Monster in the founding Richard Brinsley Peake, English Opera House (Lyceum), adaptation of Mary Shelley's *Frankenstein*, then renamed as *Presumption! or, the Fate of Frankenstein* (1823), passing on the understated advice that 'appearance may be the main feature of [the] part' in the context of advising on make-up.[8] He also gave warnings on such practical matters as the levels of fines imposed by managers for professional misdemeanours ('For being obviously intoxicated when engaged in the performance, one guinea') as well as the likely salaries for varying categories of actor, for example, the different rates of pay for 'First Old Men,' 'Walking Gentlemen' ('in Dublin even, not exceeding two guineas per week'), 'Fine Ladies – Singing Chambermaids – Old Women – and Walking Ladies.'[9] His comments on acting opportunities for female players are particularly important. He thought 'the system of modern education' had made 'First Singing Ladies' 'more numerous than male vocalists,' suggesting that a good general education was the best prerequisite for a profession that regularly required actors to adapt swiftly, retain mobility and learn lines rapidly. According to Rede's testimony, the attractions of becoming one of the 'First Singing Ladies' were compelling: 'Any young lady embracing this line, and possessed of even a moderate share of talent, could seldom lack a provincial engagement, and would stand excellent chance of metropolitan distinction.'[10] This, indeed, was the road to the stage.

One of the underlying propositions of this book is that burletta, drama set to music, was the dominant dramatic mode for the majority of Romantic-period playhouses and for the London theatres in particular. This was because burletta was the only dramatic form to have legal meaning. The original insight into the role of burletta in the development of Georgian drama was convincingly laid out in Joseph Donohue's study of over 30 years ago, *Theatre in the Age of Kean* (1975), yet its

implications have been neglected.[11] Much of this book will trace particular burlettas, how they developed, and why melodrama is a misleading
literary category with which to designate the principal modes of writing
for the stage. In the age of speaking actors such as John Philip Kemble,
Sarah Siddons or Edmund Kean, all dependent on the monopolistic
theatres, the majority of London playhouses were restricted to singing
or miming. This is why Rede advised that employment opportunities
were plentiful for theatrical 'Singing Ladies' and it explains why they
outnumbered the available male roles in the burletta houses.

As a rough rule of thumb, on any average winter's night in London
(the main theatrical season), the capital's licensed theatres would
scarcely have been able to support eight speaking roles for actresses, and
then only assuming the uncommon likelihood that Covent Garden and
Drury Lane were both playing dramas from the Elizabethan or Restoration period or else modern tragic or comic drama written for speech. The
practice of having a mainpiece and an afterpiece each evening would
not have increased the number of female speaking roles because the
afterpiece was likely to have been a pantomime or burletta. Information about relative quantities of costume property provides definitive
evidence of the gender imbalance. An inventory and valuation of the
wardrobe department at Drury Lane (a speaking house) in August 1819
gave the value of men's clothing as £2966.18s. in contrast to the
playhouse's stock of female clothing valued at a mere £807.4s.10½d
(although it is likely both sexes shared the £165.15s. 6d worth of 'Hats &
feathers').[12] Not only was the profession of acting generally precarious,
but for women who sought speaking roles the monopoly system ensured
that employment opportunities were particularly slender. In turn, this
explains why actresses were sometimes inclined to protest both at asper-
sions on their private conduct and at perceived managerial unfairness.[13]
For those prepared to carry on working within the monopoly system,
such restrictions on speaking ensured not only financial success but also
national celebrity. The celebrity of individual actresses such as Sarah
Siddons was a cultural phenomenon unparalleled in British theatrical
history and her iconography was readily assisted by leading socialite
painters such as Sir Joshua Reynolds, yet it was founded upon her work
for London's theatrical cartel.[14] For male speaking actors, the circumstances were scarcely more equitable when compared to the majority
of performers. In protests made by Covent Garden actors in 1800 over
the theatre's charges to actors for holding benefit night performances
(which gave the whole night's takings to one named player), the playhouse realized that its ability to operate was 'governed and controlled

by Eight Performers.'[15] As far as speaking roles were concerned, there would have been another eight equally crucial male performers at Drury Lane but, otherwise, Londoners were left to Rede's 'Singing Ladies' of burletta and pantomime.

In 1827, Rede estimated that there were 'six thousand individuals who are known to possess claims to the titles of actor and actress.'[16] In London, those (approximately) 8 female actresses and 16 male actors employed on any one winter's evening in speaking roles were catering for an impossibly large nightly catchment of around 10,000 persons attending some kind of theatrical entertainment. In other words, for most people spoken drama was the preserve of an elite although this did not incapacitate their desire to experience other kinds of theatrical entertainment. While it is notorious that Nahum Tate's *King Lear* (1681) still held the stage during this period, it is far more remarkable that the monopolistic system intentionally restricted the number of people in London who had any chance of seeing it. The figure of 10,000 people as London's nightly audience may seem exaggerated but it is a reasonably reliable 'guess-timate' based on theatre capacities and denotes the enormous demographics of the capital's theatre-land, its economic and social importance and the size of the populations theatres served. The rebuilt and refurbished royal theatres, Covent Garden and Drury Lane, each held audiences of about 3000 by the early 1810s. Although the royal theatres can seldom have been full, there were a number of other theatrical spaces available in London although, of course, all of them lacked permission to perform spoken drama. In 1817, the Lyceum Theatre (also known as the English Opera House), a few hundred yards along Bow Street from Covent Garden, had an estimated capacity of 1750 while the Olympic Theatre, Wych Street, a stone's throw away from the Theatre Royal, Drury Lane, was offered for sale in 1820 with the *Particulars and Conditions of Sale* registering a capacity of some 1320 places.[17] By 1827, Thomas Dibdin (ex-manager of the Surrey Theatre, a Lambeth playhouse derived from the Royal Amphitheatre in 1817), counted 22 public places of dramatic entertainment in London which, he noted, 'amounted to nearly one for every letter of the alphabet,' plus six or seven so-called private theatres bordering on illegality.[18] In 1836, Leman Thomas Rede's brother could count 22 London playhouses – all with regularly defined seasons – quite apart from 6 private theatres (discussed below) which he considered to have become more or less regular venues.[19] Up until the late 1820s nearly all of these theatres survived precariously, avoiding litigation by the royal theatres or withdrawal of licenses by local magistrates by mounting burletta and pantomime. In other words, in the age of Siddons and Kean or of Wordsworth, Coleridge and Keats, spoken drama in London was performed by an elite group of actors and actresses working in just two playhouses. About half of those Londoners visiting the theatre nightly had no possibility of experiencing the 'national drama' even in the form of Tate's *King Lear*.

The economic and monopolistic obstacles placed in the path of Londoners wishing to attend spoken drama were frequently noted. As the prolific but neglected Jacob Beuler protested in his song of 1833, 'Major *versus* Minors, A Petition to the Lovers of the Drama' performed from the stage of The Surrey Theatre:

> But great men's law is not the poor's
> When talent it condemns, sirs,
> And lets the giants take from us
> What we may not from them, sirs.
> E'en *you* must not see Shakespeare's plays
> Perform'd, unless you're willing
> To toddle six or seven miles,
> And pay down seven shillings.[20]

Apart from Beuler's estimate of the carriage fare and seat price, Horace Foote's *Companion to the Theatres* (1829) corroborates the expense by giving the hackney carriage fare for someone travelling from Blackfriars Road to Astley's Amphitheatre in Westminster Road as 1s.6d as opposed to 3s. to reach Drury Lane.[21] As the Surrey Theatre was also in Blackfriars Road, only extraordinary reasons of literary devotion could have pursuaded anyone living in that vicinity to make the journey across the river to hear something like Tate's *King Lear* at a patent theatre.

While these were the basic physical and structural conditions of drama, there were many more regulatory conditions of great intricacy governing Romantic-period theatrical representation. These considerations permeate the substance of this book. Chapter 1 will describe in more detail why the issue of vocalization, dramatic sound, was the controlling fundamental condition of drama and what this means for the role of music in Romantic drama and why melodrama should not be considered as the period's principal generic form. Chapter 2 extends the discussion of theatrical regulation by examining how one specific drama of the early 1790s, Robert Merry's *The Magican No Conjurer*, managed to circumvent the censor and allude to topical events. Chapter 3 turns to the representation of black people on the Romantic-period stage, with particular emphasis on the Haymarket's *Benevolent*

Planters (1789) and the Royalty's pantomime, *Harlequin Mungo; or, A Peep into the Tower* (1787). In this chapter, some of the problematics of black-mask harlequinade and black-face make-up, together with the presence of differing audiences and theatrical environments operating within different regulatory conditions in London, are shown to have led to highly varied responses to slavery even in the context of a single city. Chapter 4 examines William Henry Ireland's *Vortigern* Shakespeare forgery of 1796 in relationship to the feasibility of attempting to write spoken drama under a system which militated against it. Chapter 5 examines the rise of Cockney characters in the burletta playhouses, particularly during the immediate era of William Thomas Moncrieff's *Giovanni in London; or, The Libertine Reclaimed* (1817), and argues that the notorious *Blackwood's Edinburgh Magazine* attacks on the Cockney school of poetry during that year should be viewed in the context of how Londoners were represented on the stage and how they increasingly participated in fugitive private theatres of the type visited by John Keats in 1818. Chapters 6 and 7 extend this discussion by focusing on the burlettas surrounding adaptations of Pierce Egan's *Life in London* (1820), a series of entertainments generically known as 'Tom and Jerry' plays, showing how the enthusiasm for Moncrieff's Adelphi Theatre burletta of *Tom and Jerry* encoded a model of emerging types of social behaviour based upon youthful delinquency. The Conclusion focuses on an extraordinary incident in Canada where a murder was committed during a performance of a Tom and Jerry play.

What is meant by a plebeian public sphere of drama? The core of the answer is that this was a contemporary drama deliberately displaced from the conventional canon of literary writing by hegemonic forces and where playhouse venues became increasingly located in London's working-class areas. The basic structural conditions of a 'Theatrical Oligarchy,' largely within the terms described here in connection with the late Georgian period, had been in place since the early eighteenth century and were repeatedly enforced.[22] William J. Burling's *Summer Theatre in London, 1661–1820, and the Rise of the Haymarket Theatre* (2000) has noted about the period immediately following the 1737 Licensing Act that 'The hegemonic legal system, in this instance, served well to affirm the monopolistic "rights" of the holders of the patents, who reasserted their power in the face of those aspiring newcomers [wishing] to establish themselves.'[23] These terms were well understood and amounted to a cartel over spoken drama. As early as 1743, the author of *Tyranny Triumphant! . . . Remarks on the Famous Cartel Lately Agreed on by the Masters of the Two Theatres* repeatedly alluded to the 'monopolizing

Cartel' of Covent Garden and Drury Lane, which affected the careers of both actors and writers (p. 17). From its inception, as John O'Brien's *Harlequin Britain: Pantomime and Entertainment, 1690–1760* (2004) has shown, the beginnings of the imposition of theatrical censorship were borne more readily by the patentees on account of the reassurance it gave that their privileges would be honoured.[24] Right into the nineteenth century, this literary monopoly (strictly a *duopoly*) was jealously guarded and actively policed by the patentees. Or, as the theatre manager and playwright Thomas John Dibdin ruefully called them, 'the Gog, Magog, and Little David of legitimate monopoly.'[25]

Once displaced, the development of contemporary writing for the stage tended to arise not from the established canon of literary drama but from its association with other types of production in more closely related venues. This intricate intertextuality, nearly all of it occurring outside London's two winter royal theatres in Covent Garden and Drury Lane, will be the subject of extended study in Chapters 5–8. The intertextualities between playhouses at this time, and also across differently licensed playhouses, have been carefully examined by Moyra Haslett in the 1810s, with respect to adaptations of the Don Juan story. Although Haslett is principally concerned with following the context and precursors of Byron's poem *Don Juan* (1819), she accurately concludes that 'burlesques ... became increasingly inter-referential as the proliferations of Don Juan productions caused a considerable degree of mutual awareness and cross-comparison between literally competing versions.'[26] Unaccountably, the role of the theatrical context in the inception and reception of Byron's *Don Juan* – even though both Dibdin's *Don Giovanni; or, A Spectre on Horseback!* and Moncrieff's *Giovanni in London* preceded Byron's poem by nearly a year – has since been dismissed in Jane Stabler's more recent study of *Don Juan* as 'the surrender of the particular to the general.'[27] Such diminutions may successfully recommodify Byron as a Romantic poet but they do little to urge a reconsideration of drama in the context of contemporary popular culture, even when it seems a matter of simple demonstration that extremely popular dramas about Don Giovanni had been performed in the months before Byron wrote *Don Juan*.

The study of this subject has been assisted in recent times by two ground-breaking monographs that have fundamentally transformed our understanding of the drama of this period. The first is Gillian Russell's *The Theatres of War: Performance, Politics, and Society, 1793–1815* (1995) which establishes, beyond any doubt, that theatricality and the playing of plays were deeply embedded in the rituals, pastimes and everyday life of the British military, whether serving at home or overseas.[28] Russell's book elects for an anthropological approach to Georgian drama and marks a divergent direction of approach to studies such as Betsy Bolton's *Women, Nationalism, and the Romantic Stage: Theatre and Politics in Britain, 1780–1800* (2001), which opts to trace the 'theatrical anology,' the performativity of theatre within political or gendered discourses.[29] Russell's book uncovers a previously neglected side of the literary life of the nation, one which is as surprising and unexpected as it is distant from the concerns of conventional prescriptions of what constituted the role of Romantic-period authors and their readership. Russell's *Theatres of War* forces an awareness of the sheer social incommensurability of apparently co-existing late Georgian literary forms. The issues raised by Russell's book for our understanding of the social role of Georgian-period English literature begin with the realization that the dissemination of dramatic texts was not only supported by an increasingly popular print culture, one conclusively capable of reaching the furthest outposts of the empire, but Russell's study also demonstrates that printed drama, perhaps uniquely, prompted new and unexpected social configurations. This contemporary propensity to theatricality was likely to be far more culturally complex, much more dependent upon reorganizing physical space and personnel, than were the consequences of acts of solitary or domestic reading. In other words, Romantic-period drama's sociability was more far reaching than either the subject matter of its plays or the audience composition of the playhouses. My own study is similarly concerned with providing a social historiography or anthropology of drama after the pattern of Russell's *Theatres of War*.

The second major monograph on the period's drama is Jane Moody's *Illegitimate: Theatre in London, 1770–1840* (2000). Moody's book sets out much of the underlying preconditions of contemporary drama. Of particular significance is her attempt to uncover not only the 'spectacular conflagration, urban entrepreneurship and social metamorphosis of drama,' but also to try to capture the shift from a verbal, rhetorical drama (after all, the perquisite of the royal theatres) to a 'corporeal dramaturgy which highlighted the expressive body of the performer.'[30] The recovery of contemporary dramatic techniques, their contribution towards further levels of meaning – each with its own particular cultural, gender or political significance – is beyond the scope of the present writer. Moody's discussions of the careers and artistic development of such famous burletta house players as Eliza Vestris, Joe Grimaldi and Charles Mathews all provide important information for our understanding of what she terms the age's 'illegitimate celebrities.'[31] The areas of drama's verbal and visually performative discourses laid out in Moody's book provide the essential underpinning for my own contribution to the study of this field. Even a cursory reading of *Illegitimate* will reveal the recovery of an often bewildering and, for most scholars trained in canonical Romanticism, decidedly unfamiliar literary terrain. My own book will set out some of the cultural implications of a drama which, as Moody consistently argues, had largely developed independently from the major canonical writers of this period when an interest in poetry and the novel dominated. Where Moody's study swiftly and effectively maps out the principal boundaries, my own will concentrate on the relationship between drama, and the political and plebeian culture. In summary, my study will examine the workings of the kind of plebeian sphere outlined in the wider print culture of Kevin Gilmartin's *Print Politics: the Press and Radical Opposition in Early Nineteenth Century England* (1996), drawing on the historical framework of Romantic-period drama laid out in Moody's monograph *Illegitimate*, but with a working methodology owing much to Russell's *Theatres of War*.

For anyone trying to come to terms with the intricacies of the period's drama, a number of studies have significantly contributed to establishing both the vigour and the diversity of Romantic-period theatre as well as the economic basis of its survival. The manner in which a specific genre was explored on stage, and how vital texts in drama's representation of slavery for London's audiences were configured, can be examined in Jeffrey N. Cox's two important and lucidly editorialized anthologies, *Seven Gothic Dramas, 1789–1825* (1992) and *Slavery, Abolition and Emancipation: Writing in the British Romantic Period, Drama* (1999). Since theatre, at basis, is concerned with the physical processes involved in manoeuvring audiences into theatres and players onto stages, on a nightly basis, both the economic and legislative framework of the playhouses are bound to have developed into extremely well-elaborated practices during the Romantic period. William J. Burling's *Summer Theatre in London, 1661–1820, and the Rise of the Haymarket Theatre* (2000) focuses on a particular London playhouse, and documents its finances and repertoire, while Tracy C. Davis's *The Economics of the British Stage 1800–1914* (2000) fills out the broader picture, noting that by the beginning of the nineteenth century, there already existed a complex economic network of monopolistic assertions and counterclaims to a theatrical free trade.[32]

To answer the question of what is meant by a plebeian public sphere of drama in more detail involves reconstructing the specific historical conditions under which dramatic writing and theatrical representation took place during this period. The basic conditions may be simply stated but, inevitably, their actual cultural manifestations were rather more complex in practice. To anyone new to the drama of this period, its starkest difference from either early-modern or modern writing for the stage was the severe curtailment of speech, and it can be taken as axiomatic that the censorship of stage texts seriously disables any notion of a bourgeois public sphere. In the land of Shakespeare, where the Bard was swiftly progressing to iconic status, the performance of spoken drama was highly restricted. Here follows a series of discussions relative to the principal regulatory and structural components of Romantic-period theatre. A more detailed exposition of genre, censorship, legitimacy, vocalization and music will then be pursued in Chapter 1.

The rules were these: for all the British theatres falling under the jurisdiction of the Lord Chamberlain's Examiner of Plays (effectively the official censor), burletta was the only permissible dramatic form, except for the royal theatres holding patents of operation whose origins dated back to the Restoration.[33] As William J. Burling has noted, at the beginning of the taste for burletta – which he dates to 1758–1762 – when the new burletta companies appeared to be competing directly with the Haymarket's licensee, Samuel Foote, 'For reasons we shall never know, the Lord Chamberlain did not license *both* the burletta company and Foote's troupe.'[34] As so often in the narrative of eighteenth-century drama, the legislation continually acted to retard not only the development of new dramatic forms but also the playhouses in which they could be performed. As to what constituted burletta, for the modern reader the working definition can be taken as a drama where the words are set to music. Unnervingly, burletta was never subjected to a precise definition. This lack of generic precision struck right to the heart of the regulatory process. In 1824, George Colman the Younger, the incoming Examiner of Plays and a considerable veteran playwright of burletta himself, could not define the genre when it came to imposing it on a non-patent theatre which was chancing its hand with a new Examiner and testing the rules. But the Lord Chamberlain could not explain burletta when Colman asked him for assistance, although both were able to agree that it involved words set to music.[35] Nevertheless, burletta was the dominant literary form for stage performance in London and this stipulation was repeatedly enforced in practice.

As Joseph Donohue has pointed out, burletta is a primary feature of the period's stage drama. For the non-patent theatres in London, the musical setting was not an option but a legal requirement. The implications of continued enforcement mean that other genres were effectively subsumed within categorizations of either burletta or burletta's contrary, the drama of the spoken word. The principal issue at stake governing the prevalence of dramatic genres in stage representation during this period was not connected to the availability or extent of conventional literary forms (such as comedy, tragedy or the emerging form of melodrama), but to theatrical vocalization. It was not the particular literary genre in which a dramatic piece was located which helped situate it within its contemporary context but, rather, its sound. If this appears bizarre, then it seemed no less odd, vexatious and confounding to contemporaries. It is important to outline the complexities of the prevailing legal rulings governing theatrical performance because, in the absence of free choice, they significantly affected the distribution of stage genres.

Since the issue of vocalization was of crucial legal importance in defining the so-called illegitimate burlettas and pantomimes from 'legitimate' spoken drama, what follows here is a discussion of the role of sound in the period's drama. It will be shown that melodrama, although it had a close relationship with music, was quite distinctive from the burlettas which are the formats of the dramas discussed in Chapters 5–8. While it was entirely possible for a Romantic-period dramatist to be asked to write a piece which was melodramatic in character, this was a secondary issue in comparison to whether it needed to be a burletta. In London, outside of the patent theatres, no one could feasibly be asked to write a melodrama (or comedy, or tragedy, or pastoral or anything else except a pantomime) unless it was also a burletta. In the patent houses, melodramas could be written with or without music – in the non-patent theatres they were always required to be musical. It will be shown that although Thomas Holcroft's *A Tale of Mystery* (1802), the first piece on the English stage to be formally designated a melodrama, had its action accompanied by the carefully orchestrated musical colouring put together by Thomas Busby, its context and origins were quite distinctive from Moncrieff's *Giovanni in London* (1817), a burletta which drew on English folk song and traditional melody in the manner of John Gay's *Beggar's Opera* (1728). Although particular considerations of the musicality of burlettas are beyond the scope of this book, the issue about the vocalization of sound into speech or song, because it was attended by crucial implications over theatrical legitimacy, provides a good starting point for introducing the special conditions prevailing in Romantic-period drama for the stage. Music, and not melodrama, was the precondition for theatrical representation during this period. The discussion will begin with pantomime, then move to melodrama and then turn to burletta, all of which had an intricate and often paradoxical historical development. Although melodrama began in the patent theatres, the prohibitions on spoken drama, together with oppressive intervention by the censors, ensured that within a theatrical environment which was highly regulated, burletta came to be a dramatic form whose evolution took place within a plebeian public sphere.

Theoretically, pantomime was not regulated because its harlequinade component was silent apart from its sporadic use of song. The Lord Chamberlain demanded to inspect only items with texts, or as one magistrate put it, everything except ' "Tumbling and Fencing" – because no copies of these amusements can be sent to the Lord Chamberlain, for his appropriation, previous to the Acting.'[36] Robert Merry and Charles Bonnor's Covent Garden pantomime of *The Picture of Paris. Taken in the Year 1790* (1790), discussed in Chapter 2, deftly circumvented regulation by offering up for licensing by the Examiner of Plays only the parts of the piece containing spoken dialogue. The most substantial parts of *The Picture of Paris*, however, were silent so that its politically risqué pantomime content portraying Harlequin and Columbine's adventures in revolutionary Paris did not come to the censor's attention.[37] Occasionally, and in conditions of uncertainty as to the outcome, managers allowed onto their stages something they occasionally refer to as 'speaking pantomime.' The advertisement prefixing *Hurly-Burly; or, The Fairy of the Well* (1788) alluded to its being 'a novel species of Entertainment,' a hybrid of 'Italian Comedy' and 'English Pantomime' with 'much of the plot depending on dialogue' and, indeed, with its principal comic innovation being a speaking Harlequin (Harlequin Clack) and a Harlequin who has been magically struck dumb. As late as 1820, the then Lord Chamberlain's Examiner of Plays, John Larpent, was insisting to R.W. Elliston, the then manager of Drury Lane and the Olympic, that he had to be sent 'any Words...introduced in the Pantomime entitled *Shakespear versus Harlequin*' and reprimanded him for not sending him new 'Songs,' one of which, 'in a late Instance...was much disapproved' after it was performed uncensored.[38] In 1787, the beleaguered actor-manager, John Palmer, whose Royalty Theatre was under constant threat of suppression (and whose remarkable anti-slaving pantomime, *Harlequin Mungo or A Peep into the Tower* (1787), is discussed in Chapter 3), tried to escape suppression by declaring that 'Speaking pantomime I shall not perform, because they might, by a forced construction of the statute, be deemed *comedies*.'[39] The 'statute' he refers to ultimately conferred speech exclusively on the two patent theatres, Covent Garden and Drury Lane. However, despite sharing the genre of pantomime, Palmer and Merry were subject to completely different regulatory regimes even though both playhouses were in London. Of the two, although his pantomime remained subject to the censorship process, only Merry's piece at Covent Garden could include spoken dialogue because this is what that theatre's monopolistic royal patent permitted. Palmer's fear at the Royalty was that if he produced 'speaking panto-mime,' he would be deemed to be performing spoken comedy and, therefore, through 'a forced construction of the statute,' he would infringe the patentees' jealously guarded privileges.

For Merry and Palmer, in their different London theatres, the defining characteristic of theatrical performance was not genre but vocalization. Merry could put speech into *The Picture of Paris* and, after making sure its text was politically innocuous, send it off to the censor for licensing while, at the same time, not being obliged to seek approval for the silent pantomime. For Palmer, working at the Royalty outside of the royal theatrical patents, speech had to be avoided and he was clearly fearful that any infringement might create an excuse for closure by the local magistrates. Despite the generic similarities between their work, and that the pieces were to be performed at more or less the same historical moment only a couple of miles distant from each other, their exper-ience of the same theatrical genre was utterly different. Merry could vocalize his pantomime into speech, Palmer could not. The issue is of some importance to this book because all the pantomimes discussed here, although they appear to share identical generic designations, existed under diverse regulatory regimes. The same is true of burletta. In London, burletta was the only legitimate form (other than silent panto-mime) for the non-patent theatres. By contrast, the royal theatres were free to choose any combination of text, mime and music as long as the textual component had been approved by the Lord Chamberlain's Examiner of Plays.

If pantomime was the dramatic mode least susceptible to regula-tion (because of its tendency towards textual attenuation), its status still remained sufficiently uncertain as to present constant problems to producers. As it happens, and his declared precautions notwithstanding, Palmer appears to have been arrested during the actual delivery of the pantomime section of a playbill on the grounds of his holding an illicit performance ('a *pantomime* was represented; and several of the performers...taken into custody on a warrant granted by a magistrate acting within the Tower hamlets').[40] It is within this context of different regulatory regimes, sometimes controlled by the Lord Chamberlain's Examiner of Plays, at other times by local magistrates ultimately influ-enced by the exertions of the patentees, that all of the pantomimes discussed or referred to in this book existed. As far as the magistrates were concerned, in 1822 Thomas John Dibdin, the manager of the Surrey Theatre, took great care to produce a play adapted by 'Mrs. Evance,' the wife of one of the Kingston licencing magistrates, in order to secure the continuation of his licence; and he clearly thought through very carefully his relationship with this licensing magistracy.[41] The cultural complexity of this dramatic control, existing quite irrespective of generic designation, should not be underestimated. It is this differentiation of genres, not distributed by the free election of dramatic forms through unregulated or unrestrained choice, which is a cornerstone of this book's claim about differing public spheres of drama.

It has not been possible in this book to do more than hint at the different social functions and interactions across dramas emanating over these divergent regulatory regimes. Again, even for pantomime, the differentiation of theatrical public spheres meant that there were intricate intertextual relationships between dramas. Even if at first sight they appear to share similar formats, dramas often existed under different social and cultural validations. One of the first adaptations of Pierce Egan's *Life in London* (1820) came in the form of a drama entitled *Tom and Jerry; or Life in London* (1821) discussed in Chapter 6. This particular version of *Tom and Jerry* not only subtitled itself as 'Pantomimical' (i.e., represented after the manner of pantomime), but it was also designated as an 'equestrian drama,' the type of dramatized horsemanship show with which Davis's (ex-Astley's) Royal Amphitheatre was strongly associated. The Davis Amphitheatre *Tom and Jerry* indeed introduced the figures of Harlequin and Clown before quickly modulating itself into something much nearer to burletta or, more accurately, a burletta with horses. If it may appear that 'pantomimical' equestrian burlettas are sufficiently generically complicated to make finding their conventional literary equivalence less than straightforward, Davis's Royal Amphitheatre simultaneously existed in quite another regulatory regime to that appertaining to the Adelphi Theatre, the venue which staged Moncrieff's highly successful adaptation of *Tom and Jerry* later in 1821. Whereas Davis's Amphitheatre, like the Royal Coburg, was licensed by local magistrates, they were still required to avoid speech because of the threat of legal enforcement by the patentees but, as George Colman confirmed in 1824, their location south of the Thames meant that they were otherwise not obliged to submit their texts to the Lord Chamberlain for censorship.[42]

However, the conviction of the Royal Coburg in 1821 for preparing to perform Colley Cibber's adaptation of Shakespeare's *Richard III* meant that speech still lay beyond their permit.[43] It was a significant legal judgment in marking a late stage in the power of the patentees. One contemporary commentator called the Coburg conviction 'truly the bathos of legislation,' marvelling how – because the monopoly meant no further licenses for legitimate performance could be issued – 'a man is convicted under an act for not having in Surrey, what the same act declares cannot be granted to him, out of Westminster.'[44] For Moncrieff's *Tom and Jerry* at the Adelphi in the Strand, on the north side of the Thames, the censorship conditions were different because its location meant that all Adelphi texts had to come before the Examiner. The subject of Chapter 7 will be much concerned with not only the popular cultural resonance of Moncrieff's *Tom and Jerry*, but also how it appears to have been inadvertently – and irreversibly – passed for performance by the aging John Larpent. In other words, although the regulatory processes were complicated, the accidental contingencies of history were also instrumental in governing the type of dramas actually produced on the Romantic-period stage. The intersections between regulation and location makes unqualified generic designation unusually difficult. Whatever these dramas were, they had little equivalence to the conventional spoken modes of comedy or tragedy which, with minor variations such as romance, gothic or pastoral, have passed down into the literary canon.

With these contemporary practices apparent, and with generic considerations of whether texts were comic, tragic, melodramatic or romantic entirely subsumed under the features of their vocalization, it can readily be seen that the basic conditions of exclusion, policing and restrictive circulation of drama's representative practices had all the features and preconditions preparatory for a distinctive public sphere of drama, one which can be easily differentiated from the canon of conventional literary history. If the practices of pantomime alone were complex enough, even though the vocalized projection of words was permissible under the limited and unpredictable practices of 'speaking pantomime,' the Coburg ruling in 1821 came as a reminder that speech was persistently disallowed very late into the Georgian period. These matters are of some importance to my study since some recent scholarship has been quite misleading in underestimating both the intrusiveness of direct censorship and the longevity of theatrical regulation.[45]

For example, the proposal in 1811 by Robert W. Elliston to vary the terms of his original permission to convert the Pantheon building, Oxford Street, into a theatre typifies the complexity of theatrical licensing in London during this period. Elliston had petitioned the

Lord Chamberlain to 'substitute Dialogue for Recitative,' hoping such a license would allow him to perform 'Opera with Dialogue,... Ballet, Burletta, Pantomime, Spectacle, and other similar Entertainments.' An undated letter, *c.*1809, from Henry Francis Greville to Elliston signifies his relief that the Lord Chamberlain 'consents to *Dialogue* so our business is done.' However, another letter from the Lord Chamberlain's office to Elliston states that the original license had been exclusively granted to Greville as an individual, and could not be transferred. The Crown official advised Elliston of 'his Lordships determination not to grant any new licenses.' The arguments were vigorously pursued with at least one public meeting where it was stated that Greville's license, in any case, was limited to performances 'by children under seventeen years of age.' Elliston later proposed building the theatre by subscription, using an extraordinary category of 'Hereditary Governors' to form the principal body of ownership, but nothing came of it.[46]

Chapters 2–4 of this book discuss dramas presented at the patent theatres, demonstrating that no drama written for the Romantic-period stage existed in an arena which enjoyed natural and civic rights equivalent to those available to users of the contemporary print culture. Given these circumstances, it would be exceptional to find that writing for the stage was not materially affected by the operation of the prevailing regulatory regime coupled to the net structural effects of the theatrical patents. Chapter 2, focusing on Covent Garden's production of the ex-Della Cruscan poet Robert Merry's comic opera, *The Magician No Conjurer* (1792), examines a drama which commented obliquely on the circumstances and implications of the 1791 Birmingham riots. Unexpectedly, *The Magician* signifies that topical commentary could, if sufficiently diffused, remain responsive to contemporary events. While social and political commentary could be achieved in the theatre, it operated under extremely attenuated conditions. Under the prevailing circumstances of theatrical monopoly, censorship and exclusion from speech, Romantic-period drama reacted in complex ways. Writing a drama with music shrewdly multiplied Merry's chances of finding a production since it would have had no trouble representing itself as a burletta, but it is also likely that his designation of *The Magician No Conjurer* as a comic opera was also aimed at maximizing the audience. Even by the early 1790s, Covent Garden held slightly over 3000 people.[47] Merry successfully bypassed many obstacles by exploiting the apparently unpromising vehicle of comic opera. By contrast, Chapter 4 will argue that the 20-year-old Shakespeare forger, William Henry Ireland, fell foul not only of the cultural muddle of differentiating between originals and copies, within a theatrical context which borrowed plot lines heavily, but that the very project of writing serious spoken drama for stage performance was a high-risk aspiration given that burletta was emerging in the newer playhouses. Indeed, the contrast with the fully emerged burletta of Moncrieff's *Giovanni in London; or, The Libertine Reclaimed* (1817) for the Olympic Theatre, although it creates something of a gap in the chronological narrative of this book, exemplifies how fully this change in dramatic culture had developed into a shape now favouring playwrights able to meet the musical requirements of playhouses. Although the Olympic was only a few hundred metres from the doorstep of Drury Lane, *Giovanni in London* had been rapidly adapted from Thomas John Dibdin's semi-equestrianized *Don Giovanni; or, A Spectre on Horseback!* (1817) at the Surrey Theatre, on the other side of the Thames. Moncrieff's *Giovanni in London* was the product of an alternative public sphere of drama exemplified in these theatres, one which was forced to be musical but need only optionally be equestrian.

1
Busby, Burletta and Barnwell: Music, Stage and Audience

The terms of the restrictions imposing burletta as the principal dramatic form in Georgian London were perfectly well understood by contemporaries of Ireland, Dibdin and Moncrieff. The curtailment of speech was, inevitably, subjected to withering popular ridicule. The song writer Jacob Beuler, in his 'Major *versus* Minors, A Petition to the Lovers of the Drama,' sung from the stage of the Surrey Theatre, satirized how 'The Great Theatres charge the Small / With open means and latent, / Infringing on prerogative / And Charles the Second's patent.' As well as deploying the traditional option of marking how Covent Garden and Drury Lane abused their privilege by replacing literary drama with animals and acrobats ('Instead of Hamlet's ghost, a snake / That "could a *tail unfold*," sirs!'), it is striking that Beuler's song also notices the restrictions on vocalization:

> It's said the rigours of the law
> Shall be our tongue correctors;
> Unless we keep to pantomime,
> To placards, gongs, and spectres.
> So sentenced us a learned Wig—
> A judge we hold in awe, sirs,
> We know it is the law keeps him,
> And we must keep the law, sirs.[48]

The 'placards' Beuler refers to are a version of the 'flags' that David Mayer, the modern historian of pantomime, remarks were sometimes displayed to the audience at the non-patent playhouses to carry dialogue or brief textual exposition.[49] In turn, they had also been devices lowered from the galleries by protestors at Covent Garden during the 1809 Old

19

Price (OP) riots.[50] Beuler's 'gongs' and 'placards' are reminders that the non-patent theatres were obliged to provide sound without speech and supplemented action with non-verbal sound. The exasperated theatre manager Henry Lee, who owned a range of provincial theatres in Taunton, Barnstaple, Wells, Dorchester and Bridgwater, claimed that 'in the Minor Theatres, the Drama is supposed to be *legalized* by any sort of NOISE, if called Accompaniment, made during the repetition of the words of the Piece. SENSE (alone) is thus considered insufferable; while SOUND (though senseless) is approved, authorised, and applauded.'[51] The placards and gongs, like the 'spectres' which provided visual stimulation, are reminders that, as Beuler observed, the 'rigours of the law' were enforced by the 'tongue correctors': speech would be corrected (perhaps in this formulation by the 'learned Wig' Lord Chief Justice Abbott's 1821 ruling against the Coburg).

Apart from entirely silent pantomime, or pantomime interspersed with songs, the only other legal form for the non-patent theatres was burletta. It was under the imposition of burletta that managers like Lee were confounded, attempting by desperate measures to envelope dialogue within a 'NOISE' 'Accompaniment.' Once again, the issue was around vocalization rather than genre, the quality of sound rather than the piece's place within its literary genre. Indeed, as Lee perfectly put it, London was a theatrical environment in which 'SOUND (though senseless) is approved, authorised, and applauded.' Clearly, the issue revolved around the degree of burletta's musicality and its relationship to text since a burletta which merely nodded towards musical content was not a burletta and, therefore, not permissible. When James Winston, who had been manager of both the Haymarket and Drury Lane, was asked by the 1832 Select Committee on Dramatic Literature (which was inquiring into the rights of the patentees and the workings of the Lord Chamberlain's dramatic responsibilites), 'What do you consider a burletta to be?' his reply was in alignment with the opinion given by the Duke of Montrose, the Lord Chamberlain who had initiated George Colman into his duties in 1824. According to Winston, burletta was 'Recitative and singing; no speaking whatsoever.'[52] Montrose's crucial discussion had advised Colman that 'tho'' there [may] always remain the question, whether a Burletta must not be in verse, & the whole sung, not *said*,' the issue 'makes the question dangerous, for These [non-patent] Theatres, as the Great [Royal] Theatres may prosecute, under the Licence granted to the Minor Theatres.'[53] In other words, the only licensing granted to the non-patent theatres in Westminster and, in general, on the north side of the Thames, was for burletta. By the

early 1820s, the rise in the number of playhouses in London neces-
sarily meant that the majority of the playhouses in the capital were
performing burletta and pantomime: it was legally too 'dangerous,' as
Montrose put it, to attempt anything else. Just as Montrose had affirmed,
the Theatres Royal were extremely sensitive to the possibility that their
rights over speech were being infringed. As Robert Elliston, the then
manager of The Olympic Theatre, wrote in 1818 in repeating the sense
of the patentees' complaints against him, it was their own belief that
the new theatres competing with the two royal theatres were allowed
'to perform whatever pieces they may chuse; for, thus (as we find) the
term, "burletta," is now construed at these Theatres. But it can easily
be proved, that burletta is distinguished from tragedy, comedy, opera,
farce, &c. by its being A PIECE IN VERSE ACCOMPANIED BY MUSIC.'[54]
   What did this mean for performers? The consequences of so much
music were quite drastic. According to Leman Thomas Rede, who acted
'melo-dramatic characters in the provinces' and at the Adelphi during
the early 1820s, the sheer quantity of music made his professional life
difficult because, with an indifferent ear for music, he found it hard
to judge his cues for going on stage. Rede specifically records that
this was particularly a problem with 'melo-drame, and serious pantomime' where 'the cues ... for entrances and exits are frequently only the
changes of the air [melody].' He warned newcomers that 'unless the
ear is cultivated ... performers will be led into error.' His own solution
was the rather inelegant expedient of getting his younger brother, the
playwright William Leman Rede, to 'attend me behind the scenes to
tell me when my music was on.' With William giving him a signal,
Thomas could walk on at the right moment but, as he warned others,
'nothing but learning the music, or counting the time, can insure[*sic*]
correctness.'[55] Rede's advice was primarily aimed at new entrants to the
profession in the provinces who needed to heed local circumstances ('A
provincial actor's judgement should not be scouted from the circumstances of his locality') where the repertoire could freely elect the canonical repertoire of spoken drama mixed with the newer 'melo-drame' or
burletta. However, Rede also noted that because of the expansion of
interest in theatre and theatricality – which the occasion of his own book
reflected – 'now ... we have first appearances by dozens, and persons
absolutely learning their business before a London audience.'[56] In other
words, he was aware that many more newcomer actors were likely to
encounter burletta (or melodramas written as burlettas) because this was
the definitive format of the lesser London theatres where new actors
were most likely to gain their first metropolitan lucky breaks (as Rede

himself had done in the Adelphi's *Capers at Canterbury*), and where there was a constant demand for new dramatic writing conformable to the regulatory regime. Of course, as will be discussed below, music was only one example of an array of specificities making Romantic-period drama quite different from modern Western theatre or even from the spoken heritage from which such drama is usually derived.

In 1818 the owners of Covent Garden and Drury Lane feared that the Olympic in nearby Wych Street was performing speech in William Thomas Moncrieff's *Giovanni in London* (1817) and, thereby, infringing their patents. Indeed, when R.W. Elliston bought the site from Astley in 1813, it was known for a while as his 'Little Drury-Lane Theatre.'[57] The patentees insisted that the Home Office despatch an official to visit a performance to verify its musicality.[58] The Olympic's billing of the performance as a 'Broad Comic Extravaganza Entertainment' – plus the piece's immediate commercial success – may have triggered alarm in the patentees that it was rendering the Don Juan story through speech. Nothing could have been further from the truth because *Giovanni in London*'s importation of traditional English tunes into its numerous songs, together with its Cockney dialogue and London setting, were really the key ingredients of its acclaim. Even illicit contemporary biographers of Madame Vestris (who later owned the Olympic) knew well enough that her first success had been in an early 1820s production of 'the musical burletta of Giovanni in London.'[59] Colman kept to this understanding of burletta and continued to enforce the restriction. For example, 10 years later when in 1827 a non-patent house manager sent him the manuscript of William Bayle Bernard's *Casco Bay or the Buccaniers*[sic] containing, as Colman put it, 'only one song in Two Acts of Dialogue,' he replied that it 'is not, therefore, a drama of that description which your Theatre is permitted to act.' He added by way of explanation that 'Although there is a question whether a Burletta should be wholly musical there is no doubt of it's[sic] being a musical Piece – which "Casco Bay" decidedly is not.'[60]

The reason why the specification of burletta within this study is important is because burletta alone, unlike melodrama, had a legal meaning. This meaning, as has been shown, was repeatedly upheld on a number of occasions: by the investigation of the Olympic by the Home Office in 1818, by Lord Chief Justice Abbott's ruling against the Coburg *Richard III* in 1821, by the advice give to Colman by Montrose in 1824, as well as by Colman's subsequent practice including decisions such as that concerning *Casco Bay* in 1827 and his continuing role up to 1836 as Examiner of Plays. Burletta is a key generic concept for understanding eighteenth- and nineteenth-century drama and it will be the reason why this study is concerned very little with discussing melodrama. Recent critics have discussed the contemporary Romantic-period stage in terms of the tropes of the gendered or political performativities it conferred either on its players or else on its audiences. Within such interpretations, the complexities of the role of vocalization in the Georgian theatre have mattered very little. At its most basic, even our understanding of the role of language in popular song and drama has been poorly understood. What Chapter 5 describes as the increased presence of London working class, Cockney, speech on the London stage, a phenomenon which paralleled *Blackwood's Edinburgh Magazine*'s contemporary attacks on the Cockney school of poetry, was accompanied by the burlettas which set native English traditional tunes or popular contemporary melodies composed or collected by people who doubled as actors, managers, singers and musicians. To the newly founded *Blackwood's*, it may have seemed as if Cockney characters in the playhouses, and the new radical press, were set to dominate the cultural landscape. Not only did the Olympic secure a hit with *Giovanni in London* set in the Borough and Blackfriars, but T.J. Wooler had moved from editing *The Stage* (17 November 1814–23 December 1815) to editing the radical journal, *The Black Dwarf*. From being stereotyped stock theatrical figures in the late eighteenth century, by the mid-1820s the popular comedian and impressionist Charles Mathews in the Duncombe-pirated *Home Circuit; or, Cockney Gleanings* (1827) had no discernible characters speaking stage Cockney, while the related caricature print, 'The Mathew-orama for 1827 – or Cockney Gleanings – Aint that a good un Now?' showed his figures (all played by himself, of course) comfortably viewing and idling at the Royal Academy exhibition.[61] The popular playhouses and the radical press presented a powerful challenge to emerging notions of culture.

An understanding of the contemporary impact of popular theatricality as a social affect needs to be extended not only to cover the print culture developing to serve popular political and dramatic tastes but also to encompass the sociability of London's transient spouting clubs and private theatres where amateurs paid to act. The intervention, innovation and sociability of these popular cultures require a modification of the modern analyses of 'canting' and 'slang' dictionaries, as if they created simple taxonomies of working-class speech in order to improve the efficiency of social regulation. While Janet Sorensen has noted the changing function of vulgar dictionaries, and how they developed in order to both celebrate and codify British self-belief in the heritage of liberty and freedom of expression, the absence of a consideration of contemporary song and theatre from her study tends to reinforce the passivity of working class speech while omitting an understanding of the sharp curtailments on dramatic speech necessitated by complying with the privileges of the royal theatres and the interventions of the Lord Chamberlain's censor.[62] Songs in burlettas and the reproduction of Cockney speech patterns, as much as choice of dramatic genre, may have proved attractive methods for evading suppression or intervention.

If the issue of the vocalization of speech, whether musical or permeated by slang, was the subject of varying pressures of control, some studies have emphasized a sort of melodramatic free-for-all or posited complete liberty of expression. Elaine Hadley's *Melodramatic Tactics: Theatricalized Dissent in the English Marketplace, 1800–1885* (1995) has attributed a wholesale 'melodramatic mode' to nineteenth-century public consciousness, describing the melodramatic as a 'behavioural and expressive model for several generations of English people.'[63] Such hypotheses are misleading. In particular, Joseph Donohue set out quite clearly 30 years ago that 'the one dramatic form whose repeated use epitomizes the struggle of the minors [theatres] for survival ... is not melodrama but *burletta*.'[64] It is simply not true that melodrama 'was originally associated with the illegal popular drama emerging from the unlicensed cheap theaters that catered to the less elite peoples of London' or that 'most of the plays associated with the cheap theaters are lost to the historical record.'[65] The only truly unlicensed theatres in London until the 1830s were the private theatres in the Strand, Holborn, Camden and Soho, down-at-heel venues of the type visited by the poet John Keats in early 1818.[66] These were extremely fugitive establishments; and although they were quite often associated with financial fraud and prostitution, in practice the magistrates were prepared to look leniently on them, if only because imposing English statute law would have risked implicating the legality of the type of country-house theatrical famously described in Jane Austen's novel, *Mansfield Park*.[67] No new dramas ever emerged from these private theatres because their transience ensured they were only in a position to produce established dramas from the bigger playhouses. Indeed, to think of melodrama as the dominant genre, and to extrapolate its performativity into a mass cultural phenomenon of the English people, seems tendentious. Much of contemporary writing for the London stage was undoubtedly melodramatic in literary character but it was a genre, at least in the non-patent playhouses, already subsumed under the burletta form. The real question ought not to be about the dominance or otherwise of theatrical melodrama but, rather, how melodramatic writing was accommodated within its requisite musical structure. On the contemporary stage, this meant that melodrama was permeated by music. Again, this is a matter of some importance to this book because not only will Chapters 4–7 be concerned with burletta, but the larger context of my discussion of Merry's comic opera *The Magician No Conjurer* (1792) in Chapter 2 is conceived within the terms that Merry's choice of a comic-opera format was a rational decision, a choice multiplying its chances of finding a performance since, if it failed to be taken up by either Covent Garden or Drury Lane, it still stood some chance of performance at the Haymarket (the summer-season opera house) or Sadler's Wells, both of which were houses closely connected with music.

The Haymarket, the playhouse in which Chapter Three's *The Benevolent Planters* (1789) was performed, was in yet another paradoxical or anomalous position. Initially designated as London's summer opera house with a capacity of around 1500 persons (making it a little less than half the size of the two larger theatres), the Haymarket occupied an ambiguous zone as far as its permission to speak was concerned.[68] Although it had the status of a royal theatre for the performance of opera, it seems to have required special dispensations from the Lord Chamberlain to perform speech. When James Winston, who by that time had spent 15 years as stage manager of the Haymarket, was asked in 1832 by the Parliamentary Select Committee whether the Lord Chamberlain had the power to 'grant a licence to perform the legitimate drama... for a single night,' Winston affirmed that the Haymarket had been awarded '12 or 15' such licenses during its winter opening that year.[69] Clearly, licences to speak were available but were subject to individual application and their granting could not be considered as a foregone conclusion. The constraints upon Merry's *Magician No Conjurer* being written as a spoken drama instead of a comic opera, like the chances of Bellamy's spoken-format *Benevolent Planters* finding performance at the Haymarket, all depended upon imponderable exigencies dictated by the Lord Chamberlain and, secondly, by the litigious mood of the Theatre Royal patentees.

Not only did music permeate the drama of the day, it was also employed within theatricalized repertoires of popular protest. This is quite an important feature for understanding the contemporary social culture since it shows the extent to which it is impossible to disaggregate music from Romantic-period theatricality. Something of the age's elaborate response to theatrical music, quite apart from the specific demands of burletta, can be understood by examining how music was deployed during conditions of near riot at Covent Garden in 1795 as part of an elaborate popular political repertoire. In other words, far from being confined to exquisite differences of legality – although these were serious enough – music also had a significant role in the deployment of contemporary customary practices surrounding the theatre. The day after the so-called Pop-gun Plot of October 1795, when an air-gun missile or stone struck the King's carriage en route to the opening of Parliament – prompting the excuse for that year's Treasonable Practices Act – George III appears to have made a conscious decision to visit Covent Garden theatre, safely surrounded by a massive entourage of horse guards, foot soldiers and constables. John Barrell, in *Imagining the King's Death: Figurative Treason, Fantasies of Regicide, 1793–1796* (2000), has written of how that October, 'the theatre became an important site of political conflict in the days following the attack on the state coach.' Sheridan and John Philip Kemble's version of Thomas Otway's political drama *Venice Preserved* (1682), with its tableau of martyred conspirators, had been withdrawn after a few days' performance at Drury Lane.[70] Following the official party's arrival at Covent Garden theatre, with the crowds on the streets having already displayed a kind of traditional 'rough music' of '*damning*, and ... *hissing*' the king, once the royals were inside the theatre, 'the whole *Band of Music* ... [was] forced to repeat the well known sounds of *God save the King*, till the ears of the facetious were made to tingle; yea, and many of the hissers were knocked down, and thrust out of the house.' There then followed an elaborate popular manipulation of music at the nearby Drury Lane theatre when 'the [playhouse] Musicians treated the call of the house for the tune of *God save the King*, with *contempt* ... and even when obliged to play this constitutional air, they evinced the most indecent reluctance, and performed it in so spiritless a manner, as to excite the indignation of all who observed their conduct.' What is striking is that, as far as this incident is concerned, on the whole it was the players in the pit band and on the stage – rather than the audience – who were the more radicalized. After this purely instrumental rendition of the anthem, the audience also called for the words to be sung, but '*Young* [John]*Bannister* [the comedian] sung it' in an 'insipid manner,' especially when compared with his 'energetic delivery of the Songs in the farce.' As the contemporary commentator noted, 'the disposition of the audience ... was far different from that of the Band; as every person, *except a dozen or two* of the LONDON CORRESPONDING SOCIETY stood up.'[71] In other words, the players and the (alleged) members of the London Corresponding Society in the audience were in unison as to this anti-monarchist demonstration within a royal theatre. Music, its communal ownership and conditions of its rendition were fundamental to the elaborate encodings of contemporary loyalist and reformist registers of popular political expression in Romantic-period theatre.

The involvement in playhouses of composers of considerable stature is indicative of music's premier role within theatricality. Contemporary commentators were well aware that 'music is decidley becoming daily more popular in this country, [and] first singers are proportionably[*sic*] in request,' with newcomers, even in provincial Liverpool, commanding wages of £5 per week by the mid-1820s, a figure quite respectable compared with the extremely physically dangerous tumbling of James Pack who had earned as much as £22 per week at the genteel Richmond theatre much more proximate to London in the early 1810s.[72] Some musicians eventually achieved great respectability. Sir Henry Rowley Bishop (the first composer knighted by Queen Victoria in 1842 and the founder of the Philharmonic Society) began his career working alongside writers of burlettas. Bishop provided scores for George Colman's *The Gnome-King; or, The Giant-Mountains: A dramatic legend* (1819), Isaac Pocock's *The Miller and His Men, a melo-drame* (1813) – with its sensational exploding-windmill ending – as well as *The Vintagers, a musical romance* (1809), the latter produced in collaboration with Edmund John Eyre whose *The Maid of Normandy; or, the Death of the Queen of France, A Tragedy in Four Acts; as Performed at the Theatre Wolverhampton* (1794) was refused a licence for performance at the Theatre Royal, Bath, and the Theatre Royal, Norwich, 10 years later.[73] Even in the rougher and more plebeian venues, music was of great importance. During his visit to the private playhouse off the Strand, John Keats observed 'the Musicians . . . pegging and fagging away at an overture – never did you see faces more in earnest' before they went off to reconvene in the 'Pothouse.'[74] The presence of quasi-theatrical venues utilizing musicians and drawing audiences away from the theatres provided a constant tension with the more regular playhouses. In *The Road to the Stage* (1827), Rede warned that 'Places of amusement are deserted for public houses' providing music and where 'individuals mart[*sic*] their exertions for liquor, and . . . thin the benches of our theatres.'[75] Bagnigge Wells was one such venue, its manager offering stronger beverages by Rede's time than the tea and medicinal waters for which it had been traditionally associated since the 1760s, yet its entertainments also clearly merited a place (alphabetically immediately before Covent Garden) in Thomas J. Dibdin's list of all London's active playhouses that year.[76] Rede's account also demonstrates something of the changing uses of the capital's buildings and their varying relationship with music, theatre and politics. Rede complained that the Rotunda in Blackfriars Road, a venue later taken over by the veteran radical pressman Richard Carlile and retro-converted into a theatrical space, had a worse reputation for its combination of music and drinking than Bagnigge Wells. If the medicinal Bagnigge Wells spa was indiscriminately given over to any 'ignorant fellows... capable of roaring forth' their songs, the Rotunda. had put forward an even 'more formidable' attempt at matching alcohol with music and theatre. Noting that at the Rotunda 'a set of singers are regularly engaged, and the auditor... admitted for the sake of the wine he is expected to consume,' Rede can hardly have known that by 1829 the comic singer Charles Sloman and the parents of Dan Leno, the star of the Victorian music halls, prospered in this unpromising setting.[77]

It is in the context of this highly varied, rapidly developing, arena of theatricality that the musicality associated with burletta and melodrama should be placed. From the post-Pop-Gun protests to rowdy singing at the Rotunda and Beuler's satirical songs, music remained closely in touch with the popular culture of the venues licensed only for burletta. By contrast, melodrama was a format whose origins were closely involved with the patent theatres and whose music was far more decorous. Generically, English melodrama had begun when Thomas Holcroft's *A Tale of Mystery, a melodrame* (1802) was first performed at Covent Garden on 13 November 1802. Although the principal qualities of melodrama, such as exaggerated gesture, extreme physicality of acting, sharp differentiation of morality, under-development of characterization, rapid foreshortening of plot and unequivocal conclusions, are present in many of the dramas of the period, one of *A Tale of Mystery*'s main innovations for the British stage was its extended use of music.

While many aspects of the dramaturgy of Holcroft's play, staged at a Theatre Royal and employing speech as its principal dramatic vehicle, can be found in the dramas which preceded it, *A Tale of Mystery* also presents a founding musical dramaturgy of melodrama. Holcroft's Francisco is a reminder of the complex interaction between different modes of performativity on the Romantic-period stage. His dumbness and signifying through gesticulation registers what Peter Brook has described as 'melodrama's constant recourse to acting out, to the body as the most important signifier of meanings... [and] the genre's frequent recourse to moments of pantomime, which are not simply decorative, [but] which in fact convey crucial messages.'[78] However, Francisco's frequent recourse to written messages to supplement gestural communication ([S.D.] '*Fran. [Gives a sudden sign of Forbear! and writes—Music.]*

"Must not be known." ') also interacts intricately with musical sound.[79] These qualities, of pantomimic gesture amidst a complex relationship with music, made *A Tale of Mystery* a significant development in the period's drama. It drew upon established conventions of mime and signmaking through gesture and yet also developed emergent uses of music drama. For example, the 1799 Astley Amphitheatre adaptation of Sheridan's *Pizarro* had drawn favourable comment on its use of 'perspicuous scrolls and...recitative,' as the circus strove to both comply with licensing yet also exploit the piece's astonishing success.[80] Interestingly, *The Times* announced *A Tale of Mystery* as 'a New Melodrame...consisting of Speaking, Dancing and Pantomime,' a description which not only encompasses its legitimacy as a spoken drama in a monopolistic theatre but which also hinted at Francisco's 'pantomime' role.[81] Ironically, the feature of the *Tale of Mystery* melodrama which most clearly signified its potential to the non-patent playhouses, its music, was omitted in this brief newspaper notice. 'Speaking' melodrama was of little practical interest to the burletta houses, yet *A Tale of Mystery*'s suggestive use of music needs to be considered within the complex legislative context of Romantic-period drama. The feature of *A Tale of Mystery* most likely to have been of material interest to the non-patent theatres was not its melodramatic form but its musical orchestration.

Viewed retrospectively, the tendency of melodrama was to move in the direction of burletta. Since only the two patent houses could play melodrama as a spoken form, all the rest had to accommodate melodrama within burletta. One later commentator of the 1820s, looking back nostalgically on the spoken dramas played in 1760s Bristol, already recognized that music and melodrama were inextricably linked. Since that time, he wrote, 'the monster *melo-drama* (that ridiculous substitute of *sound* for *sense*, wherein the author, when at a fault for appropriate language in which to convey his meaning, has recourse to a flourish of music) [has] appeared on our boards.'[82] It is clear from this account that, during performance, music tended to substitute for speech, a facility which is not only congruent with the stage directions of Holcroft's *A Tale of Mystery*, and other melodramas of the early 1800s, but which particularly rendered its suitability for the burletta houses more compelling. Whereas for the Bristol theatre historian, melodrama was a 'monster' because of its substitution of music in place of linguistic text, for the London playhouses compelled to perform burletta, this kind of melodrama perfectly suited their legal predicament, with only limited adaptation. *A Tale of Mystery*'s stage directions had over 60 markings calling for direct musical supplement and it is clear that music's dramatic role was aimed at intensifying emotional colour, working to give both atmosphere and intensity to action and dialogue.

That melodrama and burletta were, at first, virtually exclusive genres, the former best suited to the patent theatres and the latter a legal requirement of the emerging theatres, can be demonstrated by analysing the role of musical accompaniment in the first melodramas. The music for Holcroft's *A Tale of Mystery* had been composed by the academically inclined Thomas Busby (1775–1838), whose *Complete Dictionary of Music* (1786) remained in print throughout the Romantic period although, at the time of the Holcroft commission, he had been editing *The Monthly Musical Journal* (1800) as well as writing music criticism for Joseph Johnson's liberal *Analytical Review*. Busby was more used to composing (or compiling) publications such as *The Divine Harmonist; or, Sunday Associate* (1792) but Holcroft's request in *A Tale* for extremely precise musical accompaniment strongly suggests that he had a good grasp of the composer's ability and how he might use his talents to advantage. A separately published printing of the fully engraved musical score for orchestra of Busby's music is indicative of its popular stature quite distinctive from Holcroft's text.[83] The success of *A Tale of Mystery* was sufficient to ensure that Busby later provided the music for both Matthew Gregory 'Monk' Lewis's Covent Garden *The Captive* (1803), as well as his *Rugantino; or, The Bravo of Venice: A Grand Romantic Melo-Drama* (1805).[84] The manner in which the music in *A Tale of Mystery* and Lewis's *Captive* echoes dramatic dialogue implies that their common composer, Thomas Busby, also had a currently unrecognized but significant role in the development of melodrama. If he is mentioned at all today, Busby is remembered as the disgruntled, rejected, Drury Lane opening-address entrant of 1812, when the playhouse had declared a competition to find a poetic address or prologue. It was supposed to have been an open competition but Drury Lane dismissed all the entries and, at the invitation of Lord Holland, the committee overseeing the arrangements commissioned a poem from Byron. The irate Busby got his son to read out his own entry to the opening-night audience, an incident memorably ridiculed by Byron in 'The Waltz: An Apostrophic Hymn' ('Oh! for the flow of Busby, or of Fitz...') and a parodic 'Parenthetical Address. By Dr. Plagiary.'[85] Where modern commentary exists at all, despite the theatrical location, the episode is invariably examined from the point of view of Byron's poetry rather than the context of Busby's role as an experienced composer for the stage.[86] In particular, Byron's satire appears to have obscured Busby's significant place in the development of early 1800s melodrama and how that genre was closely related to music. Not least, Busby's humiliating experience – like Byron's in its own way – exemplified the workings of the embedded theatrical monopoly.

Busby's settings for Lewis's *The Captive*, produced a year later, provides even more evidence of how music and drama coincided. *A Tale of Mystery* had called for numerous, precise, musical requirements including the following: '[S.D.] Music to express contention,' 'Music expressive of horror,' 'Music to express disorder,' 'Confused music,' 'Music loud and discordant,' 'Music expressive of terror,' 'soft and solemn music,' 'Music expressive of terror and confusion,' 'Music of sudden joy,' 'Cheerful music gradually dying away,' 'music [which] inspires alarm and dismay,' 'Violent distracted music,' 'Music mournful, then changes to the cheerful pastorale, etc.'[87] Similarly, Lewis's 'Mono-Drame, or Tragic Scene,' *The Captive* (which was really little more than an interlude), put Busby's music to extensive dramatic effect, specifying not only an extraordinary amount of music but, as with the Holcroft piece, designating the precise emotional qualities needing to be mirrored. The reviewer for *The Times* commented that the overture has 'no particular and settled key, for although it clearly commences in *C. Minor*, the ear is conducted through a wild, yet masterly maze of modulations, which anticipate the frantic perturbation of the scene to which it forms a prologue.'[88] As *The Captive*'s modern editor Jeffrey Cox notes, the combined effect of the drama and the music was immediate and Lewis appears to have been sufficiently unnerved as to withdraw it from the stage on account of the audience's well-documented hysterical reaction.[89] *The Times* reviewer reported that 'a lady in the back part of the pit shrieked, and fell into convulsions. Another near the orchestra fainted away.'[90] Busby's contribution to English melodrama was important. Within the dramatic literature of this period, only James Kenney's Covent Garden *The Blind Boy: A Melo-Drama* (1807), with over 30 stage directions specifying its musical requirements in a range of expressive registers supplementing the dialogue, even approaches the quantity of music required in *A Tale of Mystery* or *The Captive*.[91] *The Blind Boy*'s music had been composed by John Davy, whose other settings ranged from arrangements of Lewis's ballad 'Crazy Jane' to a hymn for the colours of the Loyal Hampstead Association as well as a dance in the Scottish style, suggestively titled 'Merrily Danced the Quaker's Wife.'[92] Thomas Busby must also have known something of John Davy because the latter published a forte piano arrangement of one of his theatrical pieces in 1802.[93]

Indeed, the further intricacies of these networks of sociability between authors and composers, even within the perimeters of London's theatrical scene confined to the period around 1800, should not be underestimated.[94] They confound the difference between melodrama and burletta and extend the range of influences far beyond the conventionally literary. As well as his work with Lewis and Kenney, Busby also provided the score for the young poet and novelist Ann Maria Porter's Covent Garden musical entertainment, *The Fair Fugitives* (1803).[95] Like François-Hippolyte Barthélémon (discussed below), who worked at Marylebone gardens, Busby appears to have entered the profession in a similar manner, being first engaged as a singer at Vauxhall Gardens at the age of 14 (*DNB*). In other words, the theatrical careers of Busby and Barthélémon emerged from a complex network of London's theatrical venues far beyond the boundaries of the two patent houses. As the modern historian William J. Burling has noted, Marylebone and Ranelagh Gardens not only originated English burletta, their various troupes (including another burletta troupe based at the Grotto Gardens) managed to survive in a state of precarious, outdoor, summer-season existence from 1758 to around 1774 despite the Lord Chamberlain's denial of a permanent licence.[96] These metropolitan connections of personnel ensured that innovation and influence were disseminated quickly between different personnel working at Marylebone Gardens, Vauxhall, Bagnigge Wells, the Rotunda, Covent Garden, Drury Lane, the Royalty and the other playhouse venues, quite irrespective of their status. Behind these connections, however, lay still deeper sets of influences as continental music was absorbed and adapted to the English vernacular theatrical settings.[97]

As Busby and Davy must have been aware, assisted by the advocacy of Sir Joshua Reynolds, composers such as Christoph Willibald Gluck (1714–1787) were becoming better known in London. Gluck's musical dramatizations, such as the ballet-pantomime *Don Juan* (1761) and the operas *Orfeo ed Euridice* (1762), *Iphigénie en Aulide* (1774), *Alceste* (1776) and *Iphigénie en Tauride* (1779), did much to eliminate interruptive orchestral ritornellos and minimize recitatives in order to blend the music more fully into the role of supporting dramatic action. However, rather than the Theatres' Royal or Haymarket being exclusive innovators in this German *opera seria*, Gluck's music had been enthusiastically taken up by playhouses such as the Royalty Theatre which, of course, had a highly restrictive existence dependent on sustaining the visibility of its commitment to musical or pantomime forms and avoiding spoken formats. By 1787, long before the initiation of melodrama as a

distinctive generic description for some types of contemporary performance, the Royalty theatre had successfully adapted Thomas Shadwell's
The Libertine, a Tragedy (1676) as *Don Juan; or, The Libertine Destroy'd*,
a dance pantomime (or 'tragic pantomical[*sic*] entertainment') orchestrated with new songs by the prolific theatrical composer William Reeve,
but mainly comprised of 'The Music composed by Mr. Gluck' from his
Don Juan (1761).[98] Although Moyra Haslett has noted Gluck's founding
presence amongst the English adaptations of Don Juan, his role has not
been commented on before as providing a precursor of the type of music
for drama where the melodies and tonalities were increasingly being
figured as expressively supportive to the action and characterization.[99]
The London transmission route for this type of music, a type intended
to approximate to the different sets of emotional states being portrayed
on stage, can be traced back to the adaptations of Gluck's *Don Juan* for
performance at the Royalty Theatre. In turn, Drury Lane's pantomime of
1817, *Harlequin Libertine Founded on the Interesting Story of Don Juan*, was
influential – along with the Surrey Theatre's *Don Giovanni; or, A Spectre
on Horseback!* – in spurring Moncrieff to write *Giovanni in London; or,
The Libertine Reclaimed* (1817) for the Olympic Theatre, Wych Street.[100]
As will be shown in Chapters 4–7, these developments of drama passing
between playhouses and permutating between pantomime and burletta
are typical features of how plebeian drama developed in the metropolis
within their distinctive public sphere.

The influence of Gluck's music on such an obscure and fugitive playhouse as the Royalty tells us much about the diverse theatrical discourses
available in London as well as, not least, their links to the capital's
surprising spiritualities. With transposition from orchestral scoring into
arrangements specific to domestically playable instruments being essential for spreading a composer's popularity from the playhouse or concert
hall to the drawing room, intermediaries providing such arrangements
for domestic instruments were extremely influential. By 1785, music
from Gluck's *Don Juan* was arranged for harpsichord, violin, flute and
the (newly introduced) pianoforte by the Swedenborgian François-
Hippolyte Barthélémon.[101] Working in London later, in company with
his composer daughter, Cecilia Maria, by 1776 Barthélémon had gradu-
ated from the difficult conditions of directing the music at the semi-
theatricalized Marylebone Gardens pleasure grounds to leading the
orchestra at the Haymarket King's Theatre opera house. Like the painter
and scene designer Phillip de Loutherbourg, Barthélémon is representative of a number of contemporary London immigrant communities
working on the edges of London's theatre world while, at the same

time, sharing mystical religious beliefs.[102] Disseminated and popular-
ized by Barthélémon's arrangement of 1785, the Royalty Theatre quickly
followed his lead with Carlo Antonio Delpini's production of the
William Reeve and Christoph Willibald Gluck version of Shadwell's
Libertine with music imported from Gluck's 1761 *Don Juan*. This version,
published as *Don Juan; or, The Libertine Destroy'd: A Tragic Pantomimical
Entertainmen*...*Performed at the Royalty-Theatre, Well-Street, Goodman's
Field*...(1787), printed in tandem with a set of *The Favorite Dances in the
Entertainment of Don Juan, performed*...*at the Royalty Theatre, etc.* (1787),
was adopted 3 years later by Drury Lane as 'a Grand Pantomimical
Ballet.'[103] The real link between the Royalty's production of *Don Juan;
or, The Libertine Destroy'd* (which appears to have been derived from the
prose narrative, *An Historical Account of the Tragi-Comic Pantomime, Intit-
uled[sic] Don Juan; or, The Libertine Destoyed[sic]* (1782)) and Moncrieff's
contrastingly titled *Giovanni in London; or, The Libertine Reclaimed* (1817)
comes in the way in which the role of music came to be crucial to the
very survival of playhouses such as the Royalty or Olympic.

　　While Holcroft's heavily musicalized *A Tale of Mystery* melodrama
for Covent Garden could, if it wished, take the option of moderating
its commitment to music by emphasizing the 'Speaking' qualities
announced by *The Times*, no such alternative existed for the non-
patent houses. Clearly, for them the route towards finding legality and
prosperity lay in exploiting the musicality of pantomime and burletta.
For the non-patent houses, whether burletta was embodied within melodrama was irrelevant to the process of regulation. Nevertheless, there
are a number of contributory reasons why Moncrieff and the Olympic
Theatre had so much success with *Giovanni in London*. Amongst them
must be cited the burletta's adaptation of familiar elements within the
Don Juan story and its various Romantic-period theatrical incarnations,
its risqué storyline played out within disreputable Cockney dialect, its
showing at an 'alternative venue' easily accessible alongside the patent
houses and, not least, Moncrieff's comic vitality. Moncrieff was a very
capable theatrical song writer whose music was distinctive and popular
enough to fit quite readily into the less theatricalized requirements
of London's pleasure gardens. Again, Moncrieff's work for Vauxhall
Gardens, which carried on well into the 1820s and long after his initial
stage successes at the Olympic and Royal Coburg theatres, parallels the
careers of Busby and Barthélémon 30 years earlier in its association with
the plethora of music venues available in contemporary London.[104]

　　Of course, *Giovanni in London*'s ultimate progenitor was John Gay's
ground-breaking Theatre Royal, Lincoln's Inn Fields, *Beggar's Opera*

(1728) which drew its ballad melodies from nearly 70 popular tunes. *Giovanni in London* is clearly a development of a genre first suggested by Gay but, by 1817, as will be explained below, much had changed within the context of London's popular culture. Moncrieff's 1817 hit had nearly 60 songs, almost as many as in Gay's success of nearly a century earlier. *Giovanni in London* decisively rejected the musical accompaniment of the type which can be associated with Busby's scorings for the melodramas of Holcroft's *Tale of Mystery* or 'Monk' Lewis's *The Captive* and, instead, Moncrieff drew on the more populist formats of contemporary commercial hits and traditional folk song. Some of the music in *Giovanni in London* looks back to the early eighteenth-century aftermath of *The Beggar's Opera* in developing a distinctive burletta tradition. For example, a melody from Kane O'Hara's Covent Garden *Midas; An English Burletta* (1764), sometimes taken as the national originator of the form, transformed its original lyric, 'Pray, Goody, please to moderate the rancour of your tongue! / Why flash those sparks of fury from your eyes?' into Giovanni's riposte to the Female Furies who surround him, 'Pray, Demons, please to moderate the fury of your fire, / Nor flash those sparks of sulphur from each link.'[105] In turn, the 'English Burletta' of *Midas* had borrowed this particular tune from Charles Burney's Drury Lane piece *Queen Mab* (1751).[106] Although *The Beggar's Opera*, O'Hare's *Midas* and Burney's *Queen Mab* inescapably originated in the patent theatres, their subsequent cultural appropriation had caused them to be significantly popularized. Elsewhere, Moncrieff himself had contributed to the tradition, adapting August Voigt's then recent 'Copenhagen Waltz' (1810) melody into a song, 'Dearest Ellen...The daylight has long been sunk,' in a musical arrangement by the dramatic composer John Addison. Like Moncrieff, Addison also wrote for the plebeian venue of Vauxhall Gardens, yet again marking how music – and collaboration – continued to be important ingredients in building a successful career on the Georgian stage.[107]

However, most of *Giovanni in London*'s melodies were traditional folk songs. Tunes such as 'Then farewell my trim-built wherry' ('Then farewell my trim-built wherry / Oars and coat and badge farewell! / Never more at Chelsea Ferry, / Shall your Thomas take a spell!'), like many more, were still known to Charles Dickens nearly 50 years later.[108] Other *Giovanni in London* tunes included 'Gramachree Molly,' 'Robin Adair,' 'Hey Randy Dandy,' and 'Peggy of Derby, oh!,' the latter a chap book favourite.[109] What particularly differentiated *Giovanni in London* from the musicalized melodramas begun by Holcroft, where the permissible combination of music and speech turned out to be a winning formula for the patent theatres, was Moncrieff's ability to draw on this popular culture of English folk song and to use this to supply the burletta playhouses. Rather than melodramas comprised of music and speech, burlettas replete with song were a necessity for the newer theatres to maintain their licence and not have their work rejected by the Examiner. Moncrieff was a habitual collector of traditional English music and this must have significantly contributed to his success as a playwright and manager. His collection, *Songs of the Gypsies* (1832), was part of a lifetime's scouring of the countryside for folk tunes.[110] His Surrey Theatre *Van Dieman's Land* (1830) incongruously chose to fit into its Tasmanian setting a song Moncreiff had first heard 'sung at a small road side [public] house, in the little village of Lillishul, Warwickshire.'[111] In the 1850s, towards the end of Moncrieff's life, the composer Sir Henry Rowley Bishop, who was acquainted with the playwright not least by their common employment at Vauxhall Gardens in the 1820s, corresponded with the dramatist to collect his archive of songs at a time when Moncrieff's blindness had largely confined him to the Smithfield Charterhouse. One of the songs Moncrieff singled out for Bishop's attention was a melody used in *Giovanni in London*, 'Wapping Old Stairs.' It is clear from reading these late letters that he had been a lifetime collector of 'old country ditties...picked up in my rambles' and even claiming to have 'one or two North country airs...which have never yet been committed to paper.'[112]

The conclusion which may be drawn from these circumstances is that melodrama and burletta were quite distinctive forms with quite different legal connotations for the playhouses who produced them. Whatever inferences may be deduced from the presence of melodrama as a mass-behavioural cultural condition of nineteenth-century England, or as a type of social performativity allegedly implicit in several kinds of economic, domestic and political activity, it could never have become a primary genre of the stage because it remained only a secondary dramatic feature, placed after the primacy of burletta. Music helped define the boundary between legal ('legitimate') and illegal ('illegitimate') dramatic forms. As has been argued, it was the manner in which vocalization was performed, rather than its position within a literary genre, which governed what appeared on the Romantic-period stage.

If, from one perspective, melodrama was distorted by its near-obligatory use of music (actually fully obligatory in the burletta houses), the culture of theatrical regulation produced a number of other unpredictable effects distorting drama's purity. Despite attempts by some playhouses to risk playing spoken drama in a kind of 'Sing-song,' the paradoxes of the overall regulatory regime persisted.[113] As a consequence of this material condition of the London stage, several unexpected consequences resulted for those trying to manage or produce performances on a regular basis. In order to better suit dramas written in prose to a musicalized production, prose dramas were sometimes transliterated into verse in a bastardization of the original play texts, turning them into the type of 'Sing-song' Dibdin witnessed. In 1811 *The Times* attended a performance at The Surrey Theatre of what it described as 'The *Mountaineers versified*.' The reviewer was intrigued that George Colman the Younger's Theatre Royal, Haymarket, prose comedy, *The Mountaineers* (1794), had been '*versified*' for The Surrey production. It is possible to detect a degree of malice embedded in the reviewer's insinuation that they 'could not help anticipating some fun, if not pleasure' from the production: 'the idea filled us with ludicrous delight.' The Surrey Theatre manager was obviously trying to fit Colman's play into the more musicalized or 'Sing-song' format that might circumvent the restriction on the spoken word but *The Times* merely poked fun at the consequent '*hum-drum* of the versification.'[114] In 1832, Charles Kemble recalled that Sadler's Wells, Astley's and Hughes's (ex-Surrey) Theatre performed 'in a sort of doggerel[sic] verse...accompanied by a piano-forte...in the orchestra.'[115] Similarly, in 1817 Thomas Dibdin altered for the Surrey Joanna Baillie's tragedy *Constantine Paleologus* (1804) into a 'melo-drame,' fitted out with newly composed music and choruses.[116] If he wished to produce it, he scarcely had any alternative. Taking greater risks, Jane Scott's management of the Sans Pareil theatre included French works intended as spoken drama but which she 'rendered Burletta.'[117] Sometimes the reverse circumstance obtained. An anonymous Irish commentator noted that Moncrieff's verse burletta *Giovanni in London* was 'transpose[d]...into *Prose*' because 'the people of Dublin (however easily imposed on) cannot be brought to swallow the trash that goes down on the other side of the water.'[118] Rather than perform burletta, Dublin's solitary patent theatre availed itself of the option of transposing *Giovanni* into spoken form. One may also speculate that there was a resistance to the kind of native English tunes Moncrieff had featured. While it is not clear how widespread these practices were, such customs inevitably affect one's understanding of contemporary reception history.

The effects of regulation were an inescapable virus operating within the structure of contemporary theatre. That actors' livelihoods were affected is clear even from how benefit nights operated. Benefit nights were the custom whereby individual actors were allowed to receive the takings of a whole night's performance. Leman Thomas Rede warned newcomers to the stage of some of the more arcane regulations. According to Rede writing in 1827, 'Performers are not permitted to curtail pieces; but any pieces that has been compressed in either of the patent theatres in London, may be acted from the same copy at Birmingham.'[119] So-called compressed versions were play texts abridged for performance but the 'Birmingham' rule (there was a Theatre Royal in that city) may have been an unofficial local permutation known only to Rede (who had begun his career at Stafford). It was obviously a regulatory minefield. Giving evidence to the Parliamentary Select Committee in 1832, Thomas Baucott Mash (who had acted as a deputy Examiner of Plays) claimed – erroneously but with conviction – that the Lord Chamberlain's powers of censorship extended across the entire country.[120] Rede also reminded benefit-night performers in London not to introduce new songs, such as special one-off ballads or impromptu ditties, since each and every new text required separate licensing by the Lord Chamberlain and, therefore, required the payment of an examination fee.[121] As he put it, 'though this work is not addressed to metropolitan performers, it may be as well to hint, that no song can now be sung at a benefit unless it has passed the licenser's ordeal, and he has received two guineas for his sanction.' As well as involving the difficulties of possible censorship, such licensing inevitably amounted to 'a heavy tax' on the night's takings and reduced the actor's benefit income.[122] The examiner's two guineas for a song is not only an incidental reminder of the economic privileges enjoyed by holders of this government office but also an indicator of how disincentives towards literary creativity were built into the system.

Even without resorting to theorizing a subaltern status for the burletta form, or for the newly emerging London theatres, it is easy to appreciate that any dramatic writing which evolved within these preconditions was bound to represent a closed public sphere. How could there be an influence of Shakespeare if Shakespeare was banned? Or, as Jacob Beuler's song 'Major *versus* Minors' put it from the stage of the Surrey Theatre in the early 1830s, 'Stop! – Shakespeare's words we must not speak, / So sentence has been past, sirs. / ... And *farther* say, we have no right / To speak our *mother*-tongue, sirs.'[123] As soon as one appreciates the long-term effects of these several material conditions, it is not difficult to predict that the species of drama which evolved in the London East End and Surrey side theatres would soon become much more influenced by practices within their own sphere of production than by what went on outside. It is the cultural and political practices of these plebeian spheres of dramatic writing which are the subject of this book.

Having discussed the generic and regulatory environment of Romantic-period drama, it is now necessary to attempt to materialize some of its most plebeian audiences. The presence of journeymen and apprentices at theatres was an issue with a long history by the time of the Romantic period and it is difficult to underestimate both the extent and the complexity of London's theatricalized popular culture. It certainly amounts to the civilian version of the anthropologies of behaviour uncovered in the military sphere by Gillian Russell in *Theatres of War* (1995). Street cavalcades such as those mounted by Astley's Amphitheatre were well-documented events in London's East End at the beginning of the 1800s.[124] Reactionary activists at the turn of the century, such as Thomas Thirlwall of the Society for the Suppression of Vice, were keen to eradicate such cavalcades precisely because 'journeymen are called off from their work, by the sound of a trumpet, to see pass their [work]shop windows a Company of dressed-up men, and boys, and girls on horseback, with the Taylor of Brentford, exhibiting his antic tricks amongst them.'[125] The seduction of journeymen from their work by theatre was the target of a number of patrician countercampaigns in the early eighteenth century. John O'Brien has drawn attention to how an early eighteenth-century concern with the theatrical tastes of apprentices was a considerable issue in the development of metropolitan culture and to attempts by the authorities to regulate the populace.[126] O'Brien argues that Samuel Richardson's *The Apprentice's Vade Mecum* (1734), a kind of conduct book for apprentices, and George Lillo's, *The London Merchant; or, The History of George Barnwell* (1731), detailing the temptations and remorse of a wilful apprentice, were aimed at using the theatre to engage with London's potentially disaffected young men and carefully steering their behaviour. According to O'Brien's shadowing of Foucault and Habermas, such apprentices were simultaneously members of an emerging public sphere finding itself suddenly represented in the public gaze through public theatricality and also one transfixed by authority's modulation of their conduct through the agency of texts such as *The Apprentice's Vade Mecum* and *George Barnwell* (as Lillo's play was inevitably titled on late-eighteenth-century playbills). While the Society for the Suppression of Vice and its fear of trumpets may sound like a continuation of the same narrative, closer examination reveals that by 1800 the opposite was true.

However long-lived the moral influence of *The Apprentice's Vade Mecum* and *George Barnwell*, by 1756 Arthur Murphy's Drury Lane farce

The Apprentice (1756) was meant to influence very much the same group of people and to 'repress, by timely ridicule, a passion then growing to excess among the younger branches of the commercial community; that of assembling in spouting clubs.'[127] Spouting clubs were taverns which encouraged drinkers to attend public houses by providing a regular venue for amateur actors to perform in front of each other. In Murphy's play, Dick is in the last year of his apprenticeship to Gargle, an apothecary, but ruining his training by going 'Three Times a Week to a Spouting-Club.' Murphy's play mirrors much of the contemporary public anxiety about youthful conduct with Gargle patiently explaining to Dick's naïve father, Wingate, that a spouting club was 'A Meeting of Prentices and Clerks and giddy young Men, intoxicated with Plays... [who] meet in Public Houses to act Speeches; there they all neglect Business... and think of nothing but to become Actors.'[128] Murphy's play harmoniously reunites the comically incredulous father ('Spouting-Club! wounds, I believe they are all mad') with his son and there can be little doubt of its position as a direct riposte to both *The Apprentice's Vade Mecum* and *George Barnwell*.[129] Although immediately before its premiere Lillo had chosen to omit Barnwell's execution scene, his fate of hanging would have been well enough known to contemporaries.[130] Whereas *Barnwell* had treated the execution with pathos, Murphy's *Apprentice* transforms the possibility of hanging into comedy. Not only does Wingate blame his son's spouting habit on 'that damned *Shakespear*!' ('Zookers! if they had hanged him out of the Way, he would not now be the Ruin of honest Men's Children') but the farce's reconciliation scene between Wingate and Dick also mirrors the staged version of the Lillo play in humorously displacing a possible hanging for the errant apprentice apothecary into a facetious punchline: 'The Scoundrel, you know, has robbed me; so, d'ye see, I won't hang him, – I'll only transport the Fellow.'[131] More significantly, in creating an analogy through distance between Lillo and Murphy, one of Dick's spouting companions mocks how he had tempted him from his earlier sobriety, 'when you lay like a sneaking Fellow under the Counter, and swept your Masters Shop in a Morning? when you read nothing but the *Young Man's Pocket Companion*, or the *True Clerks Vade Mecum*.'[132] Within a 20-year period, the position of *George Barnwell* as a component within a theatrical scheme for the social containment of youthful and plebeian excess had been comically disrupted, and even its intertextual proximity to Richardson's *Apprentice's Vade Mecum* allusively challenged by Murphy's farce.

These were not the only permutations within a Romantic plebeian public sphere of drama that was developing differently from its mid-eighteenth-century manifestations. Although Murphy's *Apprentice* featured a potentially disruptive apprentice who spurns his *True Clerks Vade Mecum* and engages in ale-house amateur theatricals, thereby displacing the carefully embedded lessons of *George Barnwell*, the drama indicates that no immediate social consequences resulted. By the century's end, Murphy's *Apprentice* was playing less frequently than the more morally didactic *George Barnwell*. For about three decades on either side of 1800, it was customary to play *George Barnwell* as an afterpiece in tandem with the yearly changing mainpiece on Boxing Day pantomime programmes. For example, when Thomas John Dibdin's *Harlequin and Mother Goose* (1806) started its 92 night Covent Garden run, it had been paired with the Lillo tragedy.[133] However, by the 1820s, contemporaries were noticing that the proto-burletta *The Beggar's Opera* and *George Barnwell* were both still playing to packed audiences but in different types of theatre.

An eyewitness account by an anonymous 'Friend to "Fair Play and a Free Stage",' written during the lobbying for what would eventually become the 1832 Parliamentary Select Committee of Inquiry on Dramatic Literature, fascinatingly describes London's separate public spheres of drama:

> While one of the great Theatres was edifying its audience by the representation of the Beggars' Opera, the rabble, as they have been termed, were giving a tear to the fate of George Barnwell at one of the smaller ones!...On Easter Monday last, it is said there were three thousand persons assembled at one of these proscribed theatres...soon after the second piece had begun, which was of an extremely affecting nature, the ...holiday multitude...melted into silence, and in very many instances into tears.[134]

The writer creates an equivalence of emotional capital between both audiences, one tearful at *George Barnwell*, the other edified at *The Beggar's Opera*, but it is a commonality of sentiment enjoyed separately rather than communally, one London audience housed in the legitimate 'great Theatre,' the other in the illegitimate 'proscribed theatre.' The pamphleteer even suggests that the stabilities of conduct promoted in Lillo's play are morally superior to the 'great' house's celebration of the criminal underworld in their *Beggar's Opera*. Even the relative sizes of the audiences appear intent on expressing moral equivalence within legal disparity.

However, there were also other social forces at work by the beginning of the nineteenth century, creating striking new differences in the anthropology of apprentice behaviour. Although the date of *George Barnwell*'s decline was probably rather later than Lucinda Cole has suggested, the involvement of apprentices in theatricality during this period was greater than at any other moment in history.[135] But apprentices were no longer mere passive spectators absorbing dramatic representation or delinquent excitement, they were now mounting the stage and hijacking the theatrical repertoire for their own amusement as the late-eighteenth-century spouting clubs evolved into more regular urban private theatres. Garrick's Prologue to Murphy's *Apprentice* hinted at how the 'Stage-struck Mind, / Nor Fate could rule, nor... Indentures bind.' 'The SPOUTING-CLUB' ('a glorious Treat!') made 'Prentic'd-Kings – alarm the Gaping Street!' By night the apprentice playing 'Brutus starts and stares by midnight Taper; / Who all the Day enacts – a Woollen Draper.'[136] Well into the nineteenth century, spouting clubs were still recollected as popular 'among the younger branches of the commercial community,' and it is clear they persisted way beyond the date of Murphy's play.[137] More genteel versions survived to give occasional recitations as 'The Stamford Spouters' in rural Lincolnshire in 1801.[138] However, in London the Cockney 'spouters' were transposed into the urban private theatres, at once regularizing impromptu theatricalizing into something provisionally costumed and staged but, moreover, turning the apprentice spectators into apprentice actors. Ultimately, these young men and women would become the purchasers of Rede's *The Road to the Stage*.

Opportunities for financial irregularity in the private theatres arose not only from their subscription system, but also from direct fraud. By the early 1820s it had become commonplace that London's private theatres defrauded customers, as even the upstart Olympic was quick to point in a speech set in Brixton prison:

> I am not Actor Sir; only an Amateur
> Last week at Camden Town to pass away
> Our winter's night, we tried a private play,
> Took money at the Door, which was a rarity,
> But pocketed it ourselves, & called it charity.[139]

As early as the 1790s, the Lambs Conduit private theatre in Holborn could charge a one guinea joining fee plus two shilling weekly subscriptions, with a higher scale of charges for those joining after the first night of each production. The area's association with the legal profession probably ensured a well-heeled clientele but, except for the joining fee, the weekly charge only equates to a good seat at one of the royal theatres although, of course, it was payable weekly with no possibility of arrears. The Lambs Conduit theatre also insisted that 'members and Ladies are strictly forbid to introduce any political conversation in this Society, on pain of excommunication.'[140] With its elaborate array of fines and little specification as to the facilities guaranteed (no playtext library is mentioned), enterprises like these were ripe for exploitation by less scrupulous organizers. Some of the most sustained surviving records of these fugitive venues came in the form of an irregular 'Private Theatricals' feature that ran for some time in *The Rambler's Magazine; or, Man of Fashion's Companion* in the early 1820s. Their series of articles provides a rare chronicle of the extraordinary existence of such theatres. The dubious private playhouses in Berwick Street, Rawstone Place, Wilson Street and Francis Street in Newington noticed in *The Rambler's Magazine*, also document the coincidence of a taste for theatricality merging with a contemporary semi-criminal London subculture. *The Rambler's* reviewed many of the private theatre productions, including dramas such as Shakespeare's *Richard III*, *Othello* and *The Merchant of Venice*; Matthew Lewis's *The Castle Spectre* (1797); George Colman the Younger's *Heir at Law* (1797), *Poor Gentleman* (1801), *John Bull; or, The Englishman's Fireside* (1803), *Who Wants a Guinea?* (1805); William Thomas Moncrieff's *Rochester; or, King Charles the Second's Merry Days* (1819) and *Tom and Jerry; or, Life in London* (1821), *Monsieur Tonson* (presumably in John Fawcett's Covent Garden monologue version rather than Moncrieff's 1824 farce of that name); R.B. Sheridan's (after August von Kotzebue) *Pizarro* (1799) and James Kenny's *Raising the Wind* (1803). Unlike the highly regulated spaces of the burletta houses, most of these texts are spoken dramas. In other words, as a reaction to – or consequence of – the deliberate attempts to regulate popular behaviour witnessed in Richardson's *Apprentice's Vade Mecum* and Lillo's *George Barnwell*, the tables had turned in the late Georgian period.

Ironically, the same rules governing the independence of private property and which secured the big country-house theatrical parties from legal intrusion also protected their lower-class imitators in London's seedier streets.[141] This meant that the metropolitan private theatres were free to perform spoken drama in much the same way that country house parties might include a performance of Shakespeare. The social and economic implications of these metropolitan private theatres is quite considerable. Sometimes the audience seemed mainly 'composed of hackney writers, and [legal] scribes of the lowest order' and the actors usually paid to act, overseen by a manager who earned a living 'by selling the characters [in the plays] to wretched would be actors for extravagant prices' which he would 'dub up [to] a large price.'[142] One irate correspondent writing to *The Times* in 1808 noted that the private 'Theatres are frequented principally by apprentices, and the inferior clerks of attornies and bankers' and were associated with 'females ... decoying unwary young men' amidst the consumption of 'liquors.' Ironically, not only did these private theatres extend the type of apprentice disaffection feared by Richardson and Lillo, but also *The Times* correspondent related that they performed *George Barnwell*.[143]

If, as John O'Brien has argued in *Harlequin Britain: Pantomime and Entertainment, 1690–1760* (2004), the role of the staging of *George Barnwell* has considerable implications on how we understand the role of drama within the mid-eighteenth-century public sphere, then the presence in the late Georgian period of numerous private urban theatres populated by 'apprentices' and attornies 'clerks' signals the reversal of an older order. Not least, the obvious energy with which these playhouses were attended by young people, and financed by marked signs of disposable wealth (although allegedly frequently stolen from masters and employers), signaled the breakdown of a wider consensus as to rank and station, the disintegration of the cultural function of display and the demise of a commitment to the social good, marked by modern scholars such as J.G.A. Pocock as being paralleled by the rise of the Enlightenment's Other, enthusiasm.[144] Although apprentices were obviously conspicuous frequenters of the private theatres, other social groups were equally drawn to these venues. In *The British Stage, and Literary Cabinet*'s recording of a private theatre performance, it was reported that a 'company of amateurs (consisting chiefly of gentlemen in public offices)' acted out ('in a creditable manner') Colman's *John Bull; or, the Englishman's Fireside*, despite the presence of an inebriated actress ('one of the ladies seemed to have an unusual allowance of *spirits*').[145] The levelling of social and sexual distinctions disclosed through the potent agency of a combination of alcohol and amateur dramatics were more disturbing features of the late Romantic-period metropolitan scene than had been the experience of their 1730 precursors.

Perhaps the most celebrated visitor to one of these private theatres was the poet John Keats who probably went to the Minor Theatre, Catherine Street, off the Strand, in January 1818 describing the visit in a letter.[146] Indeed, Keats's current cultural valency may be perceived as offering compelling evidence as to the importance of the private theatres' social and historical function. Certainly, his description remains one of the most extended documentations of these fugitive playhouses. While the private theatre Keats visited cannot be absolutely identified (Keats gave no name), he implies it was in the area of the Theatre Royal Drury Lane. By a process of eliminating too-distant candidates, one can be fairly certain he attended The Minor.[147] Tracing these urban private theatres provides a useful overview not only of Keats's milieu but also how theatricality was closely allied to plebeian self-fashioning. The vicinity teemed with emerging theatricality, most of it surviving on the fringes of legality. These were playhouses adapting rapidly to serve a self-improving, boisterous, plebeian metropolitan audience, the Cockney Londoners with whom Keats came to be so closely associated. The Minor was not even unique in the Strand where the The Adelphi (then known as the Sans Pareil) already provided a regular burletta venue.[148] Also in the Strand during the 1810s stood 'Mr. Bologna, Jr.'s Theatre,' a venue eventually transmogrifying into Bologna's 'Mechanical Theatre.'[149] The existence of such theatres are good indicators not only of how Londoner's sought out alternatives to the Theatres Royal but also how contemporary entrepreneurs sought to exploit the commercial opportunities resulting from the displacement of would-be theatre-goers from the monopolistic playhouses.

The Minor was well known to Keats's circle: John Hamilton Reynolds's successful Lyceum farce of 1819, *One, Two, Three, Four, Five; by Advertisement* specifically refers to 'Macbeth at the Minor [and]...Harlequin at the Cobourg.'[150] That Shakespeare was performed at the Minor is confirmed by *The Rambler's Magazine* reporting a performance there four years later of *Macbeth* played by 'a company of bakers, most of them very raw and inexperienced lads.'[151] The bakers' apprentices seem to have been ardent amateurs, *The Rambler's* having reported a couple of months earlier that at Minor Theatre performances of William Dimond's *The Foundling of the Forest* (1809) and Colman's *Mountaineers* (1793) in December 1821, 'A gang of bakers butchered these pieces in the most cruel manner.'[152] There can be little doubt that Keats's experience would have brought him into close contact with a largely plebeian company of impromptu actors, perhaps the 'apprentices' described in 1808 by *The Times* correspondent, or perhaps something more akin to the 'very... inexperienced lads,' who 'butchered' Shakespeare, Dimond and Colman a few years later.

Keats's experience of London's illegitimate theatricality was a long-way removed from the monopolistic playhouse he and Charles Armitage

Brown targeted for their (unperformed) spoken tragedy *Otho the Great*. Ironically, Keats could have learned much about the changing conditions of contemporary theatricality if he had taken advice from his two friends.[153] Not only does Reynolds's farce refer to both The Minor and the newly opened Royal Coburg, but *One, Two*'s principal plot device is that Harry Alias is an amateur actor who fools his lover's disgruntled father, Old Coupleton, by appearing to him in a variety of disguises borrowed from an amateur theatrical troupe. In other words, deeply embedded into Keats's contemporary knowledge of recent changes in London's theatricality were the essential components of its increasingly plebeian, Cockney nature and its attractiveness to a youthful, increasingly delinquent audience whose appetite for theatre was based on an expectation of participation as much as of passive viewing. Nor was John Keats, apprentice surgeon's dresser, a unique dramatic aspirant. The bakers' boys who butchered *Macbeth* were similarly removed from the malleable and deferential apprentices envisioned by *George Barnwell*. By the 1820s, intoxicated apprentices might act *George Barnwell* in front of their girl friends, but they certainly were not guided by its moral message.[154]

The picture of Romantic-period theatricality presented in this chapter may seem counterintuitive. As has been argued, it was the manner of vocalization which defined whether dramatic texts were legal ('legitimate') or 'illegitimate,' with the degree of a playtext's musicality being the co-ordinate around which legality was fixed. Within their jurisdiction, the decision as to the legality or illegality of individual dramas was determined through the statutory powers of the Lord Chamberlain and the Examiner of plays who correlated vocalization against venue. In London, burletta and silent pantomime were the only permissible genres outside of the royal theatres. In the patent houses, in London as in the provinces, all forms and genres were allowable, subject to censorship. Outside of the royal theatres, melodrama – like pantomime or other non-textual dramaturgies such as fencing and tumbling – could be optionally incorporated into dramas as long as they remained burlettas. Shakespeare, as well as the rest of the heritage of Jacobean and Restoration spoken drama, was proscribed from all of the London playhouses not bearing the King's patent. Theoretically, all the theatres in Great Britain (including Ireland) were subject to censorship, but in practice this intervention and surveillance was confined to the Westminster playhouses and the provincial Theatres' Royal. On balance, burletta was the optimum dramatic form to write or produce since it could be performed by the greatest number of playhouses. By contrast, new writing for speech had to attract the attention of just the two royal playhouses or find a one-off Haymarket permit during the summer season (and, of course, survive the censorhip process). Meanwhile, displaced from these complex networks of regulation and intervention lay plebeian appetites for personal self-validation, independence from monopoly and a growing awareness that the burletta and burletta playhouses most nearly reflected their concerns and aspirations.

2
Dramatic Topicality: Robert Merry's *The Magician No Conjurer* and the 1791 Birmingham Riots

The main purpose of this chapter is to demonstrate that drama retained the ability to respond to topical debates affecting contemporary political culture. In many ways, registering topical representations in the theatre is the evidential precondition for much of this book's contents.[155] The chapter aims to prove that theatre, despite consistent attempts at suppression, had both the willingness and the context of experience with which to develop responses to turbulent political conditions. The example chosen examines how the Birmingham Riots of July 1791, one of the most unsettling incidents of civil disturbance between loyalist and reformist groups, were reflected through the unlikely medium of a comic opera.

Unexpectedly, the ex-Della Cruscan poet Robert Merry's comic opera *The Magician no Conjurer*, composed for a February 1792 Covent Garden performance, was a surprisingly vivid evocation of the consequences of Birmingham's loyalist riots. Merry's choice of comic opera notwith-standing *The Magician* was an unexpected and surprisingly prescient response to a dangerous summer of events during which the radical scientist and Unitarian minister, Dr Joseph Priestley, came close to death at the hands of a Birmingham Church-and-King mob. Merry's opera was a realization that, with London's theatre audiences capable of being numbered in their thousands, drama was a highly significant genre for topical expressivity.

Despite state-promoted censorship and the hegemonic role of the Royal theatres, London's theatres managed to represent controversial events but such commentary was not achieved without an aware-ness of the potential for the Lord Chamberlain's political interference. Just how intricate and sophisticated these theatrical responses could become is discussed below. By 1791–1792, England was riven by the

48

national reaction to events in France. For example, at the theatre in Buxton, Derbyshire, and in London's Haymarket in 1791, William Francis Sullivan's play *The Rights of Man* was performed 'to expose those self-created reformers, who, from a love of innovation, adopt and spread political opinions, which they have neither sense nor argument to support.'[156] The Buxton staging of Sullivan's loyalist play helps define the transmission of a conflictual political debate about Paine's *Rights of Man* (1791–1792) not only onto the stage of London's Haymarket but into playhouses deep in the English provinces. If the theatres could successfully represent some of the larger political issues under debate in contemporary Britain, it was also true that dramas responding swiftly to more contingent events had sometimes to turn to covert means to express their political concerns. *The Magician no Conjurer* simultaneously contemplated, satirized and defused the public reception of one of the most alarming contemporary incidents of civil disturbance, the Birmingham riots of July 1791.[157] That summer's several days of riots and attacks on property, during which at least one person was killed, had focused on loyalist vendettas against local dissenters allegedly centred on Priestley. It is probable that the original titling of the work as *The Magician* in the manuscript sent to Larpent was Merry's own formulation of a reference to Priestley as a scientist who was already pre-eminent for his work on invisible gases, those apparently mysterious agencies which perhaps materialized a metaphor for the dissenting spiritualities which the enraged Birmingham mob associated with Priestley. The operatic form may simply have been a demand of the Covent Garden schedule but, as one favourable commentator put it, 'seeing 'twas an opera – it should pass; / Why look at operas thro' nature's glass? / In these, dramatic laws are never kept,' which suggests that, much like harlequinade, comic opera simply permitted greater dramatic freedom than conventional tragedy or comedy. Although this critic thought it 'here and there possest / Of brilliant genius,' Merry's opera only played for four nights without revival but, nevertheless, not only was its ability to comment on the Priestley affair significant, but the choice of a musical form may have been a contingent factor aimed at securing performance – if it had been a success – at playhouses licensed for burletta.[158]

Although this remained an era immediately prior to the moment when pro- and anti-Paineite agitation had thoroughly polarized popular opinion, and a couple of years before the outbreak of the war with France, a contemporary eyewitness account of the Birmingham riots written by a local dissenter and minor legal official, William Hutton, still makes chilling reading. Hutton concluded that 'more mischief was done in the Birmingham riots, than in the overturning the whole French government.'[159] Priestley's subsequent *Letter to the Inhabitants of Birmingham* (he was to emigrate to America in 1794) still reads as a highly charged, if dignified, open accusation of the local mob who attacked and burned his home and those of several others. As Priestley wrote of them, few of the rioters were ever brought to trial, and even fewer convicted of serious offences, yet 'you were prepared for every species of outrage.'[160] In reading the accounts of the disturbances today, it was obviously lucky that the injuries to dissenters, their families and property was not more extensive. Priestley wrote, and it is easy to agree with him, that 'Happily, the minds of Englishmen have a horror of *murder*, and therefore you did not, I hope, think of *that*; though, by your clamorous demanding of *me* at the Hotel, it is probable that, at that time, some of you intended me some personal injury.'[161] Contemporary public interest in the extent of the damage done to property is exemplified in the set of plates issued as *Views of the Ruins of the Principal Houses Destroyed During the Riots at Birmingham* (1791) showing shells of burned-out houses and villas with an accompanying text in both French and English, indicating an anticipated readership in revolutionary France.[162] Perhaps something of the ever-present danger of fire, although accommodated into a comic scene of undress, is sublimated into Thomas Rowlandson's 1 August 1791 aquatint etching, *Inn Yard On Fire*, published barely two weeks after the riots.[163]

That the Birmingham riots were the manifestation of latent bigotries in provincial English society should not be underestimated, nor their structural connections with the ruling elite. One has only to read the strained, superficially reasonable arguments of the local divine, Samuel Parr's *A Letter From Irenopolis To The Inhabitants of Eleutheropolis; or, A Serious Address to the Dissenters of Birmingham* (1792), to see the fractures in contemporary provincial English society. Parr's *Letter*, written three months after Merry's *Magician*, is not only predicated on positing two separate Birmingham communities where dialogue has been disabled, but its argument inevitably circulates around its insistence on how Priestley's presence had (somehow) provoked the local neighbourhood, and that this perception had been the immediate cause of the riot. However helpful the *Letter* was intended to have been, Parr's preferred solution for this local problem was for Priestley to adopt covert political practices, to 'Study ... the French Revolution in your closets ... Celebrate, if you please, the glorious destruction of the Bastile in your own private houses,' implying that a mute and passive politics were the only way to ensure the preservation of the peace.[164] It is perhaps a realization of the depths implicit in such a dispiriting acknowledgement of contemporary English society riven by factionalism which made Merry respond with the unexpected form of a comic opera. If he had been able to look further, there would have been even worse for him to contemplate in a trail of social connections leading all the way up to the office of the Examiner of Plays. Although John Larpent's wife may herself have been unaware of the relationship before 1794, her husband was a good friend of Justice Carles, a loyalist allegedly forcibly ejected from the French Revolution dinner in Birmingham in 1791. This activism resulted in Carles subsequently being appointed to a Clerkship of the Privy Seal, a government sinecure which allowed him to appoint John Larpent's brother as his deputy.[165] In such a society, the links of friendship and kinship between government offices could be surprisingly narrow. Such close ties – evidenced also by the perceptibly claustrophobic atmosphere of the factional Birmingham religious circles – formed the material conditions in which Merry was working. No doubt unwittingly, John Larpent soon had to read Merry's comic opera as a part of his official duties. Loosely based upon the events in Birmingham, Merry's *The Magician no Conjurer* provided a thoughtful critique of the mob violence Larpent's friend Carles had helped initiate.

On the day the Birmingham rioting began, sparked by celebrations commemorating the anniversary of the French Revolution, Robert Merry is said to have attended a parallel meeting held at the Shakespeare Tavern, London, along with Horne Tooke and Tom Paine.[166] At a similar meeting at the Crown and Anchor tavern in the Strand (before it became a famous loyalist venue), one of Merry's revolutionary odes written for the occasion was sung.[167] Merry's *The Magician no Conjurer*, although it had only a poorly received four-night run at Covent Garden, incorporates much of the fear and anxiety felt amongst many of the public about the Birmingham riots.[168]

Piecing together Merry's career and political interests is quite difficult. He appears to have become an enthusiast for the French Revolution almost as soon as it began in 1789, travelling to Paris and being well received by the National Convention. His co-author, Charles Bonnor, who had once been a player with the 'Bath and Bristol company of comedians,' had also lived in France in the 1770s, but was now financially distressed despite his high-sounding position as Resident Surveyor and Deputy Comptroller of the Post Office.[169] Merry had already written the fulsome, if rather naïve, poem *The Laurel Of Liberty* (1790) while his popular pantomime (with Charles Bonnor) *The Picture of Paris taken in July 1790* (1790) falls into that group of 'Bastile' productions popular in

London at that time.[170] The political inflections of Merry's Della Cruscan poems can be recovered, albeit with some perseverance, but at least his *Laurel of Liberty*, very typical of much pro-Gallic poetry in the immediate French Revolutionary period, like *The Picture of Paris*, shows that Merry was engaged with certain types of topical politics and how they might be represented. Certainly, by late 1792 he was an active member of the Society for Constitutional Information, one of the precursors of the London Corresponding Society, attending their meetings along with the playwright Thomas Holcroft.[171] His personal interest in the stage is signified not only by his marriage to the actress Anne Brunton, but later when Merry published and produced mock playbills such as 'Wonderful Exhibition!!! Sigor Gulielmo Pittachio' (1794), satirizing Pitt in the aftermath of the collapse of the London Corresponding Society treason trials.[172] Although this open confrontation with the Government came later, the earlier *The Picture of Paris* is not without its ironies. *The Picture of Paris* is important in establishing Merry's willingness to use the stage as a vehicle to express his political views.

The plot of the spoken part of the pantomime mainly concerns the arrival in Paris of the English gentleman, St. Alban, who has come to seek his lover, Louisa, confined by her parents to a convent but 'By a late decree of the National Assembly, all Nuns are set at Liberty. The moment I heard the happy tidings, I flew hither on the wings of hope.'[173] Merry and Bonnor made predictable fun of the freed nuns ('Nun: Why, the Lady Abbess has been married this fortnight to Major Spine, late Prior of St. Anne's – I saw her yesterday & she's so happy') but there were also some gentle political ironies in the presence of the Irishman Captain O'Leary and his servant, Patrick: 'Ah, now they may talk what they please but little Ireland's the only free Country at last, for there, if you don't like the cut of a Jontleman's face, you've always liberty to fight him, and what can any loyal subject wish for more?'[174] While it would be foolish to make too much of the irony of O'Leary's observing that the much-colonized 'little Ireland's the only free Country at last,' Patrick also quietly, within the medium of the humour, alludes to the congeniality of France to many Irishmen, 'By my Soul, 'tis the little Dublin Hotel, kept by Dennis O'Dermot of Tipperary, who left Ireland, and is settled here on t'other side the Channel, and where we may drink whiskey & Potatoe Puddings.'[175]

There is, however, a further conundrum with *The Picture of Paris taken in July 1790* in that the copy sent for licensing to the Lord Chamberlain, prefixed *The Dialogue, Airs, Duetts &c in a New Pantomime called...,'* omits the '*Pantomime*' part entirely. The reason for this is that the pantomime itself was a dumb show, containing no text: only the text of the *Dialogue, Airs, Duetts &c* needed to be sent to the Examiner of Plays. According to James Fennell, who acted in it, the piece contained barely a 'ligature of dialogue.'[176] The difference between Larpent's manuscript of *The Picture of Paris taken in July 1790* and the one actually produced is enormous. Such differences between the available texts of these performances present enormous pitfalls for the unwary. Perhaps understandably, one recent commentator has missed them entirely.[177] The printed version shows that Larpent was sent only one small scene which, apart from the reprinting of the songs, is summarized in two brief paragraphs.[178] In other words, Larpent only received the sub-plot. He can have had little idea of the actual pantomime as performed. This illustrates a considerable problem in analysing the political content of performed drama, particularly within the Lord Chamberlain's purview. It is clear that *The Picture of Paris* has substantial, sub-textual, topical political reference but that only the merest hint of it was present in the text they were obliged to send to Larpent. This may suggest that pantomime, under these conditions of censorship, was one of the most forward means of staging political commentary.

The capacity of pantomime to push against the boundaries of political commentary was long established by the end of the eighteenth century. The 1746 Drury Lane production, *Harlequin Incendiary: or, Columbine Cameron*, came hard on the heels of the 1745 Jacobite Rebellion, a moment which Linda Colley has argued was of immense significance in the formation of British national identity and political cohesion.[179] In *Harlequin Incendiary*, the predictable celebration of Britannia's triumph at the end of the piece takes place amidst the reassuringly peaceful surroundings of 'a beautiful Garden,' a tableaux immediately subsequent to a 'Noise of... Battle' scene showing 'Several English Soldiers plundering a Waggon belonging to [Jacobite] Glenbucket's Regiment.'[180] Even the gift of a 'Present of China' passed between Harlequin and Columbine seems to emphasize the establishment of luxury trades and leisure pursuits ('A Play, or Romance, / A Drum, or a Dance, / Is all the Fatigue our nice Frames can support; Delights and Expence / Engage all the Sense') as English prosperity was reasserted.[181] The risks *Harlequin Incendiary* takes, however, were in its dramatization of Columbine and Harlequin's apparent support for the character called 'Pretender,' an obvious reference to the Stuart dynasty instigator of the uprising. In one scene, Columbine appears disguised as the legendary Jenny Cameron of Glendessary (hence the piece's subtitle), a staunch supporter of the Young Pretender. Unexpectedly, *Harlequin Incendiary* appears to toy with treason when 'The Pretender and his Party meet *Columbine*, who, with all the Affection of *Jenny Cameron*, embraces and receives him; after many compliments, she invites him and his Friends to her House; they go out together.'[182] In the end, this apparent collaboration with treacherous forces is unfolded as a ruse of entrapment. Furthermore, the harlequinade augments anti-Jacobite propaganda by elaborating older, more traditional, popular suspicions of dubious characters in the form of the lecherous figures of a Justice of the Peace, a Beau, a Miser and a 'Scotch Laird.' When these stock figures (with the laird perhaps a new addition, topical to post-1745) try to arrest Columbine 'by Force,' '*Harlequin* charms all their Swords out of their Hands; while they stand amaz'd the Pretender &c. enters, and *Harlequin* promises to restore all they have lost, provided they'll join the Pretender's Cause.'[183] Again, Harlequin and Columbine appear to sanction Jacobite rebellion. Save for the audience's comforting awareness that the convention required a just ending, *Harlequin Incendiary* appears to directly flirt with treason by apparently giving comfort and sustenance to the Stuart Pretender. However, predictably enough, the episode is merely a trick. Harlequin's scheme has been to lay a trap for the lot of them, emblematized when 'A Standard rises, with three Crowns and a Coffin, which they all list under.'[184] Of course, the 'three Crowns' refer to the patriotic Union of England, Scotland and Ireland with the 'Coffin' device an omen of the rebels' demise after they enlist under the Pretender's cause. This downfall comes when they are led into '*An* English *Palace*' (accurately memorializing the successful penetration of elements of Jacobite troops into the English Midlands), where the 'Party of Scotch, headed by the Pretender, rush in Sword in Hand' only to find that the 'Palace immediately changes into a Prison, where Harlequin leaves them, and sinks.'[185] In other words, with song and mime being *Harlequin Incendiary*'s only modes of expression, the early eighteenth-century English pantomime had already become a significant vehicle for remarkably risqué dramatics.

In the French Revolutionary *Picture of Paris* harlequinade, 'Harlequin [is] disguised as a Silversmith, [who] accompanies a Painter and a Stone Carver to execute the decree of the National Assembly' to mutilate or modify armorial and heraldic imagery. Harlequin saves Columbine's father, an aristocratic Marquis (the Pantaloon figure), from injury and is eventually joined to her in marriage. If that is the narrative, the scenic details described in the printed version, *Airs, Duetts, and Chorusses, Arrangment of Scenery, and Sketch of the Pantomime Entitled The Picture of Paris. Taken in the Year 1790* (1790), show a rather more violent setting for the Revolution. Significantly, the printed *Sketch of the...Picture of*

Paris had reached at least four editons in 1790. The pantomime's third scene portrayed the near-lynching by the *poissarde* mob of 'a Victim,' by hanging him from one of the 'fatal *Lanterne*'s' of the type known in London from the one hanging a French bishop in James Gillray's contemporary print, *The Zenith of French Glory; – The Pinnacle of Liberty* (1793).[186] Such a scene may represent the theatre's attempt to be 'lenitive to the feelings of the principal performers' by having 'a touch at the sublime,' as one of its actors, James Fennell, recollected.[187] The murder is stopped by the intervention of a party of National Guards who advise them to have the sentence ratified by the magistrates. When the magistrates refuse to 'pass sentence of death upon the object of the Poissards' savage resentment, they propose to make the Magistrates themselves the victims of their vengeance' but are saved by Harlequin who 'exert[s] his transforming power... [and] coverts the three Magistrates into emblematical Figures of *Justice, Mercy,* and *Truth.*'[188]

In other words, Bonnor and Merry's pantomime at least contemplates a rational and judicial response to near-rioting, but one which is perhaps unexpectedly, given the national context, embodied within the new revolutionary National Guard and judiciary. *The Picture of Paris* also featured scenes, similar to several other London representations of the time, showing a 'Perspective view' of Louis XVI's Federation Oath at the Champ de Mars on the first anniversary of the Revolution, 14 July 1790. Compared with the East End Royalty Theatre's *Pantomimic Preludio, And...Paris Federation* (1790) of the same year, however, Merry and Bonnor's *Picture of Paris* was mild stuff, largely de-politicized save for its marked willingness to represent the potential savagery of the revolution.[189] Indeed, anti-Revolutionary violence was also sublimated into the presentation of the harlequinade where Harlequin is attacked in a coffee house by the vicious Clown figure (called Grotesque) and is forced to escape by imprisoning Grotesque under a metal grille over a fireplace, making him 'in imminent danger of being burnt to death,' but also allowing Grotesque to escape by running 'with his clothes in a blaze, followed by the waiters with a pail of water and a wet blanket.'[190] *The Picture of Paris* ended with a distinctly royalist, pro-Christian, procession of 'Vicars-general carrying the sacred books, supported by a body of the Clergy in their canonicals,' a far cry from Lafayette's increasingly de-Christianizing emphasis.[191] Although Examiner Larpent was probably not aware of it, *The Picture of Paris* portrayed at least some aspects of the street violence by mobs, which accompanied the Revolution. At the least, Larpent might have been pacified to figure that the role of the French National Guard in preventing a lynching could be interpreted as showing that order could be restored out of anarchy. The role of the textless pantomime in the production may also, more simply, show that Merry and Bonnor were astute enough to realize that only the more vulgar comedies based on national stereotypes and distant sexual innuendo would actually get past the Examiner. Nevertheless, their pantomime is revealing of how an awareness of violence was something Merry and Bonnor thought important enough to need to portray.

As far as his *The Magician no Conjurer* is concerned, its representation of some of the anxieties initiated by the Birmingham riots of 14 July 1791 may have been partly precipated by Merry's own contribution to that evening's second French Revolutionary anniversary celebrations. At the Crown and Anchor, Strand, that same night the assembled radicals (allegedly amounting to some 1500 people) had read out Merry's *Ode For The Fourteenth Of July, 1791, The Day Consecrated To Freedom.*[192] With the hindsight of the physical violence of the Birmingham riots, Merry may later have felt the ode's vainglorious closing chorus, 'Assert the hallow'd Rights which Nature gave, / And let your last, best vow be Freedom or the Grave,' was hopelessly unrealistic. Merry would certainly have been acutely aware that the 'Paris Federation' sequence of his *Picture of Paris* had portrayed an event which had taken place exactly a year earlier, on the first anniversary of the Revolution. William Hutton's contemporary account of the Birmingham riots makes clear the components of religious and political violence of that evening, relating how the Revolution anniversary dinner was broken up ('The Gentlemen will not suffer this treatment from the Presbyterians, they will be pissed on no longer') and two dissenting meeting houses burned to the ground while the mob prevented local fire engines from extinguishing the flames.[193] The rioters then 'undertook a march of more than a mile, to the house of Dr. Priestley, which was plundered and burnt without mercy, the doctor and his family barely escaping.'[194] What might have passed through Merry's mind was that the backlash of the French Revolution, in its English incarnation, was now targeting intellectuals like himself. At the subsequent trials, of the 12 men indicted, only two were executed with two further death sentences respited.[195] The religious bigotry of the Birmingham riots must have seemed to starkly refute Merry's hopes for the sort of revolution optimistically declaimed in *Ode for the Fourteenth of July, 1791*. In the Ode, Merry had visualized the exposure of 'The Mass, vile mummery! the Priest's deceit' but, on that very night, he would have found the worst excesses of papacy replaced by Protestant persecution.

An indication of the potential ideological fractures inherent in British society over the Birmingham riots, and to which Merry was responding, is even visible in the apparently polite, but also politically polarized, correspondence reprinted from *The Bath Chronicle* between the Earl of Dunmore's chaplain and the anonymous 'Publicola.'[196] More disturbingly, a full year before the riots, local agitation against Priestley had grown almost physically threatening. Even before Hannah More's manifestation as 'Z,' earlier loyalist ideologues had concocted the figure of 'John Nott,' a church and state 'Button Burnisher,' one of the trades associated with the area's growing industrialization. Nott's *Very Familiar Letters, Addressed to Dr. Priestley, In Answer to His Familiar Letters to the Inhabitants of Birmingham* (1790) was 'Earnestly recommended to the... Mechanics and Manufacturers of the Town of Birmingham.' The *Very Familiar Letters* had enough local knowledge to be able to taunt Priestley about an (apparently real) incident when 'one of our Birmingham gunners shot at a flight of sparrows in your garden thinking no harm.' The four-penny pamphlet went on to describe with some relish Priestley's alarm and discomfiture, relating how 'you set a ringing your great bell and whirling your ratrle[*sic*] and so you rais'd the neighbonrhood[*sic*].'[197] Without quite hinting that such intimidation might be repeated, the anonymous nature of these *Very Familiar Letters*, 'Earnestly recommended' to the local inhabitants of one of England's greatest gun-making districts, is distinctly threatening in tone. They were the outcome of a sense of grievance that Priestley was an interloper and nuisance come 'to throw us into hot water, and kick up such a dust as you have done.'[198] In other words, the hostile mob experienced by Priestley a year later seems also to be encountered in the storming of Thomas Talisman's house in *The Magician no Conjurer*.

One of the key events during the Birmingham riots was not simply the destruction of Priestley's home but also the destruction of his manuscripts and the scientific apparatus in his 'Elaboratory' [*sic*].[199] Hutton commented that 'the greatest loss that Dr. Priestley sustained, was in the destruction of his philosophical apparatus' while Priestley himself wrote in his *Letter to the Inhabitants of Birmingham* (1791) that the rioters 'have destroyed the most truly valuable and useful apparatus of philosophical instruments that perhaps any individual, in this or any other country, was ever possessed of.'[200] The scientific loss was similarly remembered in September of 1791 in an address (with reply) by students of the dissenting academy at New College, Hackney, who deplored 'The loss which the world of science and of letters, must sustain, in the destruction of your MSS and interruption of your studies.'[201] *The Times,* only two weeks after the event, was far less sympathetic and published a satirical piece announcing that Priestley's 'Philosophical Apparatus consisted of a wheel which could grind Monarchy into a Republic' and 'electrifying machine which, when charged with Republican Fire, would give the most violent shock to any Monarchy.'[202] As far as the wider public was concerned, as the modern historian of science Jan Galinksi has pointed out, Priestley was especially notable amongst his contemporaries for the thorough dissemination (in order to stimulate amateur replication) of knowledge about the scientific apparatus used in his laboratory experiments.[203] It is this idea, of the destruction of the scientific property of a gentleman, which forms the central scenes in Merry's *The Magician no Conjurer*.

The exact origin of Merry's title can also be determined. The riots themselves quickly entered into popular consciousness. A sixpenny pamphlet (not cheap but still inexpensive) published by the radic-ally inclined London publisher Joseph Johnson, *A Letter from Timothy Sobersides, Extinguisher-Maker, At Wolverhampton, To Jonathan Blast, Bellows-Maker, At Birmingham* (1792), tried to catch the manufacturing region's idiom in its choice of occupations. The pamphlet portrayed a local parish clerk, Obadiah Gape, telling Sobersides about the rioting, explaining that Priestley had escaped personal injury because 'he being a conjurer, flew away by the magical black art, or the power of Satan, in the form of a blue dragon.'[204] The demonination of Priestley as 'a conjurer,' as with the title of Merry's drama, appears to confirm a now largely lost contemporary idiom of characterizing the Enlighten-ment scientist. For example, one local minister – who was not averse to describing himself as 'a Chemical Member' of the Church of England – wrote to condemn 'the whole tribe of *Priestleyan Infidels*' by allegorically subjecting 'this *Birmingham coin*...in the crucible of reason...[to] melt it with the red heat of the sacred scriptures...[and] discover it to consist of base metal...a spurious composition.'[205] The tropes of alchemy versus rationalist scientific inquiry are very much at the centre of the Priestley controversy and of Merry's response to it. Equally, Merry's *Magician no Conjurer* takes advantage of the popularization of electrical experi-ments in therapeutic animal magnetism sometimes conducted in what one sceptical visitor described as 'Grand Magnetical Theatres.'[206] The subsuming of animal magnetism within Merry's play was probably not accidental since Priestley's own rationalist experiments on gases involved probing a medium which was equally invisible and largely intangible to the human senses. In other words, to some extent at least, the effluvia of animal magnetism ridiculed in *The Magician no*

Conjurer becomes a metaphor for Priestley's exploration of the distinction between the material and the immaterial discussed in works such as *Disquisitions Relating to Matter and Spirit* (1777). As will be argued, the riotous plundering of Thomas Talisman's laboratory in Merry's *Magician* incorporates into it not only the anxieties raised by civil disturbance but also more subliminal fears concerned with Enlightenment science's apparently covert links to occult practices. Merry's *Magician no Conjurer* also seems to subsume fears of the co-option of progressive Enlightenment by popular occult beliefs. *The Conjuror's Magazine; or, Magical Physiognomical Mirror* which began in August 1791, two months after the Birmingham riots, and which was conveyed about the country by 'newscarriers' ran a New Year piece in 1792 listing 'Remarkable Fires in 1791' including 'JULY.—Birmuham[*sic*] fires' (January 1792 p. 176) which it explained by plotting the solar, lunar and zodiacal conjunctions.

If the amount of Merry's political investment in meaning and allusion in *The Magician no Conjurer* seems surprising, it was nothing when compared to the further directions his responses to the French Revolution took. In his eight-page, separately published, *The Wounded Soldier, a poem* (1795), written in the last three years of his life, Merry turned to examining the social distress caused by the ongoing war with France. In doing so, he achieved the sort of nobility of diction now most closely associated with Wordsworth's *Old Man Travelling* (1798):

> On Crutches borne, his mangled Limbs he drew,
> Unsightly remnants of the Battles rage;
> While Pity, in his youthful form, might view
> A helpless Prematurity of Age.[207]

Merry's poem, in noticeable contrast to his earlier poems about the French Revolution, ended with a pointed criticism of the current Government:

> O may this Tale, which agony must close,
> Give deep Contrition to the self-call'd great;
> And shew the Poor, how hard's the lot of those,
> Who shed their Blood, for Ministers of State.[208]

Remarkably, Merry's publisher for this work was the little-known Bedford Court, Covent Garden, radical pressman, 'Citizen' T.G. Ballard.[209] In the advertisements printed in *The Wounded Soldier*,

Ballard puffed an array of ultra-radical imprints, including works by Thomas Thirlwall as well as a number of journals including Daniel Isaac Eaton's *Politics for the People*, Thomas Spence's *Pig's Meat* and *The Philanthropist*. Ballard was also a co-publisher of ultra-radical pamphlets. For example, Ballard co-published one of *Jockey Club* libel-indicted Charles Pigott's extraordinary satirical political lexicons, *A Political Dictionary For The Guinea-Less Pigs; or, A Glossary Of Emphatical Words* (1795). Intriguingly, in 1795 Ballard was also closely involved with the various transformations of the London Corresponding Society in its more physical-force configuration subsequent to the collapse of the 1794 treason trials. Citizen Bailey's two cheap pamphlets, *The White Devils Un-Cased. Being The First Discourse Upon Ecclesiastical Tyranny, And Superstition, Delivered At Section 2 And 7 Of The Friends Of Liberty* (1795) and *Prince Brothers's Scarlet Devils Displayed, Being The First Discourse On the Origin of Nobility, Delivered At Section 2 And 7 Of The Friends Of Liberty* (1795) were commentaries on the role of the imprisoned millenarian Richard Brothers, at least one of which works may be attributable to the black-Jamaican slave's son, Robert Wedderburn (see below). In the mid-1790s, Ballard was joining up with a starry array of radical pressmen including Daniel Isaac Eaton, H.D. Symonds, Richard Lee, Thomas Spence and George Ribeau, the follower of Brothers, to publish *The Correspondence Of The London Corresponding Society Revised And Corrected, With Explanatory Notes And A Prefatory Letter* (1795) exactly at the point where the running of the London Corresponding Society was taken over by hard-core Spenceans.

How Merry's *Wounded Soldier* found its way to such an extreme publisher is not known but Ballard's connection with physical-force radicalism provides an unusual twist to Merry's writing career. In particular, *The Magician no Conjurer*, seen through the anachronistic hindsight of 1795, now seems a work appearing to recognize the reality of a domestic propensity for violent disturbance amongst the British population. When taken together with the pantomime part of *The Picture of Paris*, it looks very likely that Merry himself, at a psychological level, was becoming more and more obsessed with different kinds of violence. Della Cruscan poetry (perhaps most simply defined as the exchange of poems between Robert Merry and Hannah Cowley, largely in *The World* newspaper) hovered and meditated within what Jacqueline Labbe has described as 'the erotic and violent world of the Della Cruscan poets.' As Labbe and Judith Pascoe have argued, Merry's theatricalized poems on the actresses Sarah Siddons, Kitty Wells and Mary Farren were also 'dramatically associated with violence itself.'[210] The near-lynchings and mob riots of *The Picture of Paris* pantomime and *The Magician no Conjurer* show that the confined poetics of violence could also erupt, embodied, on the London stage.

In much the same way that Birmingham locals must have viewed the mysterious Joseph Priestley, the discoverer of dephlogisticated air, Merry's Thomas Talisman, lives outside of the village in a castle, where the servant, Peter Panick, learns that 'every Body in the Village where we slept, says, that... [Talisman] is a most tremendous Saucer[*sic*], that he can snuff out the Moon with his fingers, and make it Mid night all day long.' Alongside the rumour that Talisman is a 'Saucer' (sorcerer), even his own sister says of him that he 'conceits himself to be a Necromancer.' The character name may even have been picked up from a popular publication such as *The Conjuror's Magazine; or, Magical Physiognomical Mirror* whose January 1792 issue had included a piece on 'The doctrine of Talismans or Telesmes' which explained that 'Secrecy is the very soul of Telesmes' (p. 183).

The complex relationship between Robert Merry's play and Joseph Priestley's portrayal in contemporary popular culture is provokingly glimpsed in another piece in *The Conjuror's Magazine* which figured Priestley under its explanation of the conundrum of '666,' the name of the beast in Revelation. The networks of popular belief which stimulated *The Conjuror's Magazine* found it equally possible to sustain an interest in the occult sciences of palmistry and astrology alongside a bitter suspicion of the invisible gasses, electrical forces and radicalized dissenting polemics espoused by Joseph Priestley:

Has not DR. PRIESTLY'S life been an open war with those, who would shelter humanity... Has he not avowedly, through his life (his death I should and do say) maintain what I have described as the principle of anti-christ and death... Has he not been 'a persecutor and injurious?' Has he not under a lamb like frontispiece, emitted the hissings of a dragon? HE HAS.

The author of this piece found 'the fountain head of folly in philosophers' before *The Conjuror's Magazine* returned, on the next page, to more letters on 'Talismans.'[211]

The plot of *The Magician no Conjurer* is that both Somerville and Darvall wish to obtain entrance to Thomas Talisman's home in order to be suitors to his daughter, Theresa. Talisman has locked up his daughter for a year 'on account of a warning from the stars.' Darvall realizes that the only way he can ingratiate himself into the Castle's interior is by striking up a friendship with Talisman's 50-year-old spinster sister ('But I was formed for Affection'), and pretending to be a necromancer called Fugacious Phosphorous ('Talisman: I have heard of thee, Great Bosphorus!'), Darvall comes to visit Talisman. Miss Talisman (the spinster), amidst much mesmeric language, willingly co-operates in the deception practised upon her brother:

Miss Talisman: I came to tell you, that an inordinate Man like yourself, who possesses magical abilities, and who says, he has carried Magnatism[*sic*] to its highest protuberance is anxiously propelled, to hold a sublime conversation with you on immaterial operations...
Talisman: Magnatism to its highest protuberance! Of magical abilities! O let me see the honoured Personage!

The tone is comic but implies that Talisman is a dangerous and potentially malicious lunatic (not least confirmed by locking up his daughter) and that his anger is directed at the locals:

Talisman: Ecod I'll soon kick up such a dust in the skies, and so fertilize the land with fogs, that there sha'n't be a blade of grass, or an ear of corn in the whole country, or a living creature to eat them, if there were. They shall be convinced that Talisman is no Triffler[*sic*].

It is Somerville who foils Darvall's attempts to court Theresa Talisman, exposing him to her father as a dowry hunter. Darvall's dreams of wealth provide their own commentary on the politics of the time:

Darvall: I'll buy a Borough, and become a Representative of the People. And then I'll be a Whig, and Tory, and a Patriot, and a Royalist, and a Republican... In this happy Country, let a Man have but plenty of Money, and he may do any thing without hurting his Character.

This comment on political insincerity and corruption escaped Larpent's pen but Thomas Talisman's sexual innuendo about his daughter (spoken in her presence) was excised, 'if she has not Magic enough to raise up a Man, I'll take my leave of the Art.'

With his bounty hunting exposed, Darvall needs a ruse or diversion to abduct Theresa. Remarkably, at this pivotal point in the opera, Darvall finds that such a diversion is already in hand when he realizes that the Castle is just about to be stormed by an angry mob who hate Talisman:

Darvall Solus: Damme, I'll alarm the Country, I'll set fire to the Castle, and take her by storm ... but who comes here? Why the Country seems to be alarmed already.

Darvall finds he has a readymade mob to hand:

(*Enter Sammy Sapling, with Peggy and Nelly having hold his arm – and a Mob of Countrymen ...*)

Sammy: We'll see if Justice Browbeat won't put a spoke in his wheel – it's a shame he should be suffer'd in a Christian Land. He's worse a deal than crazy Jane.

Countryman: That he is, why he made my Cow die last week.

Another: Aye, and he gave my little Girl the measles.

Another: All our Beer turn'd sour the other day owing to He.

The hints of religious bigotry ('it's a shame he should be suffer'd in a Christian Land') are allied with traditional fears and rumours about Talisman's alleged malice as 'the Old Villain who inhabits these parts, and frightens honest folks out of their wits, but he shan't go on with his wicked pranks much longer,' as well as the hint of the existence in the village of a loyalist Church and King Club, 'I wish I may die if I an't afraid to cross our Church Yard of a Night – though I am not apt to be very timmersome when I come from the Club.' What is striking about this episode is that, while Merry's plotting is considerably shortened by doing away with any need for Darvall to provoke a riot amongst the rural populace, *The Magician no Conjurer* finds it unexceptional to visualize a readymade, self-assembled, mob. Merry's point seems to be that such popular disquiet is always latent in provincial England. Certainly, Merry could have learned much about local Birmingham attitudes to Priestley expressed through the loyalist press. The pseudonymous John Nott's Birmingham published *Very Familiar Letters, Addressed to Dr. Priestley* (1790) put the real meaning of local loyalism in terms which are no less chilling for being phrased in a homespun fashion, 'But now do be advis'd by a friend; come to church, as a Christian should do, and hear what our rector Mr. Madan and Mr. Burn preach, and I'm sure you'd soon think as we do, and then, when we saw you quietly minding your own business and not troubling yourself with our's[sic], we shou'dn't repent, as we do now, that you ever came among us.'[212]

But what follows is a wonderful piece of comic writing when Darvall seizes on the opportunity offered by the rustic countrymen to assert that he is the 'the Great Vice Chancellor of England':

Sammy: I'll be hanged if you are n't a Vice Chancellor.

(*Darvall after some consideration*) You are a Lad of penetration, I am a Vice Chancellor, the Great Vice Chancellor of England.

Nelly: We had better not stay here in presence of his eminence, or we may perhaps be committed.

Peggy: What should we be committed for?

Nelly: Why, for what we have committed.

Nelly and Peggy, as the feisty abettors of Sammy Sapling, with their self-directed sexual innuendo are the perfect comic foil to the occasion but, within the political meaning of the time, Darvall is also quick to suggest that his project against Talisman is backed and supported by the Government:

Darvall: You're right! The whole race of Wizards must be exterminated; I was sent from London by order of all the foreign Ministers who preside in the great judicial Courts, to see the business compleated...I have a full and absolute commission to regulate all disorder.

Merry's commentary on the Birmingham riots shows that ordinary provincial folk are always led by their social betters into disorder. William Hutton commented that 'Every political mob has an owner...this [one], I am sorry to say, by some of our principal inhabitants.'[213]

There then follows a revolutionary transition of authority as the true leader of the mob, Darvall, confers local power onto a simple rustic ('Sammy: Be n't you a Londoner, Eh? Darvall: I am'):

(*Enter Sammy Sapling, with a Constable's Pole in his hand, and followed by Nelly & a Mob of Country men & women*)

Sam: His Lordship the Vice Chancellor of England, having appointed me Constable for the Time being, with positive Orders to seize the body of that wicked Wight Tobias Talisman, I thus approach his Castle to execute my Commission.

As the Castle is stormed, there is a mixture of threatening violence and comic confusion. Nelly's song appears to have been excised by

Larpent on account of its threat of intimidation and the flouting of legal process:

> Altho' the Old Villain should be in a rage,
> I think we may hustle him into the Cage,
> And if he should there be unwilling to stay,
> Why, Let's get him a verdict for Botany Bay.

And when the path of the mob is temporarily blocked by Talisman's servant, Grub, the comic misprision half-suggests allusions to the contemporary language of de-Christianization or deism:

Sam: What, do you defy us?
Countrymen: He don't dare to *deify* us, does he?

Once inside the Castle, the scene moves to Talisman's '*Observatory in the Castle An Orrery – Globes – & a very large Telescope.*' He hides from the mob inside the telescope which is quickly destroyed in the mob's rage at being unable to find him. Again, Merry emphasizes that mobs act with little regard for how their actions might 'Prejudice' them at any subsequent trial or judicial retribution:

(*Countryman looking at the Orrery*) Won't this here do one Prejudice.

Sam: No you fool, smash it.—

(*Countryman throws down the Orrery; and Others overturn the Globes –*)

Just as it had been at Priestley's house, the mob's destruction of the scientific property of a gentleman scientist is complete.[214] They then move towards ducking him in the moat. Despite the slapstick comedy of the incident, Talisman protests that 'I can't swim, and if I should be drowned, there seems to be little Chance of my being recovered by a humane Society,' the anxieties seem to mirror the Birmingham riots. Sam Sapling's reply is, 'Never mind what he says, but drag him on.' Clearly, Merry's scene has rather frightening recollections of Priestley's fear expressed in his *Letter to the Inhabitants of Birmingham* that 'some of you intended me some personal injury.'

  The Magician no Conjurer ends with Somerville's appearance bringing about a daunting command over the mob which safely disperses itself and allows Talisman to be rescued. Darvall owns up and says he is not the Vice Chancellor and encourages everyone to return to their homes 'peaceably, and like true Men.' Talisman makes amendments by suggesting that he has learnt that 'To confer a kindness, and to make People happy, is the best way of enchanting after all.' Almost as if it is a precursor to *Frankenstein* (which in some ways it is), he also adds 'I am glad I have got rid of my magical vagaries, for I begin to think there was something wrong in my upper story[*sic*].' The townspeople are reconciled to Talisman when he orders Grub to 'throw open the Cellar' to celebrate the double marriages of Somerville and Theresa, Darvall and Miss Talisman, with 'Mirth and Hospitality.'

What is curious about *The Magician no Conjurer* is the fidelity with which it parallels the incidents of the Birmingham riots. In late 1791, after Merry's initial flirtations with Revolutionary optimism in his *Laurel of Liberty* and *Ode For the Fourteenth Of July, 1791*, along with many of the population, he was obviously beginning to take a gloomier outlook on the future. As his *Magician no Conjurer* of 1792 and the later *Wounded Soldier* poem show, the results of violence brought about by the effects of Government, either in war or as a consequence of domestic unrest caused by persecution, began to trouble him. His opera, in particular, seems to dramatize the volatility of the provincial or rural poor and to imagine the result when their attentions are directed towards an apparently aloof intellectual. Merry would have known, for example, that at the trial of three men accused of firing and plundering Priestley's house, Daniel Parker Coke (the crown brief at the trials and M.P. for Nottingham) had claimed that he had 'heard it in the streets' that 'the Jury...will not convict any one of them.'[215] The trial witnesses gave a vivid picture of the rampage at Priestley's house where 'They went through the house, sometimes into one room, and sometimes into another; most of the mob got in at the windows, and began immediately to destroy windows, doors, and furniture.'[216] If these were events which, as the trial judge said, had 'occasioned alarm in the whole country,' Talisman's 'Magnatism' is only a more comical parallel to Priestley's abstruse inquiries into de-phlogisticated air; and, of course, Talisman's kind of spiritualized pseudo-science was taken seriously enough in the 1790s.[217]

Attacks on magnetism in the theatre, particularly at Covent Garden – Merry's venue – were a source of intense irritation to practising mesmerists. The near-contemporary magnetizing dream analyst George Baldwin, author of the *Book of Dreams*, told of a patient's dream representing 'the conflagration of Covent Garden Theatre, where the exclusive greatness of God, in the operation and effect of magnetism, had been so often and so shamelessly derided.'[218] In other words, the kinds of complete separation of discourse and activity which modern interpreters may make in distinguishing between the activities of Priestley and Merry's Talisman were, in their time, much less firmly capable of discrimination. For example, Priestley had himself engaged in a rationalist polemic against local Swedenborgians whose New Jerusalem Temple had opened only weeks before the riots. Priestley's own incredulity at Swedenborgian doctrines of influxes and correspondences uncannily mirrored the loyalist attacks on his own brand of dissent, something which local Swedenborgians did not fail to notice.[219] In many ways, Merry's *Magician no Conjurer* puts forward Talisman as a kind of comic Victor Frankenstein, the sort of literary character that would have been created not by Mary or Percy Shelley but by their good friend, Thomas Love Peacock. For all of its generic constraint within the form of a comic opera, Merry's *Magician no Conjurer* reveals the proximity of political expression afforded by contemporary drama. Indeed, the opera's oblique approach to an otherwise serious subject (public disorder, anti-intellectual bigotry) was probably the one mechanism which allowed it to pass practically unscathed as it fell beneath Larpent's blue pencil.

By examining the treatment in the theatre of how drama responded to a highly specific topical domestic incident such as the 1791 Birmingham riots, this chapter has demonstrated the engagement of dramatic writing with political culture in late-eighteenth-century London. The variety of forms, from comic opera to spectacular pantomime, show that there is a reliable continuum of engagement with the political in contemporary drama. The combination of the practice of close reading plus a high degree of historical specificity typified in this chapter rehearses a critical mechanism to ensure that such relationships, in all their complexities, are capable of recovery and analysis.

3
Blackface and Black Mask: *The Benevolent Planters versus Harlequin Mungo*

This chapter will analyse the portrayal of slavery in two late-1780s dramas, William Bates's *Harlequin Mungo; or, A Peep into the Tower* (1787) and Thomas Bellamy's *The Friends; or, The Benevolent Planters* (1789), and how this issue provoked dissimilar responses in London's East End and West End playhouses. Different audiences, varied regulatory provisions and inconsistent attitudes to slavery initiated markedly diverse representations of the topic of slavery even in playhouses barely a few miles apart and within a couple of years of each other. Despite these apparently polarized situations, the underlying story of their separate circumstances tells us much about the structural and social complexities of how such a highly charged political issue was portrayed in the capital's theatres. This chapter will particularly discuss the issue of black mask and blackface (the former being a convention in the representation of pantomime harlequins), and will attempt to recover the materiality of the black presence in London and how the existence of different types of audience catchments in the capital provoked these dissimilar theatrical responses. It will be shown that the opportunities afforded by the Royalty Theatre performing their pantomime of *Harlequin Mungo* using the traditional black-masked harlequin provided a mechanism more easily able to accommodate that theatre's racially diverse audience and celebrate an interracial marriage between Harlequin (the West Indian ex-slave, Mungo) and the plantation owner's daughter, Columbine.

Despite their apparent convergence as dramas about slavery, even the most rudimentary of introductions to their performed status rapidly encounters highly variant specificities. The principal texts are Thomas Bellamy's spoken prose drama *The Friends; or, The Benevolent Planters*, first performed on 5 August 1789 at the West End, summer season, Haymarket Theatre, and a pantomime produced over a year earlier

68

in London's East End, the Royalty's *Harlequin Mungo; or, A Peep into the Tower* written by William Bates with music by William Reeve and first performed on 12 November 1787.[220] While Bellamy's prose play received two performances, the Royalty's pantomime was performed at least 37 times.[221] *The Benevolent Planters* had been offered to Larpent for licensing with the revealing suffix *Slavery But a Name*. Unlike *The Benevolent Planters, Harlequin Mungo* was later assimilated into the cultural history of Georgian drama: Drury Lane's *Furibond; or, Harlequin Negro*, a pantomime of 1807, adapted much of its narrative, an outcome which was probably the result of movements amongst players crossing between the two playhouses.[222] Although not a topic of this chapter, *Harlequin Mungo's* transposition into *Harlequin Negro* is a good example of the reverse influence of the popular playhouses on the royal theatres.

Both dramas contain love stories concerning slaves in Caribbean plantation settings. Remarkably, *Harlequin Mungo* features a white plantation owner's daughter, Columbine, who falls in love with the West Indian slave, Mungo. As the harlequinade convention demanded, they marry at the end of the pantomime. In this respect, in its tale of miscegenation between the planter's daughter and a slave, its plot is closely similar to *Furibond*. However unlikely it may appear, the plot of *The Benevolent Planters* concerns an annual archery contest organized by Jamaican plantation owners for their slaves in which marriage and freedom are the prize for the competition's winner. Its narrative probably reflects anxieties that plantation owners, the 'Friends' of the title, had too much sexual licence with their female slaves. Roxann Wheeler's *The Complexion of Race: Categories of Difference in Eighteenth-Century British Culture* (Philadelphia: University of Pennsylvania Press, 2000) points out that many contemporaries concluded that 'white male sexuality ha[d] run amok in Jamaica and inverted power relations between colors and genders,' and that Edward Long's *The History of Jamaica* (1774) had argued that unbridled white male sexuality had impoverished the genetic pool from which future colonialists would need to emerge.[223] The basic plot of *The Benevolent Planters* is situated within this discourse of promoting the kind of same-race sexual partnerships that Long thought was missing on the plantations. The archery contest is its sublmination of these concerns. *Harlequin Mungo*, on the other hand, is just as specific in celebrating Harlequin and Columbine's interracial marriage. In *Harlequin Mungo*, the conventional structure of the love match within the harlequinade dictates that this marriage must not only take place but also be celebrated by the audience. Its 37 performances testify to how much the audience approved of such an outcome.

During the late 1780s, under the management of George Colman the Elder and his namesake son, playwright and future Examiner of Plays George Colman the Younger, the Haymarket was an affluent, profitable and fashionable theatre. By contrast, John Palmer's Royalty in 1787 was not only under severe and repeated attempts to bring about its closure, but the playhouse's location in the vicinity of the Tower of London adjacent to the Thames sugar-warehousing and shipping industries meant that it remained unusually aware of its racially mixed audience. Its very survival was based upon the Royalty's precariously optimistic claim that it fell within a separate legal jurisdiction controlled by the Constable of the Tower.[224] However, these plays, produced at similar temporal moments and fairly proximate locations, managed to produce different political and philosophical insights into the same set of problems. The degree of regulation imposed upon the Romantic-period stage, with its monopolistic and censored drama, was bound to throw up sharp differences in how subjects were treated and presented before different audience groups.

Both of the plays presented a number of roles for black-faced white actors and actresses. In *The Benevolent Planters*, these are Oran and his slave lover, Selima, plus various male and female 'virgin' slaves, including a group who must perform in an archery contest organized by the planters. *Harlequin Mungo* was more complicated in how its blackness was portrayed. The piece embeds within its title the pantomime's main action, the transformation of the slave Mungo into Harlequin. The setting is a West Indian 'Sugar Mill, &c.' with '*Several Slaves discovered at work at different parts of the Plantation.*'[225] Only with the black-American Ira Aldridge's appearance on the stage of the Royal Coburg Theatre in 1825 would a coloured actor perform before a London audience.[226] In *Harlequin Mungo*, before his transformation into a conventionally black-masked Harlequin in brightly lozenge patterned costume, Mungo and his fellow slaves would have been represented with coloured faces. After the transformation, Harlequin would almost certainly have followed the convention for that role of wearing a black mask. From blackface to black mask, the Romantic-period stage presented some extraordinary complications for the representations of race mediated through the conventions of pantomime. Some of the contemporary possibilities of make-up and face colourings for actors, which sometimes extended to the use of coloured textiles, are discussed below.

The current dominant critical mode for discussing stage blackface is within the culture of North American minstrelsy, as laid out by Eric Lott's influential *Love and Theft: Blackface Minstrelsy and the American Working Class* (1993). Lott argues that white people blacking up is both a comic appropriation and a controlling subjugation of black people, a practice denying racial authenticity and displaying blackness as counterfeit. Not only did the working-class taste for minstrelsy from the 1830s affirm racial difference, it reaffirmed the exclusion of black people from a place within that class. Lott's work has been enthusiastically extended by a number of cultural historians, for example James P. Byrne has argued that the nineteenth-century Irish in the United States of America were appropriated in much the same way and with similar racial implications.[227] Mikko Tuhkanen insists that 'the minstrel mask perhaps continues to be a central figure in how "racial" visibility functions in the United States,' attributing to Lott's work the wider claim that minstrelsy is a current cultural practice in that country.[228] By contrast, Sean X. Goudie has historicized these minstrelizing modes more specifically by discussing the function of blackface in J. Robinson's farce *The Yorker's Stratagem; or, Banana's Wedding* (New York, 1792). Robinson's play was produced in New York and Philadelphia but never found a production in the southern states. In southern towns such as Charleston, South Carolina – much to the surprise of the contemporary British-visitor John Lambert – Goudie argues that blackface was prohibited and no black people allowed into the theatre, 'lest the negroes in Charleston should conceive, from being represented on the stage, and having their colour, dress, manners, and customs imitated by the white people, that they were very important personages.'[229] Whereas Goudie discusses a play written in North America, a work very much the product of a dialogue with these conditions, Felicity A. Nussbaum migrates minstrelsy to eighteenth-century Britain. Nussbaum argues that Isaac Bickerstaff's popular comedy *The Padlock* (1768) and the Rev. Henry Bate's *The Blackamoor Wash'd White* (1776) were 'precursors of minstrelsy . . . an example of what Eric Lott has called "minstrelsy's mixed erotic economy of celebration and exploitation" and of a white culture's fascination with black skin.'[230] However, this embryonic minstrelizing – if that is really an apt description – was highly contested in the British setting.

It is easy to see why one might wish to trace the heritage of minstrel shows as a theatrical import datable to the last colonial phases of British sovereignty, but they were a phenomenon of nineteenth-century American popular culture which was much less obviously important in Britain. Eric Lott's *Love and Theft: Blackface Minstrelsy and the American Working Class* (1993) particularly cites working-class American melodrama playhouses in the 1830s and 1840s as a premier site of the emergence of minstrelsy, places of 'antebellum "racial" production, inventing or at least maintaining the working-class languages of race' and moving from 'solo songs and dances in legitimate theaters' as 'an art of brief burlesque and comic relief through much of the 1830s' through to 'partial absorption into the Uncle Tom's Cabin melodramas in the early and mid-1850s' as a 'major part of urban popular culture.'[231] The problem with this approach lies in its detachment from contemporary attitudes to coloured people in eighteenth-century Britain and how they were represented on the stage. Arguably, *Harlequin Mungo* and *The Benevolent Planters* hold a balance between working-class and elite tastes. At its starkest, *The Benevolent Planters* is a drama about the moralities of patrician ownership (of slaves and of plantations) while *Harlequin Mungo*, inhabiting a more plebeian genre in London's docklands, poses the dilemma of what it might be like to actually be a slave. Beyond the scope of this book are the two remarkable burlettas, William Barrymore's *El Hyder; the Chief of the Ghaut Mountains. A grand eastern melo-dramatic spectacle. In two acts* (1818) and H.M. Milner's *Tippoo Saib; or, The Storming of Seringapatam. A Drama, in Three Acts* (1823), both produced for the Royal Coburg Theatre, the playhouse where, in 1825, the black actor Ira Aldridge was to become the first black actor on a British stage. These two Coburg dramas, which may have sometimes have been played blackface, looked determinedly eastwards to the India as much as they did to the slaving west Atlantic. For *El Hyder* in particular, the public was presented with a heroic, patriotic, Indian Islamic ruler whose real-life model had been the scourge of the East India Company, and in *Tippoo Saib*, a similarly heroic figure whose martial prowess, patriotic spirit and filial devotion were equally admired. Of course, these were all roles played by white actors yet they appear to have been written to celebrate rather than denigrate the Islamic rulers of Mysore. The absence of any strongly perceptible tradition of minstrelizing Asian roles is a limitation to the relevance of Lott's thesis on the British model. Furthermore, within the British context, dramas such as these tend to show that orientalist cultural practices were the province of elite rather than popular representations.

Within this fluid but nationally specific attitude to race, even the title of *Harlequin Mungo* is itself a curiously revealing piece of British cultural equivocation. While 'Mungo' was a racial diminutive, as in the phrase used of another eighteenth-century Jamaican black, 'an uncommonly smart and intelligent little Mungo,' it was also a term capable of conveying personal affection between white people.[232] The playwright and composer Charles Dibdin named one of his sons Charles Isaac Mungo after Dibdin Snr had inaugurated the blackface role of Mungo in the first production of *The Padlock* in 1768, the year of his son's birth.[233] In an age when the radical pressman Richard Carlile was proud to name his son Thomas Paine Carlile, it is unlikely Dibdin Snr intended any diminution. A decade after Charles Isaac Mungo Dibdin's birth, it is possible to glimpse Dibdin Snr's own racial awareness in the unpromising context of Covent Garden's *The Mirror; or, Harlequin Every-Where* (1779), which included a Negro consigned to the infernal region of Tartary after being whipped to death ('... me work dam hard; and yet, Massa, Heaven forgive him, strip, and whip, and cut, poor Negro man all to piece[*sic*]'), a complaint subsequent to the character's emancipation to 'the pleasures of Elysium.'[234] In addition, and as will be argued below, the transformational conventions of the harlequinade problematizes many assumptions about the racial denigration of black characters. However, arguments about minstrelsy as a historical British condition which then migrated to North America are significantly complicated by contemporary stage practices concerning make-up and costume.

Some American blacks recognized that conditions in Britain relative to coloured people were markedly different to those appertaining in the United States of America. The black-American actor James Hewlett, who perhaps preceded Ira Aldridge onto the British stage, wrote a highly significant letter to *The Times* in July 1824 complaining about the satirical mimicry of Charles Mathews's hit sketch, 'Opossum up a Gum-Tree,' a comic scene contained within his larger entertainment known as the 'Trip to America' and apparently based on Mathews's experience of having seen the Mercer Street African Theatre in New York in which a black actor was performing *Hamlet*.[235] Hewlett's letter is important, not least because the specificity of its historical episode was imperfectly narrated in Eric Lott's *Love and Theft: Blackface Minstrelsy and the American Working Class* (1993).[236]

Lott concludes that Aldridge had been the target of Mathews's sketch and relates how Ira Aldridge 'coolly disavowed the imitation: "The truth... is that I never attempted the character of Hamlet in my life, and I need not say that the whole of the ludicrous scene so well and so humourously described by Mr. Mathews never occurred at all." ' As Lott points out, Aldridge was subsequently besieged by requests to perform 'Opossum up a Gum-Tree' and he soon incorporated it into his performances, enabling 'one of Mathews's most profitable caricatures becoming one of Aldridge's most profitable performances.' Lott concludes that 'Its influence is a foretaste of the way the minstrelization of black practices helped to obscure them.'[237] This pivotal example in Lott's narrative is based on the wrong black actor. *The Times* letter not only gives credibility to Aldridge's avowal of never having played *Hamlet*, it also complicates the validity of the lesson Lott draws from it – that this was the minstrelizing of a black actor (Aldridge) by a white man (Mathews). Not only does it appear that Aldridge appropriated Mathews's caricature of a black performance, but Aldridge also appropriated Hewlett's original performance on which the sketch was based. However, much more important is the insurgent voice of Hewlett's address to Mathews in his letter to *The Times*. His riposte was not only an important critique of American racism, it was also a defence of British interracial practices as perceived by Hewlett in the early 1820s.

Lott provides the background to Mathews's visit to America but does not make it clear that the punch line of Mathews's sketch lay in transposing the last phrase of the black-American's rendition of Hamlet's words, 'Or to take arms against a sea of troubles, / And by opposing end them?' into a song, 'Opposum up a gum-tree.'[238] Mathews's sketches were invariably pirated and unauthorized, but Hewlett seems to have been personally offended upon receiving details of the sketch, strongly implying that he believed it was his own performance Mathews had witnessed.[239] He accused him of having 'burlesqued me with the rest of the Negro actors, as you are pleased to call us – mimicked our styles – imitated our dialects – laughed at our anomalies – and lampooned, O shame! our complexions.' It is not certain whether Mathews blacked-up for the sketch, which was quite short, but it is certainly a straightforward example of the type of minstrelizing Lott has identified and not comparable in its racial specificity to Mathews's parodying of the imaginary Yankee yeoman Jonathan W. Doubikin, similarly included in the 'Trip to America' entertainment.[240] However, mustering some dignity, Hewlett's letter continued:

> In our free and happy country, custom and a meridian sun have made some distinctions and classifications in the order of society relative to complexions, 'tis true, 'tis pity, an pity 'tis, 'tis true'; but in England, where these anomalous distinctions are unknown, nay, where international marriages and blending of colours are sometimes seen, what warrant can you have of lampooning our complexion?[241]

His ironizing about 'our free and happy country' apart, Hewlett's comments about the United States's 'distinctions and classifications in the order of society relative to complexions' is contrasted to that of 'England, where these anomalous distinctions are unknown, nay, where international marriages and blending of colours are sometimes seen.' From Hewlett's point of view, it was 'our complexions,' the signifying skin colour, which had fixed him 'relative' to the American 'order of society' and which he feared was now being reiterated and affirmed in Mathews's 'Opossum up a Gum-Tree' sketch. The 'Trip to America' was certainly taken up enthusiastically by the British. As Lott points out, Mathews frequently performed the 'Opossum' song until his death in 1835, but the 'Trip to America' passed blithely even into Richard Carlile's *Newgate Monthly Magazine; or, Calendar of Men, Things and Opinions* and found provincial adaptations as *Mr. Mathews' Trip to America* even in the rural town of Stamford, Lincolnshire.[242] However, Hewlett's experience of London caused him to differentiate between racial practices in America and Britain, crucially acknowledging that, 'in England...anomalous distinctions are unknown...international marriages and blending of colours are sometimes seen.'

Whatever the American case, in London black men had long been accepted as ideological leaders amongst the working class, but usually because of what they said and how they spoke rather than because of what they wrote or how they were represented on stage. In the context of a contemporary metropolitan sociability which verged on theatricality, it is important to reconstruct the black presence so that texts are not defined within a set of critical concerns deriving from the North American situation where, as followers of Lott such as Mikko Tuhkanen have argued, the legacy of minstrelsy permeates the current cultural situation.

Radicalized black men in Georgian London were not subaltern voices nor were they passive recipients of their theatrical representation. Whatever interpretation may be put on literary texts, the ideologically marked presence of black spoken discourse retained in the historical record enables a fairly accurate degree of historical recovery: one assumes that those black voices less ideologically marked were not the less distinctive or assertive. First of all, as has been argued above, the Romantic-period stage was not a free arena of expression, not for anyone – excepting the patentees (assuming they could satisfy the Examiner). Ironically, and this may be a sad subtext to Hewlett's letter, as far as the British context is concerned, both he and Mathews were subject to specific restrictions on their natural and civic rights in pursuit of a theatrical career. Mathews's satirizing was based upon how he heard black actors speak Shakespeare in New York. Paradoxically, although Hewlett could perform Shakespeare in New York – although clearly running the risk of Mathews's racial mimicry – in London the number of male performers of Shakespeare was legislatively confined to the two patent theatres, perhaps 14–16 speaking roles per winter's night across the two theatres (assuming both houses were performing the Bard that night). Such were the economics of monopoly that Wordsworth's evaluator, Thomas Knight, was one of the eight crucial performers the Covent Garden management identified in 1800 as being able to close the theatre if they refused to act.[243] Mathews was well aware that his own shows, such as the 'Trip to America,' traversed risky territory because they relied on impromptu spoken material which could not be easily submitted to the Examiner of Plays.[244] In other words, although his comments were racist, there was nothing particulary patrician in Mathews's views, nor even in his own situation as a performer who had already felt acutely the 'injurious monopoly' of the patent houses and how their managers had displaced his earlier 'At Home' shows to the smaller venue of the Lyceum.[245] As far back as 1814, some years before Mathews ventured out solo, some of his Haymarket benefit nights had featured 'Hamlet's advice to the Players in *IMITATION* of several celebrated Performers!!!'[246] In other words, his mimicry existed in a continuum of theatrical parodies of actors in that role.

However, if the theatre tended towards making the majority of players either mute performers of pantomime or else musical actors in burletta, it is also important to bring the speaking black men of late Georgian London, and their intransigent but articulate voices, into an account of the capital's black presence and to attempt to populate the playhouses and their environs with their sounds. Figures such as Robert Wedderburn, the son of a Jamaican slave, have been all but silenced as a speaking presence in London because modern critics have attempted to re-create them as writers. Wedderburn's lack of passivity and well-documented, highly vocal, radical activism ran concurrently with black-faced actors on the London stage. It is in this void – between blacked-up minstrelizing white actors and articulate and vocal black Georgian Londoners – that the culturally assimilative racial attitudes proclaimed by James Hewlett existed.

Despite devoting a chapter to him, one recent writer has little to say about Wedderburn's oratorical power and the popular following forged by his speech making.[247] According to Richard Carlile, writing at a time when both he and Wedderburn were incarcerated in Dorchester gaol in 1820, Wedderburn was illiterate.[248] It would be foolhardy to contradict Carlile's evidence about Wedderburn's illiteracy from the vantage point of the twenty-first century. On the other hand, enabling our picture of Wedderburn as someone whose powers were principally those of an orator and leader resituates his stature amongst London's working class and, by implication, makes him someone charismatic enough to have his speechmaking worthy of transliteration into writing by an amaneuensis. Viewing Wedderburn as a black leader within an ultra-radical grouping of mainly white followers linked to the various post-1794 treason trials incarnations of the London Corresponding Society (and later United Irishmen), together with a provisional body known as The Friends of Liberty, makes sense of a possible political and theological divergence. Wedderburn's splintering from the religious-enthusiast pressman, George Ribeau, the publisher of his *Truth, Self-Supported; or, A Refutation of Certain Doctrinal Errors, Generally Adopted in the Christian Church* (1790) and many of Richard Brothers's writings, brought him before a new group of largely Spencean activists who based themselves on physical-force revolution and British and Creole versions of the biblical Jubilee.[249]

With his mid-1790s millenarianism challenged by Riebau's increasing adherence to the self-styled prophet Brothers, Wedderburn came to be associated with a diverse group of radical pressmen including Daniel Isaac Eaton, T.G. Ballard and Thomas Spence himself. Their publication of 'Citizen Bailey's' *The White Devils Un-Cased. Being The First Discourse Upon Ecclesiastical Tyranny, And Superstition, Delivered At Section 2 And 7 Of The Friends Of Liberty* (1795) was a straightforward attack on Brothers and his usurpation of the prophetic role. The *White Devils Un-Cased*'s supplementary, 'Lecture the Second: Prince Brothers's Scarlet Devils displayed,' is almost certainly a speech of Wedderburn's partially rendered as a transliterated re-creation of the 'Creole' identity Wedderburn had claimed for himelf in identifying his authorship of *Truth, Self-Supported*.[250] In a convergence of radical cultures associated with different types of theatricality and performativity, the group coalescing around Eaton, Ballard, Spence and (probably) Wedderburn were also the same group with which the dramatist Robert Merry came into contact to publish *The Wounded Soldier* (1795). If true, Wedderburn's position in the mid-1790s looks forward to his ascendant role, together with other black men, amongst London's radicalized working class in the late 1810s and early 1820s. Throughout, the impact of their charismatic presence and speech-making skills are stressed as intransigent voices within London's radical movement.[251] The speeches of black working-class radicals were listened to attentively by the general London working-class population. Exactly as Hewlett put it in his letter to *The Times*, there were fewer 'anomalous distinctions' amongst London's working class and perhaps more 'blending of colours.' The destructive tension between working-class identity and colour which Lott identifies as present in early-nineteenth-century North American minstrelsy was not a part of the British experience. Instead of minstrelsy, British black performativity was authenticated by a highly vocalized political message in a resurgence which occupied a quite distinctive performativity.

Occasionally, black people can be glimpsed in places specifically associated with theatres and theatricality. According to Paul Edwards and James Walvin, the black street entertainer Billy Waters appeared on stage playing himself at the Adelphi Theatre between 1821 and 1823 in W.T. Moncrieff's *Tom and Jerry; or, Life in London in 1820* (1821), but on what evidence this claim is based remains obscure.[252] The one-legged ex-sailor Waters was a well-known figure in the environs of the Adelphi on the Strand and figured as a black-faced character played by white actors in Moncrieff's *Tom and Jerry*. It is not clear whether appearing as one's authentic self as a street musician amounts to North America's practices of minstrelsy although Moncrieff's minstrelizing of him is quite clear-cut. Nevertheless, it is possible to be more certain about the lives of a number of other black Londoners. A spouting club at the Jacob's Well tavern in the Barbican had been visited in the 1790s by Henry Angelo, a trainer of swordsmanship for actors, where he had witnessed the black man Julius Soubise practising Othello.[253] In the late 1810s, a Home Office spy found Wedderburn and another black man haranguing nearly 300 post-Peterloo protestors at the selfsame Jacob's Well tavern, strongly suggesting not only the extraordinary continuities of the black presence in London in highly specific locations but also their association with oratory and theatricality.[254]

In the aftermath of Cato Street, a Home Office informer found 'R[ev.]. Dr. Wetherburn[sic], the Hay loft Preacher' in Holywell Street (leading off Drury Lane and near to the Olympic Theatre), where his followers immediately 'recognized him ... [and] he was surrounded presently by a Grope[sic] of those that come out of the Tavern.'[255] The 'Hay loft' where Wedderburn ('their Black Prince') had preached his blasphemous, atheistical, sermons was located in Hopkins Street, Soho.[256] Hopkins Street, and maybe even the very hayloft Wedderburn vacated subsequent to his arrest, was probably also the location of one of London's contemporary private theatres or ' "preparatory barns" for green-horns to study in,' as their facetious owner claimed in *The Rambler's Magazine; or, Fashionable Emporium of Polite Literature* during a correspondence relative to the illegality of these establishments.[257] Whatever the currency of Wedderburn's published narratives on slavery, he was clearly a considerable figure on the metropolitan scene capable of verbally articulating radical political views. This kind of vocal, and highly social, black presence can be traced further back into the eighteenth century. Whatever interpretation one puts on the theatrical practice of blackface, the historical record continues to throw up a visible, vocal – and sporadically intransigent – coloured element in the environs of the playhouses.

The reception of James Townley's Drury Lane farce, *High Life Below Stairs* (1759), provides a rich example of the cultural complexity of a blackface comic drama in a storyline which sets a West Indian landowner against his black servants. The plot features Lovel, the ostentatiously rich white-Jamaican landowner ('I have seen it delight your Soul, when the People in the Street have stared at your Equipage; especially if they whispered... 'That is "Squire *Lovel*, the great *West Indian* " ') who exposes his servants' laziness and high living at his expense.[258] The farce was the subject of a series of well-documented riots by servants on account of the play's portrayal of their aping of their master's ways and consuming his food and drink.[259] Disquiet at Townley's farce was sufficient to provoke at least one servant, Oliver Grey, to write a pamphlet about the riots, *An Apology for the Servants* (1760), which also drew attention to contemporary proposals aimed at withdrawing the practice of 'vails,' extra payments (like modern tipping) made to servants.[260] Vails were frequently paid at theatres where servants controlled access to their employers by charging this unofficial fee. Grey reckoned the practice was common in Germany; but there were also similar riots, again centred around performances of *High Life Below Stairs*, in Edinburgh and London ('No sooner was the piece begun, than a prodigious noise was heard from the footmens gallery') where again the issue of vails appears to have been prominent.[261] However, the disturbances at the Jacob's Well Theatre, Bristol (owned by the comedian John Hippisley whose daughter played in the first Drury Lane production), are more revealing because, in addition to the threat to vails, it seems highly probable there would have been a racial dimension to the rioting since the city's association with slaving implies the presence of a higher proportion of black servants in attendance than would have been the case in most provincial cities.[262] Both the text of the drama and its production history make it clear that *High Life Below Stairs* was frequently perceived as having a racial dimension.

There were two specific blackface roles, but a number of comic servants were prominent in *High Life Below Stairs*. Lovel, a white 'young West-Indian of Fortune' recently returned to England, is the employer of seven servants, two of whom – Kingston and Cloe – are black ('Why, Man, in *Jamaica*, before I was ten Years old, I had an hundred Blacks kissing my Feet every Day').[263] Returning in disguise to the servants' hall, Lovel witnesses their laziness and extravagance at first hand. At the Bristol production, the theatre's contemporary historian recorded the 'violent hissing, hooting, and pelting, which continued unabated until a favourite comedian of the name of [Robert] PALMER (who played the *Duke's Servant*), took occasion, during the supper-scene, to drink, "To the confusion of all masters and mistresses who refuse to give vales[sic]," ' thereby allowing the play to proceed. Palmer's brother was later to become the owner of the Royalty Theatre in Tower Hamlets, the playhouse of *Harlequin Mungo*. John and Robert Palmer worked in close professional association, so John would probably have been aware of this Bristol episode when he opened the Royalty two years later, close to the docking facilities associated with the West and the East Indian traffic. However, the *High Life Below Stairs* blackface roles had further cultural resonances.

Oliver Grey's protests notwithstanding, Townley's farce was popular with the employers of servants who performed it at their country house theatricals. Predictably enough, Townley's farce was enthusiastically taken up in the patrician class's private theatres. The Governor's gardens in Madras, India, was the setting in 1788 for productions of Bickerstaff's *Padlock* and Townley's *High Life Below Stairs*, both staged by European women and white army officers in aid of a local charity for female orphans (presumably Indian girls).[264] The blackface roles of *The Padlock's* Mungo and *High Life's* Kingston were played by British army captains but, more remarkably, the latter's female black servant, Cloe, was played by one, Lieutenant Grant. Some years earlier around 1774, at Cassiobury House, Hertfordshire, the seat of the Earl of Essex, the amateur actor Thomas Orde-Powlett (1746–1807) made a souvenir print etching, probably for fellow players, of the servants' hall scene in *High Life Below Stairs* which had been played at a Cassiobury country-house party. Unique impressions of this print in the Lewis Walpole Library show that players endorsed copies with own recollections of their roles in the private theatricals ('Blackee you go! ... Cookey you go! ... Sambo = Answer the Door'). While Lovel peremptorily summons his servant Kingston by one of these names ('What Blackey, Blackey'), the derogatory term 'Sambo' is not present in Townley's published text, implying a specifically Cassiobury private theatrical interpolation. Indeed, in Orde-Powlett's print, the drunken, stupefied black manservant, slouched in a wooden chair in the servants hall, is a prominent figure in the composition.[265] Within the seclusion of the English country-house private theatrical, or the Indian colonial garden party, it is clear that black-faced white gentry delighted in counterfeiting coloured people, perhaps in performances where complicated nuances of rank and authority were mixed with transgressive sexualities. In the British public theatres, however, the depiction of minstrelized 'blacks,' especially when contextualized within perceived threats to financial customs, was popularly perceived as unacceptable and resulted in rioting.

While people of colour continued to be played by white actors, the depiction of vocal and resistive blacks on stage was gradually increasing. Although heavily censored on account of its references to grain forestalling, and eventually withdrawn, Thomas John Dibdin's musical entertainment written for Covent Garden, *The Two Farmers* (1800), contained in its dialogue a confrontation between a hoarding English farmer, Locust, and his black farm labourer, Caesar, who is remarkably self-sufficient and assertive of his legal rights of entitlement to protection under British law. When threatened with a beating by Locust, the black man affirms his rights in a remarkable passage:

> Top, Massa, top! Slave once, not now...No Slave here – You pay, I worke – You kick, I tell Massa Kenyon – he speak twelve men in a Box – dey take poor Negerman's part, & you kick black man nor more, I warrant, Massa.[266]

Caesar's allusion is to Lord Chief Justice Keynon's currently impending judgement about grain forestalling (a circumstance which no doubt contributed to its suppression).[267] Like the Chinese plaintiff at the Old Bailey, discussed below, Dibdin's unperformed and intercepted drama seems to accurately reflect knowledge and awareness of how black people were empowered to access the legal system of judge and jury ('twelve men in a Box').

The social polarities evident in *High Life Below Stairs* in the 1760s, from riotous Bristol servants to the kind of exclusive securities implicit in white players blacked up as coloured male and female servants, implies a complex cultural context where racial denigration was present but contested. Blacking up for *High Life Below Stairs* tended to take place either as a prelude to riot or else under conditions where the possibility of rioting had been deliberately excluded. However, blacking up was also a practice which, in the regular theatres at least, took place within a spectrum of similar practices. As was the cases with the Indian locations of *El Hyder* and *Tippoo Saib*, the ex-actor Leman Thomas Rede made it clear in his advice to young actors that black African roles were to be differentiated from Arab, east Asian or Indian subcontinent roles. Rede's *The Road to the Stage* gave carefully detailed advice to aspirant performers about preparing skin colouring. The main reason he gives for Othello's brown 'coloured countenance' (rather than black 'sables') was that such blackface was 'destructive of the effect of the face, and preventing the possiblity of the expression being noted, [and] has become an obsolete custom.' The need to increase Othello's expressivity transposed his portrayal from black 'sables' to what Rede described as 'a tawny tinge,' an effect produced by applying to the face a compound known as 'Spanish brown,' a dark reddish-brown pigment whose principal colouring ingredient was usually sesquioxide of iron. By the first decades of the nineteenth century, particularly in the English provincial theatres where Rede had worked, Othello may well have been represented more red than brown, and certainly not black. However, for other plays in the late-eighteenth- and early-nineteenth-century repertoire, there are many pitfalls for modern commentators adhering to the minstrelizing theory of white actors in blackface.

The Road to the Stage also serves as a reminder of the extent (and modern unfamiliarity) with the range of the coloured roles in the standard dramatic Romantic-period repertory. Rede confirms that, as well as being the colour for Othello, Spanish brown was also used in the roles of Bajazet in Nicholas Rowe's *Tamerlane* (1702); Zanga in Edward Young's *The Revenge* (1721); Sadi in John Brown's *Barbarossa, A Tragedy* (1755); Bulcazin in George Colman the Younger's *The Mountaineers* (1794); Muley in Charles Isaac Mungo Dibdin's *The Wild Man* (1809); and Rolla in R.B. Sheridan's *Pizarro* (1799). Although the 'Muley' in this list may refer to a character in Matthew Gregory Lewis's *The Castle Spectre* (1797), a role of the same name is more prominent in Dibdin's *The Wild Man* where the text describes him as a 'Black Moor.' As with Othello, in the eighteenth century a 'Black Moor' might be brown. To complicate matters further, another character in *The Wild Man*, Allahmar (whose name may sound Arabic to modern ears), is also described in Dibdin's cast list as a 'Black Moor.' That is, there may have been many 'Black Moors' appearing on the eighteenth-century stage who were actually coloured a reddish 'Spanish brown.'

Conversely, Rede also advised actors of the 1820s that Wouski, a female native-American role in George Colman the Younger's *Inkle and Yarico* (1787), ought to be coloured the same 'sables' black colour as Mungo in Isaac Bickerstaff's *The Padlock* (1768) or the 'African' Sambo as in Frederick Reynolds's *Laugh When You Can* (1799).[268] To complicate matters further, Rede related that the character of Hassan (almost certainly referring to the character in Lewis's *The Castle Spectre*) was played as a black-faced negro even though (as with Dibdin's Muley) the name may sound Arabic to modern readers.[269] Lewis commented in the printed text of *The Castle Spectre* that many of his contemporaries had compared his Hassan to the character of Zanga in Young's *The Revenge*: if Zanga wore Spanish brown (as Rede suggested), it means Hassan's black-face was no particular obstacle to the audience transposing Arabic characteristics into black faceroles and *vice versa*.[270] Oddly, Rede does not comment on *The Castle Spectre*'s character of Saib, Hassan's confidant, but the absence of comment implies Saib was not a blackface. Out of all these bewilderingly coloured-up characters, it is perhaps the 'sables' black native-American, Wowski, in *Inkle and Yarico*, who is the most disturbing to modern minstrelizing interpretations because, although Colman's drama is specifically set in 'in the wilds of America,' Rede confirms she was played as a black woman, suggesting theatre managers and actors were following the original 1711 *Spectator* narrative (reprinted in *The Times* in 1787 when the drama first appeared) rather than working from the hints contained in Colman's text.[271] However, to complicate matters further, Rede claimed that in all of the roles referred to above, 'it is very common... to use only an extraordinary quantity of vermillion or carmine spread over the whole of the face,' which implies a reddish hue derived from mercuric sulphide and red iron oxide.[272] Blackface was achieved by first applying 'a thin coat of pomatum' ('or what is better, though more disagreeable... lard [animal fat]') topped off by burnt cork soaked with 'beer' – 'which will fix the colouring matter' – and all applied 'with a hare's-foot, or a cloth.'[273] Considering the crude pigmentation methods used, true 'sables' blacking up may well have been quite widely avoided by many actors. Indeed, they might more accurately be described as having 'reddened up' for their roles.

However, these were not the only colouring agents employed by contemporary actors. Commenting that 'Wigging is a science in itself,' Rede remarked that many contemporary practices of theatrical costume and colouring had become so stylized as to be arbitrary as signifying referents: 'Custom has established red wigs for countrymen, and black ones for Roman and all tragic characters, though it would be difficult to assign a reason for either practice. The English rustic is not generally seen with carroty locks... and the Romans were not partial to raven ringlets.'[274] In other words, blackface as a theatrical signifier existed within a spectrum of contemporary expedient theatrical practices selected to approximate various tangible and intangible qualities in the text.

Face colour and dyed wigs were complemented by a further battery of devices which similarly complicate our attempts to understand the signifying role of colour, as it might be construed as if relating to the real politics of race. For example, Rede refers with distaste to the 'unnatural' effect of 'wearing black gloves' to represent 'sables' roles, 'for the colour is too intense to represent skin, and negroes invariably cover themselves with light clothing.'[275] Black-faced renditions were not only sometimes complemented by gloves but also by 'armings,' sleeves coloured to approximate the colour of the character represented. Rede relates that Hassan in *The Castle Spectre* was often played costumed with 'Arms of black silk' which he considered had 'a very bad effect.' These 'armings' as they were known were 'dyed with a strong infusion of Spanish annatto,' a red seed actually tending to give a yellow or reddish colour.[276] The use of coloured textiles also extended to European roles. The great Edmund Kean disastrously played Macbeth in Dublin wearing 'flesh-coloured arms, and gloves of one piece' fixed to the rest of his costume which, in the short interval after the murder scene, 'did not allow him to disengage himself from his flesh-coloured arms and gloves, and he entered with his hands as bloody as before.'[277] The introduction of coloured textiles to represent skin appears to have been the sort of counterfeiting which drew attention to its own impossibility – and yet it was obviously a sufficiently widely distributed contemporary theatrical technique for Rede to feel obliged to warn against.

It is in the context of these highly contextualized contemporary theatrical practices concerning racial representation in the Romantic-period playhouse that Bellamy's *Benevolent Planters* and the Royalty's *Harlequin Mungo* existed. If considerations of the production location were not complicated enough, and *High Life Below Stairs* shows that plays were both performed and received very differently according to whether the venue was a Theatre Royal, a country-house theatrical or a colonial garden party, there were also a number of separate differentials possible concerning how these plays were performed. The 'science' of 'Wigging' apart, it is perfectly conceivable that *The Benevolent Planters* was performed with its slave roles fully blacked up in burnt cork fixed with beer or else, less drastically, coated in Spanish brown with the exposed upper limbs covered in black gloves and black silk 'armings' dyed reddish Spanish annatto. To add to these grotesque paradoxes of presentation, Bellamy's equivocation as to the play's meaning is indicated by its first having been submitted to Larpent as *The Benevolent Planters Slavery But a Name*, but first performed as *The Friends; or, The Benevolent Planters*.[278] Both revisions strongly suggest that Bellamy's interests are in reforming the planters rather than in freeing the slaves. The presence of carmine- or vermillion-coloured white actors dominating the drama may have helped specify the European dimension of slavery as a moral issue to be tackled within the context of patrician authority and sociability, rather than as an affect on the (blacked up) slaves. Certainly, the predicament of slaves appears to come somewhere near the bottom of Bellamy's list of priorities.

In addition to these imponderables of performance, the Royalty and Haymarket theatres staged their plays under entirely different regulatory regimes. The Haymarket, which has been the subject of William J. Burling's meticulously researched *Summer Theatre in London, 1661–1820, and the Rise of the Haymarket Theatre* (2000), had a certain amount of freedom to indulge in spoken drama. James Winston's evidence to the Parliamentary Select Committee in 1832 suggests that such occasional licensing arrangements were reasonably frequent, at least in the first decades of the nineteenth century.[279] Burling also points out that the Haymarket at this time, under the management of George Colman the Elder, was not only economically thriving but, during the period 1777–88, its repertoire was being rejuvenated by a deliberate policy of programming new writing.[280] His son George Colman the Younger's opera *Inkle and Yarico*, first performed two years before Bellamy's *Benevolent Planters* on 4 August 1787 and also linked to issues of slavery, had also been a Haymarket mainpiece. Colman may well have had a deliberate strategy of producing plays about slavery, stemming from his own success with *Inkle and Yarico*. Bellamy's possible connections with Oladauh Equiano, discussed below, may suggest that Colman thought he was drawing on these links. Certainly, taking into account that summer seasons at the Haymarket were much shorter than the winter openings of Covent Garden and Drury Lane, *Inkle and Yarico*'s run of 20 performances in 1787 was impressive.[281] Indeed, the drama proved to be of enduring popularity. Burling notes that it went on to become the playhouse's sixth most popular mainpiece in the period up to 1800, making it, as its modern editor Jeffrey N. Cox has pointed out, as popular as *Hamlet* in the repertoire during the last quarter of the eighteenth century.[282] By contrast, *The Benevolent Planters* only received two performances. Certainly, Bellamy had a well-heeled audience in prospect. Under Colman Senior's direction, the Haymarket had become not only a fashionable venue but also one which was highly profitable. Burling has calculated that it was a more profitable playhouse during the early 1780s than Drury Lane, and had risen to be more profitable than Covent Garden by the end of the decade. The Haymarket's affluent popularity brought with it 'every night a very crowded and brilliant audience,' and sometimes when royalty attended, 'twice as many persons were turned away, as were admitted.'[283]

By contrast, at the other end of the metropolis, the East End Royalty, in Wellclose Square, Goodman's Fields, was a much-oppressed theatre, the target from its very inception of strenuous efforts at its suppression by the patentees of Covent Garden and Drury Lane.[284] In its attempts to evade closure in the 1780s in a campaign led against it by the patent theatres, the Royalty had quickly developed a variety of musical formats by way of complying with the patentees. Their *Apollo turn'd Stroller; or, Thereby hangs a Tale* was described as 'A Musical Pasticcio' (*c*.1787), John and Charles Thomas Carter's *The Constant Couple; or, Though Out of Sight, Ne'er Out of Mind* (1788) was a 'Musical Entertainment' and the Royalty's *Hero and Leander, A Burletta* (*c*.1787) – the last being a generic designation which the playwright Isaac Jackman was pleased to reaffirm in the title of a supportive pamphlet he wrote for the beleaguered theatre.[285] Such 'Pasticcios' and burlettas were pieced out with pantomimes which inevitably incorporated songs.

The opening of the two-act pantomime, *Harlequin Mungo; or, A Peep into the Tower* (1787) was set in the 'West Indies.'[286] The drama presents Mungo as a negro slave working on a sugar plantation. The plantation owner's daughter, Columbine (named like Pantaloon and Clown as the convention required), falls in love with Mungo who, later, is transformed into the magical Harlequin. With many adventures, and pursued by Columbine's father, Pantaloon and the Clown, they escape across the Atlantic to London where they marry. Its significance for what it tells us, both about a marginal London theatre and the racial issues it represented, has been overlooked by most modern commentators. Felicity A. Nussbaum has recently referred to its existence in passing but apparently unaware of its content and certainly unaware of the significance of its performance history at the Royalty.[287] The chronological boundaries of David Mayer III's *Harlequin in his Element: The English Pantomime, 1806–1836* (1969) and John O'Brien's *Harlequin Britain: Pantomime and Entertainment, 1690–1760* (2004) have also meant that it has fallen outside the parameters of these important studies. However, some indication of the longevity of *Harlequin Mungo's* plotting is that, paradoxically, the pantomime's basic formula of Columbine's falling in love with a West Indian slave, and their both fleeing to London and marriage, was taken over in the Abolition Bill year of 1807 by James Powell, the highly dangerous and covert London Corresponding Society spy and playwright, who used the formula for his *Furibond; or, Harlequin Negro* played at Drury Lane as their December pantomime.[288] Without commenting on *Harlequin Mungo*, *Furibond's* modern editor, Jeffrey N. Cox, rightly remarks on the significance of *Furibond* as a work whose central figure takes on 'the trappings of the London stage's most popular figure of resistance' and whose black-masked face (the traditional costumed property associated with playing harlequin) forms a 'metadramatic moment of commentary on the various forms of being "black" on stage.'[289] Indeed, *Harlequin Mungo*'s apparently unpromising form of harlequinade and its expressive vocabulary of mime and music made it ideally suited for audiences at the London end of the transatlantic traffic in sugar and other commodities. Jane Moody has argued that in the dramaturgy of harlequinade, 'pantomime and melodrama invested that which is seen and made visible with a moral power which far outweighed that of words.'[290] *Harlequin Mungo* and *Furibond* were ideal forms within which the moral issues of slavery could be represented.

What is at stake in comparing these dramas is making a determination of the extent to which London's black people, most of whose birth and family relationships would have been derived from the consequences of slavery, were fairly represented in a society whose recognition of individual value was strictly limited. Felicity A. Nussbaum has written of the 'eighteenth-century stage ... [as] a peculiar interlude between the presumably all-white, all-male stage of Shakespeare and the appearance of the first black male actor in a patent theatre in 1833.' According to Nussbaum, 'White actors in blackface reassured their audiences that race is as easily removed as washing or smudging.'[291] The principal example Nussbaum draws on is *The Blackamoor Wash'd White* (1776), a Drury Lane comic opera hissed off the stage after three nights, only one night longer than Bellamy's *Benevolent Planters* of 13 years later. The short-lived fate of both plays may tell their own stories of audience intolerance for the unrealistic racial rhetorics the dramas deployed. The absence of black actors from the regular playhouse venues is not so surprising if one calculates that, for white female actresses intent on taking speaking parts, there were no more than about eight roles nightly available on the winter-season London stage throughout the Romantic period; in summer there would have been even fewer. With such a shortage of speaking roles available, this may help explain why actresses such as Elizabeth Macauley were so professionally and financially wounded at what they took to be their unfair dismissal and why they complained at being 'Driven from the Regular Exercise' of their profession.[292] Whatever make-up was worn, and however Colman himself may have conceived his programming, plays like his own *Inkle and Yarico* were permeated with repetitious racism:

Wowski: Iss! all white like you.

Trudge: Yes, all the fine men are like me: As different from your people as powder and ink, or paper and blacking.[293]

Unlike the case with a lot of playwrights of this period, it is possible to extrapolate something of Colman's personal political views. Most markedly, in later life he would go on to become the Lord Chamberlain's censor of drama. He was a vigorous censor with a rigorous agenda. He drew up, and privately disseminated to members of Parliament, the period's most formulated set of arguments for the continuation of theatrical regulation, insisting that 'our Theatres...should be under a Controlling Power' and warning that 'If Theatres were opened, and Dramas exhibited, at the will of every Adventurer, they would be productive of infinite moral and political evil...the Stage, instead of an engine directed by the hand of Government, for defence, would become a catapult, to batter it to pieces.'[294]

In other words, these texts are not simple embodiments of normative attitudes, they were the product of precise mentalities unpredictably enabled by certain sets of material circumstances. *Inkle and Yarico* reached the stage because it was incorporated into a comic opera (and so did not breach the playhouse's licence), and, not least, together with his father, Colman owned the lease of the playhouse in which it was performed.[295] The reasons for the hissing of *The Blackamoor Wash'd White* (1776) may never be recovered but the audience reaction may well be indicative of their vocal objections to songs such as:

> Must a Christian man's son born and bred up,
> By a *Negar* be stung in disgrace, –
> Be asham'd for to hold his poor head up,
> 'Cas'se as how he has got a white face?

Nussbaum's imperative to secure *The Blackamoor Wash'd White* as 'a precursor to American minstrelsy' seems also to ignore the slippage this song incorporates between African and Indian ethnicities:

> M'hap the nabob, that brought the poor creature
> From his father, and mother, and all,
> Is himself of a blackamoor nature,
> Dark within as the tribe of Bengal.[296]

As commented above, under the contemporary stage practices described by Rede, the 'blackamoor' from 'Bengal' probably looked reddish brown. As with the much later examples of Barrymore's *El Hyder* (1818) or Milner's *Tippoo Saib* (1823), British writers often had their attention drawn to the Indian subcontinent where the issue of slavery did not dominate but which they were able to identify as different to the Atlantic slaving predicament. As the afterlife of Townley's *High Life Below Stairs* shows, audiences did not sit quietly when racial stereotypes or social denigrations were represented.

The prose format of *The Benevolent Planters* (1789) at the Haymarket employed almost a separate register of discursivity compared to the Royalty Theatre's *Harlequin Mungo*. *The Benevolent Planters*'s prose demonstrated the Haymarket's access to the patent monopoly. The examples of the 1811 Surrey Theatre '*Mountaineers versified*,' and the reverse transposition into prose of Moncrieff's verse burletta *Giovanni in London* at the Dublin patent theatre demonstrates how these basic structural conditions of stage writing impacted. Despite these adverse conditions, the Royalty's pantomime was more nuanced in its commentary on slavery because it retained an awareness of its location near to the transatlantic shipping and sugar warehousing activities. Just as differences in venue radically affected the presence or absence of riots for *High Life Below Stairs*, *The Benevolent Planters* and *Harlequin Mungo* indicate the existence of an alterity in dramatic writing, a definable set of dissimilar political and literary discourses co-existing at virtually the same historical moment even within the highly communicative, mobile and socially promiscuous confines of London's theatreland.

Thomas Bellamy's *The Benevolent Planters* for the summer-season Theatre Royal at the Haymarket was sent for licensing by the Lord Chamberlain's Examiner, John Larpent, at the end of July 1789, a truly momentous month in European history which had seen the storming of the Bastille in Paris and the onset of the French Revolution.[297] *The Benevolent Planter*'s discarded subtitle, *Slavery but a Name*, gives some indication of its stance, as does the diction of the piece's opening lines spoken by English slave-owning planters who are discussing the annual sports festival they organize on behalf of their slaves:

Goodwin: Good morrow to my worthy neighbour, are your jetty tribe in readiness for the diversions which are to commence this day? Mine with glad hearts, and happy countenances look forward to their yearly Jubilee with rapture.

Steady: Yes my friend, my sable and grateful family are impatient to meet thine on the plain appointed for the sports.

The setting of *The Benevolent Planters* is specifically Jamaica. But just at the point where the language of the play tends to suggest that it is hopelessly ignorant and out of touch with reality, Goodwin's stray reference to the slaves' 'Jubilee' links it to the much more potent, still under-researched, subculture of the Afro-caribbean ideal of a jubilee return to freedom and black ownership of the slaving plantations. In other words, *The Benevolent Planters* may suggest a deep, almost irrecoverable, affinity with the discourse of slaves. Years later the son of a slave, Robert Wedderburn, addressed his fellow Caribbean blacks, '...follow not the example of St. Domingo, let not your jubilee, which will take place, be stained with the blood of your oppressors, leave revengeful practices for European kings and ministers.... Above all, mind and keep possession of the land you now possess as slaves.'[298] The apparently decorous diction of *The Benevolent Planters* suddenly erupts into the semi-covert discourses of the Atlantic diaspora of slaving with its language of freedom and restitution inexorably trafficked to-and-fro across the oceanic roads.[299]

One route to Bellamy's own knowledge of slaves and slavery may come from his possible acquaintance with Olaudah Equiano. *The Benevolent Planters* was sent to Larpent on 29 July 1789, some five months after the publication of Equiano's *Interesting Narrative* which had been registered at Stationers' Hall on 24 March of that year, published by subscription with 'Mr. Thomas Bellamy' listed as a subscriber to the first edition.[300] The networks of sociability which can be inferred from Equiano's subscription list have not been studied before but they have far-reaching implications for understanding the dialogue between different strands of the London slavery debate at the close of the 1780s. Even if Bellamy did not meet Equiano face-to-face, he would have received his copy of the *Interesting Narrative* by the time he was working on *The Benevolent Planters*. Bellamy's personal attitude towards slavery probably closely approximated to that of other subscribers on Equiano's list, showing how *The Benevolent Planters* embodies a number of contemporary European views, however unrealistic, for ameliorating rather than abolishing slavery.

The open generosity of spirit shown by the planters Steady and Goodwin was intended to be taken as an example for incoming planters such as the English gentleman Heartsfree, who comes 'to settle among us in order that by tenderness to his slaves he might exhibit to his brother planters the happy effects of humanity.' However, the plantationers' annual sports day for their slaves was also designed by them to be the means of distributing liberty on an extremely narrow and highly qualified basis. The sports themselves consisted of an archery contest with a breathtaking set of rewards: 'The youth who speeds the arrow farthest is to be declared victor and to gain in consequence, the Maid of his choice, a portion of land for his possession, – and freedom for his life.' Apart from the fairly gender-specific drawbacks of archery contests and having 'the Maid of his choice' as first prize, the rules also set out what was to happen to the runner-up in the event: 'in order that the unsuccessful party may have no cause to complain, they are to receive a present at the same time, and if they continue deserving, they will be made happy before the returning Sports, with the gift of liberty and the reward of well placed affection.' Quite apart from the issue of this very formalized language being scarcely the stuff of theatre drama, the prize of freedom only goes to the 'deserving' slave (who does not get the girl, just the enigmatic 'reward of well placed affection').

In part, Bellamy's play reverts to notions of servitude in order to blur the issue of slavery. Roxanne Wheeler points out that such attitudes are common in literature at least as early as Defoe's *Robinson Crusoe* (1719) and arguably re-emerged during the 1770s and 1780s as Britain debated the moral and economic implications of abolition.[301] Patrician attitudes equivocating uncertainly between outright denial and envisioning some kind of weird slave-owning utopia were still circulating amongst many liberals in the summer of 1789.[302] Charles Bernhard Wadström and August Nordenskjold that summer proposed their *Plan For A Free Community Upon The Coast Of Africa, Under The Protection Of Great Britain; But Intirely[sic] Independent Of All European Laws And Governments* (1789), a project to establish a Sierra Leone colony based upon Emanuel Swedenborg's principles of conjugal or plural marriage. Wadström had already made at least one expedition to Africa.[303] Like Equiano, in 1788 he had given a witness statement at the Board of Trade investigation into slavery, recounting his familiarity with the practices of slavers, including French slaving captains poisoning slaves with mercury and 'English Captains ... [who] throw them Overboard at once, when provisions fall short.'[304] Nevertheless, the principle of the emancipation of slaves was only a secondary objective of Wadström, with him proposing, in conformity to Wheeler's analysis, a reversion to servitude.

However, Wadström's *Plan For A Free Community* and Bellamy's *Benevolent Planters* reveal wider networks of transmission and sociability underpinning contemporary drama. Bellamy's drama was obviously surrounded by a context of sociability implying a high level of awareness about the conditions of slaves. By the spring of 1789, Bellamy's circles of friendship included both Wadström and Equiano, with the latter's *Interesting Narrative* definitively available to Bellamy by the spring of

1789. Despite this proximity to personal testimony of the slavery experience, both the *Plan For A Free Community* and *The Benevolent Planters*
decisively reject a radical abolitionist response to slaving.

Just as the Haymarket had toyed with retaining *Slavery but a name* as
the subtitle of *The Benevolent Planters*, with its implication that slavery
was a state of mind rather than a material condition, so too Wadström
and Nordenskjold's *Plan for a Free Community* began with the similarly
feeble statement that 'Every one feels a sort of Political and economical
Slavery.'[305] Indeed, *A Plan for a Free Community* is so deeply absorbed
in its own Swedenborgian principles that it is not until the second to
last page that a conditional freedom for slaves is discussed, in some
respects not unlike the one proposed by *The Benevolent Planters*: 'instead
of Slavery, a gentle Servitude is to be instantly adopted, and every
Native redeemed from Slavery shall be free after a Service or Apprenticeship of a few Years.'[306] The net effect of *The Benevolent Planters*, like
the *Plan for a Free Community*, is to enlarge, consolidate and sustain
slavery by persevering with the notion that slavery can be alleviated by
self-regulation, 'benevolent planters' indeed, moderated by reformation
rather than eradication. *The Benevolent Planters*, however, had at least
hinted at signs of possible disaffection and disturbance amongst the
Jamaican slaves when Goodwin refers to the planters' hopes to 'prevent
a repetition of disorders, which last year broke in upon the general
happiness.' The unrest was 'occasioned by the admission of those games
in which passion took too large a share.' In other words, according to
Goodwin's perspective, the excitement of the sports was the origin of
the disturbances rather than any feelings of grievance or oppression,
'And but for the timely exertion of humane authority, our honest and
deluded men would have proceeded to violence and bloodshed.'

While *The Benevolent Planters* at the Haymarket was hardly likely to
be at the forefront of radical anti-slavery drama, its venue at a fashionable and profitable summer-season Theatre Royal may have contributed
towards its distinctive demography in its literary writing. The reality of
this demographic difference, and the paradoxes of their connected soci-
abilities, is confirmed by noting that Bellamy was a personal friend of
John Palmer, manager of the Royalty, and one who took some trouble
to defend him during his struggles to keep the Royalty afloat.[307] In other
words, on the face of it, both from his links to Equiano and to Palmer,
Bellamy looked well placed to adopt an abolitionist, progressive stance
yet chose not to do so.

Something of the nature of these complex and rapidly changing
contemporary attitudes to slavery are apparent in the revisions occuring

in *The Benevolent Planters* between its submission to Larpent and its printed edition, the version perhaps more likely to reflect the piece as acted. Apart from some understandable shortening, the issue of the 'disorders, that last year disturbed the general happiness' has its emphasis fundamentally shifted in the printed edition so that the slaves can be accused of 'the folly of attacking each other without provocation.'[308] In other words, the idea of a united slave insurrection is quickly ruled out. In its place, Heartsfree pleads for the predicament of the planters to be understood as sanctioning the controlled deployment of force. 'Reasonable obedience is what we expect,' Heartsfree explains, but he also threatens that 'those who look for more, [will] feel and severely feel the sting of disappointment.'[309] The text's equivocation between physical and emotional punishment seems aimed at deliberately evading the physical cruelties of slavery. In a visual elaboration of the benevolence of the English planters, on the title page of the printed edition, an engraved vignette of an ornately dressed Selima decked out in the unlikely costume of furs and a feathered coronet is shown being graciously received into Goodwin's house. The naivety of Bellamy's position on slavery may also have been intercepted by the anonymous Prologue to the printed *Benevolent Planters* spoken 'In the Character of An African Sailor,' and which may mark the intervention of a writer less credulous than Bellamy. The Prologue evisages a route out of slavery through the personal intervention of a 'kinder master,' perhaps an optimistic parallel with the actual experience of some black slaves such as Equiano. Emancipation through service in the navy was a realistic objective if it could possibly be achieved since stepping foot into England (more or less) conferred freedom. Noticeably, the Prologue's concluding couplet outpaces the policy of amelioration by proposing unequivocal emancipation: 'Prosper the great design – thy children free / From the oppressor's hand, and give them liberty!'[310]

As a final commentary on the regulatory inconsistencies and unpredictabilities of contemporary drama, although falling under the jurisdiction of the Lord Chamberlain (who required notice of all new stage texts in Westminster), the changes made between the *Benevolent Planters* text as licensed and the (presumably) performance copy printed that year do not appear to have been resubmitted for approval and relicensing. Such a regulatory lapse was not the kind of thing the authorities were prepared to tolerate at the East End Royalty Theatre. Such oversights are indicative of the alterity of plebeian drama compared to its elite opposites. The naivety of Bellamy's *Benevolent Planters*, although it can be understood within the recoverable historical context outlined above, signals the existence of the Haymarket's elite culture, the 'brilliant,' fashionable audience promoted by the two Colmans, who were tolerant of both the racist language of *Inkle and Yarico* as well as of the essentially anti-abolitionist stance of *The Benevolent Planters*. Such decorous manoeuvrings would eventually set Colman the Younger on his route to becoming the Lord Chamberlain's stage censor. Equiano's successful authorial integration into aspects of an elite English society permeated by discourses surrounding sensibility and decorum is fascinating enough, but the very materiality of the political, economic and theatrical mechanisms which Equiano, Wadström and Bellamy traversed allows the production of *The Benevolent Planters* in the summer 1789 season at London's Haymarket to be temporalized with great accuracy.

Harlequin Mungo; or, A Peep into the Tower (1787) appears to have existed within a completely different set of dramatic, political and social registers to Bellamy's play. The issue of how Harlequin himself was represented is crucial. While Bellamy's play would have been dressed with the slave roles in Rede's 'sables' (burnt cork, beer and lard blackface), *Harlequin Mungo* provides a further complication to the issue of blacking up because the title role would have been played, at least in the harlequinade section, by a traditional harlequin wearing a black mask. The difference between blackface and black mask is an important one. Broadly speaking, whereas blackface was the mark of denigration, counterfeit or ridicule, the black mask celebrated harlequin as an enduringly popular hero. Unaccountably, Adam Lively's *Masks: Blackness, Race and the Imagination* (1998) has only the briefest discussions of blackmasked harlequins and assumes the tradition to be in decline by the time of the Jean François Marmontel's 1787 *Encylcopédie* entry on pantomime, although Lively usefully points out that this work identifies a black-African slave origin for the tradition of the mask.[311] John O'Brien's thoughtful discussion of the theatrical masking of harlequin in the first half of the eighteenth century argues that audience familiarity with gangs of thieves and poachers known as the Blacks in rural Berkshire and Hampshire also provided a point of access in which 'racial difference could be enlisted as a surrogate for distinctions of status.' O'Brien argues that not only did the Blacks share in 'a common strategy by which blackfaces helped mark the pleasure that each took in representing the common people,' but by the 1750s 'an African identity was clearly available as a referent for Harlequin's black mask,' a transformation into a racial specificity that O'Brien dates to David Garrick's *Harlequin's Invasion* (1759).[312] The implications of harlequin's black mask are quite profound, making commonplace the possibility of his African identity.

What Jeffrey N. Cox has described as the 'surprising interracial marriage' of Columbine and Harlequin in James Powell's *Furibond; or, Harlequin Negro* (1807) can now be seen as an incorporation of a pantomime tradition dateable at least as far back as the Royalty's *Harlequin Mungo*, where the transformed, black-masked Harlequin Mungo marries the plantation owner's daughter.[313]

Pantomime convention dictated that Harlequin must marry Columbine and that this is the only true love story within the drama. The harlequinade was composed of narrating their difficulties and interspersing them with comic action. This started immediately in the Royalty pantomime. As soon as Mungo has been bought (and, of course, before his transformation into Harlequin), the Clown – always his adversary – mocks his own rejection of an offer to carry Columbine's 'para-sol' by, as soon as 'they're gone, Clown perceiving Mungo following, orders him to carry the para-sol over his head, and exit. in great state.'[314] Between 1806 and 1823, as David Mayer has outlined, the Clown's business – as exemplified by the great Joseph Grimaldi – tended to dominate the pantomimes but in *Harlequin Mungo* it is still the Harlequin figure who was the centre of audience attention. This remained the case even with *Furibond* because, although it was a December 1807 pantomime (post-dating Grimaldi's entry onto the London stage), it still retained the Clown (or Clodpole) as a simple-minded figure lacking the mischievous inventiveness Grimaldi conferred on such roles.[315] Whatever the obstacles they encounter, the marriage of Harlequin and Columbine was always understood as inevitable, even if Mungo was black and Columbine white.

In the early stages of *Harlequin Mungo*, Mungo is played as a slave working on a sugarcane plantation. With Mungo still black-faced at this point, the stage directions describe the scene of slave labour as located at 'Pantaloon's House and Plantation – with a Sugar Mill, &c.' which is where 'Mungo pursues his employment at the sugar-mill.' However it was done, whether as a fabricated three-dimensional stage property, or else as painted scenery, the presence of the sugar mill reflects the economic realities of plantationing, including the long working day which is only slightly pastoralized:

> Night comes on, and the moon rises – the Plantation bell is heard to strike, the Slaves leave work, and come forward – some of them form a dance, while others sit smoking segars[cigars], drinking, &c. at length they all retire, except Mungo.[316]

Mungo's leisure time isolation leads to despair and 'disconsolate at his slavery... determines to make away with himself.' His attempt to hang himself with his loincloth is foiled by the appearance of a Wizard 'who reproves him' and changes him into Harlequin.[317] The intervention of a benevolent agent, as David Mayer has noted, was a key structural component of Romantic-period pantomime, marking the division between the first and second narratives of the plot (the second being the harlequinade proper) and magically transforming Columbine's lover into Harlequin. Benevolent agency was often retained in plebeian entertainments which were not pantomimes, for example, it crops up again in a highly adapted form as Folly, a benign character in the equestrianized burletta *Tom and Jerry; or, Life in London... as Performed at Davis's Royal Amphitheatre* (1822) (discussed below), who warns Tom, Jerry and Logic of the moral dangers and temptations of London and provides them with Harlequin and Clown as their escorts.

Apart from the transformed Slave in *Furibond, Harlequin Mungo* is highly unusual amongst the Romantic-period pantomimes in transforming a blackface character into a black-masked role. It is impossible to be certain, but the Wizard's transformation of Mungo, even though it was part of a recognizable tradition of the benevolent agent, may even hint at the pantomime's knowledge of African spiritualities dislocated by the middle passage:

> Thy guardian genius see in me,
> Who, (by the power of sorcery),
> Pursu'd thee from the Indian coast:
> Thro' wars, in which thy freedom's lost
> In slavish habit now no more be seen;
> Assume the gay, fantastic Harlequin.[318]

Helen Thomas has commented on the intricate nuances of belief, guilt and displacement associated with figures such as Briton Hammon, John Marrant and Olaudah Equiano.[319] In *Harlequin Mungo*, the attenuated format of recitative forced onto the Royalty can only briefly hint at a past history of 'Indian' origin and implicit capture as a consequence of war. For the audience, some of whom may have undergone the middle passage, or were from the Indian subcontinent themselves, this may have been a profoundly moving moment. The presence in London in the mid-1780s of ex-Nova Scotia black-American ex-slaves, eventually destined for Sierra Leone, is a reminder of this possibility. *Furibond*

similarly had a 'Fairy Benigna' and both of their journeys, of the harlequinized Mungo and the harlequinized Slave in *Furibond*, repeat the
pattern of movement across the great Atlantic slave diaspora. Again,
the effortless flight Harlequin manages in his escape to London with
Columbine must have seemed an extraordinary triumph after the tribu-
lations of the Atlantic passage.

In *Harlequin Mungo*, the original roles of Mungo and Harlequin were
first combined and played by the comic actor Charles Lee Lewes who
was then 47 years old. David Mayer has described how the role of
Harlequin needed an exceptionally energetic performer, requiring 'an
extraordinarily agile dancer and tumbler,' an actor capable of 'quick
quasi-balletic turns, leaps and gymnastic tricks:' in this case in order to
elude pursuit by Pantaloon and Clown who pursue him and Columbine
to London.[320] Perhaps in view of Lee Lewes's age, an advertisement in
The Times shows that by the ninth performance on 21 November 1787,
the role of Mungo as a slave had been parcelled out to a Mr Rayner
but with Lee Lewes still retaining the demanding Harlequin role. By the
37th performance on 1 January 1788, Rayner had taken over from Lee
Lewes, and a Mr Bourke was playing Mungo. The sexuality of Harlequin
as a black-masked lover was a traditional ingredient of the eighteenth-
century pantomime. Contemporary prints of Harlequin show him either
in a black mask courting Columbine ('What wou'd'st thou have fond
Harlequin / Why dost thou tempt my Youth to Sin?') or else similarly
black-masked as a figure in harlequin 'turn-ups' (folding prints cut to
allow different combinations of character and narrative and usually
intended as childrens' educational materials), one of which shows Harlequin actually kissing Columbine.[321] Whatever the social or political allusions within the particular pantomime, the harlequinade pursuit was
invariably a love story principally beset not by the problems of racial
origin but by an aged Pantaloon and a vengeful, sadistic Clown.

Ironically, although Thomas Bellamy was the personal friend of many
actors, his contemporary biographer Mrs Villa-Real Gooch particularly
recalled Bellamy's supportive friendship with John Palmer, the founding
manager of The Royalty Theatre.[322] *The General Magazine, and Impartial Review* devoted an engraved plate of the Royalty's interior and as
well as an opening notice in June 1787.[323] Gooch gives no further
particulars of *The Benevolent Planters* save to say that it was 'sufficiently
well received,' although perhaps also hinting that Bellamy's support for
Palmer gained him enemies amongst the West End managers.[324] There is
even a possibility that Bellamy had seen *Harlequin Mungo* himself because
the *General Magazine* included a review of the pantomime.[325] Bellamy's

contemporary biographer noted that in May 1787 he experienced problems with the literary abilities of the two journalists he had engaged, so
it seems possible that by the November of that year he would have been
obliged to go to the Royalty himself for new material. Certainly, outside
of the patent theatres, Palmer maintained good circles of friendship. In
keeping with the Royalty's consistent attempts at integration with the
local community, *Harlequin Mungo* was played as a benefit night for the
Marine Society, a charitable institution for young boys.[326] The mater-
ialities implicit in this kind of integration may account for much of
the difference between *Harlequin Mungo* and *The Benevolent Planters*. In
any event, *The General Magazine* stated that 'This Pantomime is, without
exception, the best we ever beheld.'[327]

The plot follows the basic formula of English harlequinades at this
time, with the major characters sometimes prefigured under alternative
names but still conforming to the usual conventions (which are as
explicit here as in virtually any contemporary harlequinade): Pantaloon
buys Mungo as a slave and arranges to marry his daughter, Columbine,
to a Chinese man. She is reluctant to agree because she loves Mungo.
Mungo as Harlequin transforms himself into the Chinese and signs
a marriage contract while magically impersonating the Chinese. The
presence of a Chinese character in *Harlequin Mungo* also complicates
the portrayal of race, but such a figure was traditional within British
pantomime.[328] The juxtaposition of different races in the West Indies is
not too surprising. By 1804, John Anthony, a Chinese interpreter and
'native of China,' appears to have crossed several times between Britain
and China, a pattern of travel he had adopted since 'the American war'
and a reference which perhaps implies his own involvement in it.[329]
Like Mungo, Pantaloon and, indeed, all the pantomime characters, the
Chinese was portrayed mute. Of course, muteness at the Royalty was
primarily a function of his incorporation into pantomime but, of course,
the licensing regime also insisted that no one could speak. While this
certainly enabled the audience to more easily encode onto the role their
pre-existing racial perspective, arguably reproducing race within their
own pre-conceived stereotypes, the muteness of the Royalty's pantomime was clearly a requirement of the regularity regime. Like the Indian
heroes of *El Hyder* and *Tippoo Saib*, the black mask of harlequin does not
fit easily within practices of North American minstrelsy.

Sean Metzger's study of 'yellowface' acting in nineteenth-century
American melodrama draws attention to the complications of the racial
construction of American Chinese as an immigrant people absorbed
into the heavy manual work of gold mining on the West coast, yet

also feminized by their willingness to take jobs in domestic service. In American melodrama, Metzger concludes that yellowface make-up was coupled to the 'queue' – the pigtail hairpiece – as the principal signifier of race in Chinese roles. There were probably broad similarities with the figures David Mayer reproduces from toy-theatre prints dating from 1825 of the Royal Amphitheatre's *The Mandarin; or, Harlequin in China* (1811) showing two Chinese figures whose ethnicity is largely signified by long moustaches, but in Drury Lane's *Harlequin Harper; or, A Jump from Japan* (1813) the 'queue' is more prominent.[330] However, in Britain, one assumes that yellowface make-up was simply a variation of the vermillion or carmine Rede's *Road to the Stage* recommended for most ethnic roles, that is, tending towards red. Transposing the American condition transatlantic presents difficulties within the British tradition. Not least, in the British context, Chinese were often associated with wealth.

The character in *Harlequin Mungo* is described as 'a Chinese Gentleman,' a substantial merchant accompanied by a 'Chinese servant' who arrives on the island with a sailor to carry his 'portmanteau' before heading for 'a public-house' where 'the Landlord...brings him a glass of wine,' directs him to Pantaloon's plantation to which he exits accompanied by 'several black boys, carrying baggage, &c.'[331] In England, Chinese people and Chinese imports were associated with high-quality goods: as discussed above, the 'Present of China' pottery in *Harlequin Incendiary* (1746) is a precise signifier of English civility compared to Scottish anarchy.[332] In *Harlequin Mungo*, one of the scenes shows Pantaloon, Columbine and the Chinese suitor 'discovered seated at a table' with the Chinese merchant giving out luxury presents including 'a gilt fan, a wreath of artificial flowers, and other Indian toys,' before – in a repetition of the Chinese gift motif found in *Harlequin Incendiary* 40 years earlier – presenting 'two large China Mandarine figures' which Columbine has 'placed on two pedestals in one of the cabinets.'[333] Just as Metzger carefully reconstructs the historical conditions of the Chinese in America, so too the Chinese presence in Britain presents a different set of cultural traditions. In Britain, Chinese people were strongly associated with the riches of the East India Company. A pantomime such as Thomas John Dibdin's Covent Garden *Harlequin and Fortunio; or, Shing-Moo and Thun-Ton* (1815), starring Grimaldi, presented a scenic painting of 'A Chinese Port,' a reminder of British trade with the east.[334] Occasional glimpses through law-court records of Chinese plaintiffs serve as reminders not only of individual wealth but also that the English legal system could be activated in their support when they sought the prosecution of white Londoners. Old Bailey cases strongly suggest that not only were there many Chinese in the vicinity of the Royalty Theatre, but their housing in Angel Gardens, Shadwell, organized by the East India Company but managed by Chinese personnel, provided access to interpreters, perhaps bestowing a collective sense of how the English legal system could be accessed.[335] At the Old Bailey case referred to above, where John Anthony acted as interpreter for the Chinese plaintiff Erpune, Anthony was able to swear his oath by breaking a saucer, an action signifying the London court's acceptance of a traditional Chinese oath-swearing practice. This ability of Chinese residents in London, on occasion, to be individually active within the British economic and legal system, and for it to accommodate variant religious beliefs, is an indicator of the wider impact of the Chinese presence within the community.

Whatever their representation on the Romantic-period stage, Chinese and black people in London could be forceful and articulate and both races were likely to have been present at the Royalty. It is within the context of these highly historicized realities of racial representation that the action of *Harlequin Mungo* takes place. Quite clearly, yellow-face and blackface performance had to exist within a contemporary context of cultural practices. What marks out this pantomime so clearly is that the conventions of harlequinade makes its interracial outcome utterly predictable. In *Harlequin Mungo*, Mungo and Columbine are pursued to England and into the Tower of London but finally achieve marriage and reconciliation with Pantaloon (the scenes in the Tower are a device to show off its animal menagerie and armoury). Despite its containment within a fairly strict convention, or perhaps because of it, *Harlequin Mungo* was able to explore much more freely a wholly different set of attitudes to slavery and to black people than might be expected.

Unlike *The Benevolent Planters*, which is shy of any reference to the realities of the slave trade, *Harlequin Mungo* begins with a sale of slaves, a scene containing subtle sexual undertones of miscegenation. *The General Magazine's* reviewer commented that the 'dumb show of the representatives of these helpless and abused children of nature conveyed an affecting picture to the feeling mind,' but such a critique sustaining the current ideology of sensibility rather diminishes this scene's sharp satirizing of the slave market.[336] The slave ship arrives in the Jamaican port and its captain sets up a market, but his sales pitch immediately establishes the fact that slavery depended on satisfying a vicious market of demand as much as perpetuating a vicious retailing of supply:

Captain: Oyes, Oyes, Oyes.

Come, Planters, you who wish to purchase prizes,
Be quick in buying, e'er the market rise's.
My Slaves are healthy, youthful, and well-made;
I'll deal with honor, tho' with Knaves I trade.[337]

The first person to step forward to buy a slave is a character simply called
Woman:

Woman: Dear Captain, have you got a stout young-man.

With breadth of shoulders, he will suit my plan:
I only want a husband kept in awe;
Who beats me ev'ry day, nor fears the law:

Captain: Here's one that's 5-feet-6, quite straight and boney,
Woman: He'll do my business, pray what's the money?
Captain: For thirty pounds he's yours, a strapping blade;
Woman: He's just the thing for me, the bargain's made.[338]

There is just about enough room for a dramatic pause at the end of the
second line to savour the querying of the other planters to her statement that 'he will suit my plan.' A pause would disable her attempted
pre-emptive denial of a sexual motive in the purchase. Nevertheless,
it seems pretty clear that the white Woman's motive for purchasing
the black slave is sexual in nature. However, her condemnation of her
husband's wife-beating maintains the direction of the piece's implicit
moral criticism of planters.

All the slaves are gradually sold off with the exception of Mungo.
A 20-year-old male slave the Captain calls Mahogany is sold to an Old
Man, perhaps another glance of a sexual transaction ('They well may say
Mahogany is dear; / His features please me much, so there's the cash').[339]
Interestingly, one of the purchasers is a Justice, a stock figure of popular
contempt on the eighteenth-century stage. His request for a 'black
Amanuensis – or a Scribe' may gesture towards the literacy of figures
such as Equiano, but the Justice's reference to his needing someone
capable of 'drawing out a warrant, / To serve informers, or commit a
vagrant' is a reminder that vagrancy included the Royalty's players.
Indeed, a contemporary historian of the Royalty wrote that in 1787 'an
information ... [was] laid against John Palmer for speaking Prose on the
stage, [and] a warrant was granted for his apprehension, when, from
a conviction under it, he was recorded as a rogue and vagrant.'[340] As
well as being a reminder of the criminal implications of 'speaking Prose'

from a non-patent house, *Harlequin Mungo*'s text may have even served to gesture to the audience the proximity of the theatre to the condition of its audience. The Justice's reference to how the slave's 'charcoal mazard, / Of blushing, sure will never run the hazard,' is a phrase which transforms the minstrelizing blackface comment into one readily recognizable as describing a lawyer unembarrassed by his exorbitant fees in a repetition of a common pantomime figure of derision.[341]

Mungo is 'frequently offer'd, and always refused' by buyers until Pantaloon comes along, argues about the price until, 'at the intercession of Columbine,' he is bought by Pantaloon and taken back to the plantation.[342] While it would have been a blacked-up white actor playing Mungo, the interracial love story between Columbine and Mungo is significant in that, as well as their difference of colour, there is also a sharp differential between their power relationships, with Columbine being the planter's daughter and Mungo a slave. Although this feature makes *Harlequin Mungo* unusual, it appears to be the case that, as James Hewlett was to confirm, interracial relationships were perfectly acceptable to English audiences. A 1791 Newcastle-Upon-Tyne production of a version of Sheridan's pantomime adaptation of Daniel Defoe's *Robinson Crusoe* was performed at the Newcastle Theatre Royal as *Robinson Crusoe; or, Harlequin Friday*. When Crusoe and Friday – as well as the harlequinade characters Pantaloon and Pierrot who have chanced onto the island – are repatriated to Spain and introduced to Pantaloon's daughter, Columbine, she immediately falls in love with Friday, 'Columbine's attention is taken up with looking at Friday; she endeavours to beg him from Robinson, but is refused.' This being harlequinade, their paths will be difficult but the convention dictated that their love would end in marriage. With Crusoe 'much displeased' when Friday elects to follow Columbine rather than himself, and with her father, Pantaloon, angry when 'she gives him [Friday] a miniature picture from her bosom,' Columbine and Friday are turned out of doors only to be reunited through the agency of a friendly Magician who transforms Friday into Harlequin. The sexual nature of their love, and its unconventional relationship to Friday's pagan savagery, is even hinted at in the *Harlequin Friday*'s closing scene where the Magician's verse refers to his 'wand,' his 'rod,' the powers of 'Young Cupid,' and finally their union in 'a most magnificent Temple, dedicated to Venus.' The interracial relationship of Friday and Columbine, the savage and the civilized, apparently caused no problems to the north-east-of-England Newcastle audiences.[343]

Everything suggests that pantomime could take greater risks, be more culturally adventurous, than spoken drama. In *Harlequin Mungo*, as with

Harlequin Friday, interracial relationships are only as problematic as the convention required them to be: Pantaloon always has to disapprove of Columbine's choice of lover. In *Harlequin Mungo*, the suitor approved by Pantaloon is the Chinese man but her father's traditional role as the patriarchal, flinty-souled spoilsport establishes the Chinaman's approval by Pantaloon as a suitable subject for her rejection. In its turn, the 'othering' of the oriental becomes the harlequinade's signal for the assimilation of a black man. The development of their affection into love is hastened by the cruelty Mungo experiences at the Clown's hands (in harlequinades, the Clown was traditionally the sadistic servant of Pantaloon):

> Several Slaves discovered at work at different parts of the Plantation – Columbine appears at the window reading – the Clown (with a whip in his hand) – turns Mungo out of doors – shews him his employment among the Slaves – and menaces him, unless he works fast – Columbine reproves the Clown, for his severity to Mungo, who bows to thank her – [344]

As with the exoticism of Columbine's Chinese suitor appearing in the unlikely context of the Caribbean, *Harlequin Mungo* exploits the dramatic potential of costuming and other scenic or linguistic contrasts, as the pantomime very largely rehearses its stereotypes. But the slave market and presence of the planters in a sugar-plantation setting dominate our awareness of the capital commodities produced by the slave economies of the West Indies.

Perhaps the most important factor influencing the Royalty Theatre and its *Harlequin Mungo* pantomime was the playhouse's urban environment in a port catering for West Indian shipping. Writing in 1803 in *A Solemn Protest Against The Revival Of Scenic Exhibitions And Interludes, At The Royalty Theatre*, the Society for the Suppression of Vice's critic of the Royalty, Thomas Thirlwall, had discussed the negative impact of the playhouse on local armaments manufacture.[345] John Percival, who wrote a counterpamphlet, *A Few Observations in Defence of the Scenic Exhibitions at The Royalty Theatre* (1804) in reply to Thirlwall, was more closely acquainted and up to date with significant changes in the theatre's immediate hinterland and audience catchment area. Piecing together evidence from the two pamphlets, it is possible to discover a great deal about these changes. Percival argued that the area's earlier eminence in armament manufacturing had been supplanted by industries associated with the importation of sugar. Effectively, this meant the West Indies. As Percival put it in 1804, 'the sugar-houses [now] employ a much larger number of journey-men' than the armaments industries.[346] The significance of such changes in the local economic structure is not simply that the persecuting organization was misinformed, the fact also affects the understanding of how the Royalty attempted to address its audience. Percival argued that the 'majority' of the Royalty's audience were 'foreigners of fixed habits of industry, to whom such amusements as those which occupy the Royalty Theatre, are unattractive, if not unintelligible.'[347] Percival's comments strongly suggest the cosmopolitan nature of the Royalty's audience catchment and its likely sensitivities.

Sugar, slavery and the West Indies were not merely the settings of *Harlequin Mungo*, the pantomime was being performed and offered to an audience drawn from an area of London where the sugar trade was a significant factor in the local economy, as Percival's pamphlet confirms. Materializing the local sugar trade can be readily accomplished by examining court reports. Patterns of criminal activity in the vicinity show that, by the 1780s, there were sugar refineries near Tower Hamlets and shipping 'keys' (quays) around Botolph Wharf, Lower Thames Street and towards the Tower involved in warehousing sugar. As well as thefts of hogsheads of sugar, thieves even stole a 39-shilling 'wallower wheel' (a component specifically used for grinding sugar) from a vessel revealingly named *The Generous Planter* moored up at Rotherhithe to the east of the Tower.[348]

Again, Percival makes the connection between the docklands, mariners and the Royalty Theatre explicit when he comments on 'the great numbers of seamen, and their dependants, that are placed, by the extent of our commerce, on this bank of the Thames, in the vicinity of the theatre.' Percival knew that the sugar trade, sea faring and armaments were founded on the 'great thoroughfare' of the Thames and contributed to the hinterland's extremes of wealth and poverty. While the area's affluence was derived from 'the numerous lucrative offices' associated with those industries, its poverty came about from destitute seamen who had spent all their money.[349] The Royalty, in responding to the pressures of this complex local economy, needed to explore the genres which best suited its potential audience. Percival is right to imply that *Pizarro*, *The Stranger* and *John Bull* might have proved quite 'unintelligible' at the Royalty but this was not the case with *Harlequin Mungo*. The harlequinade was the perfect generic vehicle for the Royalty to reach an audience comprised of non-English speaking 'foreigners.'[350]

Harlequin Mungo made extensive use of familiar local settings in the vicinity of the theatre and exploited the obligatory mechanism of dumb-show and stage scenery. Percival recorded that 'within the last few years' many 'considerable works and large warehouses' had been built in The Royalty's neighbourhood which, like the theft of the wallower-wheel, suggests that sugar was milled and stored in the area.[351] In *Harlequin Mungo*, a scene with 'A Warehouse, and Store-room above, with a Crane, &c.,' made a familiar local reference point for harlequin's escape from his Chinese persecutor after his work in the 'sugar mill.' That harlequin effects his escape by bursting through 'a posting bill on the warehouse' (an advertising poster making a safe *faux* wall for him to jump through) may also allude to the Royalty's local environment.[352] Contrary to Percival, the miming of Mungo's abuse in the sugar mill at the hands of the Clown would have been perfectly intelligible.

Local coloured people, literate or illiterate, would have readily understood the dumb-show harlequinade of a slave abused in a sugar mill. Older local immigrants, perhaps Jews or Huguenots, might have brought with them their own versions of European traditions of harlequin or, at least, would have understood their contemporary London incarnations. *Harlequin Mungo* and the Royalty Theatre derive from these very specific sets of local circumstances as a highly nuanced response to contemporary economic and racial conditions. Paradoxically, the flights of fancy enjoyed in *Harlequin Mungo* (with its wizards, magic swords and swift transatlantic transportations) are actually symptomatic of the Royalty Theatre's successful response and embodiment of the London East End's contemporary material culture.

To summarize, in their very different ways both *The Benevolent Planters* and *Harlequin Mungo* embody different aspects of the national response to one of the most extensive and far-reaching moral, political and social debates of the period. The venue for *The Benevolent Planters* at the Haymarket's Theatre Royal summer season was largely the determinant of the unprogressive social attitudes to slavery represented in their play, despite its timing coinciding with the beginning of the French Revolution. By contrast, *Harlequin Mungo*, with its performances located in London's East End, reflected many of the liberal or radical characteristics perhaps expected of an audience cut off by distance from the West End royal theatres and otherwise intensely connected to a gradually modernizing world of manufacture, commodity import and dockyard employment.[353] The political ideologies of *Harlequin Mungo*, ultimately derived from its local context, were remarkably prescient, having been first performed in November 1787, 18 months before the

French Revolution.[354] In other words, the social stratification of London attitudes to slavery, as represented in the theatres, was a function of their venue and location as much as it was a function of the attitudes of any individual author. A further problematic, of course, was that the writer and theatre management of the Haymarket, falling within the Westminster regulation of the Lord Chamberlain, knew themselves to be operating within entirely different terms and conditions of expressivity than was the case obtaining at the much-harried East End Royalty. At the Haymarket, the texts were regulated but not the venue. At the Royalty, the reverse situation obtained.

4
Belles Lettres to Burletta: William Henry Ireland as Fortune's Fool

The case of William Henry Ireland, probably the most famous eighteenth-century Shakespeare forger, is already well known to literary scholars through his notorious 'Shakespearean' tragedy, *Vortigern*.[355] What has not been noticed before is that the cultural conditions of stage drama in Britain in the 1790s make his activities remarkably rational and consonant. His greatest problem was that he tried to write *belles lettres* when he should have been aiming to produce burletta. With only two London venues available for spoken tragedy, if Ireland wished to write a five-act tragedy for the stage, the Royal theatrical duopoly curtailed his range of manoeuvre. Outside of the Royal theatres, in London, burletta was the only permissible dramatic genre, and it was in those alternative playhouses that the future of British drama lay. Furthermore, even if the generic restraints were surmounted, any new dramatic piece containing a text (whether song, prologue, epilogue, five-act spoken tragedy or three-act burletta), and which was deemed to fall within the jurisdiction of the Lord Chamberlain's Examiner of Plays, the piece would be further subject to licensing, cutting or even prohibition.

To an ambitious young man like Ireland, a person who later went on to fashion a precarious living from writing, the prospect of forging Shakespeare must have looked quite tempting. Not only that, it may also have appeared bordering on legitimacy in that it created for him a feasible career path amidst a contemporary London theatre which habitually borrowed and plagiarized from the works of continental authors. Ireland may even have had in mind the nobler purpose of evading the censor. After all, it may have occurred to him that a rediscovered piece by Shakespeare would not have been censored. As it proved, the conditions of Romantic-period writing for the stage were quite inflexible and the Lord Chamberlain did not exclude the Bard from his control. *Vortigern* was censored, whether its author was Shakespeare or not. However, while avoiding censorship (or at least receiving a lighter touch) may have been somewhere on Ireland's agenda, it is probably more significant for our understanding of his personal circumstances that Ireland had been brought up in a household where the boundaries between original and copy were distinctly blurred and where artisanal skills of production were quite advanced.

For Ireland, the *Vortigern* experience would be catastrophic, a life-changing event from which he never fully recovered but, in many ways, the entire circumstances of the affair were rationally based on his understanding of how the London theatre actually worked. In any event, at least as a purely symbolic moment in the history of dramatic writing, Ireland's *Vortigern* of 1796 marks a watershed where up-and-coming playwrights were forced into venturing into two major new courses of action. The first of these was that, in the future, any pretensions towards aspiring to literary qualities in tragedy or comedy which might run the risk of association or comparison with Shakespeare were decidedly ill-advised. Secondly, and this was to prove immensely influential in bringing about a renaissance in the new playhouses licensed only for burletta, any new or aspiring playwright was forced into either chancing their luck with the Royal theatres or realistically accommodating themselves to the permissible dramatic forms of burletta or pantomime associated with the non-patent theatres. It was not difficult to see, especially after Ireland's *Vortigern*, that the future lay in new writers working in accordance with the aspirations of the emerging London playhouses outside the Royal theatres.

One of the most memorable literary casualties after *Vortigern*'s opening-night failure at Drury Lane in April 1796 was that playhouse's rejection of William Wordsworth's five-act spoken tragedy, *The Borderers* (1797). In the autumn of 1797 the manuscript appears to have been forwarded by Coleridge to Thomas Harris, the manager and senior shareholder partner at Covent Garden. By 20 November 1797 it had been passed to Thomas Knight, described as a principal actor at the playhouse. Three weeks later, on 13 December, Wordsworth wrote to Joseph Cottle saying that 'Mr. Harris [had] pronounced it impossible that [*The Borderers*] should succeed in representation.'[356] Wordsworth attributed its rejection to 'the deprav'd State of the Stage at present' and a further attempt by Coleridge to send it to Sheridan at Drury Lane in 1800 reportedly resulted in Wordsworth declaring that he 'would not submit to having one syllable altered, [and said] that if in its present form it was not fit for the stage, he would try the experiment whether it was adopted for the closet.'[357] Whatever Wordsworth's views on the integrity of his text, it would never have escaped the attention of the censor. However, negotiating with Thomas Harris at Covent Garden would also have been quite formidable. The successful playwright Thomas Holcroft went from dedicating his Covent Garden *Duplicity* (1781) to him (commemorating his 'taste, as a critic'), to writing prefaces charting their tempestuous relationship. Holcroft's comedy *Seduction* (1787) was eventually produced by the 'Gentlemen, and men of honour' of Drury Lane after having been returned to him from Covent Garden 'in a bit of dirty brown paper, unsealed' by John O'Keefe's servant. His *School for Arrogance* (1791), although it was finally accepted, had to be submitted to Harris via an intermediary, a Mr Marshal who 'acted, for a time, in my behalf, as the author of the piece.'[358] Playwrights continued to struggle with such obstacles despite the demeaning and ignoble nature of such transactions because they were forced to negotiate the stranglehold of the two monopoly theatres. By 1814 John Galt had assembled *The New British Theatre; a Selection of original drama, not yet acted*, effectively an anthology of pieces rejected by the patent theatres and in which he questioned 'the pecuniary accidents by which those gentlemen became the arbiters of the dramatic cart[el] ... while they are actuated solely by motives of personal emolument.'[359]

If traversing Harris was unpredictable, the passing of Wordsworth's drama to Thomas Knight for evaluation was even less likely to have yielded an estimate of the piece's true literary value. Knight was a professional actor of comic roles, a comedian. Three days before Ireland's *Vortigern*, he had played the role of Luckless in John C. Cross's comedy sketch, *The Way to get Un-Married* (1796).[360] The day after he received *The Borderers* manuscript from Harris, he played Young Testy in Joseph George Holman's comic opera *Abroad and At Home* (1796) which, of course, was a singing role ('*Song*: ... I'm a boy that's not easily flouted').[361] Two years later he established the role of Count Cassel in Elizabeth Inchbald's *Lover's Vows* (1798), a Kotzebue adaptation best known from the private-theatricals episode in Jane Austen's *Mansfield Park* (1814). Knight was also an author himself, writing the unpublished farce *Thelyphthora; or, The Blessings of Two Wives at Once* (1783), produced at Hull as well as *Trudge and Wowski*, an unpublished prelude to *Inkle and Yarico* acted at Bristol (*ODNB*). His comic opera for Covent Garden, *The Turnpike Gate* (1799) with music by Joseph Mazzinghi, was successful enough to run to several editions. Identifying Knight is quite important since it seems highly likely that it was on his recommendation that Wordsworth's *Borderers* was turned down. However, there is no reason to think Knight was politically opposed to Wordsworth. The plot of *The Turnpike Gate* was based around a dispute between an established tenant farmer, Old Maythorn, who runs a 'small Dairy and Farm' and its owner, an incoming 'licentious, hot-brain'd, and giddy' landowner ('My master's Grand Turk here. He monopolizes all the wenches') demanding rent arrears and threatening eviction.[362] Written in 1799, shortly after the August 1798 Battle of the Nile, *The Turnpike Gate* carefully establishes how the Admiral, the deceased landlord idolized by the injured sailor John Stedfast ('but for this splintered timber of mine, I'd been by his side in the West-Indies, when the brave old boy died. Died! – I lie, he did not die; for he made himself immortal!'), headed a harmonious estate.[363] Eventually, Sir Edward is authoritatively repulsed by Old Maythorn and the estate restored to the Admiral's true heir: 'I warn you Sir Edward, not to vire[*sic*] a gun again upon my manors, or I'll zend[*sic*] you to the county gaol – I will, as sure as you're born.'[364] Although *The Turnpike Gate*'s songs made it approximate to a burletta in its format, ironically Old Maythorn's stance – and even the stereotyped 'stage' rural dialect he speaks – crudely echoes Wordsworth's concern for the predicament of small landowners or Westmoreland 'Statesmen' in *The Lyrical Ballads* (1798).[365] It may well be that Wordsworth imagined his tragedy rejected because of 'the deprav'd State of the Stage at present,' but one would have to extend the notion of depravity to encompass the structural conditions of the Romantic-period stage. At the very least, it looks likely his political opinions were not far different from his assessor's.

Wordsworth's friend Samuel Taylor Coleridge fared rather better but, again, his story is a revealing narrative of social connection, misadventure and persistence over more than a decade. By Coleridge's own account, the playwright and manager R.B. Sheridan, proprietor of Drury Lane, had initially 'twice conveyed [his] recommendation (in the year 1797),' for him to 'write a Tragedy.' The work referred to, *Osorio*, was eventually revised and produced by Drury Lane in 1813 under the title of *Remorse*. Sophie Thomas has discussed *Remorse*'s extensive adaptation and amenability towards contemporary stage practices, adding further to Richard Holmes's detailing of the context of its production.[366] While Coleridge's recollections are of events which occurred 15 years earlier, his experience was typical of contemporary authors. The young Coleridge was aware that he was 'utterly ignorant of all Stage-tactics,' but after he gave the manuscript to Drury Lane he learned 'of its having been received only by [the agency of] a third person,' and that, in 'spite of repeated applications, [they] retained my

Manuscript' and allowed it 'to wander about the Town.'[367] Five years after sending his manuscript to Drury Lane, he found one of *Osorio*'s songs set to music 'without my name' and published by William Carnaby as a glee for four voices entitled *Invocation to a Spirit* (1802). Authors such as James Powell suffered similar fates at the hands of Drury lane. Powell's preface to *The Venetian Outlaw, His Country's Friend* (1805) related how he found his adaptation of a Pixérécourt's drama performed at Drury Lane, word for word, without his knowledge but not credited to him.[368] Henry Lee's *Caleb Quotem And His Wife!* (1809), discussed below, was also plagiarized after submission to Covent Garden in 1796. However, the intervention on Coleridge's behalf in 1812 of the politician and influential Drury Lane committee member Samuel Whitbread (1758–1815) – 'I ventured to address a letter to Mr. Whitbread' – appears to have been crucial to *Remorse*'s eventual successful production. Coleridge acknowledged receiving advice on the text from Drury Lane's manager, the dramatist Samuel James Arnold (1774–1852), the author of *Man and Wife; or, More Secrets than One* (1809), as well as from its stage manager, J.G. Raymond. Longevity and persistence, allied to Coleridge's influential social connections amongst the highest levels of Drury Lane's management team, all played their part in ensuring that *Remorse* reached the stage.[369] But, as Coleridge put it in his Preface, how 'such treatment would damp a young man's exertions may be easily conceived.'[370] One such young man was William Henry Ireland. With perhaps a better appreciation of the true state of contemporary theatre than either Wordsworth or Coleridge, and with much looser personal standards of propriety, Ireland decided to take a different route.

By the time of its first (and only) night at Drury Lane in April 1796, Ireland's trickery was common knowledge to many London theatre-goers. As *The Freemason's Magazine* noted, 'From the great noise in the Theatre before the curtain drew up, it was evident, that the Audience was entirely composed either of the friends of Mr. Ireland…or those who went predetermined to resist the performance of what they conceived to be an attempt to impose upon public credulity.'[371] In a vain attempt to preempt the uproar, Ireland had caused to be distributed at the doors of the theatre a number of handbills pleading 'that the Play of *Vortigern* may be heard with that *Candour* that has ever distinguished a *British Audience*' although, as a resourcefully entrepreneurial Grub Street hack, his bill also advertised that '– The Play is now at the Press, and will in a very few days be laid before the Public.'[372] Relishing Ireland's public exposure, and the sheer enormity of the gull, the London public glee-fully thronged the thoroughfare of Drury Lane. Such was the crush to get in that one eyewitness claimed that he 'was indebted more to my height and strength for admission, than to my punctuality in attendance' finding that the 'Avenues of the Theatre were so much crouded, long before the doors were opened.' Nevertheless, this particular theatregoer was still able to find a seat 'close to Mr Ireland and it was pleasing to observe the marks of hope, fear, joy, anxiety and disappointment alternately portrayed on his countenance, as his piece at different times affected the House.' Despite Kemble's appearance on stage to try to quell the noise, 'the many gross and evident imitations,' such as Ireland's pastiche of Jacques's speech, provoked the audience into such 'a violent fit of laughter' that when 'at the end of the fourth act Vortigern speaking of the Death-bed of a King presents such a ridiculous figure of Death grown frolic...the Performers were hiss'd and order'd off the Stage,' although the performance managed to restart and limp to the end of its fifth act.[373] To a London and England now thoroughly into its third year of war against the French, Ireland's tale of a kingdom near lost by internal division, treachery and dissent was too opportune (in some ways too astute) a topical commentary on English, late eighteenth-century *angst* to ever fit credibly as the product of Shakespeare's age. *Vortigern's* image of the Saxon armies of Hengist and Horsa at the gates of London ready to murder Vortigern 'And these brave Britons by my arts and arms, / Bind to a foreign yoke' was too close for comfort.[374]

However satisfying Ireland's complete exposure was to contemporary and modern observers, what has not been commented on before is his role as a successful producer, the artisan craftsman of his own shams. But, his ability to imitate and steal, to copy and pastiche Shakespearean tropes is not the work of a naïve forger entering a culturally uncomplicated visual and literary system. Ireland produced copies into a representational culture which highly prized copiers and socially esteemed some types of forgery. Ireland's father was a copy-engraver by profession, and his son's *Vortigern* was put before a London theatre that stole and plagiarized on a regular and unacknowledged basis. One has only to try to follow the convoluted charges concerning the several stages and levels of plagiarism set out in Henry Lee's 'Prefatory Remarks' to his *Caleb Quotem And His Wife!* (1809) to witness the rapacious nature of the contemporary theatre. In an environment where the two Royal playhouses were receiving a steady flow of unsolicited manuscripts, it is easy to imagine that incompetent theatre managers, plus hectic repertory schedules, made it difficult to maintain programmes whilst ensuring accurate attribution of authorship or origin. Lee, the manager of a number of provincial theatres in south-west England, had offered Harris of Covent Garden the manuscript of *Caleb Quotem* in 1796, the same year as *Vortigern's* production, where it was first rejected only to be taken up by Harris's colleague John Fawcett for production at The Haymarket. However, in 1800 Lee found a substantial part of *Caleb Quotem* reworked, without permission, payment or attribution and being performed under George Colman the Younger's pseudonym of 'Arthur Griffinhoof,' as the two-act farce *The Review; or, The Wags of Windsor* (1800).[375] Colman's later role, from 1824, as the Examiner of Plays only makes this incident the more curious as to how it reflects on the standards of propriety of the Romantic-period stage. Certainly, Ireland's deceptions stand in a spectrum of dubious ethics, but he was scarcely unique.

Although Ireland made much in his *Confessions* (1805) of his filial emotions in wishing to satisfy his father's penchant for Shakespeare memorabilia, it must have been his father's own trade as an engraver which had first blurred the distinctions between originals and copies. Much of Samuel Ireland's day-to-day career as an engraver would have depended on copying the works of others, and supplying his own additions to suit the transfer from drawing to engraving in order to accommodate what was a translation into the technology of copper-plate printing from an original produced in an oil or watercolour medium. William Henry learned at least the basics of his father's trade, sufficient to make a picturesque watercolour of a church and chateau by 1787 and to be thought a competent enough etcher by his father to have his 'WHI' monogrammed etching after Hogarth included in his father's *Graphic Illustrations of W. Hogarth*.[376]

By 1795, the worlds of copy engraving and (what one may call) 'original forgeries' was becoming bewilderingly confused in the Ireland household. Ireland Jr gave his father a 'curious original drawing' he had bought in Butchers Row and which he had then doctored to show Bassanio and Shylock from *The Merchant of Venice*, alleging it to be a picture which once 'hung in a room at the Globe Theatre, similar to that, which is now called at our play-houses the Green Room.' In the drawing's background is a list of plays written in a pseudo- Elizabethan hand naming 'Ass you lyke itte Othello hamblott[sic] Kynge John,' implicitly the Globe's contemporary repertoire. Samuel engraved this in December 1795, unwittingly creating an almost infinitely multipliable copy of his son's forged original.[377] On the same day, Ireland Sr also put his name to an exceedingly crude copy etching of a so-called Droeshout portrait print of Shakespeare's bust on a primitive heraldic emblem while also reproducing not just one but two very shaky 'William Shakespeare' signatures, copies of forged originals presumably produced by his son.[378] Similarly, Ireland Jr created not just one but several copies of the original manuscript of plays such as the 'Tragedye of Kynge Lear,' all replete with helpful documentation as to the authorial sources: 'Ife fromme Masterrre Hollinneshedde I have inne somme lyttle deparrtedde from hymme butte thatte Libbertye will notte I truste be blamedde bye mye gentle Readerres Wm Shakspeare.'[379] While offering a potentially wondrous gift to the scholar, at one stroke self-authenticating Holinshed as the source of *King Lear*, Ireland Jr's motive is yet another example of his quibbling between copies and originals insofar as he makes Shakespeare admit he has only 'inne somme lyttle deparrtedde' from his chronicler source. In other words, Shakespeare's near-iconic status as an original genius was subverted by Ireland's manufacture of explicit source material for his genius. One immediate consequence of his son's debacle amidst this confusion between copy, original and forgery was that Samuel Ireland was forced to sell his own quite considerable print collection ensuring, as it happens, a forced dispersal of even more copies of originals into the art market. Meanwhile, Ireland Sr still preferred not to believe that his son's Shakespeare fiasco had consisted of forgeries but, rather, that they were stolen authentic originals (' – my opinion is that they have Ben[*sic*] stolen – & that he is afraid to declare y[e] truth for fear of consequences').[380]

What strongly comes across amidst all of this confusion is the role of the Ireland family as producers of their representational culture – in other words, of the Irelands' as artisans manufacturing or forging a literary environment. One anonymous contemporary caricature print entitled *The Oaken Chest Or The Gold Mines Of Ireland a Farce* shows Ireland producing Shakespeare manuscripts from out of a trunk while his mother, father and two sisters are seated in the room assisting his forgeries. While there is nothing to suggest that Ireland Jr's family assisted him, they were certainly talented enough, and capable enough, to do so. A signed drawing, now in the Folger Library, showing Jane and Anna Maria Ireland and made by their father portrays them at an easel painting a picturesque valley scene while, in the immediate aftermath of Ireland Jr's flight from London, his mother composed a long poem addressed to their friends designed to tactfully cool what must have been an almost unbearable social embarrassment.[381] Referring to the 'dreadful fracas that has lately ensued,' Ireland's mother proposed 'a new Code' to the 'all judging Eyes' of their acquaintance, which good humouredly but carefully proscribed certain types of visitors to their Norfolk Street home:

> Imprimis, no Dancer on slack rope or tight
> 'Tho in Velvet, silk, Poplin, or Broad-Cloth bedight
> No Trumpeter, Drummer, or Fidler for hire
> His Nose to thrust into these rooms shall aspire
> No Singer in Public Italian or French
> Shall dare to pollute with his set-down a Bench
> A Chair, Sofa, Stool or of Leather or Cane
> If in a whole shin he would wish to remain

The list of their acquaintances evidently included many personnel from London's theatre industry, including players from the Royal theatres ('No Player on the Stage, bad, indifferent, or good, / Not his Majesty's Servants, respect shall e'er claim / 'Tho of Actors the first, and unblemish'd in Fame') who may well have themselves been involved in the thankless task of braving *Vortigern*'s first-night audience. Commensurate with Ireland Jr's trail of forgery, what is revealed is a family surrounded by a commercialized world of actors and illusionists ('All Hair-dressers Barbers, we next do expel / And those who Perukes to red Dowagers sell').[382] Nevertheless, limiting the damage done to them by Ireland Jr was obviously of first importance to the family. A manuscript annotation in the Folger Library's copy of *The Oaken Chest; or, The Gold Mines Of Ireland a Farce* notes that the 'Caricature is of the greatest rarity as very few were disposed of prior to the Plate being bought up & destroyed,' presumably by the family.[383] Another caricature, *The Spirit of Shakespeare Appearing to his Detractors*, was illegally anonymous as to its publication details, but came from a source knowledgeable about Ireland Sr's Hogarth edition since the print was mischievously styled 'Design'd and Engraved by Wm Hogarth & found by Somebody in an old Chest,' while a play text pictured in the print's foreground opened to reveal 'Vortigern / condemned by a most Disinterested Audience April 1796.' What is common to both caricatures is that they portray the whole Ireland family, father, mother, son and two daughters as being, implicitly, fellow accomplices in the production and dissemination of the Shakespeare deception. In *The Oaken Chest Or The Gold Mines Of Ireland a Farce*, all of the family is busied at manufacturing forgeries. In *The Spirit of Shakespeare Appearing to his Detractors*, all the family cower before the retributive ghost of Shakespeare.

This is a picture of a resourceful, productive family, possibly all of whom were involved at one stage or another in helping to create or sustain the illusion of Shakespearean authenticity that they had become caught up in. Judging by the number of Ireland fake manuscripts in modern libraries, as well as the several copies of the more or less hand-produced, hand-annotated *Specimens of my* [or *W.H. Ireland's*]*Shakespearian Fabrications* extant, a surprisingly large number of artefacts were produced.[384] As well as producing fake manuscripts, their venture bordered into theatricalization, offering to the public artefacts perhaps sprung from the very 'Hairdressers Barbers' they subsequently banned from their home, including a lock of Shakespeare's hair and another lock alleged to have come from the head of 'Anna Hatherrewaye.'[385] This theatricalization cut both ways. To return to that contemporary eyewitness's account of watching Ireland Jr register 'the marks of hope, fear, joy, anxiety and disappointment alternately portrayed on his countenance, as his piece at different times affected the House,' William Henry was unavoidably transfixed by the double gaze of London theatre, at once the spectator of *Vortigern* but also spectated by the *Vortigern* audience. In many ways, both *Vortigern* and his subsequent (unperformed) play *Henry II* were highly commodified works deftly aimed to mirror the anxieties and predilections of the age. In *Vortigern*, Ireland faithfully reflects mid-1790s angst about a Britain internally riven by dissent, a nation left dangerously open to foreign invasion. In *Henry II*, Ireland's portrayal of the grasping Thomas Becket seems aimed at validating contemporary liberal misgivings about the relationship between church and state. At its basis, however, Ireland's problem as a playwright was not so much that he forged Shakespeare (*Henry II* was ingeniously trailed as the rediscovered 'Henry I. and Henry II. by Wm. Shakespeare and Rob. Davenport. [registered] In the books of the Stationers Company, the 9th of Sept. 1653' (p. ii)), but that he attempted to write a play for a Theatre Royal in the grand, five-act tragic style.

If one makes a parallel between late eighteenth-century painting, it is as if Ireland Jr had emerged, fully fledged, onto London's cultural scene as a high class history painter, a well-nigh impossible task. It is a telling detail that Ireland Jr claimed inspiration from John Hamilton Mortimer's painting *The Meeting of Vortigern and Rowena* (1779, untraced). The example of the famous history painter must have been well known to the family because 'Mortimer was particularly intimate with Ms Jane Ireland who possess'd many of his eccentric but valuable Pictures & Drawings' while Ireland Sr himself 'purchased of that Artist' a number of pictures.[386] As an attempt, in 1796, to break into the world of writing for the London theatre, Ireland Jr's strategies were pretty comprehens-ively wrong and misguided: as erroneous in terms of attracting public estimation and popularity as Mortimer's own paintings. In addition, if Ireland's personal talents as a writer lay anywhere, they were in the kinds of satiric comic verse he developed during the mid-1800s and into the 1810s.

Also unknown to Ireland Jr at the time was that the aftermath of *Vortigern* would long extinguish the careers of those budding tragic play-wrights who sought to find a realistic professional life in the London theatre. No one successfully followed or imitated *Vortigern* although, given the humdrum day-to-day production schedules of the two Royal theatres who commanded the monopoly over five-act spoken drama, many a socially well-connected Oxford MA or country parson might find their classical or biblical tragedy fitted up with a two- or three-night outing at one of the patent theatres. What Ireland had misjudged, perhaps because he was only 20 years old when he wrote *Vortigern*, was that his talents and those of his family, their sheer productive resource-fulness, were part of an emerging class of artisans whose natural home would not be in contemporary *belles lettres*, Covent Garden or Drury Lane but in the burlettas of the transpontine illegitimate theatres. For Ireland Jr himself, his subsequent career would be in the illegitimate theatres' adjacent culture of Grub Street and the political press. However, perhaps one of the most telling indications of how other dramatists viewed Ireland, quite contrary to the opinions of the London literati, was his portrayal as Sir Bamber Blackletter in Frederick Reynolds's comedy *Fortune's Fool*. Reynolds, the hard-drinking, opium-addicted (John Payne Collier alleged that he 'drinks a bottle or more after dinner, two or three glasses of brandy and water at night, and never goes to bed without a dose of fifty drops of laudanum') author of this October 1796 Covent Garden production was noticeably circumspect in his caricature.[387]

Reynolds was 'present at the first and last representation' of *Vortigern* and visited Ireland in company with the playwright James Boaden, one of the most effective exposers of his trickery.[388] Instead of lampooning Ireland, Reynolds reversed real-life and made his Ireland character, Sir Bamber Blackletter, the victim rather than the perpetrator of forgery.[389] With an alleged Chaucer manuscript as an enticing part of a proposed dowry of marriage, Sir Bamber falls foul of the scheming Miss Union and the rakish Haphazard, but he is characterized more as a cynical book-seller ('Why, the original Author is nothing nowadays') or academic literati ('The Poem originally consists of about eighteen pages, but my notes swell it up to eighteen hundred! And I haven't done yet – I'll have an Edition with additions & Revisions, and make it up two thousand') than as a forger. In fact, in *Fortune's Fool* it is Haphazard, and not Blackletter, who produces a hitherto unknown piece of Shakespeariana:

Haphazard: I look upon you as the father of the Literati, the chief of commentators, the King of blue Stockings! And therefore I'll read to you an original stanza written by Shakespeare – Written for one of the Witches in Macbeth
Sir Bamb: An original stanza for one of the Witches! Oh! Let me hear.

And it is Miss Union, from the same kind of dubious chest so closely associated with Ireland at the time, who most clearly brings forth an actual forged parchment:

Miss Union: Well, to save your life, and I've no reason for distrusting you, here (*opening Trunk and taking out M.S. in a black binding*) Here is the Chaucerian Manuscript found at Union Castle in Cumberland.
Sir Bamb: Never mind where it was found – I've got it – Oh! How the touch thrills me! Now for the Title Page *(reads)* 'Trickarinda, a Poem full of witty and conceited mirth, written by Geoffrey Chaucer.' That's it, that's the true stile of 'witty and conceited mirth.'[390]

Eventually, the gullible Sir Bamber (tricked by *Trickarinda*) good humouredly realizes his folly and the plot resolves itself peaceably but, given the context of the spring and autumn of 1796, it is remarkable that Reynolds drew back from the temptation to pillory Ireland. In the event, *Fortune's Fool* ran with modest success for 20 nights, earning Reynolds the respectable sum of nearly £500 and leaving him feeling sufficiently charitable as to consider Ireland as 'a young man of no ordinary talent.'[391]

What Reynolds must have recognized was that Ireland's forgeries represented a far more complex moral problem for fellow dramatists than straightforward financial deception. *Fortune's Fool* explicitly condemns Sir Bamber's exploitative instincts by satirizing his designs for a new Chaucer edition using Miss Union's forged manuscript prefaced by a newly engraved frontispiece taken from a portrait bust of the author brought from Wales by Haphazard (Miss Union: 'Sir Bamber with my Manuscript and a picture from your Bust will make a fortune by his new Edition'). Reynolds makes comic fun of his eagerness to be duped:

Haphazard: *(with the bust in his hand)* Ay; here's old Geoffrey – here's the father of English Poets! Look. Sir! Doesn't this remind you of Palamon and Arcite, the flower of curtesy? The Assembly of Fools?
Sir Bamb: The Knyght's Tale, & Canterbury Tales, and the money I shall make by my new Edition. Oh! That for Charles *(snapping his fingers)* you're my Heir!

Reynolds must have been perfectly aware that literary authenticity in contemporary drama was virtually non-existent. The boundaries between originality and stealing, borrowing or adapting were decidedly blurred. Making only casual reference to a play's origin was extremely common at the time. Such misappropriation, not that dissimilar in principle to Ireland's attachment of Shakespeare's name to *Vortigern* or *Henry II*, usually went without comment. Perhaps 'Vortigern, Taken from the Shakespeare,' in an era where the adaptation of the Shakespearean original (of which only Nahum Tate's *King Lear* is the best-known example) was de rigueur, would have been a more honest and accurate description of Ireland's pastiche.

A satirical light touch was also given to Ireland in Walley Chamberlain Oulton's two-act farce for Drury Lane, *Precious Relics; or, The Tragedy of Vortigern Rehearsed* (1796), whose format parodied Sheridan's *The Critic*. In *Precious Relics*, as with Reynolds's *Fortune's Fool*, the Ireland character is only part of a greater conspiracy of light-hearted deception concerning a courtship between the lovers Henry and Harriot. With the playhouse able to call on the actors who had acted in *Vortigern's* single perform-ance, Drury Lane made a virtue of satirizing the whole episode as well as celebrating their star performers (*'Prompter:* ... where's Jack Bannister? *First Player:* Oh, Bannister is on the stairs, supporting Mrs. Siddons').[392] In a revealing choice of name, the Ireland role was played by a char-acter called Craft. It is Craft who, at the instigation of Henry, has stolen allegedly Elizabethan manuscripts ('curious papers, which I verily believe were forgeries too') from the connoisseur Sir Mark Ludicrous, and has written *Vortigern* as a text to complete the deception so that Henry can pass the whole set of documents off to Harriot's guardian, Mr. Wisepate, as the eponymous precious relics which will smooth his marriage to his ward. Henry hides them in an 'iron box,' the consistent trope of the *Vortigern* episode but, significantly, his machinations are concealed from Craft. In other words, Craft (the Ireland character) is not fully aware of the purpose of the deception ('[Enter] *Henry solus.* So – Craft – my friend; ... I have deceived, even the deceiver – for he has no suspicions of my true motives for this imposture').[393] Although Craft's role diminishes sharply in the play as Drury Lane made comedy out of the ironies of its actors rehearsing the more obvious Shakespearean pastiches of *Vortigern*, and ultimately Craft is able to turn the tables on Henry after feigning his own interest in Harriot. His compensation is eventually to be paid off through a bank cheque made payable to him by Henry. As a fascinating insight into a range of issues Ireland's *Vortigern* had provoked, however, Craft's closing remark is that, if Henry had not paid him, 'I should not only have proved the forgery, but represented the play [to be] so immoral, indecent, and jacobinical, as, no doubt, to have prevented it's having a licence.' In other words, during rehearsal, Craft would have rewritten parts of *Vortigern* so as to emphasize Ireland's perceptible tendency to involve his play in sufficient incest, radical politics and a general degree of Jacobinism as to have brought about its prohibition by the Lord Chamberlain.[394] With its downplaying of the Ireland role and its summary of a range of topics *Vortigern* had provoked concerning its politics and morality, Oulton's *Precious Relics* (1796) provides a significant contemporary perspective on the cultural reception of Ireland's play.

The sort of cultural and political conditions of literary production outlined above were part of the day-to-day transactions of the writing of literary drama in late eighteenth-century London. Plays could even be censored for being too antagonistic towards Britain's enemies. Thomas John Dibdin recalled that his 'Comic Divertisement' in one act for Drury Lane, *Orange Boven; or, More good News* (1813) was prohibited with just a few hours notice before its first scheduled performance 'because... [of] two or three songs which were thought too personal against Bonaparte.'[395] Larpent's crossings out in pen have made the (just two) songs practically unreadable except that they appear to tell 'Boney' to 'let the Dutch alone' (Holland had asked Britain to assist in the removal of Napoleon's brother from the country).[396] The creator of Sir Bamber Blackletter in *Fortune's Fool* was himself no stranger to the unpredictable interferences of the Lord Chamberlain and to the effects of the exigencies of the theatrical repertoire on authorial intention. Recollecting the tumults of 1789, Reynolds commented that Covent Garden commissioned from him a 'Bastile' piece 'But, when the parts were studied, the scenery completed, and the music composed, the Lord Chamberlain refused his license' and Reynolds found two of his Bastile scenes were recycled for a piece called *The Crusade*, 'representing the deeds and manner of the Christians, and Saracens, of the eleventh century, amongst the buildings of the Parisians, of the eighteenth.'[397] Amidst such mongrel, politically propositioned and economically determined sets of practical literary values, Ireland's fabrication of *Vortigern* or *Henry II* looks extremely innocuous. Save for its rather foolish implicit self-advertisement as a sort of dramatic history painting, it is difficult to discriminate between Ireland's ethical practices and those long followed by Frederick Reynolds, the opium addict.

William Henry Ireland's subsequent career immediately took him away from dramatic writings and into the growing Grub Street print culture of the early nineteenth century, but drama and forgery were issues to which he frequently returned. Ireland Jr's artisan credentials are best established by noting that in 1798 he set up a circulating library near Kennington Cross, Lambeth, hoping to sell prints and books, and that by the early 1800s he was working for William Hone at the beginning of the latter's career as one of the era's foremost radical pressmen.[398] Hone may still have been working as a bookkeeper for a hop factory at that time, but he was obviously providing Ireland with some kind of work when Ireland was nearly destitute, and writing begging Hone for 'an advance of £2-10-0' and even asking him for financial help ('I have been living for this three weeks on borrowing &c.&c.') during Hone's own arrest for debt.[399] Around this time (*c.*1805) Ireland ventured into editing one-penny journals such as *Youth's Polar Star or The Beacon of Science!* complete with a facsimile of Queen Elizabeth's signature, the heroic deeds of the young Nelson and a collection of 'Chinese Sayings.' By 1811 Ireland was himself in York's grim castle, debtor's prison, although still managing to publish a number of poems in both *The York Herald* (of which he was then editor) and in the London published *Morning Chronicle*.[400] His flight into the popular print culture was sometimes combined not only with entrepreneurial acumen, but also with attempts at developing a niche market redeploying his knowledge of the visual-print trade. Under the pseudonym Sam Satiricus, in 1809 he ventured into anti-aristocratic scandal-mongering surrounding the revelations of the high-class courtesan Mary Ann Clarke, the lover of the Duke of York, showing a gift for rhyming couplets and arch *double entendres*. Tucked into *The Cyprian of St. Stephen's; or, Princely Protection Illustrated* (1809) was also an opportunity to purchase an engraved portrait miniature of Mary Ann Clarke at 15 shillings in a proof edition of 30, £1.5s coloured or as 10s 6d 'Common Impressions.'[401] Years later, in *Death-Bed Confessions of the Late Countess of Guernsey* (1821), Ireland was able to return to this line of work, writing for the radical pressman and printseller John Fairburn during the scandal over one of the Prince of Wales's lovers, where Ireland could excel not only at his own confessional mode but also in the miraculous production of 'Authentic Documents Never Before Published.'[402]

To return to *Vortigern* and *Henry II*, however, the best way of understanding Ireland's state of mind as the manufacturer of misattributed plays lies in his own relationship with the print trade, a trade in which he was both knowledgeable and, as shown above, entrepreneurial. Ireland's *Chalcographimania; or, The Portrait-Collector and Printseller's Chronicle* (1814) was published under the pseudonym of 'Satiricus Sculptor' or satirical engraver and was written as a verse exposé of the London printselling and collecting trade exhaustively detailed with extensive notes to every page. Ireland's target was the dubious practices of auctioneers such as Sotheby, Christie and Colnaghi who founded whole dynasties of dealers surviving into the present day. To Ireland, the point was both blunt and simple: 'For of all Tradesmen none's so glib, / As Auctioneer at telling fib.' It is likely that Ireland Jr had been severely embarrassed by his father's need to sell his prized collection of Hogarth prints shortly after the debacle following *Vortigern*, but his son had a further necessity to use the services of an auction house when disposing of the residue of his father's collection after his death in 1800.[403] Using his specialist knowledge, Ireland described the countless dubious techniques of the auction houses, such as selling completely misattributed portrait engravings (for example, an engraving said to be of Caxton but, according to Ireland, actually 'the likeness of an Italian poet'); the creation of a 'Knock-Out' or ring of insider bidders amongst a cartel of auctioneers; the sale of a so-called original likeness of young Shakespeare, 'the property ... of a Mr. P—rry, who has a taste for design' (as Ireland ironically put it); an alleged 'original' of Droeshout's famous engraving of Shakespeare put up for sale at Colnaghi's but actually a portrait of 'a *snuff-taking* German.'[404] As Ireland wrote, using the instance of the founder of Christies, auctioneering was a trade which 'In short vows ev'ry thing uncouth, / Till *Going*: – *Gone*: – knocks down *Untruth*.'[405]

One printseller was so alarmed by Ireland's work that his similarly titled *Calcographiana* (1814) – a genuine 'Guide to the Knowledge & Value of Engraved British Portraits' might be attributed to Ireland that he tried to swear an oath at Marlborough Street police office testifying that he was not the author of *Chalcographimania*.[406] Given this commercial context of double-dealing, counterfeit and fraud, about which Ireland Jr must have learned plenty during his youth (in *The Confessions* he makes it clear he was an avid and able collector of old books), then it is much more convincing to transpose Ireland across from being merely a Shakespeare forger to being a resourceful artisan negotiating his way through Grub Street and its Bond Street art-market equivalents and, during that progress, being only slightly less scrupulous than some of his more commercially successful and respectable colleagues. Even in *Chalcographimania* with its extended satire on printsellers, Ireland took care to offer for sale (at 2s.6d each) four sets of three 'already engraved' portraits 'To accommodate those Gentlemen who wish to illustrate the present volume of Chalcographimania.'[407]

Resettling Ireland into the role of aspirant artisan is much more enlightening than resigning him to the compartment of particularly ineffectual forger. There is every indication that Ireland was becoming involved in the new scene of mid-1810s urban radicalism associated with an expanding press culture. His next substantial poem, a satire on writers, *Scribbleomania; or, The Printer's Devil's Polichronicon. A Sublime Poem* (1815) was published by the radical pressmen Sherwood, Neely, and Jones who, to Robert Southey's embarrassment, went on to pirate his youthful *Wat Tyler* in 1817. Furthermore, *Scribbleomania's* printer was Thomas Davison of Whitefriars, a significant Spencean activist who moved amongst urban physical-force revolutionaries as well as being John Murray's most favoured Byron printer of the 1810s.[408] Ireland's radical sympathies can often be glimpsed throughout his career. If anything, the growing political assertiveness of the artisan print culture he worked in seems to have increased his confidence. The suggestion of an incestuous passion between the king and his daughter in *Vortigern* is consistent with the broadly anti-monarchist scandalmongering he became involved with later in *The Cyprian of St. Stephen's* or *The Death-Bed Confessions*.[409] Even more stark had been Ireland's naïve insertion of eighteenth-century radical political discourses into the supposedly Elizabethan *Vortigern*: 'Oh! you ha' struck me where I am indeed / Most vulnerable – "*The voice o'th'people!*" / For them I will surrender liberty.'[410]

On the other hand, he was also one of the many writers, contemporary radicals being the most prominent, who joined in politically nuanced outpourings of national grief at the death of Princess Charlotte in 1817.[411] In the mid-1810s he also took up the cause of Napoleon, condemning his treatment by the Allies on Elba, an issue to which he returned many years later in one of his most forthright pieces, *Britannia's Cat-O'-Nine-Tails; or, The Devil's Carols During Half a Century of Rapine, Desolation, and Blood* (1833) which attacked George III, George IV, William Pitt, Lord Ellenborough, Lord Liverpool, Spencer Perceval and Castlereagh (who 'had the effrontery to countenance and applaud the dastardly meanness of his voluptuous master, in condemning to a barren rock, the noblest enemy [Napoleon] Britain ever encountered, who had heroically thrown himself upon her mercy' (p. 11)). Although such pro-Napoleonic stances were not uncommon amongst the more extreme radicals of the post-Waterloo period, Ireland is quite unusual (and quite daring) in having shown an early interest and admiration for Britain's most feared enemy.[412] When he was only shortly out of debtor's prison, he wrote a York-published satirical poem, *The Death of Bonaparte; or, One Pound One* (1812), which focused on an almost irrecoverably obscure local legal case concerning a wager made about the life expectancy of Napoleon.[413]

Although Ireland did not return to writing for the theatre, he seems to have kept close to its developments as the new type of artisan-based playhouses expanded on the south side of the Thames. Instead of attempting to return to theatrical writing himself, where no doubt he would have been greeted with derision, Ireland carefully incorporated into his publications the steadier advantages of his knowledge of the print-selling trade. In 1814 he issued a humorous London guide book, *Something Concerning Nobody, Embellished with Fourteen Characteristic Etchings*, giving useful eyewitness accounts of most of the metropolitan theatres, including Covent Garden, Sadler's Wells, the hippodrames at Astley's Amphitheatre (where he commented on 'the great superiority evinced by the quadruped species over the more honourable creatures gifted with two legs only') as well as the 'Royal' Lyceum (then the temporary post-conflagration home of the Theatre Royal Drury Lane).[414] He was also an early visitor to the (ex-Royal Circus) Surrey Theatre (where he was 'not a little surprized at the transmogrification which has taken place ... to the total exclusion of quadrupeds'), and commented ironically on the Surrey's mode of semi-musically 'chanting forth the subject matter of the representation' in order to avoid the act of speaking, a form 'monopolized only at Drury Lane and Covent Garden' with their restrictive patents.[415] At the turn of the 1810s, with the long-running 'hits' of the 'Tom and Jerry' plays and their spin-offs based on Pierce Egan's *Life in London; or, The day and night scenes of Jerry Hawthorne* (1820), Ireland turned to making his own variation on the theme in *Gaieté de Paris, by George Cruikshank; or The Rambles of an English Party Through the French Metropolis* (1825) published by John Fairburn. This was essentially a reissuing of Cruikshank's prints for Carey's *Life in Paris* (1822) but now augmented by 'Letter-Press Descriptions of Real Life in the Vortex of that Chase Ennui' written by Ireland. With its references to the 'Tom and Jerry' slang of 'sprees,' 'flooring,' the 'set-to' and the 'row,' *Gaieté de Paris* showed that Ireland had fully absorbed the latest fashionable argot emanating from the stages of The Adelphi and Olympic Theatres.[416]

Gaieté de Paris, with the drawing power of the Cruikshank plates, was a well-chosen, elegantly produced medium for Ireland's excursion into the latest fad for the celebration of London's subculture.

The playwright most consistently associated with the 'Tom and Jerry' phenomena was William Thomas Moncrieff, the author of the Adelphi's *Tom and Jerry; or, Life in London* (1821). With its knowledge of the semi-criminal dubious practices and social and commercial promiscuities of London's entertainment haunts, Moncrieff's *Tom and Jerry*, as well as its imitators, mirrored the knowledge of the seedier side of the metropolis Ireland himself had exposed five years earlier in *Chalcographimania* and *Scribbleomania*. The possible link between Ireland and Moncrieff may have been George Cruikshank, who had worked on *Gaieté de Paris* and who had also contributed set designs for Moncrieff's Adelphi Theatre *Tom and Jerry* back in 1821. By 1823, Cruikshank was also providing etchings for Ireland's serialized *Life of Napoleon*, a troublesomely slow part-work not completed until 1828.[417]

The personal lives of the two men also mirrored each other to some extent: both wrote for their livelihood, Ireland as a Grub Street hack and Moncrieff writing short-notice commission pieces for various London theatres. They also had the shared experience of having suffered considerable financial hardship. Ireland's letters to William Hone about being owed money are paralleled by Moncrieff's letters to Drury Lane complaining of 'not having a shilling' and needing '£100 on Acct.'[418] Also, like Ireland in 1811, Moncrieff spent some time in debtors' prison in 1819 and both men achieved a certain amount of notoriety in their own lifetime, Ireland for *Vortigern* and Moncrieff for the well-publicized disturbances which broke out in the Strand during the Adelphi's performances of *Tom and Jerry*. Moncrieff was also occasionally subject to accusations about originality similar to those which had been levelled at Ireland. Charles Mathews, the great one-man-show comedian of the *At Homes*, cruelly pilloried him in the 1820s as 'the great little Moncrieff the literary thief whose wit is very brief.'[419] With little awareness of the displacement of genres necessitated by the stranglehold over five-act spoken drama enforced by the Royal theatres, at the earliest stages of his career Moncrieff, ('a name being but little known') was disparaged by an anonymous versifier who dedicated his satirical *Dramatic Scorpion* (1818) to J.P. Kemble ('that perfect Model of Theatrical Excellence').[420] It is hardly surprising, but none the less remarkable, that Ireland became acquainted with Moncrieff, the ex-forger the elder of the two by nearly 20 years, unusually settling himself into an admiration of the younger man's success. Ireland sent Moncrieff a copy of his father's book *Shakespearian Fabrications*, which gave examples of Ireland Jr's forgeries, writing into the copy that 'These specimens of my Shakespearian Fabrications are presented to my friend Mr. Moncrieff with best regards.' Ireland hoped the book would 'enrich your Theatrical Collection,' and he included with the gift an invitation to dine, together with elaborate directions as to how to reach his house.[421] It is with this kind of hindsight that one gets some kind of perspective on the revealing autograph note Ireland put into the flyleaf of a gifted copy of *Vortigern* when he wrote that the drama 'was written when my mind became a prey to the multifarious doubts and fears which my then situation gave rise to.'[422]

Apart from what must have been Ireland's dawning revelation in the early 1800s that his true literary talents lay in becoming the James Gillray, rather than the Hamilton Mortimer of literature, his flyleaf reflection on his own 'situation' in the mid-1790s and the 'multifarious doubts and fears' to which he was then subject suggests that Ireland may have even then been aware of the obstacles preventing his progress into dramatic writing. Back in 1796, unlike in the later 1810s and '20s with the emerging transpontine 'minor' theatres, the two Royal theatres still exerted a virtual stranglehold on dramatic entertainment in London: it was indeed the true 'monopoly' they so jealously guarded. Standing state sentinel over their privileges was the figure of John Larpent, the Lord Chamberlain's Examiner of Plays, and Ireland must have realized that he had written a play which, even under the cloak of Shakespeare's name, could still be subjected to his excisions.

Ireland himself appears to have toned down the 'historical fact, thought too gross for the public ear,' about the 'incestuous passion of the king [Vortigern] towards his daughter [Flavia].'[423] Whether Larpent assumed the author of *Vortigern* to be Shakespeare or not, Drury Lane was still obliged to submit any new work containing text to the Examiner of Plays. Theoretically and perhaps in practice – depending on what Larpent knew of *Vortigern*'s origins – the submission of a 'new' Shakespeare play for the consideration and possible censure (or even suppression) of the Lord Chamberlain was a bewilderingly material, but entirely legal, possibility in late eighteenth-century England. In any event, as late as the submission of the manuscript to Larpent in February 1796, Ireland still seems to have been removing whatever implications of incest had originally been present in the manuscript he had manufactured. The evidence of the scribe's handwriting suggests that lines concerning Flavia's unwillingness to tell her brother, Pascentius, the full story of her sudden flight from Vortigern's court ('Be not amazed, neither

question me / On cause o'this my unexpected flight / For if there silence
be in the cold Grave / E'en in such sort must utt'rance be with me')
were marked for excision by Ireland himself. A few pages later, however,
Larpent's manuscript copy contains a long excision which corresponds
to Vortigern's argument with his barons towards the end of Act IV. Sc.vi.
in the printed edition. An inserted page, written by a different scribe,
now bound into Larpent's copy in the Huntington Library (marked –
unaccountably – 'Page. 8.') is scored through in both pencil and in ink.
The ink's drying has left an offset on the page following the inserted leaf.
This strongly suggests that Ireland was forced to give this part of his text
a rewrite, either before – or as a supplement to – the censorship process.
In essence, Ireland's scene is a pastiche of the Magna Carta dispute, but
here transposed into late Romano-Britain. The printed edition shows few
changes from the original licensing copy except that both this inserted
leaf and the printed version reveal the contentious words Ireland had to
delete, which were concerned with the late eighteenth-century radical
commonplace of the majesty of the people and the people's willingness
to resist the king's authority:

Jacomo: The Law allows not this – it is not justice.
Vort: Be it from henceforth then, a sacred Law.
Bellarius: That power lies in the People, not the King.

. . .

Bellarius: And while the power remains that's vested in us,
We ne'er will countenance such vile injustice
To trample on our Friends, and Countries rights.
Vort: Take heed, lest for your words, you pay your heads.
Bellarius & Jacomo: Farewell, but know these threats shall cost
    you dear.[424]

If these were the conditions of literary production Ireland had to
contend with, it is little wonder he must not only have thought of giving
up writing for the stage but also thought that his dramas had their best
chance of performance under the name and aura of Shakespeare.

As has been outlined above, if Ireland wished to continue writing
dramas for the stage in the 1790s, then his room for manoeuvre was
pretty constrained by forces well beyond his control or influence. The
differences between that decade and the late 1820s were considerable.
Initially, Ireland seems to have learned little in that he still continued
writing formal tragedy in his (unperformed) play *Mutius Scaevola; or,*

The Roman patriot: an historical drama (1801). Exactly how different the context of dramatic writing would be nearly 30 years later is best indicated by two plays written by W. T. Moncrieff and C. A. Somerset to coincide with the attempt by the Shakespearean Club of Stratford-upon-Avon to celebrate Shakespeare's birth on a triennial basis. There was a remarkable degree of relaxed freedom with which both Moncrieff and Somerset could go about their writing. Even as late as 1816, a Covent Garden afterpiece outing for Garrick's *Jubilee* piece of 1769 still had its 'Grand Pageant' of plays ending in 'Sing immortal Shakespeare's praise!' only partly leavened by a degree of homely familiarization ('But the Will of all Wills was a Warwickshire Will').[425] Sensitivity to agitation for Parliamentary reform in the late 1820s still made political commentary likely to provoke the Examiner's interference but criticism about literary matters was much more open than it had been around the time of the fuss about Ireland's forgeries. Different routes, different modes, were open to writers like Moncrieff in a way which would have been unthinkable in the era of *Vortigern*. If Ireland gifted his *Specimens of Shakespearian Fabrications* to Moncrieff in the 1820s, it may well have contributed to the younger author's evident scepticism about reverence for the Bard which, of course, was nowhere more apparent than in Stratford-upon-Avon. Moncrieff's *Shakespeare's Festival; or, A New Comedy of Errors!* (1830) was described by the author as being 'written in haste, with the double object of producing a harmless laugh at the follies of some of the mad-headed commentators on the great Bard, and paying a humble tribute of respect to his matchless merits.'[426] However, Moncrieff specifically localized rather than universalised his 'tribute' to Shakespeare, making fun of the Stratford-upon-Avon Shakespearean Club (chairman: Arden Shakespeare) as the product of small-town commercialism. The financial implications of a Shakespeare birthday festival and their exploitative potential for those offering catering and accommodation are voiced in the figure of Gaius, the landlord of the Falcon Inn, Stratford, as he surveys his bulging tavern: 'Rare times for Stratford, – would we had a Shakespeare born every year! his plays, let us all play! ... if we continue to fill in this manner, there won't be a bed to be had for love nor money.'[427] Moncrieff obviously thought it prudent to observe convention and give over the entire second act to a grand civic procession through the Stratford streets featuring, in order, the Royal Standard of England, the banner of St George and the banner of the town borough and ending with a tableau of the 'Coronation of Shakespeare by the Tragic and Comic Muses,' but both the diminution of the legend and the awareness of the commodification of Shakespeare's name are apparent in *Shakespeare's Festival; or, A New Comedy of Errors!* [428] Again, its distance from Covent Garden's 1816 version of Garrick's 1769 *Jubilee* is noticeable. Furthermore, Moncrieff's play had been performed at the Surrey Theatre in April 1830, probably on a date intended to coincide with Shakespeare's birthday (23 April). Staging in a less regulated venue, beyond the remit of the Lord Chamberlain, would not have been open to Ireland in the 1790s but, of course, part of Moncrieff's success as a playwright lay in developing a comic form capable of making implicitly serious comments about 'Bardology,' all from within the unpromising genre of burletta (the only format permissible in the non-patent houses). Even in the Royal theatres, however, circumstances had changed, not least because of the successes of transpontine theatres such as the Surrey. C.A. Somerset's *Shakespeare's Early Days: An Historical Play, In Two Acts* (1829) for Covent Garden had been even quicker off the mark than Moncrieff in providing a vehicle for commenting on Statford's latest incarnation of the Shakespeare Jubilee.

Somerset's *Shakespeare's Early Days*, like Moncrieff's *Shakespeare's Festival*, is a mature exploitation of the burletta form, which makes some serious points not only about Shakespeare but also, implicitly, about the continuing role of the Lord Chamberlain. Somerset's piece stresses Shakespeare's artisan origins by identifying his father as a woolstapler. Furthermore, Somerset encapsulates the tradition of the young Shakespeare having once been caught poaching deer by having the first words of the play being his father's remark that 'our boy Willy hath not been home all night,' a familiarization immediately domesticating and de-mythologizing William's subsequent appearances. [429] Even Somerset's apparent sentimentalizing of Shakespeare by having him rescue a poor family, and being prosecuted for poaching game, is used as a cue for an eloquent pro-poaching, anti-hunting speech grounded in artisan notions of the common ownership of the natural world and traditions of customary justice:

> But a wild animal, such as a deer, or hare,
> Can have no owner...
> Where is the sin in killing such a creature,
> More than in plucking from a bush or tree
> A nut or sloe unclaimed of any man? [430]

Such attitudes were deeply engrained in popular culture. In 1822 the Adelphi's comic pantomime *Who Kill'd the Dog or Harlequins Triumph* draws on the audience's recognition of the wrongs done to the would-be poachers Blunderbuss and Gregory who accidentally shoot Squire Grim Gruffy's dog rather than the hare at which they had aimed. A false accusation for the crime ('As I'm Grim Gruffy he shall quickly swing') is enough to bring down the intervention of the divine figure of Justice.[431] If *Who Kill'd the Dog* drew on traditional and popular attitudes to poaching, by 1829 and *Shakespeare's Early Days*, the beginnings of the agricultural distress ultimately expressed in the 'Captain Swing' disturbances of 1830–1 were already being felt by rural patricians who felt themselves squeezed between the economic determinants theorized by Adam Smith and Thomas Malthus.[432] Somerset's popular commentary on the displacement of communal property by the nobility is confirmed by Shakespeare's sentence to a fine of 'fifty crowns, or twelve months' imprisonment.'[433] Escaping such injustice, Shakespeare: migrates to London where, predictably, he becomes caught up in the theatrical and tavern culture of Southwark from an alienated Stratford to the convivial community of 'the Falcon Tavern, the favourite resort of the Globe Company of Comedians, in Shakespeare's times.'[434] Again, the emphasis is on a companionable, approachable Shakespeare, someone remaining close to his artisan roots in an artificially distressed provincial agricultural community. This de-mythologising of Shakespeare is noticeably continued in the language of his tavern-based friendships with the famous Globe actors Richard Burbage and Tarleton the clown: 'Prithee, now, Tarleton, come with me, whilst thou canst walk erect, for, ere long, an' thou goest on thus, thou'lt crawl on all fours like a beast.'[435]

Somerset's deftest satire, however, is one obliquely directed at the office of the Lord Chamberlain, a circumstance he makes with a relevance much more cogent to the late 1820s than it was to the late sixteenth century. In a couple of hilarious scenes, Somerset puts the young Shakespeare into the situation which, by proxy, Ireland had found himself in with respect to 'Shakespeare's' *Vortigern*. In *Shakespeare's Early Days*, Shakespeare has to obtain a warrant of performance from the Master of the Revels, an obfuscating pedant whom Somerset names Doctor Orthodox ('Burbage: ...but first you must procure /A warrant from old Doctor Orthodox').[436] The play Shakespeare needs licensing is *Hamlet*, possibly the greatest tragedy in the English language but about which, as Somerset ironizes, Doctor Orthodox is extremely scathing. In their interview, when young Shakespeare visits the Master of the Revels to explain the delay in licensing, Doctor Orthodox is distinctly lukewarm about *Hamlet*'s suitability for the Elizabethan stage in view of its unconventional structure and content:

Doctor Orthodox: 'I recollect – hem! Hamlet: *(Looking over the MS)* and a precious Hamlet it is, too – here we have a ghost – a youth who feigns madness, and a young maiden truly out of her wits – then come a couple of grave-diggers, – now, really young man, prithee tell me, art thou not often, at the full of the moon, somewhat deranged? Out of pure friendship do I counsel thee to return home, with all convenient speed; and drive a cart, hew wood, carry water, or follow the plough – but attempt not to write tragedies, for, without Greek and Latin, how canst thou possibly hope to thrive?'[437]

Orthodox's pedantry when faced with the masterpiece of *Hamlet* ('Oh, immortal Aristotle! what wouldst thou say to this?') is an oblique criticism of the role of George Colman Jr, the then Examiner of Plays.[438] Almost at that very moment, Colman's own pedantry was excising vernacular expressions, on a day-to-day basis, in his own official role ultimately descended from the Master of the Revels. In *Caswallon; or, The Briton Chief* (1829) and *The Daughter's Vow* (1828), Colman insisted on striking out nearly all references to 'heavens,' despite making light of it: 'If the Author would, still, *thin some of his Heavens* (for I have left many of them untouch'd) his Play would not be the worse for it.' In *The School of Gallantry* (1828) he required the removal of 'Thanks, thanks, my Angel' and the poorly punning 'Her Eau de Cologne, he, he! so you gave up the flesh, but kept the Spirit.'[439]

The sorts of freedoms around the name and reputation of Shakespeare which Moncrieff and Somerset enjoyed by the end of the 1820s were mainly contingent on changes in cultural attitudes, rather than in alterations or improvements imposed by the Government's exercise of power since the 1790s over writing for the stage. The hostility which had greeted the forged *Vortigern* was mainly the result of Ireland's youthful confusion, his 'multifarious doubts and fears' over the production of both the forged artefacts or memorabilia and the staged drama at Drury Lane. Ireland's literary forte, as it turned out, was not to be in the universalized political issues of straight national history dramas such as *Vortigern*, *Henry II* or *Mutius Scaevola*, but rather in the sort of localized, highly specific, topical satires he developed in *Chalcographimania* and *Scribbleomania*. The dramatic vehicles and discourses afforded by the development of burletta in London's more experimental venues such as the Surrey Theatre were not available to Ireland in the mid-1790s. Given the structural conditions of drama in London, Ireland's *Vortigern* was an understandable attempt to short-circuit a monopolistic theatre.

That the conditions of theatrical monopoly encountered by Wordsworth in 1797 and by Coleridge in 1812–13 were still persisting into the late 1810s can be demonstrated by the example of John Keats and his five-act spoken tragedy *Otho the Great*, co-written with Charles Armitage Brown, in 1818. Jonathan Mulrooney has shown how Keats became increasingly fixed upon on the idea of one particular actor, Drury Lane's Edmund Kean, taking a principal role in *Otho*.[440] As Jonathan Mulrooney, following Jane Moody, has suggested, contemporary receptions of Kean's proletarian energy may have proved compelling.[441] This preference both for Kean and for writing *Otho* as a spoken tragedy meant that he was inevitably involved in dealing with the monopoly system.[442] Almost a generation after Ireland's, Wordsworth's and Coleridge's first experiences, Keats was about to make history repeat itself. It was not a case of exercising choice but simply moving back and forth between the two institutions. His initial opinion in August 1819 that 'The Covent Garden Company is execrable,' along with vague promises from Drury Lane about a performance – all mired by Kean's apparent unavailability – led to Keats finally admitting in January 1820 that 'Not having succeeded at Drury Lane with our Tragedy, we have been making some alterations and are about to try Covent Garden.'[443] During this process of collaboration, Brown confided to C.W. Dilke that, in the writing of *Otho*, 'Keats is very industrious, but I swear by the prompter's whistle, and by the bangs of stage doors, he is obstinately monstrous.'[444] His comments allude to Keats's lack of realism in writing for the particular conditions of the contemporary London playhouses. However, unlike the examples of Ireland, Wordsworth and Coleridge in the 1790s who were encountering the theatres unassisted and poorly advised, Keats ignored the advice of friends who had already successfully negotiated the contemporary London theatres. Crucially, as even Coleridge had realized, modern dramas needed music as well as speech. Music was not only popular with the audience (and suited to the vastly enlarged auditoriums of Covent Garden and Drury Lane), but not least, it also allowed some flexibility of venue.

Brown's Drury Lane 'serio-comic opera,' *Narensky or, The road to Yaroslaf* (1814), had not been particularly successful but it was perfectly formulated for the metropolitan stage.[445] *Narensky* had an exotic Russian location, lots of songs (the drama begins with a chorus of villagers while Scene II features the melody of a 'Russian Air'), a chorale finale ends each act and there are plenty of short speeches in the dialogue. Brown did not write the music, instead he persuaded William Reeve, a highly experienced theatrical composer, to write the songs which the popular tenor John Braham sang. Reeve specialized in writing music for dramas set in exotic lands so *Narensky*'s finale with '*a Pas Deux... to the original Russian Air*,' would not have been a problem for him.[446] Brown had deftly caught the mood of a public interested in music and spectacle as much as spoken drama. *Narensky*'s three-act format and ample musical setting also permitted it to be treated as burletta, allowing it to be potentially marketable outside the monopolistic playhouses. No doubt such considerations prompted his remark that although 'Keats is very industrious... he is obstinately monstrous.'

Keats learned even less from his friend John Hamilton Reynolds's experience of writing his English Opera House (Lyceum) farce *One, Two, Three, Four, Five; by Advertisement* (1819).[447] It is not known whether Reynolds had first offered it to Covent Garden or Drury Lane but he had clearly used to advantage the gradual changes in repertory as the English Opera House supplemented the Haymarket theatres. By 1819, Reynolds was aware of the changes in London's theatreland. The text of *One, Two* refers to both The Minor private theatre in Catherine Steet, Strand, and to the Royal Coburg. The allusion to The Minor shows that he recognized the growing popularity of social theatricality, a movement away from the limitations imposed by the duopolistic houses. *One, Two*'s principal plot mechanism is that Harry Alias is an amateur actor who fools his lover's disgruntled father, Old Coupleton, by appearing to him in a variety of disguises borrowed from an amateur theatrical troupe. If Reynolds' *One, Two* is now largely forgotten, Keats's comments were unnecessarily dismissive, relating in a letter that, while he had not seen Reynolds's 'little piece,' he thought 'Our Stage is [already] loaded with mimics.'[448] Unlike Keats, both Reynolds and Brown had successfully negotiated London's contemporary theatre by remaining open-minded and realistic and staying well informed about available performers, the importance of music and the considerable opportunities afforded by playhouses beyond London's two royal theatres.

William Henry Ireland can be placed in a spectrum of these young aspirant male authors, the least successful of them struggling to write five-act spoken tragedies for performance at just two playhouses, Covent Garden or Drury Lane. In Ireland's case, his family were too much the product of an earlier age of patronage and sensitivity to social rank rather than taking courage from their distinctively artisan talents. A generation later, as Ireland must have realized himself, newer playwrights such as Moncrieff and Somerset could focus more confidently on a more effective spirit of fun and wit. En route, Wordsworth gave up his theatrical ambitions and Coleridge succeeded only after considerable difficulty and with plentiful special assistance. John Keats, on the other hand, had access to good advice but chose to ignore it. Although it is a symbolic rather than empirical starting point, that day in April 1796 which witnessed the debacle of Ireland and his *Vortigern* can be taken as a convenient moment from which to chart the development of London popular theatre's exploitation of burletta. Excluded from spoken drama by the Royal patentees, the new playwrights learned to cater for new types of audience in different types of playhouse.

5
The Libertine Reclaimed: Burletta and the Cockney Presence

This chapter will argue that the unnoticed presence behind the attacks on the so-called Cockney School of poets which emanated from *Blackwood's Edinburgh Magazine* was the parallel growth and assertiveness of Cockneys both as fictional characters and as Londoners spectating and acting on the capital's increasingly fragmented range of stages. These were the young Londoners, legal scribes, apprentices, shopmen and women who paid to act at private theatres such as the one Keats himself visited in 1818. London's urban private theatres, the descendants of the spouting clubs, were fundamentally transforming the relationship between actors and audiences. Beyond the authority of the patent houses or Lord Chamberlain, a newly emerging class of Londoner was taking to the stage. To Ann Catherine Holbrook, an older provincial actress writing her *Memoirs of the Stage* in 1809, they were part of an increasing groundswell of 'Spouting Clubs, and Private Theatres' who threatened her livelihood, seeming to 'spring' 'from behind the Counter, from off the Shop-board.'[449] Ten years after Keats's death, London could even support *The Acting Manager; or, The Minor Spy. A Weekly Review of the Public and Private Stage* with its notices of the Shakespeare's Pavilion private theatre in the working-class Hoxton Old Town (on *Richard III*, 'Mr. Green seems to know as much about Shakespeare as a monkey knows about philosophy').[450] In an era where even Colman's Trudge could be described as 'a generous-minded cockney,' such plebeian appropriations were all part of the increasing visibility and assertiveness of London's Cockney population and which the prescient *Blackwood's* had spotted more than a decade earlier when it orchestrated its attacks on Keats and his friends.[451]

The October 1817 issue of *Blackwood's* carried the first in its famous series of essays, 'On the Cockney School of Poetry.'[452] John Keats was aware of the first essay by 3 November and, although it was largely aimed at Leigh Hunt, he must have realized the possibility of his own inclusion in future comments on the group.[453] Jeffrey N. Cox's important study *Poetry and Politics in The Cockney School* (1998) has not only traced the origin, scope and cultural context of these polemics but also how masque and pastoral drama held a special role for the Cockney school writers as vehicles with the potential to 'acquire cultural influence for a countercultural message.' Cox argues that Shelley and Hunt, after witnessing 'the collapse of the standard high genres of drama,' had turned to masque and pastoral as forms which had matured in the eighteenth century and still held considerable valency.[454] These included hybrid dramatic forms such as the English harlequinade, about which Hunt in *The Examiner* (5 January 1817) had declared that 'there is something *real* in Pantomime: there is animal spirit in it.'[455] Three weeks later, Hunt observed that 'Pantomime, at present, is . . . the best medium of dramatic satire.'[456] Reaction to the mobilization of drama's potential for circulating a countercultural message may have been behind the increasing tempo of suspicion surrounding the loose set of personal, literary and ideological associations *Blackwood's* designated as the Cockney school. The attacks on the Cockney school were already under way, not exclusively confined to *Blackwood's*, by the middle of 1817 with Cox noting that the first reference to Hunt as a Cockney had occurred as early as an issue of *The Satirist* magazine of 1 October 1813.[457] Pantomime, uniquely of the expressive dramatic forms, was immune from regulation, assuming it did not attempt to stray into the mongrel form of 'speaking pantomime.' Its potential for political commentary, especially if supplemented by the burlettas of the south-London playhouses only periodically regulated by relicensing magistrates, promised enormous access to popular audiences. A disposition towards the increasingly satirical pantomime of the post-1800 period, together with a desire to found a new type of poetry, provoked the attacks on the Cockneys because they symbolized a popularized vernacular idiom threatening to occupy English poetry. While Cockney dominance in the London playhouses could be tolerated by *Blackwood's* Edinburgh perspective, the same was not true for beleaguered readers of verse. With drama moving and innovating swiftly across the marginal theatres on the south side of the Thames and at the Olympic, *Blackwood's* was never in a position to mount a focused attack on Cockney burlettas.

It has not been noticed before that Cockney roles, and positive, celebratory images of Cockney's, had become particularly prominent in the burlettas and pantomimes of London's non-patent theatres during the

1810s, a development arguably becoming particularly noticeable during 1817. Recent scholarship has tended to look back to eighteenth-century poetic precursors such as Thomas Chatterton or Percy's *Reliques* for the origins of Keats's adherence to the native forms which ultimately provoked the *Blackwood's* articles.[458] However, this vernacular was the Cockney of the burletta houses rather than that of the aspirant literary writers typified by Chatterton or Keats. The *Blackwood's* attacks should be seen in the context of a London theatrical culture where Cockney figures, Cockney settings and Cockney language had become dominant. Jacob Beuler's outrageous song 'The Chapter of Cocks; *or, Cocky Cock, the Cocksmith, of Cock-lane, and the Coquetting Cock-eyed Maid at the Cock Public House. A Cockney Ditty'* of 1823 was only one of the more audacious and elaborated manifestations of this change in popular culture.[459] Elsewhere, *Blackwood's* might have looked askance at developments in the popular print culture prompted by the demise of *The Political Register* subsequent to William Cobbett's decision to go to America to avoid the March 1817 Suspension of Habeas Corpus. If *Blackwood's* expected to automatically occupy a place in the popular print culture vacated by the end of *The Political Register*, they were wrong. *Sherwin's Weekly Political Register*, directly aimed to supplement the role of Cobbett's *Register*, had begun in March 1817, Sherwin's collaborator being Richard Carlile who went on to edit *The Republican* in August 1817. T.J. Wooler's *Black Dwarf* also began publication in January 1817, a month before the first issue of William Hone's influential *Reformists' Register and Weekly Companion*, with Hone himself also being famously put on trial for his *Political Litanies* that year. As far as the rise of Cockney-dominated dramatics were concerned, *Blackwood's* may also have been aware that Wooler had begun publishing *The Black Dwarf* in the wake of editing the theatrical journal *The Stage*.[460] This rise in plebeian and popular involvement with the theatre, but as actors rather than audience, was noticed by many. The Dublin-based commentator David Lyddal, who hoped to prevent the stage being 'over-run by declaiming Clerks, and sentimental Milliners,' declared himself satisfied if he could 'keep one crazy Apprentice behind his counter' rather than acting on the boards.[461] It was into this new market that Wooler's *The Stage* had emerged.

Running in parallel with a visibly expanding print culture were new playhouses, of which perhaps the Olympic Theatre (opened on 30 October 1815 and owned by Astley and then by Elliston) was the most influential. As an indicator of the kinds of artistic and cultural anxieties perceived by the patentees, Elliston's initial idea had been simply to transfer the Royal Circus company (where he was tenant manager) to the new premises.[462] The Olympic's proximity to Covent Garden and Drury Lane was bound to bring them into conflict. At first it offered performances such as the 'New Ballet Dance...*Galvanism; or, The Doctor Duped*' or 'Baker, The Rochester Pedestrian,' together with the 'New Burletta...*The Man & the Monkey; or, Who Stole the Partridge?*'[463] Although it had closed by 3 April 1819 (and was offered for sale during 1820), the Olympic had ushered in not only Moncrieff's groundbreaking *Giovanni in London; or, The Libertine Reclaimed* (1817) but also a defining dramatic counterculture distinct from the royal theatres. The Olympic under Elliston's management gained a considerable reputation, but the opening of the Royal Coburg over the river in the spring of 1818, together with continuing productions at the Royal Amphitheatre (or Surrey) and the increasingly popular fugitive private theatres such as the Minor, ensured that a new type of Cockney dramatic presence continued over the longer term. In short, the mid-1810s ushered in a sort of Cockney triumphalism as far as stage plays and their audiences were concerned.

As will be argued below, with its iconoclastic approach to a classic text, Thomas John Dibdin's *Don Giovanni; or, A Spectre on Horseback!* of May 1817 for the Royal Amphitheatre parodied Mozart and, following a tradition inaugurated by *The Beggars' Opera*, transposed its traditional narrative across to native British tunes such as 'The Pretty Tawny Moor' and 'Over the Water to Charley' set within London's impoverished Borough district. By the end of the year Dibdin's burletta, in a pattern demonstrating the emergence of a plebeian public sphere of drama, had transmogrified into Moncrieff's *Giovanni in London*, first performed on Boxing Day, 1817. Originally written to fill the place of a pantomime, and sharing some of its elements like *A Spectre on Horseback!*, Moncrieff's *Giovanni* was actually a fully developed burletta, of a type precisely suited to the illegitimate playhouses. At their most effective, the Cockney settings of these two Giovanni plays entered popular culture not only on account of their success on stage but also because they lent themselves to popular amateur performance in the urban private theatres.

The London private theatres, with their audiences and paying actors indicate a crucial extra dimension of Georgian theatricality. William Barnes Rhodes's parodic farce *Bombastes Furioso* (1810), originally a Haymarket 'Burlesque Tragic Opera,' had become an extraordinarily successful repertoire piece particularly in the urban private playhouses. With Charles Mathews playing the King, and John Liston in the role of General Bombastes, the original Haymarket production paired the age's greatest comedians performing on the eve of their fame. Sharing roots with John Poole's *Hamlet-travestie* (1810) and *Othello-travestie* (1813), the plot burlesqued King Artaxominous's lovelorn passion ('I vow / Still to remain, till you my hopes fulfil, / Fixt as the Monument on Fish-street hill') over Cockney beauties such as 'Scrubinda the fair' ('O she lives by the scouring of pots, / In Dyot-street, Bloomsbury-square').[464] The private theatre Keats attended in January 1818 had *Bombastes Furioso* on the playbill although the amateur actor, 'dressed to kill for the King in Bombastes,' and in a 'very sweat of anxiety to show himself,' did not get the chance to play because the performance was abandoned amidst chaotic conditions.[465] In 1822, another performance of *Bombastes* at the Minor Theatre (probably the venue Keats attended) reportedly 'went off pretty well.'[466] That same year, the Surrey Theatre – which still retained equestrian facilities – advertised a *Bombastes* promising 'a Stud of Asses... Combats on Assback!'[467] Along with its exaggerated characterization and satirical parodic debunking of a pseudo-classical plot, the local settings of *Bombastes*, as with Dibdin's *Spectre on Horseback* and Moncrieff's *Giovanni in London*, undoubtedly contributed towards their enduring popularity. The appropriation of main-house pieces such as *Bombastes* into the metropolitan private theatres meant that in 1817 Cockneys were playing Cockneys in front of each other in extraordinary assertions of their self-identity.

The presence in the popular culture of Dibdin's *Spectre on Horseback!* at the Royal Amphitheatre, and of performances of Rhodes's *Bombastes* taking place beyond the licensing authority of the Lord Chamberlain or of the influence of the Theatres' Royal are good indicators of changes in the representation of Cockney Londoners. The ripples of these popular successes reached ever further into the country: by April 1818, the Theatre Royal Norwich had submitted a version of *A Spectre on Horseback!* for licensing.[468] The distinctive evolution of these changes are readily discernible. Keats's rare eyewitness report on (what was almost certainly) the interior of the Minor private theatre has him recording how he overheard, in the narrow backstage 'Green Room,' 'a little painted Trollop own, very candidly, that she had failed in Mary' but that she was now 'habited as the Quaker in the Review.' [469] Keats's designation of this amateur actor as 'a little painted Trollop' appears to refer to her Cockney characteristics. Although Keats makes none of the literary allusions particularly clear, the dramas being performed can be identified readily enough. The disgruntled young woman was commenting on her perception of having performed poorly in the role of Mary in George Colman's *John Bull; or, The Englishman's Fireside* (1803) which Keats had just seen acted, and he was now observing her waiting backstage, costumed in readiness for the role of Grace Gaylove in Colman's *The Review; or, The Wags of Windsor* (1801). With its class denigration and sexual aspersion, Keats's comments provide a valuable insight into these less conventional playhouses where the roles of actor and audience were thoroughly mixed and the differences between player and spectator blurred. Not least, his apparently derogatory designation of the Minor female amateur as a 'painted Trollop' is itself a fascinatingly incautious comment on urban private-theatre players whose Cockney dialect, as discussed below, caused them to sing of how ' "*hore*" the "*walleys*" she casts her rolling "*highs*." ' Keats's description almost certainly reflects the uncertainties of his own class position, a set of crises which the *Blackwood's* attacks would only intensify. But his experience is a vivid reminder of the alternative repertoire of travesty, farce and burletta in which these venues specialized. We can be sure that Keats's anonymous 'Trollop,' stealing onto the stage at the Minor, would have been a very different person to Cockney women represented in the repertoire of earlier years.

Isaac Bickerstaff's Covent Garden comic opera *Love in the City* (1767) still largely continued a seventeenth-century tradition of having its Cheapside shopkeepers (Old Cockney, Mrs Molly Cockney and Young Cockney) weighing tea and sugar. The situation had not changed very much even by the time of Andrew Franklin's popular Drury Lane musical entertainment *A Trip to the Nore* (1797) which enlisted the still durable stock figures of 'Mr Cockney' and 'Mrs Cockney' as part of the piece's narrative surrounding the naval pageantry at Greenwich in celebration of Nelson's important first victory at the Battle of Cape St Vincent and the fleet's triumphal assembly at the Nore naval anchorage. In their rush to reach Greenwich, almost inevitably, the matronly Mrs Cockney gets ducked in the Thames by a careless waterman. The comic exchange perhaps hints at the Cockney intransigence of both her husband and the waterman:

Cockney: I'll not give you another copper-penny – I belongs to the Waterman's Company...and knows what's what. Why did you jog your boat as my vife[*sic*] was stepping out, Sir, and souse her into the river? I wonder what the great folks will say ven[*sic*] dey[*sic*] see her in this pickle?...

Waterman: ...I'll have my fare...Well, I know where you live; I'll not make disturbance on such a glorious day as this is, I'm determin'd; but I'll see myself right.[470]

Crudely asserted notions of civic rights in *A Trip to the Nore*, such as the Cockney who 'knows what's what' and the waterman who will 'see myself right,' displays social fractures which are barely dissembled during the plot's celebration of the patriotic pageant. The erratically transposed 'V' and 'W' consonants ('my vife... ven'), as detailed below, were the conventional theatrical indicators of Cockney speech. However, beneath the comic characterization *A Trip to the Nore* was straining to embody divergent allegiances in London's social structure. In the year of the Nore mutiny, with its alleged Irish insurrectionary links, Franklin's musical farce had carefully co-opted a standardized loyal Irishman, O'Thunder ('I'm an Irishman and a British Sailor').[471] Elsewhere, subtle social tensions associated with differentiated classes of Cockney journeymen surface in the form of 'Mr Putty the Glazier' who stays at home 'with his 'Prentices in hopes of another Illumination,' the traditional rite of placing celebratory victory lights in windows. During these festivities, Putty wants his men to 'break all his neighbours windows' to generate work should anyone fail to illuminate.[472] In the rush to demonstrate loyalty within these various fields of class formation, the limping Buckram, a merchant and member of Lloyds insurance, weakly claims he came 'near breaking my neck in forcing my way into the Pit of Drury Lane Theatre to leave my mite for the relief of those poor Widows, whose brave Husbands fell on board ship in the *field* of battle!'[473] Franklin's *Trip to the Nore* incorporates and contains the strained social allegiances of wartime 1790s London without fracturing them. However, amidst Cockneys who 'knows what's what,' the old stereotypes were barely continuing to function. With *Bombastes Furioso* played by amateur actors at the Minor in the Strand, and *The Spectre on Horseback!* at the Royal Amphitheatre, the representation of the Cockney dialect and its people was not only popular and prevalent, it had also clearly moved beyond the confines of the winter and summer grand theatres. Instead of being satirized and contained within representations designating fixed social stations, Cockney locations and Cockney dialect dominated the popular dramas of the 1810s and moved between an array of theatrical venues. The 'little painted Trollop' caught unobserved by Keats was a young woman for whom the passivity of theatrical representation had ceased being the sole mode of her personal agency. Deep beneath the masque and pastoral dramas adopted by the literary associates of Hunt and Keats lay this further layer of Cockney drama dispersed into the side streets of Holborn, Soho and the Strand.

As far as *Blackwood's Edinburgh Magazine's* theatrical coverage was concerned, it was late in starting its own drama feature, the first one not appearing until the issue of January 1818, pretty well coinciding with the first staging of Moncrieff's *Giovanni in London* on Boxing Day 1817. Despite the journal's Edinburgh base, its reviews were strictly intended as 'Notices of the Acted Drama in London' and clearly employed London-based reviewers who appear never to have travelled beyond the two royal theatres and the Haymarket. *Blackwood's* certainly never went to see *Giovanni in London* or any of the other burlettas or performances of any description outside of the patent-holding theatres. This is not too surprising since this book has argued the alterity of different kinds of theatrical structure, even within the confines of London, at the same temporal moment. The nascent differences of class, regulation and genre noticed in Chapter Three over the Haymarket and Royalty slavery plays were bound to work themselves through as structural affects determining differences in London's later theatrical environment. For its part, *Blackwood's* was fairly casual over its inception and attribution of drama reviews. Some pieces are signed 'Q' or 'AZ' but most are left unsigned and, despite *Blackwood's* drama reviews turning out to be fairly regular features, there was an unaccountable gap between July and December 1818. Nevertheless, the journal set out a reasonably coherent stance on theatre. It thought that 'A great commercial city without an acted drama, would be like a world without a sun.'[474] Otherwise, many of the early *Blackwood's* drama notices obediently conformed to the prevailing metropolitan taste, praising Edmund Kean to the hilt in Shakespeare ('If it had not been for Mr. Kean, we should never have desired to see a play of Shakespeare's acted again...In ourselves, we shall never cease to regret having seen Hamlet so often acted in our youth') while at the same time deploring contemporary tragic writing; for example, commenting about John Dillon's Covent Garden *Retribution; or, The Chieftain's Daughter* (1818) that 'any one of the scenes might change places with any other, without injury to the piece.'[475] Predictably, *Black-wood's* condemned the 'herd of Gallo-germanic monsters which have visited us of late years, under the name of Melo-Dramas,' and went on to speak of 'the apparently irrecoverable degradation, of that once noblest portion of our national literature, the Acted Drama.'[476] Such sentiments were critical commonplaces of the conservative mode but, by the beginning of 1819, *Blackwood's* theorizing of the condition of drama had become noticeably more formulated.

In January 1819 *Blackwood's* drama review gave a revealing insight into the reasons for the 'irrecoverable degradation, of...the Acted Drama.' Underlying *Blackwood's* perspective was a sense of nostalgia or loss, a perception of drama's function to be that of facilitating a removal from the present: 'The drama is a world in which age is carried back to youth, without forfeiting the wisdom of its experience; and youth is carried forward to manhood, without losing the still better wisdom of its inexperience.'[477] Even from its first introductory essay on drama, *Blackwood's* appears to have specifically contradicted Hunt's verdict that 'Pantomime...is...the best medium of dramatic satire.' For the *Blackwood's* author, there was only loss: 'We shall never again see such a pantomime as Mother Goose as long as we live!...Is it that the art of making a pantomime is lost – or that we can never again be so young as when we saw that?' In place of the satirical debunking of contemporary authority which Hunt found exemplified by the great clown Grimaldi ('the bullies and coxcombs...he...imitates come in one respect nearer to the truth than in the best dialogue'), *Blackwood's* longed for a 'Pantomime...mixed with a little wonderment.'[478] Instead of 'a lumbering heap of unmeaning monstrosity,' 'Let them give us another *Pastoral Pantomime*, with the scenery among corn-fields and cottages, and the characters among plougboys and milkmaids.' Such infantilist regression was summarized in *Blackwood's* exasperated cry, 'What's all the Greek mythology in the world to compare with that of the nursery!'[479] In the context of 1817, productions such as December's Drury Lane pantomime *Harlequin Libertine Founded on the Interesting Story of Don Juan*, Dibdin's *Spectre on Horseback!* and Moncrieff's *Giovanni in London* were hardly likely to satisfy *Blackwood's* yearning for the baby room. However, the review of January 1819 seemed to gather together a number of issues which defined its attitude to the language of contemporary popular drama.

Discussing its perennial theme of the decline in quality of stage writing, *Blackwood's* castigated modern British drama's German 'disease caught from Kotzebue,' its plots drawn from 'novel writers – the "circulating medium" of the Minerva Library,' but most of all it attacked the theatre's 'language the bastard offspring of an illicit intercourse between the two *slangs* of St. James's and St. Giles's.'[480] The German influence had already been condemned in the 'Gallo-germanic monsters' of melodrama and these were now coupled to the equally melodramatic novels of the Minerva Press disseminated through the circulating libraries. However, it was clearly the 'illicit intercourse between the two *slangs* of St. James's and St. Giles's' which is indicative of *Blackwood's* latent suspicion of Cockney dialect. According to writers of the early 1820s such as Moncrieff, 'slang, as others call it, is the classical language of the Holy Land; in other words, St. Giles's greek.'[481] Moncrieff's formulation describing Cockeny slang was highly irreverent, not only was the Holy

Land the Cockney name for the most down-at-heel part of St Giles's, the underworld dialect of 'St. Giles's greek' 'flash' or 'cant' was celebrated for its alterity on the stage of the Adelphi theatre in *Tom and Jerry*.

In place of the slapstick piece of stage action between Mr Cockney and the Waterman in Franklin's *A Trip to the Nore* (1797), Dibdin's *Don Giovanni; or, A Spectre on Horseback!* provided another confrontation between a Cockney waterman and his customer but this time at Blackfriars's bridge, where an argument between the Don and the Dibdin's Italianate Cockney 'Gondolieri' results in the waterman being shot in an altercation over Lobsterina, the waterman's fishwife.[482] The scene is indicative of a number of remarkable innovations. The shooting of the waterman appears to complete the business of the scene in *A Trip to the Nore* but, through the means of Don Giovanni's adoption as a Borough hero, the Spanish lover is now thoroughly at home with his quintessentially Billingsgate fishwife. Not least, Dibdin was portraying not merely the Cockney accent but also its dialect ('Lobsterina: Vy vont you? Gondolieri: Vy because I vont.'). As the contemporary linguistic historian Samuel Pegge had pointed out in 1803, Cockney was still a true dialect in that it waywardly transposed consonants, particularly exchanging 'W' sounds with 'V' sounds (saying 'werry' [very], 'vidow,' 'niegh-bourwood,' etc).[483] That such Cockney pronunciations were reaching into the theatres is evidenced by a satirist in *The Dramatic Scorpion* in 1818 mocking private theatre shop-girl performers similar to Keats's 'painted Trollop,' but this time witnessed at the bare-earth floored Berwick Street private theatre, singing of how ' "*hore*" the "*walleys*" she casts her rolling "*highs*." '[484] Not least, Dibdin's *A Spectre on Horseback!* demonstrated the extent to which Mozart's classical opera had been debunked by the maturity of the burletta form, with traditional English and Dibdin's own tunes largely displacing Mozart's music. By the time *Blackwood's* came to press home its attacks on the Cockney school of poetry, Cockney burletta had already triumphed in the popular playhouses.

In April 1817, the King's Theatre, Haymarket, had staged the first English production of Mozart and Lorenzo da Ponte's opera *Don Giovanni*, sung in Italian.[485] The story of its appropriation by popular, more plebeian, playhouses was a major aspect in this Cockney presence. That *Blackwood's* viewed the London playhouses in class terms is nowhere better seen than in their complaint about Covent Garden's Easter 1818 pantomime of *The Marquis of Carabas; or, Puss in Boots*. The reviewer appears never to have seen it, but he immediately contrasted – albeit with some level of irony – 'the plebeian managers of this theatre

[and] ... the noble example of the lords and gentlemen at the other house [Drury Lane].'[486] The class designation of the two playhouses might pass as simply opportunistic or incidental comment were it not for the fact that *Blackwood's* had recently deployed exactly the same language about Hunt, judging him to be (when compared to Lord Byron) as 'completely a Plebeian in his mind as he is in his rank and station in society.'[487] The highly successful production of Mozart's *Don Giovanni* – and the entire season of 1817 – was remembered by John Ebers, the manager of the King's Theatre, as a turning point marking a whole new 'era in the history of the Theatre,' 'both as regards performers, performances, and receipts.'[488] In many respects, the King's Theatre represented the epitome of London's theatrical exclusivity. By virtue of a trust deed established in 1792 between the managers and the theatre owner, the King's Theatre had leased out 41 of its boxes for a period of nearly 25 years at £1000 each. The purchasers of the leases on the boxes (and eventually 68 were sold) not only gave unlimited access to the owners, their family and friends but the leaseholder also retained the right to sublet the boxes with Ebers acting as their agent. This two-fold income stream is indicative of the capitalization of such theatres operating, in this case, within their royal monopoly on operatic performance. Not only did the theatre raise capital when the boxes were leased, but its agency services for subletting allowed it this further income source.[489] This meant that the audience profile obtaining at the King's Theatre was very different even from the other royal theatres. The effect of these financial arrangements was to heighten the social elitism of the King's Theatre. The social rank of the audiences in the boxes can be studied in some detail by examining extant lists of box subscribers. Probably under Ebers's direction, since this seems to have begun when he took up managing this aspect of the theatre's affairs in 1802, an annual *Plan of the Boxes At the King's Theatre, Haymarket, With an Alphabetical List of the Subscribers* was published, providing exact details about the ownership of the boxes together with their relationship and adjacency to others.[490] William Lee's *Plan of the Boxes* provides authoritative empirical evidence for our knowledge of the elitist profile of the King's Theatre audience during this period. Even the language of ownership differed from its contemporaries. The King's Theatre boxes were specifically termed 'property boxes' on account of their status as being the leasehold property of others, whereas elsewhere in the capital theatrical space was viewed

as being under common ownership. As late as 1819, the pseudonymous satire *Histriomastix; or, The Untrussing Of The Drury Lane Squad* declared:

> The STAGE... – a subject fair and free –
> 'Tis yours – 'tis mine – 'tis common property...
> To clap or hiss, all have an equal claim,
> The cobler's[*sic*] and his lordship's right the same.[491]

It is easy to see why any threat to the relatively democratized public space at Covent Garden was greeted by such extensive rioting in 1809.

A month after its first opening, Isaac Pocock's adaptation of Thomas Shadwell's Don Juan story, *The Libertine*, at Covent Garden countered the King's Theatre production of Mozart's *Don Giovanni* although it took care also to incorporate its music.[492] William Hazlitt went to see *The Libertine* during May 1817 where he found that despite the fact that 'Almost everything else was against it... [Mozart's] music triumphed' save that the audience repeatedly 'hissed' the players out of 'unconscious patriotism... as well as sheer stupidity.'[493] However, despite Hazlitt's rather lofty judgement, interest in the Don Juan story went from strength to strength. Dibdin's semi-equestrianized *Don Giovanni; or, A Spectre on Horseback!* (1817) was produced for his newly managed theatre, the Royal Amphitheatre, otherwise known as The Surrey. The popular development of the Don Juan/Don Giovanni story within the context of London theatre begins with this production of *A Spectre on Horseback!* As discussed in the Introduction, it appears to have been the Royalty Theatre's 1787 'tragic pantomical[*sic*] entertainment' of *Don Juan; or, The Libertine Destroy'd* which had originated this popularized version of the story, eventually developing into the 1817 Drury Lane pantomime *Harlequin Libertine Founded on the Interesting Story of Don Juan*. In other words, when Dibdin developed the Don Juan story as *A Spectre on Horseback!*, spurring Moncrieff to create the intensely musical *Giovanni in London* for the exclusively burletta conditions of the Olympic's license, there already existed these pre-existing developmental transmission routes for the narrative as it emerged through working-class popular culture.

The Surrey's context in working-class culture can be readily outlined. The Surrey or Royal Circus is the subject of a section of Humphreys's contemporary *Memoirs Of J. Decastro, Comedian* (1824). The Royal Circus, Lambeth, opened in 1782, was steeped in the plebeian culture of the theatre.[494] Its situation on waste ground in close proximity to King's Bench prison made it one of the first venues adjacent to the newly developing audience hinterlands to the south of the Thames.

Before the building of Waterloo Bridge in 1818, the Circus was a major theatrical space which helped develop the sort of working-class audiences which the later houses, such as The Royal Coburg (built nearby in 1817), Olympic and Adelphi Theatres on the north side, were able to develop further after the building of Waterloo Bridge.

The Royal Circus's strong association with plebeian culture was of long standing by the time of Dibdin's *Spectre on Horseback!* The productions it mounted, and its connections with politics, show how marginal theatrical spaces drew the attention not only of radically inclined sections of the populace but also of the authorities intent on maintaining surveillance. John Cartwright Cross's Royal Circus pantomimes, for example, signalled approval of the St Domingo slave insurrection in his 'Grand Spectacle' *King Caesar; or, the Negro Slaves* (1801), while his 'Serio-Comic' pantomime *The Golden Farmer; or, Harlequin Ploughboy* (1802) confronted the subject of grain forestalling.[495] In the 1790s, The Royal Circus was associated in Government circles with alleged attempts to drill an insurrectionary army linked to the London Corresponding Society. Secret informers spoke of a request by two revolutionary activists who 'wish'd to have the Ring or Riding place in the Royal Circus for the purpose of learning divers persons Military Exercise.'[496] The informer and the two would-be revolutionaries, as the London Corresponding Society Treason Trials of 1794 brought out, were in reality already in the Government employ, acting as agitators intended to incriminate the likes of Thomas Hardy, the dramatist Thomas Holcroft and the other London Corresponding Society members accused of treason that year. Nevertheless, the association of The Royal Circus's equestrian compound with local artisan activism was clearly a connection which, if it had succeeded, would not have initially stretched public credulity. Similarly, in the spring of the following year, 1795, Philip Astley may have also been aware that the Government was displeased at his Circus productions (although, since a disastrous fire in 1794, the rebuilt venue was known as the 'New Circus'). The capital's *de facto* chief of police and spymaster, the Bow Street magistrate Richard Ford, indicated (but 'not in a public manner' the Home Office file noted) that the authorities were displeased with the Circus's repertoire and that 'if he [Astley] persists in making similar allusions in his Bills, it may be the means of the Magistrates refusing a renewal of his license.' The Government note went on to remark that 'The Bills of this Evening's Performance are also in the same respect objectionable.'[497] The specific aspect of the published performances which had offended the Government is not known but there can be no doubting London circus's deep association with plebeian rather than patrician values. Not least, one of the Royal Circus's pantomimes of 1809 had carefully dissociated itself from stereotyping the Cockneys who probably formed part of their audience catchment. *Harlequin Cockney; or, London Displayed* started with a view of Bow Church (within the sound of whose bells all true Cockneys are reputed to originate), and took in not only 'Bartholomew Fair, at Night' but also the Bank of England, the Royal Academy exhibition room and Westminster Hall. Its two Cockney roles of Cockney Harlequin and Harlequin Cockney included a transformation scene where Cockney Harlequin is a foundling saved and educated by the sexton of Bow Church before his change into the magically endowed Harlequin Cockney. In *Harlequin Cockney*, London looked as if it was owned by the Cockneys it celebrated. In its pantomime of social aspiration, Cockney meets his Columbine – John Bull's daughter – in the Bank of England, the very centre of Britain's economic empire. Its elaborate spectacle of an historical procession traces London's origins back to the Druids and Romans, including its establishment as a capital by King Alfred the Great, but *Harlequin Cockney* also celebrated 'Commerce' with lawyers carrying William Blackstone's *An Analysis of the Laws of England* (1756), together with processing emblems of charitable institutions such as the Philanthropic Society, Bluecoats School and Greenwich Hospital. Noticeably missing are any references to monarchy or aristocracy. Instead, its Cockney hero is celebrated as the product of social responsibility and self-reliance.[498]

Eight years later, *A Spectre on Horseback!* began a run of more than 100 nights as 'the great hit of the season.'[499] Its burlesque qualities familiarized and localized the Mozartian original by dispensing almost entirely with Mozart's music and replacing it with traditional or topical English tunes. Mozart's overture was retained but the first piece of narrative music is to the tune of 'The Pretty Tawny Moor.' When the music changes later to the tune 'Over the Water to Charley,' Leporello immediately says 'I know that tune – I've heard it at the Surrey' (p. 28). This type of localization is made implicit not only by references to Charing Cross but also by the intense de-mystification of the Commandantore role ('old Stony Batter') whose declamations include such lines as 'For Rabbits and Onions I don't care a Damn' (pp. 26–7). By December 1817, both Drury Lane and the Olympic Theatre in Wych Street were also aiming to produce versions of the Don Juan story.

The repercussions for these theatres of the processes of censorship and the enforcement of monopoly are worth following. Drury Lane's

Harlequin Libertine had been sent to Larpent on 16 December 1817, just in time for its obligatory licensing prior to a Christmas performance.[500] Elliston also ought to have sent a manuscript of Moncrieff's *Giovanni in London* to Larpent before its first performance on 26 December 1817, but it is not extant. Larpent's manuscript record book notes *Giovanni in London* as 'not ret[urne]^d by Elliston' (but that the Examiner took his two guinea fee), an occurrence suggesting that Larpent, quite irregularly, licensed it by watching its first performance.[501] The long-term effect of the Olympic's success with *Giovanni in London*, perhaps partly enabled by Elliston deliberately avoiding the Examiner of Plays – apparently without official consequences – or else taking advantage of the confusion in the Examiner's office, was to have a number of lasting consequences of great significance on the rise of popular drama in the late 1810s and afterwards.

Moncrieff wrote that his *Giovanni in London*, like *Harlequin Libertine*, was 'intended to supply the place of a Christmas Pantomime,' and it drew on traditions of the Don which were plebeian in origin.[502] *Harlequin Libertine* was cast to include two players for Harlequin and two for Columbine, doubled up from the roles of Don Juan, Octavio, Elvira and Leonora, respectively. This sort of doubling continued with the characters of 'Two Fishermen ... [and] their two Wives.' The two wives were 'afterwards Changed to Punch and his wife,' a sure indication of the plebeian Punch and Judy heritage imported into the Don Juan story. It was very much the model of the 'Pantomime ... mixed with a little wonderment' that *Blackwood's* relished, although also here actually mixed with the violence of Punch and Judy: when 'Leporello makes free with fruit [and] is detected by [a] Fruiterer – They nail his Nose to the door post – .' A fight between Don Juan, Leporello and several 'Gentlemen' demonstrates the astonishing brutality of the Christmas pantomime ('some lose Arms others heads legs ... – Leporello amuses himself by joining the mangled limbs to the several bodies &c &c *The figures which Leporello has repaired all march off*').[503] *Harlequin Libertine* follows many of the conventions common to both harlequinade and Punch and Judy and draws the Don into a native tradition. It demonstrates very clearly the diversity of theatrical conventions and narrative which could be incorporated into a story line given a new twist by the popularity of Mozart's *Don Giovanni*.

It was into this fertile series of crossed conventions and genres that Moncrieff wrote *Giovanni in London*, taking it as his aim to give the Don 'a new lease for life, and throw open the metropolis to him.'[504] Moncrieff had already seen Dibdin's 'very cleverly Burlesqued' *Don Giovanni; or,*

A Spectre on Horseback! at the Surrey. Although equestrianism played a considerable part in the finale of Dibdin's work (*'the Statue gallops across on his poney'*), he had also developed its local scenes such as the one on Blackfriars' Bridge ('Come, who is for a row with the jolly young watermen, / Who at Blackfrairs' bridge cheerily ply?') where the Don meets the fishergirls Lobsteretta and Shrimperina and kills the Gondolieri waterman.[505] With its cluster of songs which ensured that it remained permissible under the licensing laws, *Giovanni in London* is a brilliant piece of comic writing, innovative, quick-witted and taking enough liberties with the original to still render its overall direction intelligible, but newly helped by his use of London locations.

Giovanni is confined in Hell where he 'makes love' to the Furies ('see to wile the sultry hours away, by all my hopes, a Fury comes – I can't say that I'm much enamoured of Furies, n'importe – I'm man, she wears a petticoat, so here goes!') until Pluto and Proserine (whom he has jilted) decide to throw him out.[506] Charon, the boatman of the Styx, arrives bringing with him a Lawyer and a Methodist: 'lawyers we have always *plus quam suff.* – Not a term passes but plenty of your tribe come here to practice in our courts below – walk in, walk in, we've lots of room for you; and you, my methodical genius *(to Methodist,)* Erebus will always find room for one of your cloth.'[507] The incorporation of the Methodist and the Lawyer into the story, stock figures of anti-theatricality and avarice, was bound to ease the process of translating the Spanish story in an English setting but Moncrieff's masterstroke was to bring Giovanni to the backstreets of London. Throughout, the Cockney dialect is readily apparent. Charon's water ferry, with its Cockney diminutive nomenclature (where the ferryman become 'Chary') and street argot of 'brass' and 'rhino' (money), plus the water cabbie's quibbling over the fare – another throwback to *A Trip to the Nore* – economically establishes both the Styx's locality as the Thames and the scene's contemporaneity:

Giov: Come Chary turn your boat and ply your oar...
Cha: With all my heart, but pay me my fare first, if you please – lug out your brass, you know I never trust.
Giov: Plague on't, I've none – treating the fiends to drink, with hot and hot, has swallow'd all my rhino.[508]

Moncrieff locates another scene, between Giovanni and three newly deceased wives returning to haunt their homes, in the Magpie and Punch-bowl tavern in the Borough, one of the most working-class areas on the south side of the Thames. The wives have been sent to Hell for sexist reasons: scolding, shrewishness and adultery ('Mrs. Simpkins: If I must tell you – though really it makes me blush – I was sent below for – for a slight faux paux, Don.').[509] Quite apart from the sort of unreconstructed chauvinism which is typical of working-class culture at this time (their husbands sing, 'This fellow! has come from the Regions infernal, / And brought back our wives, who as dead were as door nail. / Disturbing our quiet with click clack eternal'), Moncrieff's writing is also a subtle reminder that Hell is a parallel world to London, with the classical underworld of Pluto and the Styx mirroring through its street argot London's mortal underworld.[510] Exploration of London's underworld was returned to, with even greater public success, in Moncrieff's *Tom and Jerry* of 1821 with its aura of the distinct worlds of *Day & Night Scenes!*, as the Royal Amphitheatre's titled it, set inside London's illicit gambling 'Hells' (as contemporary gaming houses were known).[511] Pierce Egan's specific usage of the metaphor to describe the criminal Samuel Hayward's journeys to gambling 'Hells' being like those of 'a second Giovanni' shows how contemporary urban discourses supported such vocabularies.[512]

Giovanni in London's setting in the contemporary metropolis was a significant factor in contributing to its success. Moncrieff's metropolitanization of Don Giovanni extended to having Leporello's house (he had not been consigned to Hell) located in Dyot Street, St Giles, one of the most destitute London areas, and to making Don Giovanni one whose dramatic and comic possibilities Moncrieff would memorably develop in *Tom and Jerry*. In part, Moncrieff was developing settings already traditional to pantomime. In *The Choice of Harlequin; or, The Indian Chief* (1780), Harlequin goes to squalid Dyot Street and 'a miserable looking house ... opened by a very dirty maid' before being carried to Bridewell.[513] Violence, prison and the law were all powerful ingredients of pantomime whose presence can be glimpsed even in Moncrieff's burlettas *Giovani in London* and *Tom and Jerry*. However, the gas-lit street and 'Charley' watchmen, like several other features, all help stress *Giovanni in London*'s modernity. In the same way that Pierce Egan and, subsequently, Moncrieff caricatured the dandies of the 1810s in the person of Corinthian Tom in *Tom and Jerry*, so too *Giovanni in London* satirized the cult of the fashionable Regency rake:

> If in London town you'd live...
> And be complete a Beau, Sir,—
> Cossacks you like sacks must wear,

> In a Brutus cock your hair,
> And wear of Wellingtons a pair,
>   ....
> You must get a pair of stays,
>   Like the ladies, like the ladies,
> Through an eye-glass still must gaze,
>   And stare at all you meet, Sir!
> With sham collar hide your nose,
> Wear false calves like other beaux,
> And still a brazen front disclose,
>   With brass heels on your feet, Sir.[514]

The 'brazen,' be-monocled, Cossack-trouser wearing, quiff-haired 'beaux' in Wellington boots and a cardboard collar was a topical characterization for Don Giovanni. The Don's subsequent adventures include a duel (where the ball passes through his ghostly body), the would-be cuckolding of County Deputy Lieutenant's wife, Mrs English, as well as the Don's arrest by Bailiff and imprisonment in King's Bench debtors' prison ('Over the water and over the bridge, / And into the King's Bench, Giovanni; / And over the water we now must trudge').[515]

Moncrieff's burletta neatly mirrored, satirized and yet made familiar and accessible several London landmarks. In *Giovanni in London*'s symmetrical three-act structure, the scene in King's Bench prison balances that of Hell in the first act, both are places of incarceration and, supposedly, of torment but are also seen as perfectly comfortable residences. Again, a pantomime such as *The Choice of Harlequin; or, The Indian Chief* (1780), with its Bridewell scene, prefigured *Giovanni in London*. In *The Choice of Harlequin*, Bridewell enumerates London's corruption with its 'French macaroni – a modern beau – a well dressed Jew – two genteel harlots – a black one dressed in white – an insurance office keeper – and a hackney coachman, discovered beating hemp. Keepers overlooking. One...comes forward and strikes at Harlequin with a rattan.'[516] Similarly, in *Giovanni in London*, a King's Bench corrupt prison officer (like all contemporary watchmen, a 'Charley') brings illicit alcohol into the gaol, a place with its own miniature system of taxation: 'Sponge: We find a way to evade the law, Don; rum Charley helps us: every morning, a gallon of rum, walks in within his wooden leg. You'll pay your entrance, of course: 'tis usual, sir').[517]

However, *Giovanni in London* also announces a moral reversal which makes it utterly different from *The Choice of Harlequin*. Whereas the latter ended with 'Harlequin, Columbine...brought on by Virtue and

Pleasure' and their marriage solemnized, *Giovanni* makes its hero triumphant, as in Moncrieff's subtitle, with the 'Libertine Reclaimed' rather than returned to hell.[518] The Cockney debunking of morality is unmistakable. In one of the last scenes, Leporello burlesques the Commandant's statue scene from the original story of Don Juan by climbing onto the equestrian statue ('old Stony Batter') of King Charles at Charing Cross. Instead of a haunting, accusatory denouement, Leporello sings him a slightly reworded version of the tune 'Barney leave the Girls alone.' Indeed, the entire escape from his would-be cuckolding of Deputy English's wife is a gigantic hoax perpetrated on Don Giovanni where he thinks Deputy English is suing him in a 'crim.con' adultery action (a topical contemporary contraction of the legal indictment 'criminal conversation with the plaintiff's husband/wife'). In an extraordinary indication of Moncrieff's challenge to conventional morality, he becomes the 'Libertine Reclaimed,' a neat moral inversion over the theatrical tradition of Shadwell's 'Libertine Destroyed.' Rather than being reformed, everyone – including the work's most obvious figure of authority, Deputy English – admires and is friendly with him:

Deputy: ... a hoax, played to try you; I have been made acquainted with every thing; you must pardon all our tricks now that they're over, and join with us in soliciting the support of our kind friends to a Libertine Reclaimed.

With the Libertine Reclaimed rather than reformed, the finale scene calls for Don Giovanni's name to be quite literally emblazoned in lights:

(*A grand display of fireworks takes place during the singing of the Finale; in which Giovanni's name appears in illuminated characters.*)[519]

Even here, Moncreiff's roots can still be traced to a vernacular tradition of pantomime. *The Choice of Harlequin* had ended with 'The Procession at an Eastern Marriage,' with 'Cooleys, spearmen, tom-toms, dancing-girls, ticktaws, seapoys, hircarars, chubdahs, chuta-chubdahs... cosmadors [and] debershes,' set amidst 'moving pyramids of different-coloured fires.'[520]

By so thoroughly setting Giovanni's inversion of conventional morality into the vastly popular – and permissible – burletta format, one which had been developed from the plebeian proving ground of the Royal Amphitheatre's *Spectre on Horseback!*, and with much of its action expressed in Cockney dialect, Moncrieff's *Giovanni in London* and the celebration of its hero mirrored in music, dance and song many of the worst fears of *Blackwood's* and its contemporaries. Indeed, the sexual anxieties which motivated many of the attacks on the Cockney school appear to be epitomized in Moncrieff's predatory, unstoppable and celebrated hero of 1817. As Jeffrey N. Cox has pointed out, the word 'Cockney' meant both wanton and effeminate and *Blackwood's* and other magazines drew on both meanings for their attacks.[521] Hunt's politics were condemned in *The Gazette of Fashion, and Magazine of Literature* for their mixture of libertinism and radical politics, declaring in 1822 that Hunt's 'politics were debased by a noxious and disgusting mixture of libertinism and Jacobinism.'[522] Nor was this an isolated accusation. In November 1818, when the popularity of *Giovanni in London* was still at its height, *The Eclectic Review* complained of Hunt's 'creed of the heathen and the morals of the libertine.'[523] Against this backdrop of the *Blackwood's*-led attacks on the 'libertinism' of the Cockney school, the hero of Moncrieff's burletta subtitled 'The Libertine Reclaimed' must have seemed a provoking figure.

As it proved, the backlash for the Olympic's owner and manager, Robert William Elliston, was even more intimidating. With successes in 1817 at the Surrey for Dibdin's *A Spectre on Horseback!* and at The Olympic for Moncrieff's *Giovanni in London*, the royal theatres became worried about loss of revenue as audiences were pulled away. At the time, supporters of the royal theatres were careful to distinguish Dibdin's *Don Giovanni...on Horseback!* from the 'worse' 'patchwork piece, called "Giovanni in London," produced at the Olympic Theatre.'[524] However, the importance of the ensuing confrontation between the royal patentees and the Olympic was that their campaign spoke so eloquently of how the hegemony of the royal theatres could coerce the minor theatres. Quite categorically, as long as the non-patent theatres performed burletta, they were safe even if, within Westminster, their scripts (including new prologues, epilogues and interspersed songs) had first to be licensed by the Examiner of Plays. Although no copy of the licensed playhouse manuscript is now extant, *Giovanni in London* must have passed into legality and, in any event, performances were never challenged by the Lord Chamberlain. However, the social reach of the royal theatres into the ruling culture ensured that the true legalities would not be followed.

Understandably, the grievances of the royal theatres were dressed up under the cover of their supposed guardianship of 'the National Drama,' indicatively five-act spoken tragedy and comedy. The immediate consequence for Elliston at the Olympic was that the royal theatres made a formal request to the Lord Chamberlain to intervene and close down both the Olympic and the smaller Sans Pareil Theatre, Strand, on the grounds that they 'have become Theatres for the performance of the regular drama' instead of the performance of burletta, the only permitted form outside of the patents.[525] The incident was not without both its short- and long-term consequences for the Olympic Theatre and the two Royal-patent playhouses. The attempt by the royal theatres to get the Lord Chamberlain to intervene, and the movement of the case file in the official bureaucracy to the emerging Department of the Home Office, marks an important shift in the relationship between theatre and Government. The transferral of the case to the Home Office indicates that Government was beginning to both question and take seriously the advisability of continuing its role of licensing patent theatres.

Events such as the 1809 OP riots at Covent Garden, with their accompanying politicized protest rhetoric, had alerted Government not only to the dangers of civil disturbance but also to the vulnerability of the royal theatres to their appropriation as local, more easily identifiable, aspects of a larger Reform movement.[526] There were also issues of the extent to which Government wished to be involved with the fate of the royal theatres since, quite visibly, audiences were shifting of their own accord to the more attractive offerings at the other theatres, including new theatres such as The Royal Coburg (now Old Vic) which had opened on 11 May 1818. Unless it took evasive action, with respect to the legislation governing performance, Government was also in danger of becoming entrammelled in the contradictions between modern social reform and English statute law. In the wake of the establishment of the Society for the Suppression of Mendicity in 1818 arose the unresolved problem of whether actors were vagrants, a judicial legacy reaching back to Elizabethan times.[527] While Government might welcome control of the poor, it also risked encountering the zeal of charitable organizations who were also likely to express anti-theatrical sentiments. That the rudiments of Elizabethan Poor Law remained in force was memorably summarized by the barrister John Adolphus in his *Observations on the Vagrant Act* (1824), 'How wonderfully it must exalt our morals and our patriotism to know, that if a miserable English stroller were to murder Hamlet at half-a-crown per box-ticket, he might spend his next six months in the house of correction.'[528]

Elliston (who was, paradoxically, also owner of the Birmingham Theatre Royal) was forced to write a lengthy rebuttal to the allegations of the royal theatres, taking care to file it with the Home Office and, for further publicity, publishing his comments as a pamphlet.[529] As one indication of the pace and intensity with which this debate moved, by the first week of March 1818, the Home Office had sent informers to both the Sans Pareil and the Olympic Theatres to report back on whether their productions fell within the burletta genre. George Wilson, the official who went to the Olympic, witnessed a performance of *Giovanni in London* on 2 March but could only comment that it was 'performed in a kind of Doggrel[sic] the whole of the performances were well received by a respectable and crowded Audience.'[530] While, no doubt, still attracted to retaining rights of regulation through the role of the Lord Chamberlain's powers of censorship, Government was not likely to have been overly worried with the decline of Covent Garden's box office, and while the ultimate outcome would be the Parliamentary *Report from the Select Committee on Dramatic Literature* (1832) in the short term the agreement which appears to have been reached was for Covent Garden and Drury Lane to switch from being gamekeepers to poachers by both of them mounting productions of *Giovanni in London*. Moncrieff, for his part, wrote bitterly that 'It was sorely against the Author's will that Giovanni was ever produced on the Patent Boards, conscious they was[sic] not its proper sphere.'[531]

Even though he was in self-imposed exile by 1817 and prior to his beginning *Don Juan*, Lord Byron would probably have encountered at least something of the deluge of popular publications spawned by the popularity of Moncrieff's *Giovanni in London*. The habit of popular singing was a typical vehicle both for disseminating and further reflecting the burletta's success. Jacob Beuler sang a Don Giovanni song in the same collection as his 'Death of Liberty' song on the 1819 Peterloo Massacre, probably written shortly after the event.[532] Although a lot of Beuler's songs were performed by other singers, Beuler himself sang at the actors' tavern, the O.P. ('Opposite Prompter') in Russell Court, Drury Lane.[533] His local fame at the O.P. tavern is symptomatic of the growing eminence of specific cultures not only located in London's theatreland but also coincident with mass popular followings typified in the national grief at the death of Princess Charlotte in 1817 and popular disquiet over the Queen Caroline affair of 1820. Beuler's 'Don Giovanni' with its comic rhymes ('O hear the life of Don Giovanni. / Alias John and alias Juan, / Who play'd the deuce with wives and widows, / And proved so many maidens' ruin') was placed alongside the kinds of alarmingly crude and unreconstructed sexism still popular before the full impact of working-class affection for Queen Caroline was felt ('Both day and night her clapper goes, / She talks and talks for ever … O my wife's tongue's like the black, black crow's / That caws from morn till noon').[534] However unsettling to modern sensibilities concerning gender, songs like this show that Beuler reliably reflected the tastes of the day, including the rising public interest in drama and where the Giovanni dramas figure strongly:

> [Song] "Clod's Review of the London theatres"
> To Lunnun I came t'other day,
> In spite of the tears of old granny;
> And first night went to Drury Lane play,
> Where I saw *Lear* and *Giovanni*.
> *King Lear* seemed to be play mad,
> *Don Giovanni* seemed mad for a revel;
> But I thought 'twere acting too *bad*,
> When I saw a man *playing the devil*.[535]

The sexual libertinism picked up by *Blackwood's* in the Cockney school was amply paralleled in the popular playhouses. Beuler's comments on Astley's Amphitheatre noted its immodest dancing:

> To see horses at Amphitheatre
> I went, but the riders, in dancing,
> As far outstripped modesty o'nature,
> As the horses outstripped them in prancing.

Beuler's songs are a reminder that Dibdin's similarly equestrianized *Don Giovanni, Or, A Spectre on Horseback!* at Astley's rival Royal Amphitheatre may have owed much of its success to its female actresses and singers, or *'may'rs* from this stud.'[536] Beuler's songs are a reliable reflection of changing cultural attitudes embracing a wide range of theatres, transforming attitudes to sexuality and their reception into popular culture at a highly definable and demonstrably metropolitan level.

Giovanni in London ushered in a whole series of 'Giovanni' dramas capitalizing on Moncrieff's success at the Olympic. Although it cannot be claimed that Byron began *Don Juan* in July 1818 in response to *Giovanni in London* and its spin-offs, it is quite clear that Byron's audience was well prepared for its comic writing. Excluded from spoken drama by the duopolistic cartel of the royal theatres, other playhouses had little alternative but to develop successes achieved in the burletta form. The run of spin-offs from *Giovanni in London* only began to slacken in early 1822, and then only as the attention of writers and theatre managers alike turned to the even greater impact of Moncrieff's next success at the Adelphi, *Tom and Jerry*. The popularity of drama was exponentially increased by daily publications such as *Keene's Theatrical Evening Mirror* which, although it was published only between June and September 1820, offered an etched frontispiece and a nightly listing of the majority of London theatres, including the Surrey, Sadler's Wells, Astley's and Royal Coburg. The ability of London to support a daily newspaper dedicated to theatre, even if only on a short-lived basis, is a remarkable development within late Georgian London. The first issue of *Keene's Theatrical Evening Mirror*, published on 18 June 1820, advertised two versions of *Giovanni in the Country*, one at the Coburg and another at Astley's. Moncrieff's *Giovanni in the Country; or, The Rake Husband* for the Royal Coburg took up a political theme, with Giovanni standing as candidate for the borough of Lushington, and with the whole piece carefully timed to coincide with anti-Regent feeling.[537] William Reeves and William Barrymore's version at Astley's Royal Amphitheatre produced a droll hippodrame version, *Giovanni in the Country; or, A Gallop to Gretna Green* (sometimes billed as *Giovanni On Horseback!*), developing the mini-genre still further with its lugubrious Cockney bailiff, Sam Catch.[538] H.M. Milner's *Giovanni in Paris* for the East London Theatre (a renaming of the Royalty) that winter added little, although its penetration eastwards in the metropolis is further evidence of the wide social demography the formula could command.[539] By the autumn of 1820, *Keene's Theatrical Evening Mirror* was protesting that Theodore Edward Hook's Haymarket farce *Over the Water*, with its 'everlasting hoaxing of *Cockneyism* – like the excessive adoption of mimicry, has nearly worn itself out.'[540]

Moncrieff's own attempt at halting formulaic plotting is implicit in his *Giovanni in Ireland* (1821), although he was sufficiently tempted back once to write *Giovanni in Botany* a year later.[541] Having routed Giovanni from Spain back to London, he removed him to Ireland and then to Botany Bay. In Drury Lane's *Giovanni in Ireland*, Moncrieff posits the idea of an Irish monarch, alluding to a profound Irish nationalist tradition countering English colonial rule. Ireland's sovereign is Giovanni's friend, 'Cornelius OShaw[sic],' 'Commonly Called King Corney,' but Giovanni's real intentions are on 'his Lady Niece[sic] Glorvina Princess of Innismore.' Stray references to Corney's friendship with 'Colonel Odonnell[sic] the Chieftain' reinforce the idea of a palimpsest of colonial and precolonial Irish histories. Even the choice of King O'Shaw's residence, Castle Rackrent ('And is this all that Remains of Castle Rackrent / Once the proud palace of the Monarchs of Munster'), recognizes the realities of Irish life and alludes to Maria Edgeworth's novel (1800) of the same name. Significantly, a couple of stray references to English tithes and taxes ('The Harp that once Round Rack Rents Walls / Delighted Young and Old . . . / Tis to the Broker Sold') were censored by Larpent:

Glor: The Tax gatherer distrained upon the Poultry in our Very parlour.
Cor: Well Jewel &—
Glor: Snapall the Rector took a Tythe pig by the Tail from your Majesty's own Sty.

The plot's main direction, however, is to secure the duping of Giovanni in an elaborate hoax (not dissimilar to *Giovanni in London*) played on him by Leperello, King Corney, Glorvina and (in the go-between role) Florence McCarthy. With its structural similarities to Moncrieff's previous hit, it was little wonder that *Keene's Theatrical Evening Mirror* was complaining about the 'everlasting hoaxing of *Cockneyism*.'

Even with *Tom and Jerry* beginning its long run of success, Moncrieff wrote another Giovanni piece for the Olympic, *Giovanni in – Botany! Or The Libertine – Transported!* (1822) where Giovanni is a convicted bigamist 'doomed to cross the herring ferry for only marrying two wives!' When he arrives in Botany Bay, he finds Leporello already established as a successful 'Hop merchant' who has 'sav'd a little blunt [money] already and [is] . . . a favourite with the Governor.' The ending is very weak. In another Cockney hoax, when Giovanni tries to elope with young Wilhelmina, the Governor's wife manages to outwit him and the Governor gives orders for his and Leporello's 're-transportation either to the West Indies or the black settlements of America or any where else out of this, for if I suffer you to remain here another four and twenty hours, damme, if you won't corrupt the whole Colony!' This may simply have been a case of Moncrieff keeping his options open by his suggestion of a Caribbean or American slave settlement location for another future Giovanni outing.

A letter probably written in early 1819 to the manager of the Royal Coburg gives a good indication of the Grub Street conditions under which Moncrieff worked, forcing him to maintain this stream of writing.[542] Nevertheless, the weakness of the spin-offs is evident. Just as the *Keene's Theatrical Evening Mirror* had wearied of 'everlasting . . . Cockneyism,' so too other writers competed to quell the formulaic burlettas. I.R. Planché's *Giovanni the Vampire!!! or, How shall we get rid of him?*, which began at the Adelphi in January 1821, is an interesting criticism of Moncrieff's success as well as that of his imitators. *Giovanni in Botany's* Dramatis Personae even glanced at Planché's *Giovanni the Vampire!!!*, 'Don Giovanni – (Redivivus) The Libertine, Lost, Destroyed, – Reclaim'd – Relapsed, Vampyrized, Resussitated[*sic*] and eventually – transported for marrying "Two Wives!" (A hint to Husbands).'[543]

It is quite clear from the above that much of the writing for London theatre was developing within its own distinctive popular or plebeian public sphere. If Moncrieff's *Giovanni in London*, through its allusions to Shadwell's *Libertine Destroyed* or Byron's rather later *Don Juan*, retained at least some vestigial references to the dominant literary culture (albeit anachronistically in the case of Byron), the development of the Tom and Jerry plays, based on characters from Pierce Egan's Cruikshank illustrated novella *Life in London* (1820), was a phenomenon wholly developed within this plebeian sphere of drama. The convergence of distinctive strands in the general culture which had once remained distinct was now not only occurring in drama but also being noticed in the other arts. In many ways, it is Pierce Egan's career, with his interest in pugilism celebrated in his *Boxiana; or, Sketches of Ancient and Modern Pugilism; from the days of the Renowned Broughton and Slack, to the heroes of the present milling æra!* (1812), reprinted in 1818, which brought together the components of an anonymous essay published in the March 1819 issue of *Blackwood's* entitled 'On the Connexion Between Pugilism, Statuary, Painting, Poetry and Politics.' One of the later ripostes to Moncrieff's success with *Tom and Jerry*, the Adelphi's own *The Fancy's Opera* (1823) registered both recognition and exasperation at the plebeian cultural tastes dominating the playhouses.[544] The relationship between pugilism and theatre, both of which emphasized physical agility, were closer than one might imagine. In the provincial theatres pugilism was an entertainment of last resort for managers in search of an audience. Writing in 1826, Richard Jenkins, the historian of the Jacob's Well theatre in Bristol, bemoaned how the deceased 'great actors [of the past would] have blushed to see themselves mixed up with *rope-dancers, pugilists, horses*, and *dogs!!!*'[545] It was no doubt the presence of such professional proximities in 1809 which allowed the beleaguered management of Covent Garden to fill the pit with Jewish pugilists (such as 'Dutch Sam') associated with the great boxer Daniel Mendoza, in order to intimidate the OP rioters. Certainly, *The Covent Garden Journal* saw no problem in heading a piece, 'Mendoza and Kemble.'[546]

The essay in *Blackwood's* omitted any discussion of drama but made the more elusive connection between poetry and pugilism. It was 'slang,' otherwise being rapidly taken up in drama from *Giovanni in London* onwards, that caught *Blackwood's* attention, claiming that 'Pugilism seems to have acted on poetry chiefly through the medium of its slang language.'[547] It is not difficult to see behind the *Blackwood's* essay a barely disguised discussion of the Cockney school of poetry, although here modified as a pseudo-celebration of plebeian influence. Pugilism, it argued, 'has enriched the diction of poetry (which notwithstanding the preface to the Lyrical Ballads, we and [the pugilist] Bob Gregson think essentially different from prose) with a vast accession of "choice set terms," for which there is absolutely no equipollent in any of the other languages of Europe.' It is difficult to interpret the tone and intention of this essay correctly. Its welcoming of boxing's 'choice set terms' appears to differentiate poetry from prose, and co-opts both Wordsworth and the boxer as supporters of such poetic taste, yet at the same time the exaggeration and feigning of the comparison pushes it into parody. The essay went on to argue that pugilism 'has introduced into poetry new images, and give to almost all representations of "sensuous forms" a vividness, and ... palpability for which we may look in vain throughout the works of the finest spirits.' The sensuality of the Cockney poets, together with their predilection for archaic poetic vocabularies (the 'choice set terms'), betrays Hunt, Keats and the other Cockney authors to be the real targets of the *Blackwood's* article. Indeed, the sheer intellectual audacity of an essay entitled 'On the Connexion Between Pugilism, Statuary, Painting, Poetry and Politics,' suggests its own facetiousness, as does its ultimate designation of the present as the 'pugilistic era of English poetry.'[548] Connectives run through the essay. It equates the physical and linguistic forms encountered in pugilism, statuary and painting with the way in which poetry and politics have borrowed their languages of description from these activities, thereby selecting 'choice set terms' capable of giving 'palpability' to 'sensuous forms.' Closer proximity between the physical and the verbal appears to be a phenomenon *Blackwood's* believed the Cockney school had imported into general culture. For *Blackwood's*, the terrifying 'Connexion' between these arts of embodiment and discursivity lay not only in their cultural miscegenation but also their displacement of elite aesthetics. Perhaps even more disconcertingly, Egan's *Key to the Picture of The Fancy Going to A Fight At Moulsey-Hurst* (1819), a guide to an Isaac Robert Cruikshanks print, mixes the 'flash' and 'cant' language of the underworld with discussions of the merits of Blackwood's *Edinburgh Magazine*, Campbell's *Specimens of English Poetry* and Bell's *Weekly Dispatch* (pp. 8–9).

Chapter 4 has argued that *A Spectre on Horseback!*, *Giovanni in London* and their spin-offs represented a kind of aporia in *Blackwood's* concerns about the contemporary cultural rise of the working-class presence typified by the Cockney school. Cockney London's representation was exponentially accelerated by Pierce Egan's *Life in London*. Originally produced as a monthly part-work between October 1820 and June 1821, the visual qualities of George and Isaac Robert Cruikshank's etched plates of *Life in London* greatly contributed to its publishing success, producing at least 65 editions, imitations, piratings or extensions.[549] Modern critical commentaries on Egan's *Life in London* have usually concentrated on the original novella rather than its extraordinary appropriation into popular culture and dramatic adaptations.[550] Egan's *Life in London* (1820) quickly spawned the first *Tom and Jerry; or, Life in London*, a dramatic adaptation written by William Barrymore and performed on 17 September 1821 at Davis's (ex-Astley's) Royal Amphitheatre, Lambeth. Taking its opportunities from Egan's Tattersall scenes, it was the perfect vehicle for a public theatrical space which remained an essentially equestrian venue. Barrymore's *Tom and Jerry* was followed by a flurry of variations more or less based on Egan's original. Charles Isaac Mungo Dibdin's *Life in London* was performed at the Olympic Theatre, Wych Street, on 12 November 1821.[551] Within two weeks, William Thomas Moncrieff's *Tom and Jerry; or, Life in London* was with the Lord Chamberlain for licensing and opened on 26 November 1821 at the Adelphi Theatre, around the corner from the Olympic, in the Strand.[552] It is this trajectory of a drama conceived in a circus venue, and then appearing under the noses of the royal theatres, which defines the solidity of this plebeian public sphere of drama.

Surrounding these immediate innovations on the London stage were larger changes in British culture which, as ever, found rapid representation on the stage. As if to put pressure on the reactionary and conservative viewpoints expressed by *Blackwood's*, near contemporaneously new seaside resorts such as Margate and Ramsgate (which already had a Royal theatre) seemed to exemplify the miscegenation of class. As early as 1801, William Dimond's Covent Garden opera *The Sea-Side Story* (1801) reflected the seasonal influx of holiday trippers travelling from London on the Margate Hoy, the generic name for the sloop-rigged coasting vessels acting as ferries: 'Good, sir! Another Hoy has just brought to, with a fresh cargo of cockney livestock.'[553] A song performed by the character of a 'Margate Hoy-Man' in the Covent Garden pantomime *Harlequin's Tour; or, The Dominion of Fancy* (1800) emphasized how this 'cockney livestock' were mixed together both on the boats and in the resort town in a wild melee of fun and social upheaval ('Crowding together all stations and quality, / Margate-a-hoy! As I merrily hollo[*sic*] t'ye[*sic*].'[554]

In the context of the late 1810s, Charles Mathews's 'Trip to Paris' at the English Opera House (Lyceum) propelled a more popular comic aware-ness of this anarchic levelling, the 'Crowding together [of] all stations,' in the sea-side resorts opening up to ordinary Londoners transported on the hoys. In Mathews's sketch, Lord Hildebrand Dablincourt, Sir Simon and Lady Sugarloaf, 'Mr Deputy Marrowfat and his fat fubsy wife...were followed by Solomon Simons, the slop-seller,' bringing Margate down-market, making it 'vulgar, plebeian, and insufferable for the reception of quality.'[555] It was a far cry from the Haymarket's *Summer Amusement; or, An Adventure at Margate* (1781) which taunted 'the light-heel'd troops of France' with a type of patriotic defiance noticeably marked by its decorum, 'Tho' we fight, we'll dance and sing, / And drub them with good manners.'[556] From the solidarities of the *Summer Amusement* to Solomon Simon, the slop-seller, it is clear that the 'cockney livestock' were not only on the move socially, recreationally and geographically, but that they appeared 'vulgar, plebeian, and insufferable' to the affluent readership of *Blackwood*'s.

This social ribaldry appeared to many to accelerate following the production of a series of Tom and Jerry plays. 'Tom and Jerry mania has seized all classes of his Majesty's liege subjects,' wrote an irate reviewer for Birmingham's *Theatrical Looker-on* in June 1822. At the city's Theatre Royal, the critic had just had an uncomfortable night of it when 'we had much difficulty in gaining our seat, and encountered great inconveni-ence from the curiosity of the folks around us.' Amidst much 'bawling recognition of "dear friends" from opposite sides of the gallery, together with much edifying whistling...the first act and part of the second of *Tom and Jerry* were a perfect pantomime.' To cap it all, the *Theatrical Looker-on*'s reviewer was pelted with 'showers of nut-shells and orange-peel...received in common with our neighbours.'[557] At a more domestic level, as a sure sign of cultural popularity, as early as 1823 Tom, Jerry and Bob Logic had become securely placed in childrens' alphabetical woodcut caricatures in the Monmouth Street, Seven Dials, printer James Catnach's broadside, *Christmas Gambols, and Twelfth Night's Amusements* which was itself a development from earlier broadsides deriving from such publications as *The Particulars of the Origin of Twelfth Night* (*c*.1774) where Tom and Jerry have displaced the outmoded traditional figures of Alderman Guttle, Lady Gimlet Eye and Doctor Poison Guts. Before long, just as with his *Giovanni in London*, there were many 'Tom and Jerry' spin-offs in the form of sequels and songs, as well as dictionaries and glossaries to explain and supplement the piece's 'flash' or 'cant' under-world language. Egan's *Life in London* was even imitated by publications such as *Real Life in London*, complete with coloured plates intended to parallel Cruikshanks's originals, which had appeared by May 1821. The need for writing and rewriting never stopped: nearly a year later, in a return to the original story line, yet another 'Tom and Jerry' play, *Life in London: A Melo Drama in 3 Acts*, was required by the Olympic Theatre.[558]

If there can be no doubting the cultural impact of Tom and Jerry, however distantly removed from Egan's original, its message appeared to celebrate the plebeian waywardness which cultural critics from Hogarth to *George Barnwell* had hoped to contain. Tom and Jerry's cultural importance as a dramatic phenomenon was that it staged delinquent anti-authoritarian behaviour without visible reproof, and exhibited forms of fashion and language which were dramatic mani-festations of socially covert alternatives to deference and harmony. In effect, although the minor gentry Tom, Jerry and Logic were the ostens-ible heroes of these plays, the burlettas present their 'cant' and 'flash' language as the further triumphalism of their Cockney characters.

Even before Moncrieff's Adelphi Theatre *Tom and Jerry*, Joseph Ebsworth's Royal Coburg burletta *Crockery's Misfortunes; or, Trans-mogrifications* (1821) had as its spokesman the eponymous Crockery. Crockery is the perfect example of that confident, knowing and well-travelled Cockney Londoner who, as a servant returning from India ('Hingy'), pronounces on the city's modernity complete with transposed consonants:

> Oh, dear!-vat a vonderful place is this Lunnun – but then vot changes have taken place – it's enough to make von's heart bleed .... even Lambeth Marsh is haltered, for they've built a Cobourg playhouse there, vot the big play-houses want to put down, and made a bridge over the water.[559]

The self-referentiality of his comments about how Lambeth Marsh has been 'haltered' for the building of the Royal Coburg, the newly built Waterloo Bridge and his allusions to the machinations of 'the big play-houses' of Covent Garden and Drury Lane are as defiant as they are accurate summations of the changes to his native 'Lunnun.' The import-ance of *Crockery's Misfortunes* is that it plays out, almost as a subtext, the major changes in the capital, the 'vonderful place,' Crockery fear-lessly embraces. With its 'gash' street lighting, 'it's enough to make von's heart bleed,' but vibrant enough to make the *Blackwood's* attacks on the Cockney school of poetry an outmoded irrelevance, a provincial obsolescence.

By the end of 1819, although in dire financial straits, Moncrieff would be negotiating with the Royal Coburg Theatre management by claiming that he could take his new work to 'The Great Theatres' if he did not get the co-operation he felt he deserved.[560] However, it should be remembered that the transferral of Moncrieff's *Giovanni in London* into equally successful and long-running productions at Covent Garden and Drury Lane in itself proves nothing about the liberalization of dramatic writing. Although the patent rules imposed burletta and forbade spoken drama for the other theatres, the reverse was not the case: the two major houses were free to mount as many burlettas or pantomimes as they chose. Moncrieff's *Giovanni* broached no new precedent. Nevertheless, like the moment of Ireland's *Vortigern* debacle at Drury Lane in 1796, Moncrieff's *Giovanni in London* nearly 20 years later symbolizes a turning point. Without its being a decisive defeat, the royal theatres had once again failed to stifle, as they had with the Royalty Theatre in the 1780s, the growth of alternative playhouse venues in London. In the case of Elliston's Olympic Theatre in Wych Street right on their doorstep, 'under the[ir] very noses' as one commentator had put it a few years earlier, not only had Drury Lane and Covent Garden failed to suppress the upstart theatres, Moncrieff's hit – long before the rather later impulse of popularization implicit in Byron's poem *Don Juan* – quickly established itself deep inside plebeian culture.[561] In effect, *Giovanni in London* had coincided not only with the gradual, barely perceptible, movement towards national prosperity in the late 1810s, but also with a more buoyant postwar popular culture which was creating itself on the back of a boom in cheap print. With all of these structural factors behind it, the cultural impact of a hit such as Moncrieff's was bound to be enormous.

6
The Royal Amphitheatre and Olympic *Tom and Jerry* Burlettas

This chapter, and the one which follows, are given over to demonstrating the workings of the popular or plebeian public spheres of drama specific to the non-patent playhouses operating in late Georgian London. Burletta was the optimum dramatic genre for these theatres to develop since it was also the only form available to them which could be confirmed as legally permissible. Inevitably, the narrative of how burletta developed bears little relationship to how spoken drama evolved in the royal theatres. While non-patent playhouses such as the Adelphi and Olympic continued to experience the censor's interventions, and while no playhouse in the London area was immune from the royal theatres' mobilization of litigation and political pressure to protect their monopolies, the burletta playhouses developed largely with reference to their own competitors or peers and in combination with a dialogue with their own audiences. For as long as the major contemporary canonical authors such as Wordsworth, Coleridge and Keats remained unable or unwilling to access the potential of these playhouses for reaching popular audiences, even though much of their verse was politically and theoretically derived from native ballads and was ideally suited to burletta, the manner in which dramas such as *Giovanni in London* and *Tom and Jerry* developed was unlikely to follow the patterns of literary or social history established by spoken drama. These chapters will demonstrate that successful burlettas reached exponentially large audiences within a public sphere which articulated its own set of concerns.

The cultural impact of burletta was considerable. Byron began writing *Don Juan* in July 1818, barely six months after the first performance of Moncrieff's *Giovanni in London*. It seems likely he was aware of its popular success because the burletta had travelled swiftly into the provinces and overseas. Edmund Shaw Simpson, manager of the Park Theatre,

New York, who was on a talent-scouting expedition to the Birmingham Theatre Royal as early as May 1818, witnessed a Giovanni play (probably *Giovanni in London*), observing in his diary that 'the Company has played it very often & therefore were very easy in it –.'[562] Seven years later, the conservative, Birmingham-printed *Theatrical John Bull* journal wrote of the recent Birmingham Theatre Royal production of *Giovanni in London*: 'This is of the description of pieces to which we are as much enemies as any puritan of the day. It is a medley of mockery, vulgarity, ribaldry, and nonsense; a stigma on the character of a Theatre Royal. We think it too vile an office to attempt the criticism of such a thing.' In the same issue, the reviewer – who went back to the same theatre a short time later – wrote, '*Don Giovanni* again!,' adding that 'This ridiculous production of Moncrieff (written we believe, under inspiration of poverty) was brought out at the Olympic Theatre, a place one degree lower than the *Tom and Jerry* Shop [i.e. the Adelphi Theatre].'[563] The *Theatrical John Bull* article is a good indicator not only of the continuing controversy over *Giovanni in London* now reaching the provinces, but it also acknowledges the cultural significance of Moncrieff's next hit, *Tom and Jerry*.

The evolution of the Tom and Jerry plays, as with the *Giovanni in London* dramas, are bewilderingly complex in their textual and cultural evolution. The first *Tom and Jerry* drama had been William Barrymore's, not at the Adelphi or Olympic theatres but south of the river at Davis's Royal Amphitheatre (previously Astley's), Lambeth, near Westminster Bridge.[564] Very much in the manner of the Don Giovanni dramas of 1817, the rapidity and sheer ability to change and innovate dramas at the Royal Amphitheatre and other London circus venues was remarkable. In July 1821 Astley's (this venue was often simply known locally as 'Astley's' although it changed hands and name several times) was celebrating the coronation with 'A Grand Pageant Illustrative Of Part Of The Splendid Ceremonial Of The Coronation Of ... King George IV ... [with his] Champion In Real Armour!! Mounted On The Horse Cato ...'[565] By the end of August it billed Barrymore and Reeves's *Giovanni On Horseback! Or, A Gallop to Gretna Green*, its Coburg *Giovanni in the Country* adaptation. Barely two weeks later, on 17 September 1821 (as Thomas Dibdin later corroborated), Astley's produced the first Pierce Egan spin-off, *Life In London! Or, Day & Night Scenes! Of Tom And Jerry, In Their Rambles And Sprees Through The Metropolis*, which they billed as a 'New Whimsical Local Melo-Dramatic Pantomimical Drama.'[566] What must have first attracted Astley's to quickly adapt Egan's *Life in London* was the opportunities the book afforded for equestrian display, the traditional strength of its theatricalized circus arena.

Astley's extraordinary 'advertising cavalcade' which consisted of a horse troop doing such comic stunts as 'The Taylor of Brentford' (a fine rider appearing to take inept falls) were well known in the East End streets both north and south of the Thames.[567] Their coronation spectacle strongly featured the King's Champion 'on the Horse Cato,' which had been a steed specifically chosen from Astley's stables for the actual ceremony, but even the English Opera House, Haymarket, made much of this ('almost time for the Champion, very ancient Ceremony that') in their 'Operatick Sketch' *A Squeeze to the Coronation* which featured 'The Interior of Westminster Hall filled up for the Coronation Festivities – The procession of the Champion Entrée & Proclamation of the Challenge Read according to the Annexd. Official Ceremonial.'[568] Egan's *Life in London* had emphasized his personal affection for horse racing, such as in the scene narrating the duping of Green at the horse trader Tattersall's, so it was natural for Astley's, London's most celebrated equestrian venue, to exploit the vivid 'hippodrame' potential of the book. This was also a formula Astley's repeated a couple of years later when they shoe-horned canonical British Romantic poetry onto horseback in *Lord Byron's Beutifulramatic*[sic] *tale of Mazeppa and the Wild Horse.*[569]

At first, Astley's merged much of their standard repertoire into *Life In London! Or, Day & Night Scenes! Of Tom And Jerry*, which was accompanied by a display of 'the Learned Hanoverian Horse!' and joined by a boa constrictor exhibit in October. Astley's venture into 'flash' language with 'The Road to the "Mill"…shewing the Eccentric Movements of 'The Fancy,' Peep-o'day Boys, Out and Outers, &c.' was balanced by the more traditional fare of a scene set in Vauxhall gardens 'illuminated at the late masquerade! Embracing every Description of Amusement peculiar to this Theatre, Slack Rope Vaulting, tumbling, Conjuring, Balancing-terminating with the following Brilliant Display of Fire-Works!' which allowed them to exploit their troop of actors, acrobats and horsemen.[570] Of course, the horse business in the Davis *Tom and Jerry* was much more in evidence than it had been even in horse-fancier Egan's book, with the scene at Tattersall's horse sales showing how 'The horse is run up and down' as the rich fool Green is duped into buying an overpriced aging nag in poor health.[571] 'Mr. Davis, the Celebrated Rider' (and now the owner of Astley's) was himself a famous acrobatic horseman, spectacularly shown in contemporary prints standing one legged and holding two flags on the saddle of a galloping horse.[572] In Egan's *Book of Sports, and Mirror of Life: Embracing the Turf, The Chase, The Ring, and The Stage*

(1832), the theatrical gossip was almost entirely displaced by horse-racing anecdotes. This was a rich vein of contemporary plebeian culture. Renton Nicholson, the landlord of The Garrick's Head, Bow Street, a follower of Egan and author of the *Autobiography of a Fast Man* (1863) and editor of *The Town* magazine, similarly shared connections with turf, theatre and journalism. The nearby Royal Coburg Theatre, when it opened in May 1818, quickly mounted an audience-poaching exercise against Astley's by featuring 'More Novelty, A Real Pony Race!' in *Epsom Downs; or, All Alive at the Races* which guaranteed to show only 'ponies of the highest character.'[573] By the spring of 1822, Davis's emphasized on their play-bills the speciality of a *Tom and Jerry* with 'real Pony Races.'[574]

There was also a further, completely unexpected, device which the Davis production used quite distinctively. Egan's *Life in London* consisted of a sequence of varied but relatively short scenes. Davis's Amphitheatre invoked the harlequinade convention as the mechanism enabling the scene to flit rapidly between country and town, or from race course to gambling den. The exasperated Birmingham *Theatrical Looker-on* reviewer had commented that much of the *Tom and Jerry* was a 'perfect pantomime.' It is quite possible that, just as the *Theatrical Looker-on* reviewer thought, the *Tom and Jerry* audiences actually were more bois-terous and rowdy than the average and it appealed to 'those who love bustle, and riot, and noise.'[575] This also has a number of implications for understanding the early reception of Tom and Jerry in the more working-class playhouses.

Like several others, the Davis Amphitheatre *Tom and Jerry* began by quickly establishing the fashionable 'flash' language and urban sophist-icated mores of London ('Tom: I say Jerry, don't stand to pack up any thing, for curse me if they will stand such toggery [clothing] as this in London').[576] But its most startling perspective on Egan's original was to identify all of the characters, including harlequin, within a strong morality tradition whose origins probably date back to medieval times. *Life in London*, for all its self-conscious contemporaneity and usage of covert languages, was immediately positioned by Davis's Amphitheatre into a narrative dating back to the medieval or renaissance morality play. Before Tom and Jerry set out for London from Hawthorne Hall they are intercepted by Folly, a female role complete with her place in 'Folly's Temple.' All of this is completely alien to Egan's original: there is nothing in his *Life in London* to justify anything like it.[577] Folly's highly formalized speech to Tom is didactic in nature, warning him of the traditional dangers of the big city: 'Folly: You would bend your steps to that seat of vice and folly, London.' She then delivers a homily to Tom which figures both her own reality and that of the dangers which lie in his path:

> 'Tis there that thousands in my train, daily ramble...slighting prudence and discretion into a vortex of dissipation...from which, reflection too late relieves them. To avoid this gulph of misery, take thou discretion's mirror, and you the wand of prudence, consult the one, and use the other, and little is to be dreaded from the various scenes of Life in London.

The transition to Egan's title is quite smoothly handled but, in an unexpected piece of stage business, Tom and Jerry are actually given a 'wand of prudence' and 'discretion's mirror' to carry with them ('Tom: Thanks dear Goddess...'). Furthermore, they are granted a 'boon' – to have a 'conductor' or guide, Harlequin, together with the Clown, now benign and transformed (appropriately) into 'Tom fool.' Folly also manages to shift the end of this prelude back once again to the subtitle of Egan's book (*The day and night scenes of Jerry Hawthorne*), 'Hear me folly's favourite son [Harlequin], attend these mortals, through London point the way, and shew them scenes by night, as well as day.'[578] The point of this intervention by the Davis's Amphitheatre's scriptwriter, William Barrymore, in the light of *Tom and Jerry's* later success at The Olympic and Adelphi, is very significant in indicating that south of the river and away from the West End, the way of life portrayed in Egan's *Life in London* was greeted with both caution and suspicion.

The dissolute lifestyle of Tom, Jerry and Logic is not endorsed. Folly, like 'discretion's mirror,' is actually a real presence in the Davis *Tom and Jerry*, coming into action after an episode of 'Charley' (watchman) baiting to pronounce that 'This comes of slighting discretion's mirror! 'tis easy enough to get into a Watch-house; but not so easy to get out of it.'[579] This moral commentary is continued with a sharpening of Egan's episodes dealing with the trio's pursuit by bailiffs. In the Davis *Tom and Jerry*, the rakish life does nothing to keep the Bailiff out of Logic's apartments in the exclusive Albany, Piccadilly. As Bob is arrested ('Grabb'd, as sure as my name's Logic, and go I must'), Harlequin – who has been transporting and transfiguring the various scenes from Jackson's boxing parlour through to the Albany apartment – appears on the scene to make another moral comment: 'let your friend know the horrors of imprisonment, then I'll release him – for the lesson he'll be sure to learn, that poverty in a garret, is better than splendour in a prison.'[580] With

Tom, Jerry and Logic devoid of talent, dissolute, pointless and almost nihilistic, the Davis Amphitheatre's *Tom and Jerry* is quite remarkable in putting its audience in the position of being their moral superiors. Folly is effectively the nanny of the three young men with Harlequin their patient tutor.

There was a further respect in which the Davis *Tom and Jerry* differed from its descendants at the other theatres. Not only did it fail to endorse upper-class behaviour, but, compared with its followers, it also noticeably failed to romanticize or glamourize Egan's St Giles's beggars. Dusty Bob (in the Davis's Amphitheatre version Dusty Sam), African Sall, Billy Waters and Egan's other 'gammoning' (pretending a disability) beggars were one of the great audience successes of Moncrieff's *Tom and Jerry*. In the same way that the Davis Amphitheatre's audience were invited to patronize Folly's guardianship over wayward aristocrats, so too its *Tom and Jerry* failed to endorse London beggars. In late 1821 the Albion Press had published a caricature print warning of one 'William Stevenson. / A notorious Beggar who died worth £900.'[581] Ingrained principles of working-class respectability ensured begging was not endorsed but, interestingly, the Davis production made its moral discriminations even finer by avoiding racial antagonism. An episode from Egan's *Life in London*, where the beggars dance, sing and eat hearty dinners, was adapted by Moncrieff to provide an unfavourable comment about a racist gibe.

In the Davis *Tom and Jerry*, the beggars' scenes were more equivocally handled, at least as far as the issue of begging was concerned. In the Davis production, the 'Back Slums' beggars of the Holy Land in St. Giles's could be optionally replaced by beggars 'carousing' outside the drinking den of Almack's in the East, a significantly less moral possibility of a location with its suggestion of a link between poverty, 'gammoning' and alcohol:

The Back Slums; or, Almack's in the East. Music. At the opening of the scene, a variety of Beggars of all classes are discovered carousing . . .

Billy Waters: Bravo! Bravo! Now suppose 'em dance a lilly bit, it do 'em good after hearty supper. What say you Massa Sam? Massa Dussy Sam I mean, here be very pretty partner – my countrywoman, I introduce you.

Dusty Sam: Vell Ize no objections, it vouldn't be perlite, for to go for to refuse the lady.[582]

Buried away in the subtext here is the opportunity both for a theatrical Caribbean accent ('Now suppose 'em dance a lilly bit') and for the white man, Dusty Sam, to affect initial surprise at the offer of the black woman, African Sall, as a dancing partner. His well-mannered response ('that it wouldn't be perlite' to refuse) together with his Cockney accent ('Vell Ize no objections'), quite deftly sets them up as a community of relatively honourable and civilized equals, far more truly decorous in their behaviour than the example given by the drunken 'sprees' of Tom, Jerry and Logic. Blacked up as they were, the moral direction of the piece criticizes class rather than race, begging rather than blackness.

However, amidst these subtle gradations and distinctions in the portrayal of working-class sentiment and respectability which Davis's Amphitheatre felt obliged to observe, there was a scrupulously materialist set of judgements about beggars. When the beggars are exposed (even in Moncrieff their 'gammoning a maim' is made explicit), it is through the agency of the violence of a harlequinade, recalling something of the Drury Lane *Harlequin Libertine...A Pantomime* (1817):

Harlequin: Behold! – (*He waves. – Beggar's coat flies off – shows arm tied up*)
1st Beggar: Dash my wig – here's an exposition.
2nd Beggar: Ha, ha, ha! Vy you've found your arm.

(His leg goes)

1st Beggar: Ha, ha ha! Vy he has found his leg... (*...A regular row. – They beat the Beggars off*).[583]

Harlequin's appearance is, as ever in the Davis *Tom and Jerry*, a moral intervention, a magical device to materialize the bound up arms and legs of the beggars. When the second Beggar's 'leg goes' and the first Beggar laughs, it is because his wooden leg has been knocked from under him so he quickly has to put his foot down ('Vy he has found his leg') to stop himself falling over. This materialization of the sham is a literalistic device whose moral meaning would have been readily understood by the Amphitheatre audience. Such nuanced distinctions demonstrate how socially evaluative the writing and audiences for the non-Theatre Royal playhouses could become and how the presentation of blacked up characters adhered to their class, as much as their racial, categorization.

Despite the success of Moncrieff's *Tom and Jerry*, there would always be lingering moral suspicions about its main characters, anxieties which the producers of the Davis's Amphitheatre version clearly felt they should portray. These reservations, plebeian suspicions of high life, were to have remarkable repercussions. For some reason which is not quite clear, the Olympic Theatre whose production of Dibdin's *Life in London; or, The Larks of Logic, Tom, and Jerry* had been playing since the middle of November 1821 required a second version of *Life in London* by the autumn of 1822. The 'Melo Drama' they produced was very different to both Dibdin's and Moncrieff's plays, much more critical and cautionary in tone.[584]

The 'new' Olympic *Life in London* was much closer to the original Davis's Amphitheatre's *Tom and Jerry* in its lack of sympathy with its principal characters. This may possibly have something to do both with the Olympic's being under the purview of the Lord Chamberlain (for the circumstances of the similarly situated Moncrieff *Tom and Jerry*, see below) but it may also represent a maturing of audience reaction which The Olympic thought they must respect. The first (Dibdin) Olympic *Life in London* may not have been able to adjust itself to working-class disquiet at the upper-class behaviour portrayed and the explicit breakdown in the patrician role ('my Dear Fellow Conscience does not belong to our Order') which was the very thing which made the Moncrieff version so revolutionary.[585] The second Olympic *Life in London*, performed in late 1822, was much more critical of Tom, Jerry and Logic than any of its predecessors. In other words, emerging in the second Olympic *Life in London* is a return to the values represented in the Davis Amphitheatre's first, but much cruder, *Tom and Jerry*. This migration of the concerns of a plebeian, south of Thames, equestrian circus amphitheatre into the Olympic Theatre adjacent to Drury Lane is a significant indicator of how working-class perspectives were infiltrating the regions of the Royal theatres.

The most noticeable immediate feature of the Olympic *Life in London*, something quite unprepared for by Pierce Egan's explicit novella about the gentry's life in the metropolis, is its emphasis on rural settings and on the feelings of the servant class, a quite contrary emphasis to that presented in the other Tom and Jerry plays and quite alien to Egan's original work. Furthermore, both of these settings are presented so as to cast serious doubt upon upper-class individuals alongside a more deliberate and developed role for social criticism than had been attempted in the Davis Amphitheatre's *Tom and Jerry* in autumn 1821. The opening is not in the 'Sportman's Cabinet at Hawthorn Hall,' the curtain raiser for Moncrieff's production, but rather in a rural 'Picturesque Scene, with Bushes & a Stile, Enter Patty with Milk pail.'[586] The Sadler's Wells production of a 'Pedestrian, Equestrian' *Tom and Jerry* in April 1822 also appears to have begun with a similar scene, although, apart from one song by Patty, nothing else of the text survives.[587] Compared to the ridiculing of servants in Townley's *High Life Below Stairs* (1759), the Olympic production was quite distinctive in showing servants endangered by philandering gentry.[588] The milkmaid Patty Primrose's opening words immediately establish the realities of servant life: 'Heigho! Four o'clock, & not one of my Cows milked yet? What will my mistress say to that? (*sets down Pail*) I wonder who would be a servant. Up early & down late and worry, worry, from Morn till night.' The next words heard are Jerry's hunting calls offstage ('Tally ho! Tally ho!') to which Patty immediately responds by sensing the danger she is in from Jerry's philandering, 'By Gosh! If it ain't young Squire Master Jerry. There'll be the dickens to do! He's the very devil, among the girls, and my Tim is as jealous as old scratch & if he catches me.' Patty narrowly escapes being groped by the son of her employer, even if it is handled with good humour. Again, the theatrical theme of trysts between master and maidservant was traceable at least as far back as Colley Cibber's Drury Lane production *The Careless Husband* (1704) with the topos still being depicted in paintings such as Francis Wheatley's scene from Cibber's piece *Lady Easy's Steinkerk* (1791, V&A Museum, London).

Patty's reference to her fiancé, Tim Flail, introduces a further vehicle for the criticism of upper-class mores in the Olympic *Life in London* because Tim is angry but also prepared to intervene: 'Well, whats this world come to? ... young Measter too, who always boasts of his being a thoro' bred sportsman, and a great enemy to Poachers but he doesn't mind poaching on my Manor, yet I'll spoil his sport, altho' he be young Squire.' Tim's noticing of double standards and behavioural contradictions in Jerry is paralleled by the dead-flat analysis of Mary Rosebud's first-sight verdict of Tom, '(*aside*) I don't much like the look of Tom: he appears a shocking rake.' In one of the later incarnations of *Tom and Jerry*, these misgivings are taken even further. In Thomas Greenwood's *The Death of Life in London; or, Tom & Jerry's Funeral* (1823) for the Royal Coburg, Mary Rosebud goes 'mad... dressed fantastically' at Jerry's apparent death.[589] The Adelphi had taken over the Coburg's *Death of Life in London* in early 1824 and became obliged to have it licensed by the Lord Chamberlain because the Adelphi was in Westminster (they simply sent him a printed copy). One of George Colman the Younger's first actions as new Examiner, following the death of John Larpent, was to expunge from the play a comical reference by Jerry (who is not dead, as it turns out) to Mary's pregnancy by him and its effects on her complexion and appearance: 'I left a *rosebud*, but you disclose, / The glowing beauties of a full-blown rose.'[590] These progressively severe criticisms of the trio's antics ('Patty:... for shame of yourself – Master Jerry. You can never let the girls alone') are actually quite subtly handled in the second Olympic *Life in London*. The futility of upper-class habits is surprisingly strongly presented. There is even a degree of melancholy evoked in the portrayal of the pointless and, as this production implied, empty pursuit of fox hunting. The coincidence of rural blood sports is a feature of both Moncrieff's *Tom and Jerry* and the Olympic's second *Life in London*; indeed, both of them use the same – presumably traditional – hunting toast, 'Horses sound, Dogs healthy; / Earths stopped, and Foxes plenty.'[591] The consequences of upper-class actions were quite forcibly articulated as the play progressed.

At one point, drunk and late in the night in the middle of London's West End, the trio attempt to shake off the effects of alcohol by buying coffee (an interesting indicator that such shops opened to serve this type of custom). Of course, the rake and the coffee shop were traditional but the affected 'Tippy Bob' character of the 1790s prints ('Then under this collar, / I've got a large roller, / 'Tis just like a huge German sausage; / And squeez'd up so tight, / That, by this good light, / It goes nearly to stop up the passage!') had replaced sexual innuendo ('The girls cry out "Bobby"! / "Here bobby"! – My bibidy bob!" / ... I can't get them out of my nob!') with outright delinquency.[592] In *Life in London*, Bob, Jerry and Logic drink the coffee but run off without paying and are chased by 'the Coffee shop woman with her arms a Kimbo':

Coffee: Vy don't you pay me for my Coffee, now you are a nice man indeed, and vants to rob an honest voman – I shouldn't have thought of it, that's vat I shoun't, but I'm not to be done, by such a nasty, little, imperent[sic], fellow without a mag in your pocket – so if you don't tip directly, I'll call my husband & give you in charge to the vatch, that's vat I vill.[593]

It's an excellent cameo, conforming to a style of acting still apparent in the ex-music hall British film stars of the 1930s and '40s. Her Cockney dialect and nasal rhythm of speech is swiftly sketched in by the Tom and Jerry writer. Her half mispronunciation ('imperent' for impertinent) is not a foolish measure of affectation but embedded in working-class dialect. As with much of the characterization of Cockney speech in these dramas (see the Dusty Sam of the Davis *Tom and Jerry*, above) the spelling follows accurately, rather than caricatures, contemporary

London dialect at that time. Indeed, the author of both the Davis and the Olympic's Tom and Jerry plays, as well as Moncrieff himself as early as *Giovanni in the Country*, utilize contemporary Cockney dialect. Her anger is sincere, her irony amazed ('now you are a nice man indeed') and her restraint comes about solely through being female and outnumbered by two drunken men on a midnight London street.

> Come, come – that won't do – you Gentlemen? A pair of dandies, with collars sticking out about your necks & the devil a shirt to your backs, and I tells you once for all, if I don't get my money from that green spectacle, blinking fellow there, I'll fetch my husband, to mill his glaze & the Flue Faker to thump you all round, – that's vat I vill. (*Exit Coffee Woman in a rage*).

In this brilliantly observed comic writing, the 'cant' language is vivid: she will fetch her husband to 'mill his glaze' (punch his eyes) and the 'Flue Faker' (chimney sweep) will come to 'thump you all round.'[594] However, perhaps her most telling put-down is to see through the ridiculously fashionable 'dandies, with collars sticking out about your necks' and know that they are stony broke with 'the devil a shirt to your backs' (to paraphrase, 'I'm damned if you've even got a shirt beneath your collars'). Most tellingly, however, she belittles Tom into 'that green spectacle, blinking fellow there.' The episode dramatizes the type of confrontation between Cockney and gentry patterns of language implicit in the *Blackwood's* attacks on poetry in 1817. The second essay 'On the Cockney School of Poetry' had professed itself 'incapable of understanding many parts' of Hunt's poetry because it lacked 'a good glossary of the Cockney dialect.'[595]

Whereas Davis's *Tom and Jerry* had presented a scene ambivalently located in '*The Back Slums; or, Almack's in the East*,' the Olympic version carefully differentiated between these two areas as representing two distinct types of urban poor, forcibly distinguishing between two cultures of poverty to be found in the 'Back Slums' and in 'Almack's in the East.' The 'Back Slums' were in the area of St Giles's at the eastern end of Oxford Street then known as 'the Holy Land.' The parish of St Giles's-in-the-Fields had a major problem dealing with urban poverty, with about 30 per cent of the 1815 destitutes in that parish being Irish.[596] 'Almack's in the East' was the subcultural nickname for a tavern more properly known as the Coach and Horses in Nightingale-lane, East Smithfield, London.[597] The latter was a bit of Cockney 'flash' comic naming since there had long been the fashionable salon and gambling house called Almack's in St. James's, in the West End of London. Moncrieff's Corinthian Tom warns that his friends 'must mind our flash doesn't peep out at Almack's. 'Tis classic ground there; the rallying spot of all the rank, wealth, and beauty in the metropolis.'[598] Tom's comment encapsulates the problematics of this structured mirroring of East and West Ends of the metropolis. One of the origins of the growth in the use of the term 'The Metropolis' to describe London was that it could accommodate peoples' experience of London as a city increasingly de-centred towards its peripheries. Taking care not to use 'flash' in the West End denotes that the language of the East End was distinctive from that used in the more affluent St. James's. The 'flash' comic vernacular, however, goes into much more intricate nuances of humorous complexity.

'Almack's in the East' got its name not only because of its symmetry with Almack's in the West End but also because it punned on the surname of the Coach and Horses publican, a man called Mace. The verb 'mace,' in 'flash' language, was to cheat or impose on another, usually by running up credit – an ironic verdict bestowed on Mace, no doubt by his impecunious drinkers.[599] One of the common variants in the subculture at this time was simply to call Almack's in the East 'All Max.' In this male-dominant, heavy-drinking culture, 'max' was the 'flash' term for gin. All of these things come together in an extraordinary contemporary appropriation of Tom and Jerry's 'flash' linguistic exhibitionism as well as in the contemporary working-class derision of Lord Byron in the anonymous song called 'All Max in the East' which parodied his *The Bride of Abydos* ('Know ye the spot call'd *All Max* in the East[?]').[600] The celebration (or lack of condemnation) of heavy drinking was one of the few things in the Olympic's *Life in London* that John Larpent identified as immoral or controversial enough to require to be expunged. The passage Larpent marked for excision concerned Jerry's querying of the origin of the word used to name a gin-drinking den known as The Daffy Club:

Jerry: Then pardon Sir one word more, will you explain to me the term of daffy. Is it dictionary proof.
President: Certainly Sir. The squeamish fair who take it on the sly politely name it to her friends as 'white wine,' the swell chaffs it as 'blue ruin.' The laundress loves dearly a dram of 'auld Tom.' The drag fiddler can toss off his glass of 'max' the coster monger a 'flash of lightning.' The link boy & mud lark are for some 'stark naked.' So you see Sir to have called this institution the Gin Club might have deprived it of many of its Elegant friends – they meet under the above title.

The language is rich in all the varied terms and contemporary social connotations of the 'flash' synonyms for gin, the apple seller calling it his 'flash of lightning' and the 'drag fiddler' (a thief who specializes in stealing from wagons or carts) calling it 'max.'[601] Larpent's excisions are a reminder that the Cockney dialect was capable of being policed not only by the ridicule of *Blackwood's* but also by the interventions of the censor.

The role of the censor is also apparent in another area of the Olympic *Life in London*'s portrayal of social behaviour, this time concerning mendicity. The new Society for the Suppression of Mendicity in 1818, joining the Society for the Suppression of Vice's increasing activities against Richard Carlile in the early 1820s, is a reminder of how poverty and politics were significant topics about which a stage censor might wish to intervene.[602] The scene set in the 'Back Slums' of St Giles's shows the grumbling 'gammoning' of able-bodied but indolent beggars or 'Cadgers' (a term still in use today in British English). Moncrieff recalled in later years that there were two public houses for 'beggars' in Church Lane, St Giles's, one called the Robin Hood and another officially called the Rose and Crown but locally known as the Beggars' Opera.[603] The tone of the episode is immediately established by Gammoning Jack whose opening words simply declare contemptuously, 'Vork indeed vy its all my eye.'[604] Gammoning Jack tells of how he had been 'pull'd up the other day' and that the Poor Law officers 'vanted to gammon me as how that I should become a respectable man & be able to keep myself.' The rest of the group of 'Cadgers' all agree, 'What muffs.'[605] The hardened unrespectability of the group, the antithesis of the tendency towards working-class self-improvement, marks out the 'Back Slums' 'Cadgers' as idle. Jack tells of how he was made to 'dig gravel – carry heavy loads, [and] wheel a barrow' along with 'several other gammon of our order' who were also 'served as cruel.'[606] The group's response ('Horrid behaviour indeed!') is followed by his description of how he soon 'mizzled' (absconded) because he knew he could 'pick up 16 times as much in a day with this bit of a broom at a crossing out of the Toddlers.'[607] Evasion of the Poor Law authorities was both easy and commonplace before the 1834 Poor Law Amendment Act, especially in the urban centres.[608]

The socially beneficial role of such menial parish work was highlighted in contemporary drama by such things as the dramatization in H.M. Milner's Royal Coburg *The Hertfordshire Tragedy* (1824) which introduces two parish road menders ('it's none of your sham work, like pounding of oyster shells') who find a murder victim.[609] In the Olympic *Life in London*, Gammoning Jack is quite blunt about 'vork,' 'No, no it wouldn't do for me.' His sturdy refusal of parish relief ('Let them keep such charity as that to themselves') seems to have been the cue for John Larpent to excise much of this passage, presumably on account of its criticism of the Poor Law and Gammoning Jack's ability to evade its regulation. In real life, one of the minor characters in Moncrieff's version of *Tom and Jerry*, Little Jemmy, was thought to be based upon a man called Andrew who could be seen in the Blackfriars Bridge area until his death in 1826, 'propelling himself about the streets of London in a little truck, or box on wheels, assisted by the aid of two small crutches.'[610] Andrew wore a white apron to conceal the deformity of his legs 'which were curved, and had the appearance of thin planks, having no calves.' One of the woodcuts in James Catnach's broadside *The Death, Last Will, and Funeral of 'Black Billy': Also, the Tears of London for the Death of Tom and Jerry* (1823) showed him in the funeral entourage for Billy Waters, he and his cart placed on a chair and carried in the manner of a sedan chair. Despite these disabilities, he still worked, having 'a few quill pens stuck in his coat and apron' by which sort of trade he was known locally as The Penmaker.[611]

This Tom and Jerry scene of 'Back Slums' work-shy 'gammoning' 'Cadgers' was intended to be critical of the beggars, as is emphasized by the group's admiration of Jack's deviousness ('You was always a prime gammon Jack'). These were most definitely the *un*deserving poor. Leigh Hunt's comments, quoted above (about how 'the poor people who sell the play-bills deserve... encouragement... for they prefer industry to beggary') are a reminder that the industrious as well as the idle poor would have been a very visible presence in the Strand and Drury Lane areas around the theatres in the vicinity of the Olympic. A more complex depiction of urban poverty is set out at Allmax in the East where 'A motley group' is discovered, consisting of 'Sailors, Girls, Blacks Coal heavers, a fidler[*sic*] seated, Dusty Bob & African Sal, arm in arm.' This scene presents the other side of London's urban poor, the honourable, respectable (if rather romanticized) conviviality of the street. This *Tom and Jerry* play also portrayed the publican, Mace, the keeper of the Coach and Horses, alias Allmax in the East. One of his first encounters is with Dusty Bob and African Sall (also sometimes known as Black Sall or Sarah).[612] The emphasis in the scene is on the good-humoured nature of this tavern conviviality but it also takes the opportunity to stress the relaxed inter-racial nature of the group by showing racism and sexual stereotyping being identified, confronted and then dissipated.

This is portrayed by having Mace, the publican (always an equivocal profession between host and hardman), invite African Sall to a drink with the implication – at least as understood by Dusty Bob – that she is a whore. Dusty Bob immediately intervenes in her defence:

Mace: Vell vot will you like to take my black diamond. (*to Sal*)
Bob: I say my covey, you are getting rude, none of your slum, she pays
   her vay – and does the best to yarn an honest penny; does any of
   your customers do more I axes you? Therefore I begs as how, you vill
   not take any more liberties without me in future, for if you do Mr
   Wastebutt (*doubles his fist*) I vill give you such a conker, as will spoil
   your sneezing for a month – that vat I vill, so remember no more
   chaffing. (*they all laugh*)

Dusty Bob's retort to Mace, 'I say my covey,' runs components of Cockney dialect into each other: a 'cove' was the master of a shop or house but a 'covey' was a collective term for a group of whores, so the address equivocates between respect and disrespect. When he says 'none of your slum,' he means he will not accept any fooling, but the structural meaning is to make a contrast with the St Giles beggars.[613] African Sall, Dusty Bob says, 'pays her vay' and does her best to 'yarn [an elision of "earn"] an honest penny.' The Cockney argot is thick and fast: a 'Waste-butt' is a publican (a barrel filled with the alcoholic waste of the tavern), the 'conker' is the nose (i.e. a sore nose). Although some of the terms are not described in Pierce Egan's virtually contemporary edition of Grose's *Dictionary of the Vulgar Tongue*, the sense is clear enough that Mace's immediate reaction is to back off and apologize: 'Well Mr Bob, you needn't have been so much on the high toby – I didn't mean to set your monkey up I there axes your pardon.'[614] Mace's capitulation and apology is an effective and signal piece of racial and social integration, the restoration of a convivial civilized society of industry and pleasure which is absent not only in the antics of Tom, Jerry and Logic but also in the cynical negativity of the St Giles's 'Cadgers.'
   Fortified by 'a pot of heavy wet' (beer) and 'a twopenny Buster & a slice of Bees wax' (bread and cheese), the entry of the upper-class trio reinforces the harmony when Tom (despite not having 'a mag') orders drinks all round ('Group: Regular swells these'). Jerry's comment that 'every cove that puts in his appearance, seems quite welcome, and colour & country no obstacle' is quite significant.[615] African Sall would have been acted by a blacked-up white man ('Mr Sanders' in the original Adelphi production) but, deep in the middle of London, the stage afforded the means of portraying mixed racial and class groups with very little caricature. Providing a definitive indication of

working-class attitudes in central London, James Catnach's Seven Dials printed broadside *The New Marriage Act Displayed in Cuts and Verse* (1822) lampooned a black man ('I who am black as a sloe on a bush') marrying Miss Shrivelskin, an elderly white spinster: the grounds of this satire are ageist rather than racist. The African Sall and Dusty Bob roles were a huge expansion on their original appearance in Egan's *Life in London* where, out of a book of some 375 pages, the entire scene in AllMax in the East covers just eight pages.[616] Egan recorded many constituents of London's cosmopolitan population who mixed together freely in a jumbled harmony of class, race and gender, including 'Lascars, blacks, jack tars, coalheavers, dustmen, women of colour, old and young... all *jigging* [dancing] together, provided the *teazer* of the *catgut* [the fiddler/violinist] was not *bilked* [cheated] of his *duce* [two pence].'[617] In another Olympic one-act prelude or afterpiece *The Death of Don Giovanni; or, the funeral of the Hero's*, a mixture of *Giovanni in London* and *Tom and Jerry*, the marriage of Dusty Bob and African Sall (or Sarah) is celebrated ('Oh! Massa Bob! I knows not vat to say') 'Cause color's an't no odds.'[618]

Charles Isaac Mungo Dibdin's original songs written for the November 1821 Olympic production had been dropped by the time of the 1822 printed version, but the Larpent copy neatly summarizes Tom and Jerry's revolutionary immorality:

> We three jolly boys be
> Rovers that range the Streets for a spree
> Which costs us our money and liberty
> But no matter as long as we've money.[619]

A 'spree' is 'A frolic. Fun. A drinking bout' in Pierce Egan and in the Tom and Jerry plays: this usually means a brawl involving the city watchmen or 'Charleys.'[620] The idea of ranging the streets seeking trouble and openly accepting the consequences of being caught, imprisoned and fined signals the collapse of an entire system of social deference, the breaching of accepted codes of conduct and blatant disregard for the law or its consequences.

In some ways, the 'sprees' narrate a battle between the upper and lower classes, a series of physical brawls played out on the midnight streets of London. Although a series of prints such as an anonymous set picturing the escapades of Tom and Jerry's contemporaries, Dashall and Lubin, has a moralizing intention, the caricatures themselves show well-dressed beaus punching watchmen and arrogantly appearing in front of a magistrate ('His worship's lecture is extremely trite') ahead of lower-class criminals immobilized by handcuffs. Then, when they are released without charge, 'Scot free, they *do* the *Jarvis* for a *spree*,' running off without paying the 'jarvey,' or coachman. Indeed, the belligerence of these individuals is quite specific. One scene portrays them in Offley's Cyder Cellars directly adjacent to the Adelphi Theatre, Strand, a premises run by an individual named Porson and known to be frequented by the Covent Garden actor Edmund Kean.[621] The text which accompanied the prints is quite clear (as is the etching itself) in showing a drinking den frequented by upper-class 'politicians, bucks, and bravoes' who 'Sublimed with liquid fury, thence they sally, / Choosing a most pacific term, to mark / The blows and bloodshed (not quite critically,) / Of midnight rows: *videlicit*, 'a lark.' Drunk with 'liquid fury,' Dashall and Lubin will set out from Offley's to 'floor' Charleys in a rampage of noctural aristocratic violence. By contrast, the next print depicts a lower-class gin shop, where the ubiquitous figures of Dusty Bob, African Sall and their black baby sit drinking, and where a watchman (the eventual target of the brawling 'lark'), lantern in hand, calls in to collect his own nip of gin to keep out the cold.[622] Although Dashall and Lubin drink in both places, it is only the picture of Offley's which announces this as their point of departure, 'fresh and bold' for a night of 'blows and bloodshed,' a carefully judged raid on the lower classes ending 'not quite critically.' The representation of such narratives appears to have reached the playhouses quite rapidly since Moncrieff's *Lubin Log's Journey to London; or, York You are not Wanted* (1820) played at the Royal Coburg as early as July 1820.

The contemporary problem inherent in Dibdin's song was that it was not an isolated example, nor was it an extreme indicator of the possible modes of behaviour represented within the play. However, the four lines quoted above neatly encapsulate the whole range of possible attitudes the Tom and Jerry plays narrate. The oscillation between hedonism and restraint is, of course, quite extensive in the literature of the time, but it is particularly interesting that its debate is continued as a thematic paradox written within a number of texts of the period. For example, Pierce Egan's *Life and Extraordinary Adventures of Samuel Denmore Hayward* (1822) was suffixed with 'An Address to the Rising Generation On the Imminent Danger to be dreaded from what is termed, being "On the Town!",' but, being written by Egan himself, it needed to counteract his macabre journalistic reporting of Hayward's execution at Newgate where Egan classifies the criminal as 'our hero' and reports the convicted man's scaffold sympathies for a fellow female capital prisoner.[623]

Dibdin's *Life in London; or, The Larks of Logic, Tom, and Jerry* (the title finally settled upon for the 1822 printing), which is very far from being a unique text within this phase of London drama, fully denotes the loss of the social subject, the citizens bound by honour, responsibility and tradition into harmonizing their individuality with society in an economy of exchange comprising an accommodation of personal restraint for the gain of civil freedom. The routes leading towards this state of affairs are as intricate and as circumscribed by politics, gender and class as might be expected under the circumstances, but the role of drama as the agent or symptom of social change does not lie exclusively within the author's function. Charles Isaac Mungo Dibdin, like William Thomas Moncrieff, both of them hardly household names even amongst modern literary scholars, are writers constituted by their texts rather than being their text's originators. Behind all of them, to some extent, was Pierce Egan's original *Life in London* (1820), a remarkable pictorial novella accompanied by its fashionably coloured etchings by Cruikshank. They exemplify a confident, often radicalized, contemporary print culture strongly associated with the metropolis. The plays spun off from Egan's *Life in London* are as close as it comes to being fully social texts, created within a definable metropolitan community of professional writers.

The collapse in deference and rise in delinquency manifested in the Tom and Jerry plays is signalled by subtle sharpenings in the dialogue of Dibdin's version as it settled itself into theatrical performance. In the original copy sent to Larpent in November 1821, at one point Jerry says: 'Oh, there's a Row! I must be in that – this is Life in London, Oh! its glorious fun – ' By the time of the 1822 printed edition, this has become 'Oh, there's a row! I must be in that, because it's Life in London.' The slight alteration in the printed version embodies Jerry far more consciously into his own actions, making his participation celebratory and affirmative and losing a degree of detachment. As it happens, the scene takes place in the box lobby (or 'the Fruit-Room' in the first printed edition) of one of London's theatres, and concerns a contrived scuffle in a public place, ensuring that the drama doubly validates the actions of those involved by theatricalizing itself.[624]

As Tom and Jerry evolved, working through the hands of many authors, it became apparent that censorship was becoming less and less effective. Playhouses and censors were struggling to cope with regularity requirements. When the Olympic's version was altered quite substantially, as it was between when the manuscript was sent to Larpent in early November 1821 and the printed editions of 1822, the Olympic was obliged to send their new-copy text to Larpent (together with another fee). The theatre had gone ahead with printing the retitled *Life in London; or, The Larks of Logic, Tom, and Jerry* (1822) actually before submitting it to Larpent. This was because the Olympic appreciated that the Examiner of Plays could only censor the stage dialogue and not the publication. Larpent's control was over the boards, not over the pressmen. In the event, Larpent's copy for licensing marks no excisions. There were two factors which ensured that such a radicalized, socially disruptive array of values could be openly portrayed on stage. The first is that John Larpent was old and less effective in his post. The days when he sat with his wife and young family to read aloud, censor or prohibit plays were gone. His wife, Anna Margaretta, seems to have been little involved in censorship after the mid-1790s.[625] The second reason is that the sorts of particularized culling of politically or morally sensitive words and passages was less effective at regulating larger cultural movements whose disaffections were less easy to pinpoint. Although the Examiner could, and did, use his powers of complete suppression, such tactics were only used intermittently. Suppression was meant to act as a deterrent as much as an instrument of intervention. Censorship worked well at striking out the precise language or letter of disruptive or immoral sentiments, but far less well when attempting to resist a broad change in the social temperament.

There were relatively few excisions demanded of Dibdin for his (as initially titled) *Life in London a Burletta* manuscript but some of them achieved the reverse of what Larpent probably intended. As is common in some of the other early Tom and Jerry plays, particularly those performed outside of the Royal theatres, a certain amount of moral misgiving is voiced by some of the characters about the 'sprees' of Tom and Jerry. In Dibdin's *Life in London* manuscript (the whole episode was pushed out of the version which evolved for the printed edition), there comes a point where Bob Logic tires of their games and gets rebuked by Tom.[626] Amazingly, Larpent excised Logic's reluctance to join in the sport and also cut out his noticeably personified soliloquized moralizing, but he left untouched Tom's bravado and hedonism:

Tom: Zounds if you are Sentimental, I will leave you, for between your
    Sermons and Jerry's Scrapes I'm boxed out of my life – as for your
    System & Science my Dear Fellow Conscience does not belong to our
    Order & until you get clear of that you'll never become a Corinthian
    Capital. (*Exit*)

Logic: Egad I am ruin'd myself and am determined to save Jerry, Tom is past hope; your genteel Devil is the most dangerous Vice, Ruin dress thyself in Eloquence & Plausibility and thou art soon the Fancy – while poor Virtue put out of Countenance, shrinks into a Corner dejected and disregarded.

Despite the obvious punning on Corinthian orders of architecture, Dibdin's wit is highly effective. 'Conscience does not belong to our Order' is virtually a satiric epitaph on the aristocracy and clergy of the age, from the Prince Regent, through Lord Byron, down to the sodomistic Reverend John Church. Presumably Larpent's eye fastened on the phrase about 'your genteel Devil,' and then he made the assumption (not unreasonably) that *Life in London* was critical of upper-class beaus such as Corinthian Tom. Without having noticed that the celebratory mode of their actions was far more subversive than the manner of their speech, Larpent suppressed one of the few morally improving didactic passages in the play.

The politics of this kind of suppression are extraordinarily complex in their contemporary context. When the Olympic had submitted another piece in late October 1821, *The House that Jack built Or Harlequin Tattered & Torn*, apparently just a few weeks before Dibdin's *Life in London*, it found that the Lord Chamberlain required at least one substantial deletion of a passage portraying a drunken cleric, Dr Ocasoozenem. The major modifications which Dibdin obviously made between his *Life in London* manuscript for the Lord Chamberlain and the printed version as eventually published may have been partially motivated by the Olympic management's letter to Larpent expressing 'great regret ... that you consider some of the matter in opening of "The House that Jack Built" objectionable ... I feel a little mortified at your having occasion to point out the necessity of an alteration.'[627] Despite sending the manuscript to Larpent in October 1821, the Olympic delayed its production until the Christmas of that year, presumably modifying it during the interval. This letter of 22 October 1821 went on to also 'remark that the piece of "Life in London" as acted at this theatre is wholly free from immorality.' In the light of their rebuff with *The House that Jack built*, it seems likely that Dibdin was persuaded (or forced) to carry out the further modifications to the Olympic's *Life in London*, which are apparent from the differences between the Larpent manuscript and the printed edition. However, the possibility of some even more complicated piece of evasion may be indicated by the fact that the letter of 22 October predates the 8 November submission of Dibdin's *Life in London* manuscript sent for the Lord Chamberlain's approval.[628] This to and fro of censorship, rebuttal and accommodation makes interpretation difficult.

Larpent's censorship of Dibdin probably comes about because of his misrecognition of *Life in London*'s relationship to conventional morality. The Examiner of Plays, whose duties meant he had to read new plays virtually weekly as part of his job, may himself have been torn between trying to prohibit on-stage accusations of moral disaffection amongst the 'genteel,' and a more politicized desire to remove the role of moral judgement from the likes of characters such as Bob Logic.[629] He did little to challenge the Tom and Jerry plays because they represented a phenomenon of social change which he probably did not understand. The alterations made between Dibdin's initial manuscript of *Life in London* and its 1822 printed edition (presumably a fairly accurate reflection of the piece as finally acted) reflect some of the piece's vascillation between mounting a moral or philosophical commentary and its recognition of the redundancy of these efforts as antithetical to the play's mood.

When Jerry and Bob Logic enter the theatre drunk, they attempt a philosophical exchange about their drinking:

Jerry: Why, – (*hiccup*) – Life in London's a glorious thing: we've nothing like this in the country. – How (*to Tom*) you pushed the glass about.

In the Larpent manuscript, as originally conceived, Logic then makes some comments about the 'Spirit of the Age:'

Logic: I suppose not.
Jerry: You suppose?
Logic: Why not, this is the Age of supposes, if's, buts and perhaps's.
Jerry: Perhaps you are drunk.
Logic: I suppose you are.
Jerry: But if, that shouldn't be the case?
Logic: I resign all knowledge of Casuistry. Jerry my Boy, a drunken man is...[630]

The refusal to enter into a serious discussion and to avoid the responsibility of sentient thought is a characteristic of Tom and Jerry. The 'Age of supposes' is also a neat enough tag to the era although not one to be taken too seriously, except that Dibdin's dialogue does indeed reflect some of the period's irreligious, amoral scepticism, attitudes which were already well embedded in various strands of popular culture.

Richard Carlile's contemporary, elegantly chosen riposte (although it was not original) at the Society for the Suppression of Vice's prosecution of his publishing Tom Paine's deistical *Rights of Man* Part III was that 'All the Books of Moses / Are nothing but supposes.'[631] This exchange between Jerry and Logic, for all of its expression of languor and ennui verging on nihilism, was dropped from the printed edition. The refining of *Life in London* by removing elements of introspection and of doubt was, of course, not something imposed by Larpent but rather by Dibdin reacting to how the play was running in real time as well as, perhaps to a lesser extent, by his reaction to other adaptations of Egan's Tom and Jerry.

This strengthening emphasis on the insubstantiality of Tom, Jerry and Logic was something engineered directly into the play to hide some of the economic mechanisms which allow them to function as three bachelors-about-town. This matter was not lost on some of the more working-class London audiences. Pretty much at the forefront of the portrayals of *Life in London* are the comfortable circumstances of the British gentry. Although an exact identification of the prototypes of the characters was only to be expected given their notoriety, with Isaac Robert Cruikshank claiming that Tom was modelled on himself, Jerry on his brother George, and Bob Logic on Pierce Egan, this should not detract from either Pierce Egan's or, later, Moncrieff's ability to create topicalized characters relevant to social conditions in contemporary London.[632] Unlike the often financially turbulent circumstances of the real-life character attributions, Egan's minor gentry are pretty well funded. Although Jerry Hawthorne is temporarily stumped for cash, it is only because his father is still alive and living at Hawthorne Hall. Similarly, Tom has his own London townhouse and Bob Logic his Oxonian education. However slenderly Dibdin and Egan sketched in the economic foundations of their lifestyle, the words of the song quoted at the beginning of the chapter ('no matter as long as we've money') show how firmly established they remain.

One of the best topical cameos on the financial circumstances of the gentry in Dibdin's *Life in London* comes with the entry of Primefit, the tailor, and the way the scene was cut, patched and abridged provides a fascinating insight into the dramatist's perspective on how the upper classes financed their lifestyle. The whole point about Primefit is that he has laid his business success amongst the beaus exactly by not receiving payment but, rather, extending credit ever further. Dibdin wrote and then rewrote the scene from the manuscript into the first and second printed editions, broadly cutting it by half and toning down the implications of the financial over-borrowing. Primefit's novel business strategy is to increase his number of orders through credit arrangements which entail no repayment. Primefit explains that he never needs bailiffs ('John Doe') because as his 'Orders multiplied,' his credit with the 'Drapers' or wholesalers increased proportionately:

> as the Drapers became acquainted with my plan; and Peter Primefit, who began the world with no Credit & half a pattern Card, can now call, to measure a Gentleman, in his own Carriage – and – to cut a long story short – never cut a Customer – Good morning – Gentlemen (*calling as he goes off*) Mr Primefit's Carriage! (*Exit Primefit*)[633]

By the first printed edition, Primefit (who by then calls himself a 'Decorator' of bodies) emphasizes how insulted he is that he is thought to be asking for payment: 'Bill! Heavens, Sir! Do you imagine Peter Primefit brings in his bill... like a butcher's ticket stuck with a skewer upon a leg of mutton. Oh, dear, never!... there's something so vulgar in ready money price, that no man of spirit could put with it.'[634] For the second edition, it was contracted to little more than one sentence, 'Peter Primefit, who began the world with no credit, and half a pattern card, can now call to measure a gentleman in his own carriage.'[635]

Although one hardly expects stringent economic analysis in a burletta, the gentry's lack of financial means would have evoked working-class disapproval because, as will be seen, lower-class attitudes were far more socially conservative (and financially prudent) than those of their superiors. There also seems to be a stratification of class relationships even amongst the audiences of the minor theatres as the more respectable playhouses, such as the Adelphi and Olympic, distanced themselves from the uptake of Tom and Jerry in the lesser theatres, circuses and even cheaper mediums of song and broadside. In other words, there was a certain amount of class-differentiated appropriation going on with respect to Tom and Jerry during its extraordinary embodiment into the plebeian public sphere. When the Olympic had been offered for sale in 1820, it was advertised as having a seating capacity of 1320 persons.[636] With the long runs of both *Giovanni in London* and the *Tom and Jerry* plays, London was witnessing the mass cultural phenomenon of dramas representing the effective integration of a cosmopolitan London population. It is a significant reminder that positive images of Cockney characters and racial harmony were familiar aspects of the London stage. Along with the extraordinary melee of anti-flash, anti-credit, anti-begging, pro-hunting, pro-servant, pro-delinquency, hard-drinking nuances in these plebeian dramas, racial equality must also be accommodated as a working cultural practice.

7
Moncrieff's *Tom and Jerry* and its Spin-Offs

By the time Moncrieff wrote his *Tom and Jerry* for the Adelphi in the late autumn of 1821, there was already a strong metropolitan cultural tradition of dramatic representations derived from Pierce Egan's original *Life in London*. This chapter, like Chapter 6, shows how dramas in London developed within a separate public sphere in an intertextuality gaining its own independence within the burletta form. It is perhaps worth reiterating at this point the separateness of the public sphere discussed. Occasionally, dramas masquerading as if from the regular, legitimate, canonical repertoire were advertised but, in practice, they were always distanced from the wrath of the patentees. In 1818 the Royalty Theatre advertised 'a Burletta founded on the Tragedy of Hamlet,' and later engaged Edmund Kean in 1824 in a 'Grand Tragic Melo-Drame' version of the same play.[637] At best, any Royalty *Hamlet* would have been more than usually heavily cut but, of course, it would also have been performed interspersed with imported songs and accompanied by continuous music of the type Leman Thomas Rede found so irksome. It is quite possible that further variations abounded. An 1823 Surrey 'grand Melo-Drame, founded on ... Hamlet' was curiously advertised as 108 'rounds' of speech which, although fully cast, implied that its performance was presented as an exhibition or feat of memory.[638] To many managers, bastardizing Shakespeare can hardly have seemed worth the risk. By contrast, *Tom and Jerry*'s potential was quickly appreciated by London's equestrian playhouses but it was also readily adaptable to the less flexible spaces such as the Adelphi or Olympic. Its suitability for carrying allusions to horse racing was appropriate to Moncrieff's talents because as early as 1818 he had introduced the Ascot races into *The Monk's Cowl* and *The Dandy Family* written for Astley's.[639] Remarkably, Moncrieff's luck with Larpent over *Giovanni in London* continued with his *Tom and Jerry*. The Davis Amphitheatre production of *Tom and Jerry; or, Life in London* had not been censored because the venue did not come under the Lord Chamberlain's jurisdiction, whereas the Olympic's version may have been licensed because Larpent may have detected something of the degree of moral censure present in the play.

As far as the Moncrieff *Tom and Jerry* is concerned, however, it appears to have passed through Larpent's hands quite mysteriously with very few excisions. Whatever the circumstances of Larpent's licensing of the Adelphi *Tom and Jerry*, it was a moment of acute embarrassment for the authorities. There was an almost immediate public disapproval of the Adelphi hit. Thirty years later Moncrieff recollected that the Adelphi was targeted by repressive religious groups and that 'the whole of the stock of the Religious Tract Society' was distributed by them at the doors of the theatre.[640] Whether it was old age, or being lulled into a false sense of security by the modest successes of the Davis and Olympic *Tom and Jerry* plays, Larpent failed to spot the controversy Moncrieff's version would generate. It was licensed on 23 November 1821 for production three days later.

Apart from putting his pen through a few 'Damn me's,' the only passage Larpent expunged from the *Tom and Jerry* licensing manuscript was one showing a drunken cleric at a Hawthorne Hall drinking session:

(*Parson slips under the Table Drunk*)
Hey theres one Dead Man – Who is it?
The Parish Clerk – Ah we always have to
Carry him to Bed first – take him off –[641]

However, within three weeks of its licensing, the Lord Chamberlain, the Duke of Montrose, had received a complaint (which Montrose was obliged to pursue) from a Croydon man who, although he had not seen the production personally, feared the effect *Tom and Jerry* would have on his 'young family.' Intriguingly, Montrose also received a memorandum from someone within the Government, possibly within the Lord Chamberlain's staff. This internal complaint expressed amazement that 'the Lord Chamberlain gives his sanction to this obnoxious performance.' The suspicion that the aging Larpent had an enemy lurking within the Lord Chamberlain's office is aroused by the author of the memorandum, reminding Montrose that, technically, the 'poisonous and Designing' *Tom and Jerry* was 'licensed by your grace,' that is, ultimately sanctioned by the Lord Chamberlain himself as head of the department.[642] By 1821, Larpent had already been in office as Lord Chamberlain's Examiner of Plays for 43 years. His assistant, Thomas Baucott Mash, had similarly held office for 43 years by the time he was answering questions from the panel of the 1832 Select Committee on Dramatic Literature.[643]

Much of Moncrieff's success lay in capturing the attention of theatregoers fascinated by Egan's spotlight on a world they knew little about, but, to the real inhabitants of London's underworld, there was no need for further representation. Indeed, in a confusion of reality and illusion, there is some probability that Moncrieff's original actor for Billy Waters was Billy Waters himself, a familiar busker outside the Adelphi Theatre and whose image was captured in prints by contemporaries.[644] Moncrieff was certainly aware of the exact symmetrical inversions of class and race implicit in the double punning between the respective West and East End locations of Almacks and its plebeian equivalent: 'Almack's in the East; where I'll match Dusty Bob's jig with black Sal, against all the waltzing and quadrilling of the diamond squad of Almack's in the West.'[645] Moncrieff's depiction, as with Egan's before him, of the two drinking establishments ('... as you have your *"Highflyers"* at Almacks, at the West End, we have also some *"choice creatures"* at our All Max in the East') was coincident with the plebeian perspective of *The Rambler's Magazine*, which made quite explicit the inequable contrast between the treatment of Almacks and that of its lower-class equivalents: 'whilst the "Vice Society", and the "informers", are sticking their noses in to every public-house ... the Hells, supported by nobility, under the very walls of the royal palace, are protected, and kept open even on the Sabbath day – no one daring to interfere with them!'[646] Significantly, *The Rambler's* also noted that 'a clergyman is master of the ceremonies.'[647] *The Rambler's* headed this piece 'London Hells Exposed' and, of course, in the rapid structure of high and low life, the day and night scenes which comprise the narrative of Egan's *Life in London*, the idea of exposure and revelation highlighted the contrast between upper- and lower-class social mores.

The image of the gambling 'Hell' is pervasive. It is noticeable that the groundswell of a working-class anti-gambling sentiment did not emanate from the likes of the Society for the Suppression of Vice or Society for the Suppression of Mendicity but was deeply ingrained into lower-class culture and found expression in contemporary theatricalized culture. Working-class attitudes themselves can be gauged by the letterpress and woodcut printings of James Catnach, the Monmouth Court, Seven Dials, printer. His crude woodcut of *A Full and Particular Account of Mr. John Jobling . . . He Frequented a noted Gambling-House* [and] *in a fit of madness, having lost every Farthing he had in the word*[sic] *. . . went home and killed his Wife and Child* (1832) depicts a gambling 'Hell' with 'rouge-et-noir' table, three flying satans and two gamblers in the middle of their transformation into devils. Although including a formulaic 'Prisoner's sad Lament,' Catnach's print draws on the tradition of a 'progress' rather than overtly moralizing or sermonizing its message. Indeed, the greatest contemporary exposé of gambling 'Hells' actually post-dates their appearance in Egan's *Life in London* or the Tom and Jerry plays.

The most notorious contemporary incident evoking the dangers of gambling was the murder in October 1823 of William Weare, a gambler and ex-tavern waiter, by John Thurtell, a gambler, amateur pugilist and keeper of a tavern in Long-acre, which had quickly acquired a reputation as a 'free-and-easy' singing venue in its Covent Garden locality. There was enormous public interest surrounding Thurtell's conviction and execution for the murder of Weare because, along with the publicity given to the case, full accounts emerged of the goings-on in the gambling 'Hells' recently described by Egan and staged in *Tom and Jerry*. The connection between theatricality and this highly topical murder is apparent from the case's strong links with various macabre manifestations of theatricality. Thurtell himself was said to have been once 'greatly attached to theatricals, and prided himself in no small degree upon his imitations of Kean, the actor.'[648] After the public spectacle of his execution at Hertford (at which a nearby thatched roof barn – belonging to the prison governor – was commandeered by an audience of onlookers before collapsing, minutes before the hanging), Thurtell's body was removed under court order, and then displayed and dissected in the anatomy theatre of London's St Bartholomew's Hospital.[649] 'Multitudes of persons assembled, and . . . an almost indescribable admission of the public took place, which continued for three or four days' until the 'visitors of each succeeding day were witnesses of the gradual dilapidation, if not of the decay, of the body. On one day a finger, on another an eye, was missing . . .'[650] What commentators particularly picked up on was the association of this incident with the culture of 'flash' notoriety based upon gambling and boxing: 'The murder of Weare has doubtlessly resulted from . . . that school of *fraud* and *flash*, to which not only the victim but this murderers also were attached. [They] . . . were all *sporting blades*, ultra *flash men*, and gamblers.'[651] The anonymous author of *The Fatal Effects of Gambling . . . to which is added, The Gambler's Scourge; a Complete Exposé of the Whole System of Gambling in the Metropolis* (1824) particularly emphasized the promiscuities of class encouraged by the gambling houses, where 'persons of the very highest rank in the state...from the top of nobility down to the very lowest of the low, the scum and outcasts of society' 'all commingled.'[652] The title's reference to gambling 'in the Metropolis' is itself an indicator of how the comfortable structures of 'London' had descended into being an amorphous 'metropolis,' without distinction of person or deference to rank. The particular Pall Mall gaming house *The Rambler's* identified earlier as conducted by a 'clergyman' was one of the most notorious 'Hells' whose dealings, two years later, were fully detailed in *The Gambler's Scourge*.[653] Ownership of the St James's establishments were generally, indiscriminately, ascribed to French or Greeks, but there were also other 'Sub-Hells' in the vicinity of Piccadilly alleged to be owned by 'Plebeian Proprietors' previously employed as such things as groom-porters, fishmongers' assistants and Thames lightermen.[654] In short, Weare's enthusiasm for 'theatricals, and...imitations of Kean,' together with the 'Exposé' of *The Gambler's Scourge*, is indicative of a Cockney class thoroughly linked to dramatics yet fluidly moving between upper and lower social levels amidst an increasingly heterogeneous metropolis.

One of the manifestations of these concerns, about the kinds of social breakdown involved when class divisions are traversed through the agency of gambling, is the incorporation of these anxieties into a song by Thomas Hudson, Jacob Beuler's singer contemporary at the actors' tavern, The OP in Russell Court, Drury Lane.[655] In his song 'Gentility!,' Hudson marked out a warning to working-class people not to ape the gentry in their gambling dens:

> I wanted to see all the great folks ifeggs,[*sic*]
> So I went to a house where the Gents and Nobility,
> Mix'd themselves up with thieves call'd black-legs,
> And lost their estates to support their gentility:
> And when by bad luck one got into a mess,
> By poverty struck like, bow'd with humility,
> I found that to look on a friend in distress,
> Was against all the rules of real genteel Gentility.[656]

As Hudson expressed it, the imitation of 'real genteel Gentility' would entail the loss of the roots and community which would otherwise ensure personal survival during times of hardship. But the likes of Almacks were real enough and Egan's *Life in London* did much to fascinate by its relevations about these previously obscure places. Renton

Nicholson remembered one early 1830s' 'elegant gambling house' in St James's Street where Theodore Hook, the 'improvisatore' and dramatist, made up 'flash' songs about his gambling friends assembled there.[657] Plays about the melodramatic downfall of the gambling working class were beginning to find their way onto the stage but not without official opposition.

Mystifyingly, as with so much of the censorship of drama at this time, the presentation of positive anti-gambling plays could be greeted with suppression while Almacks in *Tom and Jerry* went uncensored. The Thurtell case had become so notorious that the Surrey Theatre's *The Gamblers* was 'suppressed by Order of the Court of King's Bench' in November 1823 because of its being too closely based on those events (although it was relicensed in early January 1824).[658] H.M. Milner's *The Hertfordshire Tragedy* (1824) based upon the same crime (which attempted to spoil The Surrey's audience by opening at The Royal Coburg on the same night *The Gamblers* was relicensed at the Surrey) ended on an even more moralistic note with Freeman (the Thurtell character) declaiming in court before sentencing that 'had I never entered ... a Gaming House, I had not stood here this day.'[659] Nearly 10 years later, at the Parliamentary *Select Committee on Dramatic Literature* (1832), the legal foundations of the attempts to suppress the Coburg's *Hertfordshire Tragedy* were still being discussed.[660] The cases are interesting because they show that opposition to gambling was not a patrician imposition foisted onto working-class people by the Society for the Suppression of Vice (or its Mendicity equivalent) but, rather, plebeian and popular theatres had to struggle vigorously, and risk legal penalty, in mounting dramas voicing concern about the influence of aristocratic gambling haunts on lower-class morals.

Another Surrey production *The Treadmill; or, Tom and Jerry at Brixton*, a later incarnation of the Tom and Jerry story, indicates a more circumspect anxiety about imitating 'Corinthian' behaviour of sprees and brawls but one evidently grounded in these material fears of gambling and riotous behaviour.[661] To make the point explicit, Lowndes's edition of *The Treadmill* carried a coloured frontispiece showing, at the top, a brawl ('Life in a Slap-bang Crib. – or, how to *platter* flash') and, at the bottom, prisoners stripped to the waist tramping the newly opened Brixton gaol treadmill ('Life in a Mill'). The new reality was that the consequences of a street fight might end in the punishing hard labour of the treadmill. The treadmill at Brixton House of Correction, newly built following a decision in 1818 to build two new prisons, came into service in 1821. Prisoners spent, depending on the regime, 15 minutes treading the mill with 15 minutes for rest or sometimes 10 minutes on and 5 off. They frequently became ill and exhausted. At Brixton, the treadmill was set so that the labour of treading had to overcome the resistance of a windsail set into the roof of the building.

Grimly humorous writers, such as the author of *The Treadmill*, eagerly compounded 'milling' – the 'flash' term for fighting – with the carefully punned literary generic description of the piece as a 'Serio, Comic, Operatic, Milldramatic[*sic*], Farcical Moral Burletta.' The Surrey's latest *Tom and Jerry* truly was 'Serio,' 'Moral' and 'Milldramatic.' To the entrepreneurs of the unrespectable private theatres, the Brixton treadmill sent through a shudder of fear, 'O word of fear, – Unpleasing to a *Gamester*'s ear!' as a motto on a contemporary Tom and Jerry woodcut broadsheet by the Seven Dials printer James Catnach put it.[662] *The Rambler's Magazine* in early 1823 commented on the manager of a Camden Town private theatre ('these nurseries for pick-pockets – these schools for future bullies and prostitutes') whose 'next appearance at a private performance will probably be at Brixton.'[663] A couple of months earlier, the Olympic Theatre had staged *Two More Slaves; or, The Escape from Brixton* (1822) originally subtitled <*The Mill of*> ... *Brixton* which, in turn was a 'Burlesque Parody' of Thomas Morton's Drury Lane hit *The Two Galley Slaves* (1822). One scene from *Two More Slaves* was set in Brixton Mill. This featured amateur actor-managers who have embezzled money from a Camden Town private theatre apparently identical to the one alluded to in *The Rambler's Magazine*:

> I am not Actor Sir; only an Amateur
> Last week at Camden Town to pass away
> Our winter's night, we tried a private play,
> Took money at the Door, which was a rarity,
> But pocketed it ourselves, & called it charity.
> "The Wheel of Fortune" was the play we fix'd on,
> But that you see is chang'd to Wheel of Brixton

This reply to the Brixton treadmill's gaoler is followed by the introduction of another prison inmate who had kept 'A fashionable place called Pandemonium / Or vulgarly called Hell.' In the popular mind, fear of the hard labour of the Brixton treadmill ('Gaoler: Come boys to work, you've rested quite enough') was enough to temporarily clear the streets.[664] Even the black man Billy Waters, an ever popular and positive figure in Moncrieff's *Tom and Jerry* (1822), gives a graphic indication of the physical perils of the treadmill when he is asked by another beggar,

'Does any gemman understand these here Tread Mills, that have got such a footing? Billy: Oh, curse a de tread mill, me no like a de "here we go up, up, up," and "down, you go down, down, down, down," – an if you no work, a great lump of wood come and knock you down so – '[665] The Surrey's *The Treadmill; or, Tom and Jerry at Brixton* actually only has a kind of 'guest appearance' of Tom, Jerry and Logic although the familiar plot formula of Old Pringle, his son, Jack, and their servant Peter Pumpkinhead, visiting London from Hog's Norton Hall continues the emphasis on rural ignorance and urban chicanery, the 'Johnny Newcome' or 'Johnny Raw' of contemporary 'flash.' Introduced to a London 'Gambling Room' the rustics are, predictably, allowed to win the first games at *Rouge et Noir*, little realizing in their bravado ('let the Hog's Norton folks alone to be up to these Cockneys') that they are being tricked into over-confidence ('Peter [*impatiently*]: Laud, laud, if I had my poor three an sixpence what mort[*sic*] of money I might make. I always beats Moggy at three halfpenny tricket [*sic*]') (p. 23). The gaoling of Tom, Jerry and Logic, plus all three country men tempted into the vice of gambling, is given further moral commentary by Cerebus the turnkey's remarks: '(*unlocking the gate*) Bring 'em along, a parcel of impudent wagabonds, what a horrid thing it is to think peoples of heddication should be made turnspits on, and all through their own hignorance' (p. 26). It is also left to the gaoler Cerebus to make what is perhaps the most pointed moral commentary in the play: 'When gemmen mixes along with pickpockets and gamblers, they must be taken for what they seem, and not what they his[*sic*]' (p. 27). The gambling houses were, in many ways, symptomatic of the tendencies towards political attitudes of social levelling that were well underway in the approach to the 1832 Reform Bill. Reverting to traditional attitudes of deference which Tom and Jerry had already done so much to symbolically destabilize, Cerebus apologizes for not recognizing gentlemen 'for what they his[*sic*].' Cerebus, but not *The Treadmill; or, Tom and Jerry at Brixton*, fails to recognize that behaviour is the construction of being. Some two years before either Thurtell's trial or *The Fatal Effects of Gambling* ... [and] *Gambler's Scourge* (1824), the latter's moral point that the gambling houses dangerously mixed the classes had already found a fully staged London representation.

In the deeply moralistic Surrey *Treadmill*, the physical consequences of the new punishment were stressed. Cerebus makes the new prisoners strip down ready to tread the boards: 'Come, gemmen, don't be timbersome; the hexercise[*sic*] of the mill will soon set you all to rights. Come, off with your upper ones, and down with your toppers' (p. 27). The kinds of deep conservatism manifested in *The Treadmill* were only one expression of a complex set of working-class cultural attitudes made manifest through the Tom and Jerry burlettas. Of course, the popularity of the plays was mirrored by their uptake amongst the pressmen. James Catnach's woodcut illustrated broadsheet *The Tread-Mill...A New Song Tom, Jerry, and Logic in the Tread-Mill* (1821), featuring an adapted pirated excerpt from the Surrey's *Tom and Jerry at Brixton*, definitively discloses the dispersal of this aspect of working-class anxiety into the depressed Seven Dials area of London. Into the late 1820s or early '30s, the fugitive pornographic pocket-sized song books emanating from the 'song-and-supper' clubs, such as *The Nobby Songster, A Prime Collection as now Singing at Offleys Cider Cellar: Coal Hole &c.* printed by William West of Wych Street, opposite The Olympic Theatre, could still contain the lewd 'Swell Coves Alphabet' with its roots in the Regency taste for Tom and Jerry argot. Around that time too, Jacob Beuler who sang at similar haunts published his song collection *Bob Logic's Memoranda: an Original Budget of Staves, Nightly Chaunted by Kiddy Coves, Knights of the Darkey, &.c&c. at every Free and Easy Throughout the metropolis, by Way of Prelude to The Sprees of 'Life in London'* with its long and intricate expeditions into 'flash' language (a 'kiddy' is a thief, a 'darkey' a darkened lantern used by burglars). But the cultural dissemination of Tom and Jerry was much more rapid than this suggests. By July 1822, Tom and Jerry's popularity was such that a version had been performed by paying amateurs at the unrespectable Rawsthorne Place private theatre.[666] By January 1823, the Theatre Royal, Edinburgh, was offering *Tom and Jerry – compressed*, which entirely omitted the scenes set in St Giles's or Almacks in the East but concentrated instead on the arrogance of Tom, Jerry and Logic (Tom: Sir, I'm a gentleman & an MP & I insist – Snoozy [Constable]: Aye, Aye, we've lots of Gentlemen & MPs here who forget that they are so').[667] There were also other types of cultural influence at work. According to Moncrieff, the MP for Coventry, Mr. Butterworth, quickly became a habitué (but 'masquerading it') of the Beggar's Opera (Rose and Crown) and Robin Hood taverns in St Giles's, where he drank 'blue ruin' (gin) with 'Cutaway Moll' and toasted '*Emancipation* to the *Blacks!*' with Billy Waters, the African, one-legged ex-navy cook who became a beggar in St Giles's but who died in the summer of 1823, both of them the originals of Egan's characters.[668]

Ultimately, Moncrieff's success probably lay in his ability to depict the lives of Tom, Jerry and Logic as exciting but empty while, at the same time, foregrounding the rich diversity of natural community within

London's colourful poor. At the only point in the play where Tom appears to be reflective, he is mercilessly taunted by Bob and Jerry:

Tom (*sitting down, and soliloquizing*): And I must retire somewhere: I was not born to racket thus. Fortune ushered my entrance into the world; splendour rocked my cradle; fun, frolic, and fancy, perched upon its top, and luxury waited on my very go-cart. My leading-strings were under the guidance of tenderness and refinement; and I scarcely lisped, 'ere anxiety anticipated all my wants – my infant tears were dried by acquiescence, and surly contradiction was forbidden to cross my path – my – (*Logic and Jerry steal down on each side of him, and laugh derisively.*)
Jerry: Go it! – Bravo! beautiful! ha, ha, ha! (p. 64)

The decorous, explicitly literary diction of his soliloquy – quite apart from its allusion to a life of privilege – contrasts sharply with the 'flash' and 'cant' language he usually speaks but Bob and Jerry's mockery of his brief recantation is still quite shocking today. This single scene crystallizes much of what was socially revolutionary about Moncrieff's *Tom and Jerry* since it expresses the nadir of what Larpent had hoped to sustain in his prohibition of plays such as Eglantine Wallace's *The Whim* (1795) which had criticized upper-class mores. The collapse of any moral system of education which Moncrieff hints at in Tom Hawthorne's words reveal that he has been brought up to live a life of wilful, unrestrained passion and frolic, 'my infant tears were dried by acquiescence, and surly contradiction was forbidden to cross my path.' The artificiality of their life ends up being celebrated in the vivid 'Brilliantly Illuminated' 'Venetian Carnival,' set in Leicester Square, which closes Moncreiff's *Tom and Jerry*.

The final Venetian Carnival (organized by Logic's gambling debtor, Sir Jeremy Brag) seems to recapitulate much of what Moncrieff would have seen had he attended the Davis Amphitheatre *Tom and Jerry; or, Life in London* (1822), by its importation of a harlequinade into his Adelphi show. In Moncrieff's *Tom and Jerry*, Harlequin, Columbine and the Clown, in a dumb show, make an inversion of much of what has happened in the play. The violence of the Charley baiting during which constable O'Boozle's watchhouse is overturned and Tom and Jerry fight three watchmen apiece is mirrored by traditional quasi-Punch and Judy harlequinade stage business of Clown stealing Old Maid's Poodle, putting his own head in the dog's place under her arm until the 'enraged' Old Maid 'pummels Clown's pate till she breaks her fan – [and] Clown carries her off squalling' (pp. 30, 70). Similarly, the portrayal of St Giles's beggars such as Little Jemmy or others 'gammoning a maim' – one beggar says 'If any lady or gemman is inclined for a dance, I'll nash [quit] my arm-props [crutches] in a minute' – is mirrored in the harlequinade by the appearance of a 'grotesque Dwarf, in chintz gown and cap, with big head' (pp. 47–8). Even Jemmy Green, the wealthy cockney 'Johnny Raw' character with rustic-like simplicities, who gets sold a dubious nag at Tattersalls ('[I'm] Mr. Green from the City. I want's an orse, and I like the looks of that 'ere hanimal amazingly, and I'm no bad judge, I tell you that'), is mirrored in a piece of comic stage business where Countryman crosses the stage on Donkey (presumably a hobby horse variant) until 'he slips off; gets up very much bruised, and eventually takes Donkey under his arm, and exits in a hobble' (pp. 23–4, 71).

Community and cosmopolitanism within the metropolis, the dramatic fulfilment of Egan's title, 'Life in London,' is only truly embodied by the urban poor. Compared with the censorious Davis Amphitheatre *Tom and Jerry*, Moncrieff mixes the worlds of the St Giles's Holy Land Back Slums 'cadgers' with that of Billy Waters, the genuinely one-legged ex-sailor. The 'cadgers' (now named as Mr Jenkins, Soldier Suke, Dingy Bet, Little Jemmy, Creeping Jack, Ragged Dick) are portrayed with some level of gaiety as they sing:

> Never mind what's to pay,
> The public pays for all.
>
> Rumpti bumpti bay, &c. (p. 47)

Even their response to London's rudimentary welfare system couples derision with good humour: 'The Mende-*city* Society, I believe they calls themselves, have kindly purwided a fund for us-gemmen; so, if any body offers you less nor a mag, or a duce, vy, you may say vith the poet, "Who vou'd his farthings bear? ven he himself might his quivetus make vith a bare Bodkin"' (p. 48). When Mr Jenkins the beggar is picked up by the Poor Law officers (when they 'slapp'd a pick-ax into one of my mauleys, and shov'd a shovel into t'other') he simply tells them quite baldly, 'says I, gemmen, I can't vork, cause vy, I'm too veak—so they guv'd me two bob, and I bolted!' (p. 48). In these scenes Cockney dialect is celebrated. The social levelling and political edge Moncrieff gives his work, unlike the moralistic conservatism of the Davis Amphitheatre *Tom and Jerry* or the Surrey's *The Treadmill; or, Tom and Jerry at Brixton*, is exemplified in the derisively satirical song sung to a 'barking chorus of Beggars' who repeat the last phrase:

That all men are beggars, 'tis very plain to see,
Tho' some they are of lowly, and some they are of high degree;
Your ministers of state will say, they never will allow
That kings from subjects beg, but that you know is all bow wow.
(p. 49)

In place of the 'bow wow' is portrayed the conviviality and sociability so highly prized in the interpretations of Tom and Jerry. The scenes at Almacks in the East where Dusty Bob, African Sall, Mahogany Mary and others are eventually joined up with Tom, Jerry and Logic are set out as a sort of 'free-and-easy' which ends with music and dancing.

The whole of the extraordinary free-and-easy *Tom and Jerry* scene set in Almacks in the East is a vivid portrayal of that condition which, ironically, in Egan's original *Life in London* had been best articulated by Bob Logic: '[it is] the LOWER ORDERS of society who really ENJOY themselves... Their minds are daily occupied with work, which they quit with the intention of *enjoying* themselves, and ENJOYMENT is the result.'[669] The wild dancing in Moncrieff's *Tom and Jerry*, accompanied by a '*cracked Cremona*' violin and the noise of '*Jerry on a pair of Tongs,*' embodies values of boisterous pleasure, community and conviviality:

In the course of the Pas Deux, when encored, [African] Sal, by way of a variation, and in the fullness of her spirits, keeps twirling about; at the same time going round the Stage – [Dusty] Bob runs after her, with his hat in his hand, crying "Sarah vy, Sarah, 'ant you vell?" &c. – the black Child seeing this, and thinking there is something the matter with its mother, also squalls violently; stretching its arms towards her: at length, Sal, becoming tired of her vagaries, sets to Bob, who exclaims, 'Oh! it's all right!' and the dance concludes. (p. 62)

This anarchic revelry, fuelled by copious supplies of 'Blue Ruin' (gin) and, in African Sal's case, at least a 'kwarten [a quart] of de Fuller's earth' (gin and bitters), even in its apparent mayhem is a subtle visual, verbal and musical embodiment of a number of core working-class values (p. 62).[670] Dusty Bob's concern (' "*Sarah vy, Sarah, 'ant you vell?*" ') for his common law wife, African Sal, is immediate but also notice-ably interracial. The place of the black child (obviously not Dusty Bob's offspring) is absolutely central to this scene: however drunkenly, this lower-class interracial family functions as a unit. This familial harmony is an aspect of *Tom and Jerry* emphasized by Moncrieff's adaptation of Egan's original in which the Dusty Bob character (who is seen dancing with African Sal in Cruikshanks's 'Lowest "Life in London"' plate for the book) was actually called 'nasty Bob' whose profession was given as a coal heaver (or '*coal-vhipper*').[671] Moncrieff perhaps took the cue to convert 'nasty Bob' into Dusty Bob, as well as to initiate African Sal's wild dancing, from Egan's description about 'All Max' in the East, which said that there 'All was happiness, – every body free and easy, and freedom of expression allowed to the very echo.'[672] Moncrieff may also be hinting in his description of African Sal's dancing being 'by way of a variation, and in the fullness of her spirits... twirling about... going round the Stage' some true black-African tribal or racial origin to her exhibition.

If 'All was happiness' in Egan's and Moncrieff's versions of the working-class partying at All Macks, this happiness gets disrupted by aristocrats. Bob Logic had already, thoughtlessly, 'give[n the] black child gin out of a measure he has received from Landlord' but as the singing and dancing get under way, the drama's only piece of alarming racial abuse is spoken by him (p. 62). Bob Logic's racism is far more vicious than that of the tavern landlord. Mace, who is presented throughout as coarse and grasping, had called on Dusty Bob for a 'minnyvit[minuet] vith your ould lady in mourning, here' (p. 62). The 'lady in mourning' is, of course, a reference to African Sal's colour. Bob Logic, however, satirizes Sal's colour by inverting it into a whiteness she does not possess. When Sal says that the fiddler is drunk and can 'no play at all,' Logic says he will 'gin him a little, my Snow-ball; then he'll rasp away like a young one... (*gives Fiddler gin and snuff, and begrimes his face*) (p. 62). The racial slur of the 'Snow-ball' gibe is instantly recognized for what it is by her partner, Dusty Bob: 'Snow-ball,' – come, let's have none o'your sinnywations, Mister Barnacles; she's none the vurser, though she is a little blackish or so!' (p. 62).[673] In other words, Dusty Bob intervenes to protect his black partner from the aristocrat's racial 'sinnywations.'

As the wild dancing gets under way (Cruikshanks's 'Lowest "Life in London"' plate is a fine etching of Dusty Bob and African Sal's dancing in the crowded tavern), Bob Logic's drunkenness begins to get thoroughly out of hand. Logic may even intend a further racist allusion hidden in his song beginning 'There's a difference between...' (p. 63).

The allusion is to a popular song of the 1780s, 'The Beggars' Imitation,' made famous in the provincial theatres by the comic James Robertson:

> There's a difference between a beggar and a queen,
> And I'll tell you the reason why,
> A queen cannot swagger, not get drunk as a beggar,
> Nor be half so happy as I.[674]

Buried away in the context of the possibilities of its interpretation in Mace's tavern at that moment is the possibility of a sarcastic allusion to the racial difference between Dusty Bob and African Sal. Whether that allusion is intended or not, Jerry Hawthorne becomes concerned at Logic's behaviour, whispering to him in an aside, 'Eh! – zounds! what's the matter with you?' (p. 63). Things get even further out of hand when Logic begins to drunkenly horseplay with the tavern violinist, 'I do like this Fiddler – I will have this Fiddler. (*pulling Fiddler along*),' forcing Tom into 'taking [the] gin measure away from him' until, with 'Logic becoming obstreperous, they partly force him off, and exeunt with him' (p. 63). The incident is perhaps a typical example of an upper-class prank belying Bob Logic's supposed gentle breeding. It is quite noticeable that when they are gone (having been 'stuck... into' for cash by Mace) the partying continues, paid for out of the drunken trio's own money:

Mace: So I don't mind standing a trifle of summat all round, just by vay of drinking their healths; and vhen ve've had the liquor, ve'll kick up a reel, and all go to our dabs.
Bob: Aye, aye! but before that, mind you get us a bit of grub for me and my Sal – about a pound and a half of rump stake. –
Sal: No, two pound! Massa Bob, for her rather peckish. (p. 63)

A return to the human fundamentals of food, drink and the pleasure of dance concludes the scene ('*Comic characteristic Reel by all the Characters; who, under the influence of All Max* [gin], *at last reel off*') as Tom, Jerry and Logic are completely forgotten (p. 64).

Moncrieff's *Tom and Jerry* made its mixed-race, impoverished beggars attractive without overly romanticizing them. They are alcoholically drunk in their genuine pleasure and enjoyment, revelling in their own natural Cockney and Creole dialects as much as Tom, Jerry and Logic are intoxicated by gin, pointless rowdyism and their fascination with an urban argot they understand but which is not their native tongue. The Tom and Jerry plays point to a dislocation of English drama from its centring on the literary texts of Shakespeare and his followers to a more proletarian mode of expression. In an S.W. Fores print of the scene discussed above, *All Max in the East, A Scene in Tom & Jerry; or, Life in London* (1822), the caricaturist 'W.W.' appears to have omitted Tom, Jerry and Logic entirely and has given the picture over to a scene of dancing centred on African Sal and Dusty Bob, with a wooden-legged black fiddler providing the music, the white-aproned Mace the publican looking on benignly and an older white woman, seated on the floor, pleasurably giving a black baby a mug of gin while a fourth, grey-haired black man looks on appreciatively.[675] With the print's specific title reference to a dramatic version, *Tom & Jerry; or, Life in London*, this anonymous caricature confirms the piece's triumphal representation of working-class culture. James Catnach's woodcut and letterpress broadsheet *Life in London: or, The Sprees of Tom and Jerry; Attempted in Cuts and Verse* (1822) similarly showed the Beggars Opera tavern in the Holy Land, with 'The quintessence of Tag, Rag, and Bob-Tail,' and noticeably including many black women such as Black Molly, Mahogany Bet, Yankee Moll and 'Suke as black as any pall.' In part, the displacement into amphitheatre and broadside of such themes as Tom and Jerry was the inevitable result of a London theatre which monopolized and protected spoken five-act drama into just two playhouses.

Once the displacement of Shakespeare by burletta had taken place, it was natural that there would be a concomitant perceived linguistic shift, a phenomenon which might be aptly described as the rise of Cockney. Or, as a song in *The Fancy's Opera* (1823) put it – another Adelphi piece written just over a year after Moncrieff's *Tom and Jerry* – 'Oh, what a change, all England now are slanging it.' The Adelphi had done much to create the phenomenon upon which *The Fancy's Opera* comments, so it is notable when that song goes on to declare that 'Poor Doctor Johnson's nose [is] put out of joint by Cap[tai]n Grose':

> Slang the Current language is with Gentry & Nobility
> Their Mother Tongue they patter it [speak 'flash'] – the pedant's power defy
> The higher Classes boast they're up,and young sprigs of Nobility
> Roses, Pinks & Tulip vow they're regularly fly [knowing][676]

The linguistic displacement of the language of Shakespeare and the eighteenth-century's attempts to define an orderly English lexicon, so markedly followed by the *Blackwood's* attacks on Cockney writing, had been disrupted by Tom and Jerry at the very heart of the metropolis.

Fundamental to what has been outlined above is the displacement of Shakespeare from the contemporary London stage and his supplementation by a form of drama evolved entirely from within its own public sphere. The development of the Tom and Jerry plays from Davis's Amphitheatre in Lambeth, to the Olympic in Wych Street, through to the Adelphi in the Strand (and back again to the Olympic) reveals the workings of an intricate network of literary borrowing and adaptation exhibiting complex patterns of morality and class consciousness. The criticism of upper-class immorality which is present in the Tom and Jerry plays achieves by an oblique route what Eglantine Wallace had tried to affect in the mid-1790s. Tom and Jerry were the perfect vehicles of social criticism because they did not attempt social subversion head-on. This point would be painfully relearned two years later, at great personal frustration, by a newcomer to dramatic writing, the painter Martin Archer Shee, whose five-act *Alasco; a Tragedy* (1824) was so cut by the incoming Examiner, George Colman the Younger, that Shee felt obliged to withdraw it. Shee, probably out of his own ignorance of current conditions of censorship, had attempted to have performed a tragedy of national insurrection (closely allegorizing an Irish nationalist model) set in Poland. Shee commented in the New York edition (where *Alasco* was produced later that year) that the Examiner permitted dramas which 'sustain the decorum of our stage, by the graceful introduction of petty-larceny rogues, and man-milliner immoralities' but where the representation of the grander issues of public liberty were stifled. As he went on to say, 'How long shall we be allowed to point a shaft at a debauchee, or throw any dramatic discredit on the revels of the bacchanal, or the orgies of the gaming table?'[677] In other words, Tom and Jerry's representation of upper-class 'revels of the bacchanal' at All Max in the East or the 'orgies of the gaming table' at Almacks in the West was the most subtle – and practical – vehicle available or permissible from which to mount a criticism of upper-class behaviour on the metropolitan English stage.

Conclusion: The Canadian *Tom and Jerry* Murder

The Tom and Jerry burlettas of the early 1820s, prefigured as they were by a string of what one might call 'Giovanni in XYZ' plays of the late 1810s, mark the maturity of a genuine public plebeian dramatic sphere located at the heart of London. Whatever the arguments which might be posited about the degree of permeability of plebeian public sphere of drama this book has outlined, there clearly existed a large body of dramatic writing which had little to do with the literary canon or even the national heritage of spoken drama. The regulatory framework, and its bewildering legal and cultural intricacies, ensured that Romantic-period drama outside of the patent playhouses would develop differently from the five-act spoken format of play derived from the era of Shakespeare or the Restoration. The manner in which this drama increasingly reflected or embodied consciously working-class aspirations or sentiments may be more open to discussion, but it seems quite clear that the play-houses and playwrights themselves felt they were in the middle of a new phenomenon of class and dramaturgy. Even the Adelphi, with the hit of Moncrieff's *Tom and Jerry* firmly on its hands in late 1821, staged its own comment about the revolution in taste, which was increasingly a devolution towards the representation of the artisan, Cockney, public who comprised their audiences. In *The Prelude* (1823), the character Play Trump, the fictional, near-bankrupt, manager of an imaginary theatre rival to The Adelphi, laments that 'the Vulgar Tongue is certainly the only one that is understood and studied at present – in these days of Slang and Song of Extravaganza, Low Life and Lark and Libertinism the stirling pieces of old times have lost all their attractions.'[678] *The Prelude* was licensed to precede *The Fancy's Opera* (1823), and introduces one Mr Colley Skylark ('Poet Lauret[sic] of the Pugilistic Club – better known by the title of the Sporting Apollo') who has 'written you an

Opera to suit the present Taste...I take my Heroes from the Turf – My scenes from real life...in short, the Fancy's Opera.'[679] *The Prelude*'s 'Poet Lauret,' Colley Skylark, is a complexly nuanced reference hinting at Colly Cibber, Robert Southey, Percy Shelley and Pierce Egan, but Trump takes Colley Skylark's play not because he is desperate for new dramas (*The Prelude* also stresses that there was no scarcity of manuscripts from budding authors) but because they have all latched onto the new fashion manufactured by Moncrieff and his followers.

Indeed, when Trump asks his scene shifter whether he has 'received any fresh pieces lately,' Shifter replies 'Rather slack in that way just now, Sir, only one hundred and eighty last week.' Despairingly, Trump looks into the 'large Hamper mark'd "Tragedies" ' that Shift and two wingmen have dragged into his office:

Trump: Eh, what the deuce have you got there – Wine?
Shift: Yes, but not of the description you wish – see, Sir 'Tragedies' – Tis full of them – and Trag[ed]i[e]s[*sic*] whine –

The puns are as desperate as Trump ('I...don't want to be hamper'd in that way') is desperate himself to find a new manuscript worthy of drawing the audiences. After ignoring an 'army of French pieces,' Trump goes on to reject 'Romeo and Juliet an Opera with a Pageant and Song. By Shakespeare and Timitty Figgins,' not to mention 'Giovanni in Newfoundland or here I am again!' (' – But here you shan't stay tho').[680]

The pun that 'tragedies whine' but were in over-supply was a serious issue. William Henry Ireland's *Vortigern* (1796) had represented one covert way of ushering new drama onto the London stage. By the 1820s, burletta as exemplified by Moncrieff's string of hits including *Giovanni in London* and *Tom and Jerry* was reaching and reflecting the attitudes of a vast popular audience which can be numbered in scores of thousands. Trump's *'Hamper mark'd "Tragedies"'* signalled a lost cause. Tom and Jerry swept the world, and not just London. By 1824 Moncrieff's *Tom and Jerry* had played at theatres in New York, Philadelphia and Boston, the latter where Moncrieff was already known for his New York-produced farce *The Spectre Bridegroom; or, A Ghost in Spite of Himself* (1821).[681] The survival of a number of *Tom and Jerry* promptbooks, almost invariably based on Moncrieff's version, from the period *c.*1825–50 in the Harvard Theatre Collection are good indicators as to the frequency of its production in North America during that period. It is clear from the promptbooks that heavy cuts were sometimes made and, in at least one copy, the pages have been pinned for the insertion of new or adapted material, although it was not unusual for editors to cut or adapt these texts fairly freely. An edition for the Albany Company, New York, omits the roles of African Sal and Billy Waters entirely, possibly on racial grounds, but a handwritten cast list for the 1834 Warren Theatre, Boston, production shows that both characters were present on that occasion.[682]

It is worth following *Tom and Jerry* in North America a little further. The obscure trial for murder of a young Irish-born printer, Charles French, in the township of York in the province of Upper Canada in 1828 brings together many of the aspects of the interplay of drama, popular culture and criminality, which have been examined in this book. As his 'Dying Confession' put it, French, along with two friends, had gone to the York playhouse in June 1828 'with the intention of hearing the Play called "Tom and Jerry," or "Life in London."'[683] Although the exact identity of the particular adaptation or abridgement of Tom and Jerry performed at York cannot be determined, true to the culture of 'sprees' and pugilistic 'milling,' French found himself seated in the playhouse when he found one Edward Nowlan 'looked very hard at me.' The presence of alcohol was another consistent feature of early nineteenth-century theatregoing. French and his friends twice went out of the theatre during the performances to drink wine at Howard's bar and even made a third trip out for liquor, 'when the Farce was nearly over.' Unfortunately, earlier in the evening one of French's friends (who was acquitted at the trial) had given him a loaded pistol because, bizarrely, they believed Nowlan was carrying 'a pair of tongs in his left coat pocket.'[684] As they re-entered the theatre, French and Nowlan had a brief verbal altercation ('God damn you what are you standing there for?'), and fearing Nowlan was about to hit him with the tongs, French shot him dead. In French's (pretty well stereotyped) 'Dying Sentiments,' the convicted man told the prison minister that he blamed it all on 'BAD COMPANY AND DRINKING.'[685]

Nowlan's murder outside the theatre in Upper Canada was a case of life imitating art. 'BAD COMPANY AND DRINKING' is a pretty accurate synopsis of what happens in any Tom and Jerry play. In Charles Isaac Mungo Dibdin's *Life in London*, Jerry and Bob Logic both go to the theatre drunk ('Jerry: Why, – (*hiccup*) – Life in London's a glorious thing') but the medley of 'sprees' in the drinking dens of the Daffy Club, Almax in the East and the cellar 'rookeries' round the Surrey Theatre held out a warning that everything would end in *The Treadmill, or Tom and Jerry at Brixton*.[686] The Tom and Jerry plays with their intricate display of contemporary social nuances, discerning between the morality of such things as gambling and begging while at the same time representing its heroes as racially indiscriminate, the rakish lifestyles of Don Giovanni or Corinthian Tom came to be a remarkable reflection of the greater world which lay outside the doors of the playhouses. The plebeian public sphere was not simply a London experience but it had also become a transatlantic phenomenon.

The macabre comparisons between art and life were uncanny. Moncrieff's *Frank-in-Steam Or, the Modern Promise to pay* (deliberately parodying Mary Shelley's successful *Frankenstein*) for the 1824 Olympic Theatre season had featured its eponymous hero turning to body-snatching to stave off the bailiffs ('Should I be found out tho' – Ha! – discovered like a Vampyre preying on the loathsome tenants of the Grave – Body snatching').[687] Meanwhile, Charley the watchman ('asleep in his box') ruminates on the demise of Tom and Jerry and how 'Thanks to the Magistrates and the Tread Mills we may now sleep in some comfort without being upset by either a Tom, Jerry or Logic.'[688] Moncrieff's reference to his own hit play (and those of others) was obviously an allusion he could be completely confident would be immediately recognized by The Olympic audience. Grimly, four years later, in Upper Canada, it was the fate of Charles French's body also to be 'delivered over to the Surgeons for dissection.' Luckily, the medical men, 'humanely considering the condition of the parents, and the sympathy felt for the departed youth, merely made a few incisions and sewed them up again.'[689] In the same way that the fictional Tom, Jerry and Logic were obviously idolized by London theatregoers, cartoonists and popular songwriters, the short-tempered and drunken Charles French was similarly celebrated, despite Nowlan's murder, by the York townspeople. Their 1,100 signature petition to the Governor, Sir Peregrine Maitland, considered French 'a fit and proper object of the royal clemency.'[690] Finally, following templates prefigured in London's print culture by such publications as *The Death of Life in London; or Tom & Jerry's Funeral. An Entirely New Satirical, Burlesque, Operative Parody, in One Act* (1823); *The Death of Don Giovanni, or, the funeral of the Hero's* (1823) and the James Catnach ballad broadside *The Death, Last Will, and Funeral of 'Black Billy': Also, the Tears of London for the Death of Tom and Jerry* (1823), in the township of York, Upper Canada, French's superficially dissected body was borne by 'Four youths of this town, printers by profession' followed by 'an immense concourse of his townsmen.'[691] It is ironic that the very emergence of a distinctive Canadian print culture (French had worked in the offices of *The Canadian Frenchman*), so coincident with the growth of a popular press in London which reinforced the success of Moncrieff's *Tom and Jerry*, should also have contributed to his final journey to the grave. The wrapper of the pamphlet relating his fate, *Confession of Charles French, an Irish youth, executed... for the murder of Edward Nowlan at the play-house, on the 4th of June 1828, where they had met to see the play of Tom & Jerry* (York, Canada, 1828), lugubriously pictured a scaffold with a masked prisoner dangling above a coffin captioned 'C[harles] F[rench].'

From London's Adelphi or Olympic Theatres to the obscure play-house in York, Upper Canada, Moncrieff's *Tom and Jerry* and its spin-offs had come a long way. The enormous contemporary audiences brought in their wake other tragedies and transformations. At a *Tom and Jerry* performance in Newcastle in 1823, an alarm of fire in the theatre resulted in seven deaths, but in New York that same year, much more far-reaching changes were happening when the black actors of the African Company in Mercer Street off Broadway, performed their version of *Tom & Jerry, Or, Life in London* with their own newly written scene set 'On the Slave Market.'[692] If the unfortunate fate of the Irish-born printer, Charles French, was intimately bound up with the influence and dissemination of a distinctively plebeian dramatic culture, in scarcely 40 years, drama had itself travelled far. Far away from the colonialist embarrassments of Bellamy's *Benevolent Planters*, black actors were now taking to the stage and writing their own scripts. Like the Cockney 'Trollop' witnessed by John Keats at the fugitive London private theatre, the spouters were no longer content to remain spectators.

Notes

1. One of the most comprehensive of the gestural manuals is Henry Siddons's *Practical Illustrations of Rhetorical Gesture and Action, Adapted to the English Drama* (1807).
2. James Morris, *Recollections of Ayr Theatricals from 1809* (Ayr: Ayr Advertiser Office, 1872), pp. 5, 8.
3. Thomas Meadows, *Thespian Gleanings, A Collection of Comic Recitals, Songs, Tales, &c. Including a Variety of Comic Sketches, From Dodd's Lecture on Hearts; A Farce Called Who's to Blame; or, No Fool Like an Old One; and Many Originals* (1805). It was sold in Kendal, Northalerton, Beverley, Harrogate, Ripon, Richmond (Yorkshire), Stockton, Whitby, York, Hull, Liverpool, Lancaster, London, Gainsborough, Preston, Whitehaven and Glasgow.
4. Joseph Londale[*sic*] to R.W. Elliston, 13 April 1820, R.W. Elliston Papers, Harvard Theatre Collection Vol. 2.
5. Leman Thomas Rede, *The Road to the Stage; or, The Performer's Preceptor* (1827), p. 62.
6. *The Theatric Tourist* (1805).
7. Leman Thomas Rede, *The Road to the Stage; or, The Performer's Preceptor* (1827), p. 39.
8. Ibid., p. 40.
9. Ibid., p. 16.
10. Ibid., pp. 16–17.
11. Joseph Donohue, *Theatre in the Age of Kean* (Oxford: Basil Blackwell, 1975), pp. 46–50.
12. Ms. TS 953.7, 'Inventory Valuation of Property taken at the Theatre Royal Drury Lane Aug 1819,' Harvard Theatre Collection.
13. George Anne Bellamy, *An apology for the life of George Ann Bellamy, late of Covent-Garden theatre* (1785); Elizabeth Macauley, *Facts Against Falsehood! Being A Brief Statement Of Miss Macauley's Engagements at The Winter Theatres* (1824).
14. For Siddons and celebrity, see Martin Postle (ed.) *Joshua Reynolds: The Creation of Celebrity* (London: Tate Publishing, 2005).
15. *A Statement of the Differences Subsisting Between the Proprietors and Performers of the Theatre-Royal, Covent-Garden. Given in the Correspondence Which Has Passed Between Them* (1800), p. 67.
16. Leman Thomas Rede, *The Road to the Stage; or, The Performer's Preceptor* (1827), p. 15; his brother halved this estimate in the posthumous edition, Leman Thomas Rede, *The Road to the Stage; or, The Performer's Preceptor* (1836), p. 14.
17. Charles Beecher Hogan, *The London Stage 1660–1800* (Carbondale, Ill.: Southern Illinois University Press, 1968) Vol. 5 pp. ccix–x; Görel Garlick, *To Serve the Purpose of the Drama: The Theatre Designs and Plays of Samuel Beazley 1786–1851* (London: Society for Theatre Research, 2003), p. 24; *Particulars and Conditions of Sale of the Olympic Theatre ... 13th June, 1820* (1820).
18. Thomas Dibdin, *The Reminiscences of Thomas Dibdin* (1837) Vol. 2 p. 401.

19. Leman Thomas Rede, *The Road to the Stage; or, The Performer's Preceptor* (1836), pp. 12–13.
20. Jacob Beuler, *Comic Songs to Popular Tunes . . . Ninth Collection* (1833), p. 26.
21. Horace Foote, *A Companion to the Theatres; and Manual of The British Drama* (1829), p. 148.
22. Eugene Macarthy, *A Letter to The King, on The Question now at Issue Between The 'Major,' and 'Minor' Theatres*y (1832), p. 10.
23. William J. Burling, *Summer Theatre in London, 1661–1820, and the Rise of the Haymarket Theatre* (Madison, Teaneck: Fairleigh Dickinson University Press; London: Associated University Presses, 2000), p. 103. On the licensing of entertainments, see Vincent J. Liesenfeld, *The Licensing Act of 1737* (Madison: University of Wisconsin Press, 1984).
24. John O'Brien's *Harlequin Britain: Pantomime and Entertainment, 1690–1760* (Baltimore, MD: The Johns Hopkins University Press, 2004), p. 212.
25. Thomas Dibdin, *The Reminiscences of Thomas Dibdin* (1837) Vol. 1 p. 337.
26. Moyra Haslett, *Byron's 'Don Juan' and the Don Juan Legend* (Oxford: Clarendon Press, 1997), p. 50.
27. Jane Stabler, *Byron, Poetics and History* (Cambridge: Cambridge University Press, 2002, 1997), p. 6.
28. Gillian Russell, *The Theatres of War: Performance, Politics, and Society, 1793–1815* (Oxford: Clarendon Press, 1995).
29. Betsy Bolton, *Women, Nationalism, and the Romantic Stage: Theatre and Politics in Britain, 1780–1800* (Cambridge: Cambridge University Press, 2001).
30. Jane Moody, *Illegitimate: Theatre in London, 1770–1840* (Cambridge: Cambridge University Press (2000), p. 232.
31. Ibid., pp. 191–208; 213–17.
32. See the important chapter, 'Monopoly and free trade; fair and unfair competition,' Tracy C. Davis, *The Economics of the British Stage 1800–1914* (Cambridge: Cambridge University Press, 2000), pp. 17–41.
33. For the evolution of the patentees, see Robert D. Hume, *Henry Fielding and the London Theatre, 1728–1737* (Oxford: Clarendon Press, 1988), pp. 2–14.
34. William J. Burling, *Summer Theatre in London, 1661–1820, and the Rise of the Haymarket Theatre* (Madison, Teaneck: Fairleigh Dickinson University Press; London: Associated University Presses, 2000), pp. 114–5.
35. Correspondence between Colman and the Lord Chamberlain upon Colman's appointment as Examiner establishes this lack of generic definition, B[ritish] L[ibrary] Add Ms 42865.fol 24 March 1824.
36. *The number of little Theatres already opened . . . having greatly injured the Theatres Royal . . .* (*c*.1808–10), p. 9.
37. Robert Merry and Charles Bonnor, *Airs, Duetts, and Chorusses, Arrangment of Scenery, and Sketch of the Pantomime Entitled The Picture of Paris. Taken in the Year 1790* (1790); Larpent 886, Huntington Library, California.
38. John Larpent to R.W. Elliston, 12 April 1820, R.W. Elliston papers, Harvard Theatre Collection, Vol. 2. The pantomime referred to is a version of David Garrick's, *Harlequin's Invasion* (1759), played as *Shakespeare Versus Harlequin; or, Harlequin's Invasion,* cf. playbill, Drury Lane, 4 May 1820. A young Madame Vestris played Dolly Snip. Elliston had produced it at the Surrey Theatre as a 'Comic Burletta Pantomime,' under the title, *To be, or not to be? Or, Shakespeare versus Harlequin*, playbills, 10 April 1812.

39. Isaac Jackman, *Royal and Royalty Theatres. Letter to Phillips Glover, Esq of Wispington, In Lincolnshire; in a Dedication to the Burletta of Hero and Leander, now performing...at the Royalty Theatre, in Goodman's Fields* (1787), p. 26.
40. Isaac Jackman, *Royal and Royalty Theatres. Letter to Phillips Glover, Esq of Wispington, In Lincolnshire; in a Dedication to the Burletta of Hero and Leander, now performing...*, *at the Royalty Theatre, in Goodman's Fields* (1787), p. 22.
41. Thomas John Dibdin, *The Reminiscences of Thomas Dibdin* (1837) 2 vols, Vol. 2 pp. 148–53.
42. BL Add Ms 42865.fol. 432, 8 March 1824.
43. P[ublic] R[ecord] O[ffice] L[ord C[hamberlain] 5/164. fol. 75–6.
44. *A Letter to a Member of Parliament on the impropriety of classing Players with Rogues and Vagabonds in the Vagrant Act. By the Author of 'The Vagrant Act in relation to the Liberty of the Subject.'* (1824), pp. 17–8.
45. John Brewer, *The Pleasures of the Imagination: English Culture in the Eighteenth Century* (London: Harper Collins, 1997) 388–9; ' "The most polite age and the most vicious": Attitudes towards culture as a commodity, 1660–1800,' (eds) Ann Bermingham and John Brewer, *The Consumption of Culture 1600–1800: Image, Object, Text* (London: Routledge, 1995), pp. 341–61, 348.
46. Henry Francis Greville, *Mr. Greville's Statement of Mr. Naldi's Case* (1811), pp. 10, 14–15; *Mr. Greville and Mr. Elliston's Plan of a British Winter Opera* (*c*.1811); unidentified newspaper clipping, 8 August 1811, R.W. Elliston papers, Harvard Theatre Collection Vol. 1; *Private Subscription Theatre...On the South side of Oxford Street, East of Hanover Square...25 April 1811* (1811).
47. Charles Beecher Hogan, *The London Stage 1660–1800* (Carbondale, Ill.: Southern Illinois University Press, 1968) Vol. 5 p. xliv.
48. Jacob Beuler, *Comic Songs to Popular Tunes...Ninth Collection* (1833), pp. 24–6.
49. David Mayer III, *Harlequin in his Element: The English Pantomime, 1806–1836* (Cambridge, Mass.: Harvard University Press, 1969), p. 21.
50. 'Almost all the dress Boxes were adorned with placards, with the following descriptions...No Private Boxes, No Accommodation Boxes. No hiding-places, No theatrical taxation...No concealment in Private Boxes. No close Boxes...The whole House for the whole Public, and no Private Retreats, *Remarks on the Cause of the Dispute Between the Public and Managers of the Theatre Royal, Covent Garden, With a Circumstantial Account of the Week's Performances and the Uproar...illustrated with a large Caricature Frontispiece of the House that Jack built* (1809), pp. 25–6.
51. Henry Lee, *The Manager. A Melo-Dramatic Tale* (1822), p. 63n.
52. *Report from the Select Committee on Dramatic Literature: With The Minutes of Evidence...2 August 1832*, Parliamentary Papers (1831–32) Vol VII. Question 223.
53. BL Add Ms 42865 22 March, 24 March 1824.
54. Robert William Elliston, *Copy of a Memorial Presented to the Lord Chamberlain, by the Committee of Management of the Theatre-Royal Drury-Lane, Against the olympic and Sans Pareil Theatres* (1818), pp. 4–5.
55. Leman Thomas Rede, *The Road to the Stage; or, The Performer's Preceptor* (1827), pp. 62–3.
56. Ibid., pp. 56, 95.

57. Unidentified clipping, dated 1813, R.W. Elliston papers, Harvard Theatre Collection Vol. 1.

58. PRO H[ome] O[ffice] 119/4, 2nd and 5th March, 1818, Sans Pareil, Strand, Olympic, Wych Street.

59. *Memoirs of the Life of Madame Vestris...Illustrated with Numerous Curious Anecdotes* (1830), p. 23.

60. BL Add Mss. 42, 887, 22 November 1827.

61. 'The Mathew-orama for 1827 – or Cockney Gleanings – Aint that a good un Now?,' 26 March 1827.

62. Janet Sorensen, 'Vulgar tongues: canting dictionaries and the language of the people in eighteenth-century Britain,' *Eighteenth-Century Studies* 37:3 (2004), pp. 435–54.

63. Elaine Hadley, *Melodramatic Tactics: Theatricalized Dissent in the English Marketplace, 1800–1885* (Stanford: Stanford University Press, 1995), p. 3.

64. Joseph Donohue, *Theatre in the Age of Kean* (Oxford: Basil Blackwell, 1975), p. 46 (Donohue's italics).

65. Elaine Hadley, *Melodramatic Tactics: Theatricalized Dissent in the English Marketplace, 1800–1885* (Stanford: Stanford University Press, 1995), pp. 66–7.

66. Maurice Buxton Forman (ed.) *The Letters of John Keats...With Revisions and Additional Letters* (Oxford: Oxford University Press, 1947) Third Edition, To *George and Thomas Keats*, 23 January 1818.

67. For a magistrate's dismissal of a case against a Strand private theatre, see *The British Stage, and Literary Cabinet*, 26 May 1818, p. 294.

68. Charles Beecher Hogan, *The London Stage 1660–1800* (Carbondale, Ill.: Southern Illinois University Press, 1968) Vol. 5 pp. xliii–xliv.

69. *Report from the Select Committee on Dramatic Literature: With The Minutes of Evidence...2 August 1832*, Parliamentary Papers (1831–32) Vol. VII, Questions 209, 210.

70. John Barrell, *Imagining the King's Death: Figurative Treason, Fantasies of Regicide, 1793–1796* (Oxford: Oxford University Press, 2000), p. 568.

71. *Truth and Treason! or, a Narrative of the Royal Procession to the House of Peers, October the 29th, 1795. To Which is Added, an Account of the Martial Procession to Covent-Garden Theatre, on the Evening of the 30th* (1795), pp. 6–8.

72. Leman Thomas Rede, *The Road to the Stage; or, The Performer's Preceptor* (1827), p. 15; James Pack, *Some Account of the Life and Experience of James Pack, Late A Celebrated Actor, in the Pantomime Department, at the Theatre Royal, Drury Lane, and other Places: But Now, by the Grace of God, A Disciple and Follower of the Lord Jesus Christ* (1819), p. 29.

73. Diaries of Anna Margaretta Larpent, Vol. 1, 14 April 1794, Huntington Library, California; Ms. Larpent 1413, Huntington Library, California; BL Add Ms. 27702, 277703, 27714. On Eyre's play, see my *Theatric Revolution: Drama, Censorship and Romantic Period Subcultures, 1773–1832* (Oxford: Oxford University Press, 2006) pp. 126–31; 311–2. The licence was refused principally because of the Larpents' alarm at representing the execution of royalty, Eyre's depiction of Charlotte Corday's anti-republicanism notwithstanding. For the refusal of the 1804 Norwich license, see HM 19926 Vol. 1 folio 8 verso, Huntington Library, California, this updates Worrall (2006).

74. Maurice Buxton Forman (ed.) *The Letters of John Keats ... With Revisions and Additional Letters* (Oxford: Oxford University Press, 1947) Third Edition, To *George and Thomas Keats*, 23 January 1818.

75. Leman Thomas Rede, *The Road to the Stage; or, The Performer's Preceptor* (1827), p. 59.

76. Ibid.; Thomas Dibdin, *The Reminiscences of Thomas Dibdin* (1837) 2 vols, Vol. 2 p. 394; John Bevis, *An experimental enquiry concerning the contents, qualities, and medicinal virtues, of the two mineral waters: Lately discovered at Bagnigge Wells, near London* (1760).

77. Leman Thomas Rede, *The Road to the Stage; or, The Performer's Preceptor* (1827) p. 59; Charles Stuart and A.J. Parks, *Variety Stage: A History of the Music Halls from the Earliest Period to the Present Time* (1895), pp. 46–7.

78. Peter Brooks, 'Melodrama, Body, Revolution,' Jack Bratton, Jim Cook, Christine Gledhill (eds) *Melodrama: Stage Picture Screen* (London: British Film Institute, 1994), p. 19.

79. Thomas Holcroft, *A Tale of Mystery: A Melodrama, in Two Acts* (1826), p. 10.

80. John Britton, *Sheridan and Kotzebue. The Enterprising Adventures of Pizarro ... Also Varieties and Oppositions of Criticisms on The Play of Pizarro* (1799), p. 130.

81. *The Times*, 13 November 1802.

82. Richard Jenkins, *Memoirs of the Bristol Stage, from the Period of the Theatre at Jacob's Well, Down to the Present Time* (Bristol, 1826), pp. 101–102.

83. Thomas Busby, *The overture[,] marches, dances, symphonies, and song in the melo drame, called A tale of mystery: Now performing with universal applause at the Theatre Royal, Covent Garden entirely new, composed by Dr. Busby* (1802).

84. *Rugantino* was revived on 29 June 1825 at the Royal Coburg, although suitably interspersed with a 'Grand Allegorical Ballet' written by the manager, Leclerq. The playbill does not mention whether Busby's music was used.

85. Busby's submission, and that of William Fitzgerald, are in BL Add Ms. 27,899, 27,900.

86. Jane Stabler, *Byron, Poetics and History* (Cambridge: Cambridge University Press, 2002), pp. 65–7.

87. Thomas Holcroft, *A Tale of Mystery: A Melodrama, in Two Acts* (1826), pp. 8ff.

88. *The Times*, Wednesday, 23 March 1803.

89. Jeffrey N. Cox, *Seven Gothic Dramas, 1789–1825* (Athens: Ohio University Press, 1992), pp. 225, 229n.

90. *The Times*, Wednesday, 23 March 1803.

91. James Kenney, *The Blind Boy: A Melo-Drama* (1808), James Kenney, *A Description of The Blind Boy: A New Grand Historic Melo-Drama* (1807). See also, Simon Shepherd, 'The Blind Leading the Blind,' *Nineteenth Century Theatre* 24:2 (1996), pp. 90–107.

92. John Davy, *The Overture and Music in The Blind Boy, a Grand Melodrama* (1808), *Crazy Jane, a Ballad. Sung by Mrs. Mountain ... The Words by M.G. Lewis, etc.* (1799), *A Hymn on depositing the Colours of the Loyal Hampstead Association on Friday the 18th of June 1802 in Hampstead Church ... The words by the Revd Joseph Dixon ... Sung by Mr Incledon* (1802), *Merrily danced the Quaker's Wife, Scottish dance ... for the Pianoforte* (1804).

93. John Davy, *The Favorite Pas Seul ... in the Vale of Mystery ... by Dr. Busby, arranged as a Rondo with Variations for the Pianoforte* (1802).

94. For a variety of recent perspectives, see the essays collected in Gillian Russell and Clara Tuite (eds) *Romantic Sociability: Social Networks and Literary Culture in Britain, 1770–1840* (Cambridge: Cambridge University Press, 2002).

95. The only text surviving is the one sent to John Larpent as Examiner of Plays, Larpent 1385, Huntington Library, California. Parts of the musical score, together with Porter's lyrics, were published separately, Thomas Busby and Ann Maria Porter, *Overture; Strike the Gombay; A Duett; Why truly Sir:* [O how I should like: When Pedro first: When gazing on: Now shines the moon]; *The Favorite Trio* [Hist methought I heard] (1803).

96. William J. Burling, *Summer Theatre in London, 1661–1820, and the Rise of the Haymarket Theatre* (Madison, Teaneck: Fairleigh Dickinson University Press; London: Associated University Presses, 2000), pp. 114, 136.

97. Diane Long Hoeveler and Sarah Davies Cordova, 'Gothic Opera in Britain and France: Genre, Nationalism, and Trans-Cultural Angst,' *Romanticism on the Net*, 34–35, May–August 2004, http://www.erudit.org/revue/ron/2004/v/n34-35/009435ar.html.

98. Royalty Theatre, playbill, 7 September 1787, when *Don Juan* was being played for the 19th time.

99. Moyra Haslett, *Byron's 'Don Juan' and the Don Juan Legend* (Oxford: Clarendon Press, 1997), pp. 32, 36, 39.

100. Larpent 2004, Huntington Library, California.

101. Christoph Willibald Gluck, *Il Convitato di Pietra. Grand Ballet by Mr. Le Picq…the music by the…Chevalier Gluck in which is introducted a…Pas de Trois, part of the Music by the above Author, and the whole adapted for the Harpsichord, Piano Forte, Violin & Flute, by F.H. Barthélémon* (1785).

102. For de Loutherbourg and Barthélémon, see my Chapter 4 in *Theatric Revolution: Drama, Censorship and Romantic Periods Subcultures, 1774–1832* (Oxford: Oxford University Press, 2006).

103. *Don Juan; or, The libertine destroyed, a grand pantomimical ballet, in two parts, first performed at the Theatre Royal, Drury Lane, on Tuesday, the 26th of October 1790* (1790). There was a further edition for the theatre at Boston, Mass., in 1795.

104. As was common with successful pantomime and burletta pieces, throughout his life Moncrieff's works were sometimes separately issued as song collections, see *Songs, Duets, Chorusses, &c. Serious and Comick, as Sung in the Highly Popular…Entertainment, in Two Acts, Yclept Giovanni in London* (c.1817); *Songs, Duets, and Glees: Sung…at the Royal Gardens, Vauxhall* (1827); *Songs, Duets, Trios, Chorusses, &c. &c. in Actors al fresco, or, The Play in the Pleasure Grounds (an occasional vaudeville) First Produced at the Royal Gardens, Vauxhall, 4th June, 1827*(1827); *An original collection of Songs: sung at the Theatres Royal, etc* (1850).

105. See also William J. Burling, *Summer Theatre in London, 1661–1820, and the Rise of the Haymarket Theatre* (Madison, Teaneck: Fairleigh Dickinson University Press; London: Associated University Presses, 2000), p. 114.

106. Kane O'Hara, *Midas; An English Burletta* (1764) p. 12; William Thomas Moncrieff, *Giovanni In London; or The Libertine Reclaimed, A Grand Moral, Satirical, Comical, Tragical, Melo-Dramatical, Pantomimical, Critical, Infernal, Terrestrial, Celestial, in one word for all, Gallymaufrical-ollapodridacal Operatic*

Extravaganza, In Two Acts, As Performed At The Theatres Royal Drury Lane And Covent Garden (1825), p. 2; Charles Burney, The Songs in Queen Mab: As they are perform'd at the Theatre Royal in Drury Lane compos'd by the Society of the Temple of Apollo (1751).

107. John Addison and William Thomas Moncrieff, Dearest Ellen...Notturno [The daylight has long been sunk] written by W.G.T. Moncrieff, & Adapted to the Air of the Copenhagen Waltz, etc. (c.1815); John Addison, Stranger! Pass not, welcome to my cot: A favourite song, sung by Mr. Gibbon, at Vauxhall Gardens (1805).
108. Charles Dickens, Our Mutual Friend (1864) Vol. 1 p. 143.
109. Cf., The Virtuous Maid of the Inn; or, The Entertaining History of Margaret Sunders[sic], commonly called Pretty Peggy of Derby.... To which is added, a Collection of the Most Choice Songs (1791). See also the broadsheet, Pretty Peggy of Derby (c.1800).
110. William Thomas Moncrieff, Songs of the Gypsies: To which is Prefixed an Historical Introduction on the Origin and Customs of This Singular and Interesting People...with music by S. Nelson (1832).
111. William Thomas Moncrieff, Van Dieman's Land (1830) p. 36.
112. BL Add.Mss. 29905, 3, 22, 28 January 1852.
113. Charles Dibdin, Professional and Literary Memoirs of Charles Dibdin the Younger, Dramatist and Upward of Thirty Years Manager of Minor Theatres (ed.) George Speaight (London: The Society for Theatre Research, 1956) p. 111.
114. The Times, Monday, 4 November 1811.
115. Cited in Joseph Donohue, Theatre in the Age of Kean (Oxford: Basil Blackwell, 1975) p. 46.
116. Thomas Dibdin, The Reminiscences of Thomas Dibdin (1837) Vol. 2 p. 136.
117. Quoted in Joseph Donohue, Theatre in the Age of Kean (Oxford: Basil Blackwell, 1975) p. 49. On Scott, see Jacky Bratton, 'Jane Scott the Writer Manager,' Women and Playwriting in Nineteenth-Century Britain, Tracy C. Davis and Ellen Donkin (eds) (Cambridge: Cambridge University Press, 1999) pp. 77–98; Gilli Bush-Bailey, 'Still Working it Out: An Account of the Practical Workshop Rediscovery of Company Practice and Romantic Performance Styles via Jane Scott's Plays,' Nineteenth Century Theatre and Film 29:2 (2002), pp. 6–21.
118. Caleb Crowquill, The New Patent, or Theatrical Secrets Worth Knowing, In a Series of Familiar Epistles, Addressed to H— H— Esq. of the United Theatres of Great Britain & Ireland, Patentee, &c. (Dublin, 1822), p. 35n. Christopher Morash does not mention Crowquill's work but the patent (which appears to have passed between individuals rather amongst consortia of lessees) was transferred in 1819 from Henry Harris to Frederick Jones and a new theatre built, A History of Irish Theatre, 1601–2000 (Cambridge: Cambridge University Press, 2002), p. 77.
119. Leman Thomas Rede, The Road to the Stage; or, The Performer's Preceptor (1827), p. 21.
120. 'Question 31. Does he [the Lord Chamberlain] claim a censorship over pieces that are acted in the country? – Decidedly, under the Act of Parliament; the same Act of Parliament authorises him to do that.' Report from

the Select Committee on Dramatic Literature: With The Minutes of Evidence ... 2 August 1832, Parliamentary Papers (1831–2) Vol. VII p. 10.

121. The standard fee was two guineas (£2.2s). For 1816, Larpent recorded a total of £107.2s. in fees received, HM 19926, Vol. 2, folio 3 recto, Huntington Library, California.

122. Leman Thomas Rede, *The Road to the Stage; or, The Performer's Preceptor* (1827), pp. 56–7.

123. Jacob Beuler, *Comic Songs to Popular Tunes ... Ninth Collection* (1833), pp. 24–5.

124. Rev.Thomas Thirlwall, *Royalty Theatre. A Solemn Protest Against The Revival of Scenic Exhibitions And Interludes, At The Royalty Theatre; Containing Remarks on Pizarro, The Stranger, And John Bull* (1803) p. 9; John Percival, *A Few Observations in Defence of the Scenic Exhibitions at The Royalty Theatre* (1804), p. 31.

125. Rev.Thomas Thirlwall, *Royalty Theatre. A Solemn Protest Against The Revival Of Scenic Exhibitions And Interludes, At The Royalty Theatre; Containing Remarks On Pizarro, The Stranger, And John Bull* (1803), p. 9.

126. John O'Brien's *Harlequin Britain: Pantomime and Entertainment, 1690–1760* (Baltimore, MD: The Johns Hopkins University Press, 2004), Chapter 5, pp. 138–80.

127. John Adolphus, *Memoirs of John Bannister, Comedian* (1839) 25. John A. Thieme notes that London spouting clubs declined in popularity after the 1770s although he does not note their transmogrification into working-class private theatres of the 'song-and-supper' clubs of the 1820s and 1830s, 'Spouting, Spouting-Clubs and Spouting Companions, *Theatre Notebook* 29 (1975), pp. 9–18.

128. Arthur Murphy, *The Apprentice. A farce, in two acts, as it is Perform'd at the Theatre-Royal, in Drury-Lane* (1756), p. 8.

129. Ibid.

130. See Helen Burke, '*The London Merchant* and Eighteenth-Century British Law,' *Philogical Quarterly* 19 (1993) pp. 347–66; John O'Brien, *Harlequin Britain: Pantomime and Entertainment, 1690–1760* (Baltimore, MD: The Johns Hopkins University Press, 2004), pp. 169–72.

131. Arthur Murphy, *The Apprentice. A farce, in two acts, as it is Perform'd at the Theatre-Royal, in Drury-Lane* (1756), pp. 6, 43.

132. Ibid., p. 21.

133. R.J. Broadbent, *A History of Pantomime* (London: Simpkins, Marshall, Hamilton, Kent & Co., 1901), p. 219.

134. *Letter To The Right Hon. Robert Peel, Respecting The Proposed Introduction of a bill, to Repeal so much of the Act of 10th Geo.II.Cap.28, As Requires Notice to be Sent to The Lord Chamberlain ... and Showing that the Consequence of such an Act Would be, to Confirm the Monopoly Claimed by the Proprietors of Drury Lane and Covent Garden, and to Enable Them to Annihilate the Minor Theatres* (1829), pp. 10–11. *George Barnwell* had enough songs indicated to escape suppression by the Theatres' Royal. See also, *The songster's delight: Being a choice collection of songs. Containing, My Nannie O. Bonny Jean of Aberdeen. The Dutchess of Newcastle's lamentation. The London merchant* (1805); [songs] *George Barnwell. The Comic Phiz, &c. Anthony Brown. Fair Young Phoebe* (Edinburgh, c.1820); *The Joys of Kilfane. Together with George Barnwell* (Dublin, c.1820); Judith Milhous 'The Economics of Theatrical

Dance in Eighteenth-Century London,' *Theatre Journal* (Assn for Theatre in Higher Education) 55:3 (2003), pp. 481–508.

135. Lucinda Cole, 'The London Merchant and the Institution of Apprenticeship,' *Criticism: A Quarterly for Literature and the Arts* 37:1 (1995), pp. 57–84.

136. Arthur Murphy, *The Apprentice. A farce, in two acts, as it is Perform'd at the Theatre-Royal, in Drury-Lane* (1756) np [David Garrick] Prologue.

137. John Adolphus, *Memoirs of John Bannister, Comedian* (1839), p. 25.

138. Playbills, Theatre, Stamford, Lincolnshire, 3 August 1801.

139. Larpent 2322, Huntington Library, California.

140. *Rules and Regulations for the Lambs Conduit Private Theatre* (1799), pp. 4, 7.

141. Sybil Rosenfeld mentions lower-class private theatres only fleetingly, *Temples of Thespis, Some Private Theatres and Theatricals in England and Wales, 1700–1820* (London: Society for Theatre Research, 1978), p. 8.

142. *The Rambler's Magazine; or, Man of Fashion's Companion*, 8 January 1822 p. 81; 16 January 1822, p. 82.

143. *The Times*, Saturday, 9 January 1808.

144. J.G.A. Pocock, 'Enthusiasm: the Antiself of Enlightenment,' *Huntington Library Quarterly* 160 (1998) pp. 7–28; Lawrence E. Klein, 'Sociability, Solitude and Enthusiasm,' *Huntington Library Quarterly* 160 (1998), pp. 153–77.

145. *The British Stage, and Literary Cabinet* July 1818, pp. 159–60.

146. Harry R. Beaudry, *The English Theatre and John Keats*, Salzburg Studies in English Literature (Salzburg: University of Salzburg, 1973).

147. Harry R. Beaudry identifies the venue as either Dominion of Fancy (ex-Bolognas's, see below) or the Minor but says little about their context, *The English Theatre and John Keats*, Salzburg Studies in English Literature (Salzburg: University of Salzburg, 1973), p. 26.

148. Görel Garlic, *To Serve the Purpose of the Drama: The Theatre Designs and Plays of Samuel Beazley 1786–1851* (London: Society For Theatre Research, 2003), p. 96.

149. *The Times*, 13 July 1815.

150. John Hamilton Reynolds, *One, Two, Three, Four, Five; by Advertisement: a musical entertainment, In One Act.* (c.1829), p. 21.

151. *The Rambler's Magazine; or, Man of Fashion's Companion* March 1822, p. 129.

152. Ibid., January 1822, p. 32.

153. John Hamilton Reynolds's farce was not printed until c.1829, as *One, Two, Three, Four, Five; by Advertisement: a musical entertainment, In One Act.*

154. Walter Donaldson remembered performing 'the questionably moral tragedy of "George Barnwell," ' *Recollections of an Actor* (London: John Maxwell and Company, 1865), pp. 104–105.

155. For a study of dramatic topicality from a Foucauldian perspective, see Daniel O'Quinn, *Staging Governance: Theatrical Imperialism in London, 1770–1800* (Baltimore: Johns Hopkins University Press, 2005).

156. David Erskine Baker, Isaac Reed and Stephen Jones, *Biographica Dramatica* 3 vols (1812) Vol. 2, with MS annotations, Huntington Library, California. Reprinted in *The Thespian Magazine* (1792) Vol. 1, but untraced.

157. Larpent 933, Huntington Library, California; *The Airs, Duets, Glees, Chorusses, &c. in the Comic Opera of the Magician No Conjurer* (1792).

158. *The Children of Apollo: A Poem. Containing an impartial Review of all the Dramatic Works of our Modern Authors and Authoresses. Particularly Lady*

Wallace. Margravine of Anspach. Honourable Major North. Honourable John St. John. (c.1793), p. 27.

159. Catherine Hutton, *The Life of William Hutton, F.A.S.S. Including a Particular Account of the Riots at Birmingham in 1791* (1817), p. 233.

160. Joseph Priestley, *Dr. Priestley's Letter to the Inhabitants of Birmingham* (1791), p. 3.

161. Ibid., p. 4.

162. The prints in *Views of the Ruins of the Principal Houses Destroyed During the Riots at Birmingham* (1791) are dated May 1792.

163. Lewis Walpole Library, Farmington, Connecticut.

164. Samuel Parr, *A Letter From Irenopolis To The Inhabitants of Eleutheropolis; or, A Serious Address to the Dissenters of Birmingham* (Birmingham, 1792), p. 25.

165. Joseph Priestley, *Dr. Priestley's Letter to the Inhabitants of Birmingham* (1791) p. 8; Diaries Of Anna Margaretta Larpent, Vol. 1, 19 March 1794 , Huntington Library, California.

166. For Merry's radical circle, see Jon Mee, ' "Reciprocal Expressions of Kindsness:" Robert Merr, Della Cruscan and the Limits of Sociability,' in *Romantic Sociability: Social Networks and Literary Culture in Britain, 1770–1840,* Gillian Russell and Clara Tuite (eds) (Cambridge: Cambridge University Press, 2002), pp. 104–22.

167. W.N. Hargreaves-Mawdsley, *The English Della Cruscans and their Time, 1783–1828* (The Hague: Martinus Nijhoff, 1967), pp. 239–40.

168. For the performance reception, see W.N. Hargreaves-Mawdsley, *The English Della Cruscans and their Time, 1783–1828* (The Hague: Martinus Nijhoff, 1967), p. 254. Hargreaves-Mawdsley dismisses *The Magician* in one sentence.

169. Charles Bonnor, *A Letter to Philip Thickness, Esq ... To Which is Added, Mr. Thicknesse's Answer* (1792), p. 13; Charles Bonnor, *Facts Relating to the Meeting, Held on Wednesday, the 15th of February, at the London Tavern, Respecting the Later Delivery of Letters; and an Explanation of some Circumstances that have led to a Difference between The Comptroller General and his Deputy* (1792); Philip Thicknesse, *A Letter To Charles Bonner, Esq ... Deputy Comptroller of the Post-Office* (1792).

170. On John Dent's original Royal Circus *Bastille* (1789), see Jane Moody, *Illegitimate: Theatre in London, 1770–1840* (Cambridge: Cambridge University Press, 2000), pp. 25–8.

171. PRO T[reasury] S[olicitor] 11/966, 19 October; 16 November 1792.

172. John Barrell, *Exhibition Extraordinary!!: Radical Broadsides of the Mid 1790s* (Nottingham: Trent Editions, 2001), pp. 9–12.

173. Larpent 886, Huntington Library, California.

174. Ibid.

175. Ibid.

176. James Fennell, *An Apology for the Life of James Fennell* (1814), p. 306.

177. George Taylor, *The French Revolution and the London Stage, 1789–1805* (Cambridge: Cambridge University Press, 2000), pp. 61–2.

178. *Airs, Duetts, and Chorusses, Arrangment of Scenery, and Sketch of the Pantomime Entitled The Picture of Paris. Taken in the Year 1790* (1790), pp. 10, 17.

179. Linda Colley, *Britons: Forging the Nation, 1707–1837* (New Haven, CT: Yale University Press, 1992).

180. *Harlequin Incendiary: Or, Columbine Cameron. A Musical Pantomime. As it is Perform'd at the Theatre-Royal in Drury-Lane* (1746), p. 22.
181. *Harlequin Incendiary* (1746), p. 16.
182. Ibid., p. 19.
183. Ibid.
184. Ibid., p. 20.
185. Ibid., p. 23.
186. Mary Dorothy George, *Catalogue of Political and Personal Satires Preserved in the Department of Prints and Drawings in the British Museum, 1793–1800* (London: British Museum Trustees, 1942) Vol. VII, Cat. No. 8300.
187. James Fennell, *An Apology for the Life of James Fennell* (1814), p. 307.
188. *Airs, Duetts, and Chorusses, Arrangment of Scenery, and Sketch of the Pantomime Entitled The Picture of Paris. Taken in the Year 1790* (1790), p. 7.
189. See my *Theatric Revolution: Drama, Censorship and Romantic Period Subcultures, 1773–1832* (Oxford: Oxford University Press, 2006).
190. *Airs, Duetts, and Chorusses, Arrangment of Scenery, and Sketch of the Pantomime Entitled The Picture of Paris. Taken in the Year 1790* (1790), p. 16.
191. Ibid., p. 21.
192. James L. Clifford, *Robert Merry: A Pre-Byronic Hero* (Manchester: The Manchester University Press, 1942), p. 21n.2.
193. Catherine Hutton, *The Life of William Hutton, F.A.S.S. Including a Particular Account of the Riots at Birmingham in 1791* (1817), pp. 241, 243–4.
194. Hutton, *The Life of William Hutton* (1817), p. 244.
195. *The Report of the Trials of the Rioters, At the Assizes Held at Warwick, August 20, 1791* (Birmingham, 1791).
196. *A Correspondence Between the Rev. Robert Wells, M.A. Chaplain of the Earl of Dunmore, and A Gentleman Under the Signature of Publicola, Relative to the Riots at Birmingham, and the Commemoration of the French Revolution* (1791).
197. John Nott [psued], *Very Familiar Letters, Addressed to Dr. Priestley, In Answer to His Familiar Letters to the Inhabitants of Birmingham* (1790), pp. 13–14.
198. Nott [psued], *Very Familiar Letters, Addressed to Dr. Priestley* (1790), p. 26.
199. *An Authentic Account of the Riots in Birmingham, on the 14th, 15th, 16th, and 17th Days of July, 1791; Also, the Judge's Charge, the Pleadings of the Counsel, and the Substance of the Evidence Given on the Trials of the Rioters* (Birmingham, 1791), p. 6.
200. Catherine Hutton, *The Life of William Hutton, F.A.S.S. Including a Particular Account of the Riots at Birmingham in 1791* (1817), p. 244; Joseph Priestley, *Dr. Priestley's Letter to the Inhabitants of Birmingham* (1791), p. 4.
201. *Address of the Students at the New College to Dr. Priestly, in Consequence of the Birmingham Riots* (1791), p. 3.
202. *The Times*, 26 July 1791.
203. Jan Golinski, *Science as Public Culture: Chemistry and Enlightenment in Britain, 1760–1820* (Cambridge: Cambridge University Press, 1992), pp. 83–5.
204. *A Letter from Timothy Sobersides, Extinguisher-Maker, At Wolverhampton, To Jonathan Blast, Bellows-Maker, At Birmingham* (1792), p. 7.
205. *The Wisdom of our Modern Dissenters, Analyzed in the Crucible of Reason, By a Chemcial Member of the Church of England* (1792), pp. 3, 6.

206. Samuel Stearns, *The Mystery of Animal Magnetism Revealed to the World* (1791), p. 23.
207. Robert Merry, *The Wounded Soldier, a Poem* (1795), p. 4.
208. Ibid., p. 8.
209. 'Citizen' T.G. Ballard is how he styled himself in the broadside, *The Tree of Liberty* (1795).
210. Jacqueline Labbe, *The Romantic Paradox: Love, Violence and the uses of Romance, 1760–1830* (Basingstoke: Macmillan Press/New York: St Martin's Press, 2000), pp. 9, 46; Judith Pascoe, *Romantic Theatricality: Gender, Poetry, and Spectatorship* (Ithaca: Cornell University Press, 1997) Chapter 3.
211. *The Conjuror's Magazine; or, Magical Physiognomical Mirror*, February 1792, pp. 223–4.
212. John Nott, Button Burnisher [psued], *Very Familiar Letters, Addressed to Dr. Priestley* (1790), p. 26.
213. Catherine Hutton, *The Life of William Hutton* (1817), p. 241.
214. A contemporary inventory of Priestley's house, predictably, does indeed include several telescopes and an orrery, Samuel Timmins, *Dr. Priestley's Laboratory, 1791* [*reprinted from the 'Birmingham Post,' March, 15, 22, 29, and April 5, 1890*] (Coventry, c.1890).
215. *Trials of the Birmingham Rioters* (1792), p. 40.
216. Ibid., p. 46.
217. Ibid., p. 90.
218. George Baldwin *Book of Dreams. 1811–1812–1813* (1813), p. 29.
219. J. Proud, *A Candid and Impartial Reply to the Rev. Dr. Priestley's Letters, Addressed by Him to the Members of the New Jerusalem* (Birmingham, 1791).
220. A facsimile text, modern introduction and editorial apparatus is provided in Jeffrey N. Cox, *Slavery, Abolition and Emancipation: Writings in the British Romantic Period: Slavery* (London: Pickering and Chatto) Vol. 5.
221. Jeffrey N. Cox, *Slavery, Abolition and Emancipation: Writings in the British Romantic Period: Slavery* (London: Pickering and Chatto) Vol. 5 p. 110; Walley Chamberlain Oulton, *The History of the Theatres of London ... From the Year 1771 to 1795*, 2 vols (1796), p. 184 gives the first night of *Harlequin Mungo* as the 13 November 1787 but this seems to have been the second night. The pantomime ran until at least 1 January 1788.
222. Jean-Baptiste Laurent (who played the Clown in *Furibond*) and Mr Male were also the producers of the 'Local Melo-Dramatic Spectacle,' *British Heroes; or, the Defeat of Junot!* (1808), Royalty Theatre, playbill, 21 September 1808.
223. Roxann Wheeler, *The Complexion of Race: Categories of Difference in Eighteenth-Century British Culture* (Philadelphia: University of Pennsylvania Press, 2000), pp. 225–33, 227.
224. R. Humphreys, *The Memoirs of J. Decastro, Comedian* (1824), pp. 183–4.
225. William Bates and William Reeve, *Harlequin Mungo; or, A Peep into the Tower: A New Pantomimical Entertainment, in Two Acts: As Performing at the Royalty Theatre, Well-Street, Goodman's-Fields* (1788), p. 11.
226. Herbert Marshall and Mildred Stock, *Ira Aldridge: The Negro Tragedian* (London: Rockliff, 1958).
227. James P. Byrne, 'The Genesis of Whiteface in Nineteenth-Century American Popular Culture,' *Melus* 29:3/4 (2004) pp. 133–49.

228. Mikko Tuhkanen, 'Of blackface and paranoid knowledge: Richard Wright, Jacques Lacan, and the ambivalence of black minstrelsy,' *Diacritics* 31:2 (2001), pp. 9–35.

229. Quoted in Sean X. Goudie, 'The West Indies, Commerce, and Play for U.S. Empire: Recovering J. Robinson's "The Yorker's Stratagem" (1792),' *Early American Literature* 40:1 (2005), pp. 1–35.

230. Felicity A. Nussbaum, 'The theatre of empire: Racial counterfeit, Racial realism,' Kathleen Wilson (ed.) *A New Imperial History: Culture, Identity, and Modernity in Britain and the Empire, 1660–1840* (Cambridge: Cambridge University Press, 2004), pp. 71–90, 79.

231. Eric Lott, *Love and Theft: Blackface Minstrelsy and the American Working Class* (Oxford: Oxford University Press, 1993), pp. 72–3.

232. Henry Angelo, *Reminiscences of Henry Angelo* (1828), p. 446.

233. Ephraim Hardcastle [pseud. W.H. Pyne], *Wine and Walnuts; or, After Dinner Chit-Chat* (1823) Vol. 1 p. 277.

234. Charles Dibdin, *The Mirror; or, Harlequin Every-Where. A Pantomimical Burletta, in Three Parts. As it is performed at the Theatre-Royal in Covent Garden* (1779), p. 9.

235. For the possibility of Hewlett's appearance at the Coburg, *c.*1824, see Herbert Marshall and Mildred Stock, *Ira Aldridge: The Negro Tragedian* (London: Rockliff, 1958). Although it is not noted in the study, *The Times* letter was reprinted from the American *National Advocate*, see George A. Thompson Jr, *A Documentary History of the African Theatre* (Evanston, Ill.: Northwestern University Press, 1998), Document 61, pp. 147–8.

236. For an important corrective, see Samuel A. Hay, *African American Theatre: A Historical and Critical Analysis* (Cambridge: Cambridge University Press, 1994), pp. 136–7.

237. Eric Lott, *Love and Theft: Blackface Minstrelsy and the American Working Class* (Oxford: Oxford University Press, 1993), p. 46. Aldridge's denial of having played Hamlet is in Ira Aldridge, *Memoir and Theatrical Career of Ira Aldridge, the African Roscius* (1850), p. 11.

238. On the context of Mathews's search for black voices, see Eric Lott, *Love and Theft: Blackface Minstrelsy and the American Working Class* (Oxford: Oxford University Press, 1993) p. 45; *The London Mathews; Containing An Account of this celebrated Comedian's Trip to America . . . To Which Are Prefixed, Several Original Comic Songs, Viz. Travellers All . . . Mrs. Bradish's Boarding-House. Opossum up a Gum-Tree* (1825), p. 10.

239. Christine C. Mather, 'Acting (Each) Other: J. Hewlett, Charles Mathews, and Ira Aldridge,' *Text & Presentation: The Journal of the Comparative Drama Conference* 24 (2003), pp. 69–77.

240. *The London Mathews; Containing An Account of this celebrated Comedian's Trip to America* (1825), p. 13.

241. *The Times*, Saturday, 10 July 1824.

242. Richard Carlile (ed.) *The Newgate Monthly Magazine; or, Calendar of Men, Things and Opinions*, p. 231; Playbills, Theatre, Stamford, 12 July 1826.

243. *A Statement of the Differences Subsisting Between the Proprietors and Performers of the Theatre-Royal, Covent-Garden* (1800), p. 67.

244. John Payne Collier, *An Old Man's Diary, Forty Years Ago; For The First Six Months Of 1832* (London: Thomas Richards 1871) Vol. 1 p. 40.

245. Anne Mathews, *Memoirs of Charles Mathews, Comedian* (1838) Vol. 2 p. 472.

246. Haymarket, playbills, 5 September 1814, Harvard Theatre Collection.

247. Helen Thomas is equivocal on whether Wedderburn was a founder of discursivity, an orator, a writer or all three, *Romanticism and Slave Narratives: Transatlantic Testimonies* (Cambridge: Cambridge University Press, 2000), pp. 256–9, 263, 267–70.

248. 'I was told that Wedderburn was anxious to learn to write during his confinement, and that he expressed this wish immediately on entering his cell. I bid the turnkey tell him that I should be most happy to assist him with books, paper, or money, if he wanted, but I had no answer to this,' *The Republican* 20 October 1820, pp. 364–5. Carlile offered to pay for Wedderburn's coals and reported he was in solitary confinement, *The Republican* 1 March 1822, p. 265.

249. 'Follow not the example of St. Domingo, let not your jubilee, which will take place, be stained with the blood of your oppressors,' Robert Wedderburn (ed.) *The Axe Laid to the Root, Or A Fatal Blow to Oppressors, Being an Address to the Planters and Negroes of the Island of Jamaica* (1817) No. 1 p. 3.

250. Citizen Bailey, *The White Devils Un-Cased. Being the First Discourse Upon Ecclesiastical Tyranny, and Superstition, Delivered at Section 2 and 7 of the Friends of Liberty . . . . Lecture the Second* (1795) p. 9.

251. *The London Alfred* reported an open-air meeting in Finsbury Market Place in November 1819 addressed by 'Mr. DAVISON[*sic*], (*a man of colour*).' This was William Davidson, executed in February 1820 for involvement in the Cato Street conspiracy. Richard Carlile of *The Republican* remembered meeting him and 'his vivacity to keep the whole company alive.' See *The London Afred*, Paul Keen (ed.) *The Popular Radical Press, 1817–1821*, 6 Vols (London: Pickering & Chatto, 2003); *The Republican* 3 March 1820, pp. 218–9.

252. Paul Edwards and James Walvin, *Black Personalities in the Era of the Slave Trade* (London and Basingstoke: Macmillan Press, 1983), p. 164.

253. Henry Angelo, *Reminiscences of Henry Angelo* (1828) Vol. 1 pp. 284–7.

254. For 40 black men at The Shovel tavern, East Smithfield, see Joseph Curry, Thomas Riley, theft, 11 July 1787, *The Proceedings of the Old Bailey Ref*: t17870711-4; David Worrall, *Radical Culture: Discourse, Resistance and Surveillance, 1790–1820* (Hemel Hempstead: Harvester, 1992) pp. 146, 161; PRO HO 42/193.97, 23 August 1819.

255. PRO HO 44/1.229, *c.*spring, 1820.

256. Ibid., 44/2, 14 February 1820.

257. *The Rambler's Magazine; or, Fashionable Emporium of Polite Literature* April 1822, p. 177.

258. James Townley, *High Life Below Stairs. A farce of two acts. As it is performed at the Theatre-Royal in Drury-Lane* (1759) p. 4. The play is sometimes attributed to David Garrick. See also, Gillian Russell, ' "Keeping Place:" Servants, Theater and Sociability in Mid-Eighteenth-Century Britain,' *Eighteenth Century: Theory and Interpretation* 42:1 (2001), pp. 21–42.

259. John O'Keefe recalled 'hisses and groans, and even many a handful of half-pence . . . flung on the stage' from the footmen's gallery during a peformance of *High Life Below Stairs, Recollections of the Life of John O'Keefe* (1826), Vol. 1 p. 162.

260. Oliver Grey, *An Apology for the Servants....* *Occasioned by the Representation of the Farce called* High Life Below Stairs, *and by what has been said to their Disadvantage in the* Public Papers (1760), p. 6.

261. Ibid., p. 17; John Jackson, *The History of the Scottish Stage* (Edinburgh, 1793), pp. 376–8.

262. David Richardson, *The Bristol Slaver Traders: A Collective Portrait* (Bristol: Bristol Branch of the Historical Assocation, 1985).

263. James Townley, *High Life Below Stairs. A farce of two acts. As it is performed at the Theatre-Royal in Drury-Lane* (1759), p. 4.

264. 'Madras Theatricals of Ton,' *The Times*, Monday, 11 August 1788.

265. Giles Waterfield, Anne French and Matthew Craske (eds), *Below Stairs: 400 Years of Servants' Portraits* (London: National Portrait Gallery Publications, 2003), pp. 128–9, Cat. 67. Two impressions of the print 'High Life below Stairs' dated to 23 February 1774, signed by Orde, but with variant handwritten inscriptions, are at Call no. 774.2.23.1.1 and 774.2.23.1.2., Lewis Walpole Library, Farmington, Connecticut, USA.

266. Larpent 1301, Huntington Library, California.

267. Douglas Hay, 'The State and the Market in 1800: Lord Kenyon and Mr Waddington,' *Past and Present* 162 (1999), pp. 163–94.

268. Frederick Reynolds, *Laugh When You Can: A Comedy, In Five Acts. As Peformed at the Theatre Royal, Covent-Garden* (1799), p. 5.

269. Leman Thomas Rede, *The Road to the Stage; or, The Performer's Preceptor.* (1827), p. 38.

270. Matthew Gregory Lewis, *The Castle Spectre: A Drama. In Five Acts. First performed at the Theatre Royal, Drury-Lane, on Thursday, December 14, 1797* (1798), p. 100.

271. George Colman the Younger, *Inkle and Yarico An Opera. In Three Acts. As Performed at the Theatre-Royal in the Hay-Market* (1787), p. 3; 'The Story of Inkle and Yarico,' *The Times*, Monday, 6 August 1787.

272. Leman Thomas Rede, *The Road to the Stage; or, The Performer's Preceptor.* (1827), p. 38.

273. Ibid., p. 38.

274. Ibid., pp. 33–4.

275. Ibid., p. 38.

276. Ibid., pp. 38–9.

277. John Finlay, *Miscellanies. The Foreign Relations of the British Empire: The Internal Resources of Ireland* (Dublin, 1835), pp. 247, 282.

278. Larpent 839, Huntington Library, California.

279. *Report from the Select Committee on Dramatic Literature: With The Minutes of Evidence...2 August 1832*, Parliamentary Papers (1831–2) Vol. VII, Questions 209, 210.

280. William J. Burling, *Summer Theatre in London, 1661–1820, and the Rise of the Haymarket Theatre* (Madison, Teaneck: Fairleigh Dickinson University Press; London: Associated University Presses, 2000), p. 149.

281. One commentator claimed the Haymarket 'dares not open till May 15, and must close by September 14,' James Peller Malcolm, *Anecdotes of the Manners and Customs of London During the Eighteenth-Century Including the Charities, Depravities, Dresses, and Amusements, of the Citizens of London During that*

Period; With a Review of the State of Society In 1807 2 vols (1810) Vol. 2 pp. 310–11.

282. William J. Burling, *Summer Theatre in London, 1661–1820, and the Rise of the Haymarket Theatre* (Madison, Teaneck: Fairleigh Dickinson University Press; London: Associated University Presses, 2000) p. 152; Jeffrey N. Cox, *Slavery, Abolition and Emancipation: Writings in the British Romantic Period: Slavery* (London: Pickering and Chatto), Vol. 5 p. 2.

283. Cited in William J. Burling, *Summer Theatre in London, 1661–1820, and the Rise of the Haymarket Theatre* (Madison, Teaneck: Fairleigh Dickinson University Press; London: Associated University Presses, 2000), p. 145.

284. For the history of the Royalty, see my *Theatric Revolution: Drama, Censorship and Romantic Period Subcultures, 1774–1832* (2006) and Mary Dorothy George, *Catalogue of Political and Personal Satires Preserved in the Department of Prints and Drawings in the British Museum, 1793–1800* (London: British Museum Trustees, 1938) Vol. VI, Cat. No 7214.

285. Isaac Jackman, *Royal and Royalty Theatres. Letter to Phillips Glover, Esq of Wispington, In Lincolnshire; in a Dedication to the Burletta of Hero and Leander, now performing, with the most distinguished applause, at the Royalty Theatre, in Goodman's Fields* (1787).

286. The author was one 'W. Bates' who also wrote *Gil Blas; or, The Fool of Fortune. A . . . Pantomimic Entertainment in Two Parts* (1788).

287. Felicity A. Nussbaum, 'The theatre of empire: Racial counterfeit, racial realism,' Kathleen Wilson (ed.) *A New Imperial History: Culture, Identity, and Modernity in Britain and the Empire, 1660–1840* (Cambridge: Cambridge University Press, 2004), pp. 71–90.

288. Authorship of *Furibond; or, Harlequin Negro* is attributed to James Powell (and 'G. Male') on the basis of the BL catalogue and a handwritten Ms note on their copy of the 1807 edition. The ms. Drury Lane account book confirms payments for the 1807 Christmas pantomime distributed to 'Laurent on ac of Pant' (£25 and £35), 'Mayle' (£25), 'Powell for Pant' (£25) and 'Mrs. Richardson by Agr for Pant' (£50), BL Add. Ms. 29710, folios 374 recto, 377 recto, 388 verso.

289. A facsimile text, introduction and editorial apparatus is in Jeffrey N. Cox, *Slavery, Abolition and Emancipation: Writings in the British Romantic Period: Slavery* (London: Pickering and Chatto), Vol. 5 p. xxiv.

290. Jane Moody, *Illegitimate: Theatre in London, 1770–1840* (Cambridge: Cambridge University Press, 2000) p. 88. See also Moody's discussion of 'Mute Busines,' pp. 87–98.

291. Felicity A. Nussbaum, 'The theatre of empire: Racial counterfeit, racial realism,' Kathleen Wilson (ed.) *A New Imperial History: Culture, Identity, and Modernity in Britain and the Empire, 1660–1840* (Cambridge: Cambridge University Press, 2004) p. 84.

292. Elizabeth Macauley, *Facts Against Falsehood! Being a Brief Statement of Miss Macauley's Engagements at the Winter Theatres* (1824).

293. George Colman, the Younger, *Inkle and Yarico: An opera, in three acts. As performed at the Theatre-Royal in the Hay-Market, On Saturday, August, 11th, 1787* (Dublin, 1787), p. 30.

294. Ibid., *Observations On The Notice Of A Motion to Rescind Certain Powers of His Majesty's Lord Chamberlain* (1829), p. 2.

295. William J. Burling discusses the financial crises occasioned by Colman the Elder's poor health and how his son met the challenge of ensuring the theatre's survival, *Summer Theatre in London, 1661–1820, and the Rise of the Haymarket Theatre* (Madison, Teaneck: Fairleigh Dickinson University Press; London: Associated University Presses, 2000).

296. *Airs, Ballads, &c. In The Blackamoor Wash'd White. A New Comic Opera. As it will be performed this Evening At the Theatre-Royal, Drury-Lane.* (1776), pp. 13–14. See also the Lord Chamberlain's copy at Larpent Ms. 400, Huntington Library, California. There appear to be a number of textual variants between the published *Airs, Ballads, &c.* and the theatre scribe's copy text; Felicity A. Nussbaum, 'The theatre of empire: Racial counterfeit, racial realism,' Kathleen Wilson (ed.) *A New Imperial History: Culture, Identity, and Modernity in Britain and the Empire, 1660–1840* (Cambridge: Cambridge University Press, 2004), p. 82.

297. Larpent 839 *The Benevolent Planters Slavery but a Name*, Huntington Library, California. See also, Bellamy's *Miscellanies in Prose and Verse* (1795) containing a prologue, 'Spoken by Mr. Palmer, then Manager of the Circus: Before the Exhibition of the Destruction of the Bastille,' a reference to John Dent's *The Bastille* at the Royal Circus, 1789. Bellamy may have been the reviewer of William Roscoe's *The Wrongs of Africa* (1787) in his journal *The General Magazine, and Impartial Review,* July 1787, pp. 77–8.

298. Robert Wedderburn, *The Axe Laid to the Root; or, A Fatal Blow to Oppressors, Being an Address to the Planters and Negroes of the Island of Jamaica* (No. 1) (1817), p. 3, PRO HO 42/202. 337. My working assumption is that Wedderburn used an amanuensis.

299. For the context, Peter Linebaugh and Marcus Rediker, *The Many-Headed Hydra: Sailors, Slaves, Commoners, and the Hidden History of the Revolutionary Atlantic* (London: Verso, 2000).

300. Olaudah Equiano, *The Interesting Narrative And Other Writings* (ed.) Vincent Carretta (Harmondsworth, Middlesex: Penguin, 1995), pp. xv, 317.

301. Roxann Wheeler, *The Complexion of Race: Categories of Difference in Eigtheenth-Century British Culture* (Philadelphia: University of Pennsylvania Press, 2000), pp. 84–5, 287.

302. Gordon Turnbull, *An Apology for Negro Slavery; or, The West-India Planters Vindicated From the Charges of Inhumanity* (1786) and Raymund Harris, *Scriptural Researches on the Licitness of the Slave-Trade, Shewing Its Conformity With the Principles of Natural and Revealed Religion, Delineated in the Sacred Writings of the Word of God* (Liverpool, 1788).

303. C.B. Wadström, *Observations on the Slave Trade, and a Description of Some Part of the Coast of Guinea, During a Voyage Madevin 1787, and 1788* (1789).

304. PRO B[oard of] T[rade] 6/10 folios, pp. 388–9.

305. Charles Bernhard Wadström and August Nordenskjold, *et al.*, *A Plan For A Free Community Upon The Coast Of Africa, Under The Protection Of Great Britain* (1789), p. iv.

306. Ibid., p. 50.

307. Mrs Villa-Real Gooch, *The Beggar Boy: A Novel...by the Late Mr. Thomas Bellamy. To which are prefixed Biographical Particulars of the Author* (1801) Vol. 1 p. xxvi.

308. Thomas Bellamy, *The Benevolent Planters. A Dramatic Piece as performed at the Theatre Royal, Haymarket* (1789), p. 2.
309. Ibid., p. 3.
310. Ibid., Prologue.
311. Adam Lively, *Masks: Blackness, Race and the Imagination* (London: Chatto & Windus, 1998), pp. 15–17.
312. John O'Brien's *Harlequin Britain: Pantomime and Entertainment, 1690–1760* (Baltimore, MD: The Johns Hopkins University Press, 2004), pp. 127–37.
313. Jeffrey N. Cox, *Slavery, Abolition and Emancipation: Writings in the British Romantic Period: Slavery* (London: Pickering and Chatto) Vol. 5 p. 282.
314. W. Bates, *Harlequin Mungo; or, A Peep into the Tower: A New Pantomimical Entertainment, in Two Acts: As Performing at the Royalty Theatre, Well-Street, Goodman's-Fields* (1788), p. 9.
315. David Mayer III, *Harlequin in his Element: The English Pantomime, 1806–1836* (Cambridge, Mass.: Harvard University Press, 1969), pp. 24–8.
316. W. Bates, *Harlequin Mungo; or, A Peep into the Tower* (1788), pp. 11–12.
317. Ibid., p. 12.
318. Ibid.
319. Helen Thomas, *Romanticism and Slave Narratives: Transatlantic Testimonies* (Cambridge: Cambridge University Press, 2000), pp. 180–97, 236–41.
320. David Mayer III, *Harlequin in his Element: The English Pantomime, 1806–1836* (Cambridge, Mass.: Harvard University Press, 1969), pp. 38–9.
321. 'Columbine, Harlequin' (1745), Lewis Walpole Library, Farmington, Call No. 745.0.43; *Harlequin Junior; or, The Magic of Cestus* (1770), Lewis Walpole Library, Farmington , Call No. 784.11.17.1. The latter print, which seems to be warning children against buying 'American Bonds,' is unusual in portraying a temporarily errant Harlequin: 'And Harley vows to rove no more; / But will with faithful Columbine, / In Love, and Truth forever Join.'
322. Mrs Villa-Real Gooch, *The Beggar Boy: A Novel...by the Late Mr. Thomas Bellamy. To which are prefixed Biographical Particulars of the Author* (1801) Vol. 1 p. xxvi.
323. *The General Magazine, and Impartial Review*, June 1787, pp. 49–53.
324. Mrs Villa-Real Gooch, *The Beggar Boy: A Novel...by the Late Mr. Thomas Bellamy. To which are prefixed Biographical Particulars of the Author* (1801) Vol. 1 p. xxxv.
325. *The General Magazine, and Impartial Review*, November 1787, pp. 331–2.
326. Mrs Villa-Real Gooch, *The Beggar Boy: A Novel...by the Late Mr. Thomas Bellamy. To which are prefixed Biographical Particulars of the Author* (1801) Vol. 1 pp. xix–xx.
327. *The General Magazine, and Impartial Review*, November 1787, pp. 331–2.
328. See 'Fairlop Fair,' showing a rural fair Harlequin and Chinese, etching with watercolour, Thomas Tegg, 7 July 1815, Harvard Theatre Collection (not in BM).
329. Ann Alsey and Thomas Gunn, theft and receiving stolen goods, 5 December 1804; *The Proceedings of the Old Bailey* Ref: t18041205-56 (the theft of 17 Spanish dollars, the property of 'Erpune, a native of China,' with John Anthony, 'a native of China' acting as his interpreter).
330. David Mayer III, *Harlequin in his Element: The English Pantomime, 1806–1836* (Cambridge, Mass.: Harvard University Press, 1969) Figs 38, 39.

331. W. Bates, *Harlequin Mungo; or, A Peep into the Tower* (1788) p. 10.
332. *Harlequin Incendiary; or, Columbine Cameron* (1746), p. 16.
333. W. Bates, *Harlequin Mungo; or, A Peep into the Tower* (1788), p. 14.
334. Thomas John Dibdin, *The New Pantomime of Harlequin and Fortunio; or Shing-Moo and Thun-Ton, With a Sketch of the Story: As First Performed at the Theatre-Royal, Covent-Garden, Tuesday, December 26th, 1815. The Musick, Scenery, Machinery, Dresses, And Decorations, Are Entirely New* (1815), p. 12.
335. Mary Bush, Sarah Clarke, Elizabeth Smith, grand larceny, 17 September 1800, *The Proceedings of the Old Bailey* Ref: t18000917-106 (concerning the theft of 13 banknotes from 'a Chinese' sailor, with the Anglicized name of 'Peter Francis' and who gave evidence through an interpreter); William Rayner and Charles Moren, burglary, 17 September 1800, *The Proceedings of the Old Bailey* Ref: t18000917-29 (the theft of a coat belonging to Awing, 'a Chinese man'); Ann Alsey and Thomas Gunn, theft and receiving stolen goods, 5 December 1804; *The Proceedings of the Old Bailey* Ref: t18041205-56 (the theft of money, the property of 'Erpune, a native of China.'
336. *The General Magazine, and Impartial Review*, November 1787, p. 331.
337. W. Bates, *Harlequin Mungo; or, A Peep into the Tower* (1788), p. 7.
338. Ibid., pp. 7–8.
339. Ibid., p. 8.
340. R. Humphreys, *The Memoirs Of J. Decastro, Comedian* (1824), p. 125.
341. W. Bates, *Harlequin Mungo; or, A Peep into the Tower:* (1788) p. 9. See also, 'A voracious Hyena, to him nought's a cloyer, / So as he's no conscience we call him the Lawyer,' Charles Isaac Mungo Dibdin, *Songs, And Other Vocal Compositions, In the Pantomime, Called Jan Ben Jan; or, Harlequin and the Forty Virgins. Performing at the Aquatic Theatre, Sadler's Wells* (1807), p. 12.
342. W. Bates, *Harlequin Mungo; or, A Peep into the Tower* (1788), p. 9.
343. *Robinson Crusoe; or, Harlequin Friday. A Grand Pantomime, in Two Acts, As performed at the Theatre-Royal, Newcastle-upon-Tyne, in 1791* (Newcastle, 1791), pp. 15, 16, 27.
344. W. Bates, *Harlequin Mungo; or, A Peep into the Tower* (1788), p. 11.
345. Thomas Thirlwall, *Royalty Theatre. A Solemn Protest Against the Revival of Scenic Exhibitions and Interludes, at the Royalty Theatre* (1803), pp. 9–10.
346. John Percival, *A Few Observations in Defence of the Scenic Exhibitions at The Royalty Theatre* (1804) p. 12.
347. Ibid.
348. William Shepherd, 16 October 1782, Angus Masterman, 4 December 1782, Richard Stevens, Thomas Herbert and William Hardy, 22 February 1786, John Parker and George Mullins, 21 February 1787, *The Proceedings of the Old Bailey*.
349. John Percival, *A Few Observations in Defence of the Scenic Exhibitions at The Royalty Theatre* (1804), p. 12.
350. Percival never mentions having actually attended a Royalty performance.
351. John Percival, *A Few Observations in Defence of the Scenic Exhibitions at The Royalty Theatre* (1804), p. 14.
352. W. Bates, *Harlequin Mungo; or, A Peep into the Tower* (1788), p. 17.
353. See the account of the Royalty's 1780s licensing, John Adolphus, *Memoirs of John Bannister, Comedian* (1839), pp. 153–60.

354. Walley Chamberlain Oulton, *The History of the Theatres of London...From the Year 1771 to 1795*, 2 vols (1796) Vol. 1 p. 184.
355. For the context of literary forgery, see Paul Baines, *The House of Forgery in eighteenth-century Britain* (Aldershot and Brookfield, VT.: Ashgate Publishing, 1999).
356. William Wordsworth, *The Borderers* (ed. Robert Osborn) (Ithaca and London: Cornell University Press, 1982), pp. 4–5.
357. Ibid., pp. 5–6.
358. Thomas Holcroft, *Duplicity: A Comedy. As it is Performed at the Theatre-Royal, in Covent-Garden* (1781), p. i; *Seduction: A Comedy. As it is Performed at the Theatre-Royal in Drury Lane* (1787), pp. ix, xi; *The School for Arrogance: A Comedy. As it is Acted At the Theatre Royal, Covent Garden* (1791), p. ii.
359. John Galt, *The New British Theatre; a Selection of original drama, not yet acted; some of which have been offered for representation but not accepted; with critical remarks by the editor* (1814), p. vii.
360. John C. Cross, *The Way to get Un-Married. A Dramatic Sketch. As Performed With Universal Applause at the Theatre Royal Covent Garden, For the First Time, on Wednesday, March 30th, 1796* (1796).
361. Joseph George Holman, *Abroad and at Home. A Comic Opera, In Three Acts. Now Performing at the Theatre-Royal, Covent-Garden* (1796), p. 18.
362. Thomas Knight, *The Turnpike Gate; A Musical Entertainment...Covent-Garden. Second Edition* (1799), p. 1.
363. Knight, *The Turnpike Gate* (1799) p. 6.
364. Ibid., p. 50.
365. Alex J. Dick, 'Poverty, charity, poetry: The unproductive labors of "The Old Cumberland Beggar," ' *Studies in Romanticism* 39:3 (2000), pp. 365–96.
366. Sophie Thomas, 'Seeing Things ("As They Are"): Coleridge, Schiller, and the Play of Semblance,' *Studies in Romanticism* 43:4 (2004) pp. 537–55; Richard Holmes, *Coleridge: Darker Reflections* (London: Harper Collins, 1998), pp. 321–38.
367. Samuel Taylor Coleridge, *The Complete Poetical Works of Samuel Taylor Coleridge including Poems and Versions of Poems now Published for the First Time: Edited with Textual and Bibliographical Notes by Ernest Hartley Coleridge...In Two Volumes* (Oxford: The Clarendon Press, 1912), pp. 812–3.
368. James Powell, *The Venetian Outlaw, his Country's Friend. A Drama, in Three Acts, Now Performing at the Theatre Royal, Drury-Lane...Altered from the French of A. Pixiricourt* (1805); R.W. Elliston, *The Venetian Outlaw* (1805).
369. For details of Whitbread, Arnold and Carnaby, see the edition of *Remorse* in Jeffrey N. Cox and Michael Gamer (eds), *The Broadview Anthology of Romantic Drama* (Ontario: The Broadview Press, 2003).
370. Samuel Taylor Coleridge, *The Complete Poetical Works of Samuel Taylor Coleridge...Edited with Textual and Bibliographical Notes by Ernest Hartley Coleridge...In Two Volumes* (Oxford: The Clarendon Press, 1912), p. 812.
371. *Freemasons' Magazine* April 1796, p. 177.
372. Folger S. b.119, Folger Shakespeare Library, Washington DC.
373. Anon, 4 April 1796, Folger PR 2950 B5 copy 2 Cage, Folger Shakespeare Library, Washington DC.

374. William Henry Ireland, *Vortigern, an Historical Tragedy, in Five Acts* (1799), p. 43.

375. George Colman the Younger, *The Review; or, The Wags of Windsor. A Musical Farce* (1800); Henry Lee, *Caleb Quotem and his Wife!* or *Paint, Poetry, and Putty!, An Opera, in Three Acts. To which is added A Postscript* (1809).

376. Folger W. b. 496. fol 20, Folger Shakespeare Library, Washington DC.

377. Samuel Ireland, 1 December 1795, Folger W. b. 496 fol 119, Folger Shakespeare Library, Washington D.C.; William Henry Ireland, *The Confessions of William Henry Ireland. Containing The Particulars of his Fabrication of the Shakespeare Manuscripts* (1805), pp. 108–13.

378. 'Sam Ireland fe=,' 1 December 1795, Box 48/94, Huntington Library, San Marino, California; published in Samuel Ireland, *Miscellaneous Papers and Legal instruments Under The Hand and Seal of William Shakespeare* (1796).

379. Folger S. b. 119, Folger Shakespeare Library, Washington DC.

380. Samuel Ireland, 26 June 1797, Folger S. b. 119, Folger Shakespeare Library, Washington DC.

381. Folger W. b. 496 fol. 21, Folger Shakespeare Library, Washington DC.

382. Folger S. b. 119, Folger Shakespeare Library, Washington DC.

383. *The Oaken Chest or The Gold Mines of Ireland a Farce*, Folger W. b. 496, Folger Shakespeare Library, Washington DC.

384. For example, *Specimens of W.H. Ireland's Shakespearian Fabrications* in the Huntington Library, California, call no. 287917.

385. The locks of hair are at Folger W. b. 496 folios 93–4, Folger Shakespeare Library, Washington DC.; HM 45657, Huntington Library, California.

386. William Henry Ireland, *The Confessions of William Henry Ireland. Containing The Particulars of his Fabrication of the Shakespeare Manuscripts* (1805), pp. 132–3; extra illustrated, Folger W. b. 496, Folger Shakespeare Library, Washington DC.

387. John Payne Collier, *An Old Man's Diary, Forty Years Ago; For The First Six Months of 1832* (London: Thomas Richards 1871), Vol. 2 p. 16.

388. Reynolds's recollection of the sequence of events must be erroneous. He claims he saw *Vortigern* 'shortly' after visiting Ireland's residence 'the day following' the first night of *Fortune's Fool*, but *Vortigern* had been produced in April 1796 and *Fortune's Fool* not until October 1796. Reynolds may simply have the sequence of events muddled, Frederick Reynolds, *The Life and Times of Frederick Reynolds* 2nd ed (1827) Vol. 2 pp. 240–3.

389. Reynolds was equivocal about the extent to which the Ireland identification was justified, Frederick Reynolds, *The Life and Times of Frederick Reynolds* 2nd edition (1827), Vol. 2 p. 239.

390. Larpent 1140, Huntington Library, California.

391. Frederick Reynolds, *The Life and Times of Frederick Reynolds* 2nd edition (1827) Vol. 2 pp. 243–4.

392. Walley Chamberlain Oulton, *Precious Relics; Or the Tragedy of Vortigern Rehearsed. A Dramatic Piece. In Two Acts. Written in Imitation of the Critic. As Performed at the Theatre-Royal, Drury-Lane* (1796), p. 29.

393. Oulton, *Precious Relics; Or The Tragedy of Vortigern Rehearsed* (1796) p. 14.

394. Ibid., p. 62.

395. Thomas Dibdin, *The Reminiscences of Thomas Dibdin* (1837), Vol. 2 pp. 23–4.

396. Larpent 1788, Huntington Library, California.

397. Frederick Reynolds, *The Life and Times of Frederick Reynolds* 2nd edition (1827), 2 vols, Vol. 2 pp. 54–5.
398. There is a sketch of the building at HM Ms 287179 Vol. 2 fol. 56, Huntington Library, California.
399. HM Ms 31428–30, *c*.1801–07, Huntington Library, California.
400. HM Ms 287179 Vol. 2 fol 1–5, Huntington Library, California; *Morning Chronicle* 11 January 1811; *Biographical Dictionary of 300 Contemporary Public Characters, British & foreign of all Ranks & Professions* (1825). Ireland was now signing his works with the evasive initials, 'W.H.C.I.'
401. Sam Satiricus [William Henry Ireland], *The Cyprian of St. Stephen's, Or Princely Protection Illustrated; in a Poetical Flight to the Pierian Spring* (Bath, 1809) pp. 6, 28.
402. William Henry Ireland, *Death-Bed Confessions of the Late Countess of Guernsey, to Lady Anne H——. To which are Added The Q——'s last Letter to the K——* (1821).
403. *Hogarth's Works. A Catalogue of the Most Complete Collection of Hogarth's Works..., The Property of a Gentleman...Will be Sold by Auction by Messrs. Christie, Sharp, and Harper...May 6th, 1797* (1797), *Hogarth's Works...Will be Sold by Auction, By Mr. King...On Saturday, April 21, 1798* (1798), *A Catalogue Of...The Property of the Late Samuel Ireland...Which will be Sold by Auction by Leigh, Sotheby and Son...May 7, 1801* (1801).
404. William Henry Ireland, *Chalcographimania; or, the Portrait-Collector and Printseller's Chronicle* (1814), pp. 22n.; 46–7n.; 97n.; 99n.
405. William Henry Ireland, *Chalcographimania* (1814), p. 5.
406. James Caulfield, *Calcographiana the Printseller's Guide to the Knowledge & Value of Engraved British Portraits* (1814).
407. William Henry Ireland, *Chalcographimania* (1814), p. xi.
408. David Worrall, 'Mab and Mob: The Radical Press Community in Regency England,' Stephen Behrendt (ed.) *Romanticism, Radicalism, and the Press* (Detroit: Wayne State University Press, 1997).
409. William Henry Ireland, *Vortigern, An Historical Tragedy, in Five Acts* (1799) p. vi.
410. Ireland, *Vortigern* (1799), p. 13.
411. Ibid., *An Anthem On the Lamented Death of her Royal Highness The Princess Charlotte* (1817).
412. Other books by Ireland on the subject include, *The Last Will and Testament of Napoleon Bonaparte...* (1821); *The Napoleon Anecdotes* (1823); *The Hundred Days of Napoleon Bonaparte* (1827); *The Life of Napoleon Bonaparte* (1828).
413. Cervantes [William Henry Ireland], *The Death of Bonaparte, Or, One Pound One. A Poem in Four Cantos* (York, 1812). The basis of the wager was that a local M.P. offered to pay one guinea per day "Till Bonaparte, that scoundrel – scum –/Is dead, and gone to kingdom come' (p. 8). The legal case seems to have been an attempt by the M.P. to recover his money since Bonaparte showed no signs of dying in 1812, *Report of a Case, The Reverend Robert Gilbert versus Sir. M. M. Sykes...tried at the York Lent Assizes, 1812...Being an Action brought by the Plaintiff to recover a Sum of Money won on the life of Bonaparte* (York, 1812).
414. William Henry Ireland, *Something Concerning Nobody* (1814), pp. 162.
415. Ibid., pp. 161–2.

416. William Henry Ireland, *Gaieté de Paris, by George Cruikshank, or the Rambles of an English Party Through the French Metropolis* (1825), pp. 4, 9.
417. Robert L. Patten, *George Cruikshank's Life, Times and Art* (London: Lutterworth Press, 1992) Vol. 1 pp. 260–2.
418. BL Add Ms.33, 964 fol. 299.
419. *Mr. Mathews' Memorandum-Book, of Peculiarities, Character, and Manners, Collected by him in his various Trips* (1825), p. 5.
420. *The Dramatic Scorpion. A Satire, in Three Cantos* (1818), p. 25n.
421. HM Ms 287179 Vol. 2 fol. 225, Huntington Library, California.
422. Autographed Ms. Insertion, William Henry Ireland, *Vortigern, An Historical Tragedy, in Five Acts* (1799), Call no. 124170, Huntington Library, California.
423. William Henry Ireland, *Vortigern* (1799), p. vi.
424. Larpent 1110, Huntington Library, California. The roles of Bellarius and Jacomo were subsumed under those of the anonymous 2nd and 3rd Lords in the printed version.
425. *Songs, Chorusses, &c. in the Musical Afterpiece, called Garrick's Jubilee ... Covent-Garden, 23rd of April, 1816* (1816), pp. 4, 5, 16.
426. W.T. Moncrieff, *Shakespeare's Festival; or, A New Comedy of Errors!* (1830), p. vii.
427. Ibid., p. 9.
428. Ibid., pp. 35–6.
429. C.A. Somerset, *Shakespeare's Early Days: An Historical Play, In Two Acts* (1829), p. 13.
430. Ibid., p. 21.
431. Larpent 2325, Huntington Library, California.
432. James Thomas Law, *The Poor Man's Garden; or, A Few Brief Rules for Regulating Allotments of land to the Poor ... with remarks, addressed to Mr. Malthus, Mr. Sadler, and the Political Economists: and a reference to the opinions of Dr. Adam Smith in 'Wealth of Nations'* (1830), pp. 16–17.
433. C.A. Somerset, *Shakespeare's Early Days* (1829), p. 24.
434. Ibid., p. 33.
435. Ibid.
436. Ibid., p. 39.
437. Ibid., p. 41.
438. Ibid.
439. Folger Y. d. 483 (12), (11), (10), Folger Shakespeare Library, Washington DC.
440. Jonathan Mulrooney, 'Keats in the company of Kean,' *Studies in Romanticism* 42:2 (2003), pp. 227–50.
441. 'Keats in the company of Kean,' *Studies in Romanticism* 42:2 (2003) pp. 227–250. For a vivid contemporary painting of Kean as Macbeth, see the frontispiece to Joseph W. Donohue, Jr, *Dramatic Character in the English Romantic Age* (Princeton, NJ: Princeton University Press, 1970).
442. The fate of *Otho* can be charted through Keats's letters, Maurice Buxton Forman (ed.) *The Letters of John Keats ... With Revisions and Additional Letters* (Oxford: Oxford University Press, 1947) Third Edition. To Fanny Keats, Saturday 28 August 1819; To John Taylor, Tuesday 31 August 1819; George And Georgiana Keats, Friday 17–Monday 27 September 1819; To Fanny

Keats, Monday 20 December 1819; To Georgiana Augusta Keats, Thursday 13–Friday 28 January 1820.

443. Maurice Buxton Forman (ed.) *The Letters of John Keats...With Revisions and Additional Letters* (Oxford: Oxford University Press, 1947) Third Edition. To Fanny Keats, Saturday 28 August 1819; To Georgiana Augusta Keats, Thursday 13–Friday 28 January 1820.

444. Jack Stillinger (ed.) *The Letters of Charles Armitage Brown* (Cambridge, Mass.: Harvard University Press, 1966) To C.W. Dilke, 2 August 1819, p. 48.

445. For details of *Narensky's* production and a plot summary, see E.H. McCormick, *The Friend of Keats: A Life of Charles Armitage Brown* (Wellington: Victoria University Press, 1989), pp. 4–7.

446. Charles Armitage Brown, *Narensky; or, The road to Yaroslaf...Drury-Lane* (1814) p. 66. For his other music, see the dramas referred to below, James Cobb, *Songs, Duets, Trios, and Finales in Ramah Droog, Or, Wine Does Wonders...Covent-Garden* (1798); *The Overture Favorite Songs & Finale In the Musical Entertainment of Tippoo Saib...Sadlers Wells...The Words by Mr. Lonsdale The Music Composed by W. Reeve* (1792).

447. John Hamilton Reynolds, *One, Two, Three, Four, Five; by Advertisement: a musical entertainment, In One Act.* (c.1829), printed edition.

448. Maurice Buxton Forman (ed.) *The Letters of John Keats...With Revisions and Additional Letters* (Oxford: Oxford University Press, 1947) Third Edition, To George and Thomas Keats, 23 January 1818.

449. Ann Catherine Holbrook, *The Dramatist; or, Memoirs of the Stage* (Birmingham, 1809), pp. 48–9.

450. *The Acting Manager; or, The Minor Spy. A Weekly Review of the Public and Private Stage.* No 1, 14 May 1831, p. 10.

451. John Adolphus, *Memoirs of John Bannister, Comedian* (1839), p. 165.

452. 'On the Cockney School of Poetry No. I,' *Blackwood's Edinburgh Magazine* October 1817, pp. 38–41.

453. Maurice Buxton Forman (ed.) *The Letters of John Keats...With Revisions and Additional Letters* (Oxford: Oxford University Press, 1947) Third Edition, To Benjamin Bailey, Monday 3 November 1817.

454. Jeffrey N. Cox, *Poetry and Politics in The Cockney School* (Cambridge: Cambridge University Press, 1998), Chapter 4, 'Staging hope: genre, myth, and ideology in the dramas of the Hunt circle,' pp. 123–45.

455. Cox, *Poetry and Politics in The Cockney School* (Cambridge: Cambridge University Press, 1998), p. 140.

456. Leigh Hunt, *The Examiner*, 26 January 1817, quoted in David Mayer III, *Harlequin in his Element: The English Pantomime, 1806–1836* (Cambridge, Mass.: Harvard University Press, 1969), p. 10.

457. Cox, *Poetry and Politics in The Cockney School* (Cambridge: Cambridge University Press, 1998), pp. 16–20, 228n.10.

458. Beth Lau, 'Protest, "Nativism," and Impersonation in the Works of Chatterton and Keats,' *Studies in Romanticism* 42:4 (2003), pp. 519–39.

459. Jacob Beuler, *Comic Songs to Popular Tunes...Second Collection* (1823), pp. 34–5.

460. *The British Stage, and Literary Cabinet*, 4 December 1818, p. 292.

461. David Lyddal, *The Prompter, or Elementary Hints to Young Actors* (Dublin, 1810), pp. 5, 28.

462. Unidentified clipping, dated 8 February 1813, R.W. Elliston papers, Harvard Theatre Collection, Vol. 1.
463. Playbills, Olympic Theatre, 9 and 30 November 1815.
464. *Othello-Travestie* (1813); William Barnes Rhodes, *Bombastes Furioso; A Burlesque Tragic Opera...Haymarket, August 7, 1810* (1822), pp. 14, 18.
465. Maurice Buxton Forman (ed.) *The Letters of John Keats...With Revisions and Additional Letters* (Oxford: Oxford University Press, 1947) Third Edition, To *George and Thomas Keats*, 23 January 1818.
466. *The Rambler's Magazine; or Fashionable Emporium of Polite Literature* (1822) April 1822, p. 231.
467. Playbills, Surrey Theatre, 19 March 1822.
468. The licensing application is recorded but no text is extant, HM 19926 folio 6 recto, 10 April 1818.
469. Maurice Buxton Forman (ed.) *The Letters of John Keats...With Revisions and Additional Letters* (Oxford: Oxford University Press, 1947) Third Edition, To George and Thomas Keats, 23 January 1818.
470. Andrew Franklin, *A Trip to the Nore. A Musical Entertainment...Drury-Lane.* (1797), pp. 11–12.
471. Franklin, *A Trip to the Nore* (1797), p. 14.
472. Ibid., p. 18.
473. Ibid., p. 20.
474. *Blackwood's Edinburgh Magazine* January 1818, p. 427.
475. Ibid., pp. 428, 430.
476. *Blackwood's Edinburgh Magazine* February 1818, p. 567, January 1819, p. 443.
477. *Blackwood's Edinburgh Magazine* January 1818, p. 427.
478. Leigh Hunt, *The Examiner*, 26 January 1817, quoted in David Mayer III, *Harlequin in his Element: The English Pantomime, 1806–1836* (Cambridge, Mass.: Harvard University Press, 1969), p. 10.
479. *Blackwood's Edinburgh Magazine* January 1818, p. 430.
480. Ibid., January 1819, p. 444.
481. William Thomas Moncrieff, *Tom And Jerry; or, Life In London In 1820* (1825), p. 17.
482. Thomas John Dibdin, *Don Giovanni; or, A Spectre on Horseback!...Royal Circus and Surrey Theatre* (1817), p. 15.
483. Samuel Pegge, *Anecdotes of the English Language: Chiefly Regarding The Local Dialect of London and Its Environs* (1803), pp. 75–7.
484. *The Dramatic Scorpion. A Satire, in Three Cantos, With Explanatory Notes* (1818), p. 15.
485. Larpent 1966, 1013, Huntington Library, California.
486. *Blackwood's Edinburgh Magazine* April 1818, p. 82.
487. Ibid., October 1817, p. 40.
488. John Ebers, *Seven Years of the King's Theatre* (1828), pp. 30–1.
489. Ibid., pp. 8–9, 14–15.
490. William Lee, *The Plan of the Boxes At the King's Theatre, Haymarket...For the Season[s]of 1803[1804, 1805, 1807]* (1803, 1804, 1805, 1807).
491. Peregrine Prynne, *Histriomastix, or, The Untrussing of the Drury Lane Squad* (1819), p. 17.
492. Larpent 1973, Huntington Library, California.

493. William Hazlitt, *A View of the English Stage; or, A Series of Dramatic Criticisms* (1818), p. 440.

494. Marius Kwint, 'The Legitimization of the Circus in Late Georgian England,' *Past and Present*, 174:1 (2002) (174:1), pp. 72–115.

495. John Cartwright Cross, *Songs, Chorusses, &c. in The Eclipse, or, Harlequin in China. A New Grand Pantomime Performed at the New Royal Circus, For the first Time, On Monday, August 10, 1801*(1801); *Songs, Chorusses, &c. In King Caesar; or, the Negro Slaves: A New Grand Spectacle, In Two Parts Performed at the New Royal Circus, for the first Time, On Wednesday, September 16, 1801* (1801); *Songs, Duets, Trios, Chorusses, &c. in the New, Grand, Serio-Comic Pantomime, Called the Golden Farmer; or, Harlequin Ploughboy: Performed at the New Royal Circus, For the first Time on Monday, June 28, 1802* (1802). The latter is sometimes attributed to William Ware but Cross was the chief playwright at the Royal Circus.

496. 28 October 1794, PRO TS 11/966.

497. 18 April 1795, PRO HO 43/6

498. Royal Circus playbill, *Harlequin Cockney: Or, London Displayed* (c.1809), recto and verso, Harvard Theatre Collection.

499. Thomas John Dibdin, *The Reminiscences of Thomas Dibdin* (1837) Vol. 2 pp. 135–6. Thomas John Dibdin, *Don Giovanni; or, A Spectre on Horseback!...Royal Circus and Surrey Theatre* (1818). In June 1819, this text was relicensed by Larpent for Covent Garden, Larpent 2096, Huntington Library, California.

500. Larpent 2004, Huntington Library, California.

501. HM 19926, Vol. 2, folio 5 verso, Huntington Library, California.

502. William Thomas Moncrieff, *Giovanni In London; or, The Libertine Reclaimed...Drury Lane And Covent Garden* (1825), p. ii.

503. Unlike the case of *The Picture of Paris* where no pantomime sketch had been forwarded to Larpent, *Harlequin Libertine* shows the inconsistency of the rules governing the practice of the Examiner of Plays.

504. William Thomas Moncrieff, *Giovanni In London; or, The Libertine Reclaimed* (1825), p. ii.

505. Thomas John Dibdin, *Don Giovanni; or, A Spectre on Horseback! A Comic, heroic, operatic, tragic, pantomimic, burletta-spectacular extravaganza; in Two Acts* (New York, 1818), pp. 10–13, 23.

506. William Thomas Moncrieff, *Giovanni In London; or, The Libertine Reclaimed* (1825), p. 3.

507. Ibid., p. 7.

508. Ibid., p. 8.

509. Ibid., p. 10.

510. Ibid., pp. 15–16.

511. BL Playbills 171, Royal Amphitheatre, 17 September 1821.

512. Pierce Egan, *The Life and Extraordinary Adventures of Samuel Denmore Hayward* (1822), p. 31.

513. *The Choice of Harlequin; or, The Indian Chief. A Pantomimical Entertainment...Covent Garden* (1780), p. 16.

514. William Thomas Moncrieff, *Giovanni In London; or, The Libertine Reclaimed*, (1825), p. 21.

515. Ibid., p. 44.
516. *The Choice of Harlequin; Or, The Indian Chief* (1780), p. 17.
517. William Thomas Moncrieff, *Giovanni In London: Or The Libertine Reclaimed* (1825), p. 46.
518. *The Choice of Harlequin; Or, The Indian Chief* (1780), p. 31.
519. William Thomas Moncrieff, *Giovanni In London: Or The Libertine Reclaimed* (1825), pp. 50–1.
520. *The Choice of Harlequin; Or, The Indian Chief* (1780), pp. 30–1.
521. Jeffrey N. Cox, *Poetry and Politics in The Cockney School* (Cambridge: Cambridge University Press, 1998), pp. 24–6.
522. *The Gazette of Fashion, and Magazine of Literature* 4 (25 May 1822), cited in Jeffrey N. Cox, *Poetry and Politics in The Cockney School* (Cambridge: Cambridge University Press, 1998), p. 26.
523. *The Eclectic [Review]* (2nd ser.)10 (November 1818) p. 485, cited in Jeffrey N. Cox, *Poetry and Politics in The Cockney School* (Cambridge: Cambridge University Press, 1998), p. 34.
524. *The Dramatic Scorpion. A Satire, in Three Cantos, With Explanatory Notes* (1818), p. 43 and 43n.
525. PRO HO 119/4.
526. Marc Baer, *Theatre and Disorder in Late Georgian London* (Oxford: Clarendon, 1992).
527. *Society for the Suppression of Mendicity, established in London, March 25th, 1818: supported by voluntary contributions* (1819);*The first report of the society established in London for the suppression of mendicity* (1819).
528. John Adolphus, *Observations on the Vagrant Act, And Some Other Statutes, And on the Powers and Duties of Justices of the Piece* (1824), p. 35. Adolphus appeared a number of times as the defence counsel for R.W. Elliston, unidentified clipping, 3 November 1821, Harvard Theatre Collection, R.W. Elliston papers, Vol. 2.
529. PRO HO 119/4; Robert William Elliston, *Copy Of A Memorial Presented To The Lord Chamberlain* (1818).
530. PRO HO 119/4, 2 and 5 March 1818, Sans Pareil, Strand, Olympic, Wych Street.
531. William Thomas Moncrieff, *Giovanni In London: Or The Libertine Reclaimed* (1825), p. ii.
532. Jacob Beuler, *Comic Originals!* (*c.*1820), p. 13.
533. Pierce Egan, *Show Folks!* (1831), p. 45.
534. Jacob Beuler, *Comic Originals!* (*c.*1820), pp. 16,17–19, 23.
535. Ibid., pp. 26–7.
536. Ibid.
537. William Thomas Moncrieff, *Songs, Duets, Choruses &c.&c &c. Sung in…Giovanni in the Country; or, the Rake Husband…Royal Coburg Theatre* (1820). The first performance was 15 August 1820. BL Playbills 171, Astley's Royal Amphitheatre, 30 August 1821.
538. William Reeves and William Barrymore, *Songs, Chorusses &c in…Giovanni in the Country; or, A Gallop to Gretna Green…Astley's Royal Amphitheatre* (1820).
539. H.M. Milner, *Songs, Chorusses, Duets, Parodies &c in Giovanni In Paris…East London Theatre* (1820).

540. *Keene's Theatrical Evening Mirror*, 25 September 1820.
541. On the context of *Giovanni in Ireland* and George IV's visit to Ireland, see Jane Moody, *Illegitimate: Theatre in London, 1770–1840* (Cambridge: Cambridge University Press (2000), pp. 107–108.
542. Huntington Ms A1 247, Moncrieff to an unknown recipient, no date, Huntington Library, California.
543. Larpent 2281, Huntington Library, California.
544. Larpent 2333, Huntington Library, California.
545. Richard Jenkins, *Memoirs of the Bristol Stage* (Bristol: 1826), p. 102.
546. Daniel Mendoza, *Memoirs of the life... To Which are Added, Observations on the Art of Pugilism* (1816); *The Covent Garden Journal* (1810), 10 October 1809, pp. 309–10.
547. 'On the Connexion Between Pugilism, Statuary, Painting, Poetry and Politics' *Blackwood's Edinburgh Magazine*, March 1819, pp. 722–6, 723.
548. Ibid., p. 723.
549. Robert L. Patten, *George Cruikshank's Life, Times, and Art* (London: Lutterworth Press, 1992) Vol. 1 pp. 226–9.
550. Gregory Dart, ' "Flash Style": Pierce Egan and Literary London, 1820–28,' *History Workshop Journal*, 51 (2001), pp. 180–205.
551. Larpent 2257, Huntington Library, California.
552. Larpent 2262, Huntington Library, California.
553. William Dimond, *The Sea-Side Story, An Operatic Drama... Covent Garden* (1801), p. 9.
554. Thomas John Dibdin, *Songs, Chorusses, &c. In the New Pantomime of Harlequin's Tour; Or, The Dominion of Fancy...*, Covent-Garden (1800), p. 9.
555. R. Mitchell, *Mathews's Trip to Paris; or, the Dramatic Tourist; ... and Delivered by him at the English Opera House... Taken in Short-hand, and Dedicated to Dandy Cockney, Esq* (1819), pp. 12–13.
556. *Songs, Trios, Duetts and Chorusses in the Comic Opera of Summer Amusement; or, An Adventure at Margate... Hay-Market* (1781), p. 18.
557. *The Theatrical Looker-on* (Birmingham), 3 June 1822, pp. 5–6.
558. Larpent 2313, Huntington Library, California.
559. *Crockery's Misfortunes; or, Transmogrifications. A Burletta... Royal Cobourg Theatre* (1821), p. 4.
560. Huntington Ms A1 247, Moncrieff to an unknown recipient, no date, Huntington Library, California.
561. *Account of the Proceedings Before His Majesty's Most Hon. Privy Council Upon the Petition For A Third Theatre in the Metropolis* (1810), p. 54.
562. Folger T. a. 5 *Diary of visit of Edmund Shaw Simpson, manager of Park Theatre, New York*, 28 May 1818, Folger Shakespeare Library, Washington DC.
563. *The Theatrical John Bull* (Birmingham) (1) 5 June 1825, p. 15.
564. William Davis had been in partnership with John Astley taking over the Amphitheatre in 1821, A.H. Saxon, *The Life and Art of Andrew Ducrow and the Romantic Age of the English Circus* (Hamden, CT: Archon Books, 1978), p. 120.
565. BL Playbills 171, Astley's Royal Amphitheatre, 30 July 1821.
566. Ibid., 17 September 1821; Thomas Dibdin, *The Reminiscences of Thomas Dibdin* (1837) Vol. 2 p. 214.
567. John Percival, *A Few Observations in Defence of the Scenic Exhibitions at The Royalty Theatre* (1804) p. 31. See also R. Humphreys, *The Memoirs of*

J. Decastro, Comedian... Also An Accompanying History of the Royal Circus, Now The Surrey Theatre (1824).

568. Larpent 2237, Huntington Library, California.
569. BL Playbills 171, Astley's Royal Amphitheatre 30 May *c*.1824.
570. BL Playbills 171, *Life In London! Or, Day & Night Scenes! Of Tom And Jerry, In their Rambles and Sprees Through the Metropolis*, Astley's Amphitheatre, 17 September 1821, 5 October 1821.
571. *Tom and Jerry; or Life in London... Davis's Royal Amphitheatre* (1822), p. 16.
572. *The Sportsman's Companion (c*.1820).
573. BL Playbills, Royal Coburg, 1 June 1818.
574. BL Playbills 171, Astley's Amphitheatre, 22 April 1822.
575. *The Theatrical Looker-on* (Birmingham), 3 June 1822, p. 6.
576. *Tom and Jerry; or Life in London: An entirely new Whimsical, Local, Melo-Dramatic, Pantomimical Equestrian Drama, in Three Acts... as Performed at Davis's Royal Amphitheatre* (1822), p. 4.
577. The Caledonian Theatre, Edinburgh, version incorporated the popular figure of Sylvester Daggerwood, a character from George Colman the Younger, *New Hay at the Old Market: An Occasional Drama, in One Act* (1795); *Tom and Jerry, Or Life in London; A Musical Extravaganza. With Remarks* (Edinburgh, 1824).
578. *Tom and Jerry; or Life in London... as Performed at Davis's Royal Amphitheatre* (1822), p. 5.
579. Ibid., p. 36.
580. Ibid., p. 34.
581. Call number 821.10.1.1., Lewis Walpole Library, Farmington, Connecticut.
582. *Tom and Jerry; or Life in London... as Performed at Davis's Royal Amphitheatre* (1822), p. 22.
583. Ibid., p. 24.
584. Larpent 2313, Huntington Library, California.
585. Larpent 2257, Huntington Library, California.
586. William T. Moncrieff, *Tom and Jerry: or, Life in London in 1820. A Drama. In Three Acts. From Pierce Egan's celebrated work* (1826), p. 9; Larpent 2313, Huntington Library, California.
587. *The Songs, Parodies, &c. Introduced in the New Pedestrian, Equestrian, Extravaganza, and Operatic Burletta, In Three Acts of Gaiety, Frisk, Lark, and Patter, called, Tom and Jerry; Or, Life in London... Monday, April 8, 1822* (1822), p. 9.
588. Giles Waterfield, Anne French and Matthew Craske (eds) *Below Stairs: 400 Years of Servants' Portraits* (London: National Portrait Gallery Publications, 2003), pp. 128–9, Cat. 67.
589. Thomas Greenwood, *The Death of Life in London; or Tom & Jerry's Funeral. An Entirely New Satirical, Burlesque, Operative Parody, in One Act... Royal Coburg Theatre, 2 June 1823* (1823), p. 9.
590. BL Add Ms. 42866; Thomas Greenwood, *The Death of Life in London; or Tom & Jerry's Funeral* (1823), p. 19.
591. William T. Moncrieff, *Tom and Jerry: or, Life in London in 1820. A Drama. In Three Acts. From Pierce Egan's celebrated work* (1826), p. 10.
592. *Tippy Bob*, 28 March 1792, Lewis Walpole Library, Farmington, Connecticut, Call no. 792.3.28.1.

593. This differs substantially from Egan where the swells visit a coffee shop near the Olympic Theatre kept by Mahogany Bet where they are set upon by *kids*, Pierce Egan, *Life in London* (1820), pp. 181–3; A *kid* was a term 'particularly applied to a boy who commences thief at an early age,' Pierce Egan, *Grose's Classical Dictionary of the Vulgar Tongue, Revised and Corrected With the Addition of Numerous Slang Phrases Collected from Tried Authorities* (1823).
594. Egan, *Grose's Classical Dictionary of the Vulgar Tongue* (1823).
595. *Blackwood's Edinburgh Magazine*, November 1817, p. 198.
596. Lynn Hollen Lees, *The Solidarities of Strangers: The English Poor Laws and the People, 1700–1948* (Cambridge: Cambridge University Press, 1998), p. 220.
597. W.T. Moncrieff, *Selection from the Dramatic Works of William T. Moncrieff* (1851) Vol. 3, 'Tom and Jerry Key to the Persons and Places,' pp. 103–28.
598. W.T. Moncrieff, *Tom and Jerry: or, Life in London in 1820* (1826), p. 26.
599. Pierce Egan, *Grose's Classical Dictionary of the Vulgar Tongue* (1823).
600. *The Corinthian Parodies, by Tom, Jerry and Logic, Illustrative of Life in London* (*c.*1824), p. 19.
601. Egan explains that 'Drag' was a cart, 'The drag' or 'done for a drag' was committing or being caught for stealing from carts. 'Fiddling' still has the British meaning of stealing, hence, thieving from carts, Pierce Egan, *Grose's Classical Dictionary of the Vulgar Tongue* (1823).
602. *Society for the Suppression of Mendicity, established in London, March 25th, 1818: supported by voluntary contributions / [by] Society for the Suppression of Mendicity* (1819); *The first report of the society established in London for the suppression of mendicity* (1819).
603. W.T. Moncrieff, *Selections from the Dramatic Works of William T. Moncrieff* (1851), Vol. 3, p. 112.
604. 'All my eye,' 'A lame story. Fudge,' Pierce Egan, *Grose's Classical Dictionary of the Vulgar Tongue* (1823).
605. 'Muff,' 'a fool,' Pierce Egan, *Grose's Classical Dictionary of the Vulgar Tongue* (1823).
606. Gravel digging was common welfare work, Richard Carlile, *The Life of Swing, the Kent Rick-Burner. Written by Himself* (1830), p. 24.
607. 'Mizzled,' 'To elope, run off;' 'Toddlers,' not in Egan, but 'Toddle' is 'walk away,' it presumably means bypassers, Pierce Egan, *Grose's Classical Dictionary of the Vulgar Tongue* (1823). The 'bit of broom' is used to sweep horse dung out of the path of people crossing the street in exchange for tips, see Pierce Egan, *Life in London* (1820), p. 344–5n.
608. Lynn Hollen Lees, *The Solidarities of Strangers: The English Poor Laws and the People, 1700–1948* (Cambridge: Cambridge University Press, 1998), p. 71.
609. H.M. Milner, *The Hertfordshire Tragedy; or, The Victims of Gaming. A Serious Drama ... Royal Coburg Theatre* (1824), pp. 26–7.
610. A similar figure is shown in the S.W. Fores print, *All Max in the East, a Scene in Tom & Jerry, or Life in London*, 24 April 1822, Lewis Walpole Library, Farmington, Connecticut, Call no. 822. 4. 24. 1.
611. Charles Hindley, *The True History of Tom and Jerry ... From the Start to the Finish!* (London: Reeves and Turner, 1888), pp. 109–11.
612. Thomas Greenwood, *The Death of Life in London; or Tom & Jerry's Funeral* (1823), pp. 2, 11–14.

613. Pierce Egan, *Grose's Classical Dictionary of the Vulgar Tongue* (1823).
614. 'High toby,' meaning robbery from horseback. To 'set your monkey up' probably means, secretly stealing valuables from him. To 'suck the monkey' was 'to suck or draw wine... privately, out of a cask, by means of a straw or small tube.' Ibid.
615. African Sall orders 'fullers earth,' which was gin and bitters originating in a pub called the George Head. Bob Logic had his usual 'flash of lightning' or straight gin. Ibid.
616. Pierce Egan, *Life in London* (1820), pp. 284–90.
617. Ibid., p. 286; Pierce Egan, *Grose's Classical Dictionary of the Vulgar Tongue* (1823).
618. Larpent 2389, Huntington Library, California.
619. Larpent 2257, Huntington Library, California.
620. Pierce Egan, *Grose's Classical Dictionary of the Vulgar Tongue* (1823).
621. J. Ewing Ritchie, *The Night Side of London* (1857), p. 101.
622. This set of prints, not certainly laid out in the correct order, is in Lewis Walpole Library, Farmington, Connecticut, identifiable as 'Small brown album, gold-banded.'
623. Pierce Egan, *The Life and Extraordinary Adventures of Samuel Denmore Hayward* (1822), p. 192.
624. Larpent 2257, Charles Isaac Mungo Dibdin, *Life in London a Burletta in three Acts Intended for representation at the Olympic Theatre* (1821); *Life in London; or, The Larks of Logic, Tom, and Jerry, An Extravaganza... Olympic Theatre... Second Edition* (1822). The pagination of the first edition (1822), which was re-presented to Larpent (Larpent 2257), is slightly different, Huntington Library, California.
625. Diaries Of Anna Margaretta Larpent, Vol. 1, 1 August 1793, Huntington Library, California.
626. Larpent 2257, Huntington Library, California.
627. Larpent 2269, Huntington Library, California.
628. Larpent 2257, Huntington Library, California.
629. Eloquence, gentility and plausibility of speech were often associated with radical demagoguery, see *The English Metropolis: Or, London in the Year 1820* (1820), p. 66.
630. Larpent 2328, Huntington Library, California.
631. *Republican* 21 January 1820.
632. Robert L. Patten, *George Cruikshank's Life, Times, and Art* (London: Lutterworth Press, 1992) Vol. 1, p. 223.
633. Larpent 2257, Huntington Library, California.
634. Charles Isaac Mungo Dibdin, *Life in London; or, the Larks of Logic, Tom & Jerry, An Extravaganza in Three Acts, of Wit and Whim, Replete with High Goes, Prime Chaunts, and Out-and-out Sprees... As Performed at the Olympic Theatre* (1822), p. 4.
635. Dibdin, *Life in London; or, the Larks of Logic, Tom & Jerry... As Performed at the Olympic Theatre* (1822) 2nd edition, p. 6.
636. *Particulars and Conditions of Sale of the Olympic Theate... 13th June, 1820* (1820).
637. Royalty Theatre, playbill, 28 January 1818, East London Theatre (ex-Royalty) 9 August 1824.

638. Surrey Theatre, playbill, 16 June 1823.
639. *The Dramatic Scorpion. A Satire, in Three Cantos, With Explanatory Notes* (1818) p. 25.
640. W.T. Moncrieff, *Selections from the Dramatic Works of William T. Moncrieff* (1851) Vol. 3 p. vi.
641. Larpent 2262, Huntington Library, California.
642. Enclosures, one undated, signed 'P.W.' and 17 December 1821, signed Thomas Twigg, Larpent 2262, Huntington Library, California.
643. *Report from the Select Committee on Dramatic Literature: With The Minutes of Evidence...2 August 1832, Parliamentary Papers* (1831–2) Vol. VII, Answer to Question 80, p. 13.
644. Victoria & Albert Museum E.1070–1921 (CIS) (1804–37).
645. W.T. Moncrieff, *Tom and Jerry: or, Life in London in 1820. A Drama. In Three Acts. From Pierce Egan's celebrated work* (1826), p. 46.
646. Pierce Egan, *Life in London* (1820) p. 284; *Rambler's Magazine* 1822 March, p. 105.
647. *Rambler's Magazine* 1822 March, p. 105.
648. *The Fatal Effects of Gambling Exemplified in the Murder of Wm. Weare, and the Trial and Fate of John Thurtell* (1824) p. xvn.
649. Ibid., pp. 319–20.
650. Ibid., pp. 332–3.
651. Ibid., p. x.
652. Ibid., p. 349.
653. Ibid., pp. 354–8.
654. Ibid., pp. 364–71.
655. Pierce Egan, *Show Folks!* (1831), p. 45.
656. Thomas Hudson, *Hudson's Comic Songs* (*c*.1830), pp. 32–3; 'Black Legs. A gambler or sharper [cheat] on the turf or in the cock-pit,' Pierce Egan, *Grose's Classical Dictionary of the Vulgar Tongue* (1823).
657. Renton Nicholson, *Autobiography of a Fast Man* (1863) pp. 69–73.
658. *The Gamblers, A new Melo-Drama...New Surrey Theatre* (1824).
659. H.M. Milner, *The Hertfordshire Tragedy; or, The Victims of Gaming...Royal Coburg Theatre, On Monday, Jan. 12, 1824* (1824), p. 32.
660. *Report from the Select Committee on Dramatic Literature: With The Minutes of Evidence...2 August 1832*, Parliamentary Papers (1831–2) Vol. VII, Question 1270ff, pp. 79ff.
661. The author is probably Edward Ball.
662. James Catnach, *The Tread-Mill...A New Song Tom, Jerry, and Logic in the Tread-Mill* (1821).
663. *The Rambler's Magazine*, 1 January 1823.
664. Larpent 2322, Huntington Library, California.
665. William Thomas Moncrieff, *Tom and Jerry: or, Life in London in 1820. A Drama. In Three Acts. From Pierce Egan's celebrated work* (1826), p. 48.
666. *Rambler's Magazine and Man of Fashion's Companion*, 27 March[sic] 1822. The performance was on 15 July 1822.
667. Larpent 2331, Huntington Library, California.
668. W.T. Moncrieff, *Selection from the Dramatic Works of William T. Moncrieff* (1851) Vol. 3 pp. 113, 121–3.
669. Egan, *Life in London* (1820), p. 286n.

670. Egan, *Grose's Classical Dictionary of the Vulgar Tongue* (1823).
671. Egan, *Life in London* (1820), p. 290.
672. Ibid., p. 286.
673. 'Barnacles' is a 'flash' allusion to the (green) spectacles designated for Bob Logic (the Oxonian scholar's) costume in the Dramatis Personae. Egan, *Grose's Classical Dictionary of the Vulgar Tongue* (1823).
674. James Robertson, *A Collection of comic songs* (Peterborough: 1805), p. 3. See also Betrand H. Bronson, 'James Robertson, Poet and Playwright,' *Modern Language Notes* XLIX (1934), pp. 509–11.
675. 24 April 1822, Lewis Walpole Library, Farmington, Connecticut, Call no. 822. 4. 24. 1.
676. Larpent 2333, Huntington Library, California.
677. Martin Archer Shee, *Alasco: A Tragedy, in Five Acts...New-York Theatre* (New York: 1824), p. 16n.
678. Larpent 2334, Huntington Library, California.
679. Ibid.
680. Ibid.
681. William Thomas Moncrieff, *A Burletta of Fun, – Frolic, – and Flash, in Three Acts, Called Tom & Jerry, or, Life in London* (Boston, 1824); William Thomas Moncrieff, *The Spectre Bridegroom; or, A Ghost in Spite of Himself. A Farce* (New York, 1821).
682. William Thomas Moncrieff, *Tom and Jerry; or, Life in London; A Burletta...As Performed at the London, New York, Boston, and Philadelphia Theatres...And a Vocabulary of Cant and Flash* (Albany, NY, 1825); William Thomas Moncrieff, *Tom and Jerry; Or, Life in London: An Operatic Extravaganza* (1828), promptbooks, Harvard Theatre Collection.
683. *Confession of Charles French, an Irish youth, executed...for the murder of Edward Nowlan at the play-house, on the 4th of June 1828, where they had met to see the play of Tom & Jerry* (York, Canada: 1828), p. 4.
684. *Confession of Charles French, an Irish youth* (York, Canada: 1828), p. 4.
685. Ibid., p. 7.
686. Larpent 2328, Huntington Library, California.
687. BL Add Ms 42869.
688. Ibid.
689. *Confession of Charles French, an Irish youth* (York, Canada: 1828), p. 3.
690. Ibid., p. 3.
691. Ibid., p. 8.
692. *Awful calamity...Newcastle Theatre...at the performance of Tom & Jerry, or Life of London* (Glasgow, 1823).

Bibliography

Manuscripts

British Library

Add. Ms 27702; 27703; 27714; 27899; 27900; 29905; 33964; 42865; 42869; 42887.

Folger Shakespeare Library, Washington D.C.

Folger S. b.119; Folger PR 2950 B5 copy 2 Cage; Folger T. a. 5; Folger W. b. 496; Folger Y. d. 483 (12), (11), (10).

Huntington Library and Art Gallery, San Marino, California

Autograph Ms. insertion, William Henry Ireland, *Vortigern, An Historical Tragedy, in Five Acts* (1799), Call no. 124170.

Box 48/94.

Diaries of Anna Margaretta Larpent, Vol. 1 14 April 1794.

HM A1 247.

HM 19926, Vol. 2.

HM Ms 31428-30; 45657; 287179 Vol. 2.

Samuel Ireland, *Miscellaneous Papers And Legal instruments Under The Hand And Seal Of William Shakespeare: Including the Tragedy Of King Lear And A Small Fragment Of Hamlet, From The Original Mss. In The possession Of Samuel Ireland Of Norfolk Street* (1796).

Larpent Ms. 839, 886, 915, 933,1013,1110,1140,1301,1385,1413,1788,1966,1973, 2004, 2096, 2237, 2257, 2262, 2269, 2281, 2313, 2322, 2325, 2328, 2331, 2333, 2334, 2389.

Specimens of W.H. Ireland's Shakespearian Fabrications, call no. 287917.

Harvard Theatre Collection, Houghton Library, Harvard University

Ms. TS 953.7, 'Inventory Valuation of Property taken at the Theatre Royal Drury Lane Aug 1819.'

R.W. Elliston Papers, Vols 1, 2.

Public Record Office, Kew

P[ublic] R[ecord] O[ffice] H[ome] O[ffice] PRO HO 42/23; 42/193; 43/6; 44/1-2; 119/4.

PRO Lord Chamberlain 5/164.

PRO Treasury Solicitor 11/966.

Periodicals

The Acting Manager; or, The Minor Spy. A Weekly Review of the Public and Private Stage.

The Axe Laid to the Root, Or A Fatal Blow to Oppressors, Being an Address to the Planters and Negroes of the Island of Jamaica (1817).

Blackwood's Edinburgh Magazine.

The British Stage, and Literary Cabinet.

The Conjuror's Magazine, Or, Magical Physiognomical Mirror.

Freemasons' Magazine.

The General Magazine, and Impartial Review.

Keene's Theatrical Evening Mirror.

The London Alfred.

The Newgate Monthly Magazine, or Calendar of Men, Things and Opinions.

The Rambler's Magazine, or, Man of Fashion's Companion.

The Republican.

The Theatrical John Bull (Birmingham).

The Theatrical Looker-on (Birmingham).

The Thespian Magazine (1792), untraced.

The Times.

Primary Printed Sources

Account of the Proceedings Before His Majesty's Most Hon. Privy Council Upon the Petition For A Third Theatre in the Metropolis (1810).

Addison, John and William Thomas Moncrieff, *Dearest Ellen... Notturno* [The daylight has long been sunk]... *Adapted to the Air of the Copenhagen Waltz, etc.* (*c*.1815).

Addison, John, *Stranger! Pass not, welcome to my cot: A favourite song, sung by Mr. Gibbon, at Vauxhall Gardens* (1805).

Address of the Students at the New College to Dr. Priestly, in Consequence of the Birmingham Riots (1791).

Adolphus, John, *Memoirs of John Bannister, Comedian* (1839).

Adolphus, John, *Observations on the Vagrant Act, And Some Other Statutes, And on the Powers and Duties of Justices of the Piece* (1824).

Aldridge, Ira, *Memoir and Theatrical Career of Ira Aldridge, the African Roscius* (1850).

Angelo, Henry, *Reminiscences of Henry Angelo, With Memoirs of his Late Father and Friends* (1828).

An Authentic Account of the Riots in Birmingham, on the 14th, 15th, 16th, and 17th Days of July, 1791; Also, the Judge's Charge, the Pleadings of the Counsel, and the Substance of the Evidence Given on the Trials of the Rioters (Birmingham, 1791).

Awful calamity which happened at Newcastle Theatre on Wednesday last, the 19th February, 1823, at the performance of Tom & Jerry, or Life of London, when seven persons were crushed to death, and a great number severely bruised. The calamity was occasioned by an alarm of fire, when the whole of the audience rushed to the stair, and many were thrown down. Also, the names of the unfortunate sufferers (Glasgow, 1823).

Bailey, Citizen, *The White Devils Un-Cased. Being the First Discourse Upon Ecclesiastical Tyranny, and Superstition, Delivered at Section 2 and 7 of the Friends Of Liberty.... Lecture the Second* (1795).

Baker, David Erskine and Isaac Reed and Stephen Jones, *Biographica Dramatica* 3 vols. (1812) Vol. 2, with MS annotations, Huntington Library, California.

Baldwin, George, *Book of Dreams. 1811–1812–1813* (1813).

Ball, Edward, *The Treadmill, or Tom and Jerry at Brixton* (1821).

Bates, William and William Reeve, *Harlequin Mungo; or, A Peep into the Tower: A New Pantomimical Entertainment, in Two Acts: As Performing at the Royalty Theatre, Well-Street, Goodman's-Fields* (1787).

Bellamy, George Anne, *An apology for the life of George Ann Bellamy, late of Covent-Garden theatre: written by herself; to which is annexed her original letter to John Calcraft, advertised to be published in Oct. 1767, but which was then violently suppressed* (1785).

Bellamy, Thomas, *The Benevolent Planters: A Dramatic Piece, As Performed at the Theatre Royal, Haymarket* (1789).

Beuler, Jacob, *Comic Originals! Beuler's Collection of Original Comic Songs! And Comic and Serious Parodies on Popular and Well-Known Songs* (c.1820).

Beuler, Jacob, *Comic Songs to Popular Tunes ... Second Collection* (1823).

Beuler, Jacob, *Comic Songs to Popular Tunes ... Ninth Collection* (1833).

Bevis, John, *An experimental enquiry concerning the contents, qualities, and medicinal virtues, of the two mineral waters: lately discovered at Bagnigge Wells, near London* (1760).

Biographical Dictionary of 300 Contemporary Public Characters, British & foreign of all Ranks & Professions (1825).

Bonnor, Charles, *Facts Relating to the Meeting, Held on Wednesday, the 15th of February, at the London Tavern, Respecting the Later Delivery of Letters; and an Explanation of some Circumstances that have led to a Difference between the Comptroller General and his Deputy* (1792).

Bonnor, Charles *A Letter to Philip Thickness, Esq ... To Which is Added, Mr. Thicknesse's Answer* (1792).

Brown, Charles Armitage, *Narensky: or, The road to Yaroslaf, a new serio-comic opera, in three acts, as performed at the Theatre Royal, Drury-Lane / by Mr. Charles Brown, the music composed by Mr. [John] Braham and Mr. [William] Reeve, the overture by Mr. Reeve* (1814).

Britton, John, *Sheridan and Kotzebue. The Enterprising Adventures of Pizarro ... Also Varieties and Oppositions of Criticisms on The Play of Pizarro ... The Whole Forming a Comprehensive Account of those Plays and the Grand Ballads of Cora, – and Rolla and Cora, At the Royal Circus, and Royal Amphitheatre* (1799).

Burney, Charles, *The Songs in Queen Mab: As they are perform'd at the Theatre Royal in Drury Lane compos'd by the Society of the Temple of Apollo* (1751).

Busby, Thomas, *The overture[,] marches, dances, symphonies, and song in the melo drame, called A tale of mystery: Now performing with universal applause at the Theatre Royal, Covent Garden entirely new, composed by Dr. Busby* (1802).

Busby, Thomas and Ann Maria Porter, *Overture; Strike the Gombay; A Duett; Why truly Sir: The Favorite Trio* (1803).

Carlile, Richard, *The Life of Swing, the Kent Rick-Burner. Written by Himself* (1830).

A Catalogue of the Books, Paintings, Miniatures, Drawings, Prints, and Various Curiosities, the Property of the Late Samuel Ireland ... Which will be Sold by Auction by Leigh, Sotheby and Son ... May 7, 1801 (1801).

Catnach, James, *The Tread-Mill ... A New Song Tom, Jerry, and Logic in the Tread-Mill* (1821).

Caulfield, James, *Calcographiana the Printseller's Guide to the Knowledge & Value of Engraved British Portraits* (1814).

The Children of Apollo: A Poem. Containing an impartial Review of the all the Dramatic Works of our Modern Authors and Authoresses. Particularly Lady Wallace. Margravine of Anspach. Honourable Major North. Honourable John St. John. (c.1794).

The Choice of Harlequin; or, The Indian Chief. A Pantomimical Entertainment ... Covent Garden (1780).

Cobb, James, *The Overture Favorite Songs & Finale in the Musical Entertainment of Tippoo Saib as performed with universal applause at the Sadler's Wells Theatre the Words by Mr. Lonsdale the Music Composed by W. Reeve* (c.1792).

Cobb, James, *Songs, Duets, Trios, and Finales in Ramah Droog, Or, Wine Does Wonders; A Comic Opera in Three Acts. As Performed at the Theatre-Royal, Covent-Garden* (1798).

Collier, John Payne, *An Old Man's Diary, Forty Years Ago; For The First Six Months Of 1832* (London: Thomas Richards 1871).

Colman the Younger, George, *Inkle and Yarico An Opera ... Hay-Market* (1787).

Colman the Younger, George, *The Review; or, The Wags of Windsor. A Musical Farce* (1800).

Colman the Younger, George, *XYZ: A Comedy. In Two Acts ... The Theatre Royal*[sic] (1820).

Confession of Charles French, An Irish youth, executed ... for the murder of Edward Nowlan at the play-house, on the 4th of June 1828, where they had met to see the play of Tom & Jerry (York, Canada: 1828).

The Corinthian Parodies, by Tom, Jerry and Logic, Illustrative of Life in London (c.1824).

A Correspondence Between the Rev. Robert Wells, M.A. Chaplain of the Earl of Dunmore, and A Gentleman Under the Signature of Publicola, Relative to the Riots at Birmingham, and the Commemoration of the French Revolution (1791).

The Covent Garden Journal (1810).

Crockery's Misfortunes; or, Transmogrifications. A Burletta, In One Act. Performed for the First Time, on Monday, July 11th, 1821, at the Royal Cobourg Theatre (1821).

Cross, John Cartwright, *The Eclipse, or, Harlequin in China* (1801).

Cross, John Cartwright, *Songs, Chorusses, &c. In King Caesar; or, the Negro Slaves: A New Grand Spectacle, In Two Parts Performed at the New Royal Circus, for the first Time, On Wednesday, September 16, 1801* (1801).

Cross, John Cartwright, *Songs, Duets, Trios, Chorusses, &c. in the New, Grand, Serio-Comic Pantomime, Called the Golden Farmer; or, Harlequin Ploughboy: Performed at the New Royal Circus, For the first Time on Monday, June 28, 1802* (1802).

Cross, John Cartwright, *The Way to get Un-Married. A Dramatic Sketch ... Covent Garden* (1796).

Crowquill, Caleb [pseud.], *The New Patent, or Theatrical Secrets Worth Knowing, In a Series of Familiar Epistles, Addressed to H—— H—— Esq. of the United Theatres of Great Britain & Ireland, Patentee, &c.* (Dublin, 1822).

Davy, John, *The Favorite Pas Seul ... in the Vale of Mystery ... by Dr. Busby, arranged as a Rondo with Variations for the Pianoforte* (1802).

Davy, John, *Merrily danced the Quaker's Wife, Scottish dance ... for the Pianoforte* (1804).

Davy, John, *The Overture and Music in the blind Boy, a Grand Melodrama* (1808).

Dibdin, Charles, *The Mirror; Or Harlequin Every-Where. A Pantomimical Burletta, in Three Parts. As it is performed at the Theatre-Royal in Covent Garden* (1779).

Dibdin, Charles Isaac Mungo, *Life in London; or, The Larks of Logic, Tom, and Jerry, An Extravaganza, in Three Acts, ... as performed at the Olympic Theatre ... Second Edition* (1822).

Dibdin, Charles Isaac Mungo, *Professional and Literary Memoirs of Charles Dibdin the Younger, Dramatist and Upward of Thirty Years Manager of Minor Theatres* (ed.) George Speaight (London: The Society for Theatre Research, 1956).

Dibdin, Charles Isaac Mungo, *Songs, and Other Vocal Compositions, In the Pantomime, Called Jan Ben Jan; Or, Harlequin and the Forty Virgins. Performing at the Aquatic Theatre, Sadler's Wells* (1807).

Dibdin, Thomas John, *Don Giovanni; or, A Spectre on Horseback! A Comic, Heroic, Operatic, Tragic, Pantomimic, Burletta-Spectacular Extravaganza; in Two Acts; As Performed at the Royal Circus and Surrey Theatre ... The Action and Dances under the Direction of Mr. Bologna and Mr. Giroux* (1817).

Dibdin, Thomas John, *Don Giovanni; Or, A Spectre on Horseback! A Comic, heroic, operatic, tragic, pantomimic, Burletta-spectacular extravaganza; in Two Acts* (New York, 1818).

Dibdin, Thomas John, *The New Pantomime of Harlequin and Fortunio; or Shing-Moo and Thun-Ton, With a Sketch of the Story: As First Performed at the Theatre-Royal, Covent-Garden, Tuesday, December 26th, 1815* (1815).

Dibdin, Thomas John, *The Reminiscences of Thomas Dibdin* (1837) 2 vols.

Dibdin, Thomas John, *Songs, Chorusses, &c. In the New Pantomime of Harlequin's Tour; Or, The Dominion of Fancy. As Performed at the Theatre-Royal, Covent-Garden. With entire new Music, Scenery, Dresses, &c* (1800).

Dickens, Charles, *Our Mutual Friend* (1864).

Dimond, William, *The Sea-Side Story, An Operatic Drama, in Two Acts; As now Performing at the Theatre Royal, Covent Garden, With the Most General and Distinguished Applause* (1801).

Dixon, Joseph, *A Hymn on depositing the Colours of the Loyal Hampstead Association on Friday the 18th of June 1802 in Hampstead Church ... The words by the Revd Joseph Dixon ... Sung by Mr Incledon* (1802).

Donaldson, Walter, *Recollections of an Actor* (London: John Maxwell and Company, 1865).

Don Juan: or, The libertine destroyed, a grand pantomimical ballet ... first performed at the Theatre Royal, Drury Lane, on Tuesday, the 26th of October 1790 (1790).

The Dramatic Scorpion. A Satire, in Three Cantos, with Explanatory Notes (1818).

John Duncombe's Edition. Memoirs of the Life, Public and Private Adventures, of Madame Vestris ... With Interesting & Curious Anecdotes of Celebrated and Distinguished Characters in the Fashionable World (1836).

Ebers, John, *Seven Years of the King's Theatre* (1828).

Egan, Pierce, *Book of Sports, and Mirror of Life: Embracing the Turf, The Chase, The Ring, and The Stage* (1832).

Egan, Pierce, *Grose's Classical Dictionary of the Vulgar Tongue, Revised and Corrected with the Addition of Numerous Slang Phrases Collected from Tried Authorities* (1823).

Egan, Pierce, *Key to the Picture of the Fancy Going to A Fight at Moulsey-Hurst* (1819).

Egan, Pierce, *The Life and Extraordinary Adventures of Samuel Denmore Hayward, Denominated the Modern Macheath, who Suffered at the Old Bailey, on Tuesday, November 27, 1821, for the Crime of Burglary* (1822).

Egan, Pierce, *Life in London; or, the Day and night scenes of Jerry Hawthorn* (1820).

Egan, Pierce, *Show Folks!* (1831).

Elliston, Robert William, *Copy of a Memorial Presented to the Lord Chamberlain, by the Committee of Management of the Theatre-Royal Drury-Lane, Against the Olympic and Sans Pareil Theatres; with Copies of Two Letters, in Reply to the Contents of Such Memorial, Addressed to the Lord Chamberlain* (1818).

Elliston, Robert William, *Mr. Greville and Mr. Elliston's Plan of a British Winter Opera* (c.1811).

Elliston, Robert William, *Private Subscription Theatre...On the South side of Oxford Street, East of Hanover Square...25 April 1811* (1811).

The English Metropolis: Or, London in the Year 1820 (1820).

The Fatal Effects of Gambling Exemplified in the Murder of Wm. Weare, and the Trial and Fate of John Thurtell, The Murderer...to which is added, The Gambler's Scourge; a Complete Exposé of the Whole System of Gambling in the Metropolis; With Memoirs and Anecdotes of Notorious Blacklegs (1824).

Fennell, James, *An Apology for the Life of James Fennell* (1814).

The first report of the society established in London for the suppression of mendicity (1819).

Foote, Horace, *A Companion to the Theatres; and Manual of The British Drama* (1829).

Franklin, Andrew, *A Trip to the Nore. A Musical Entertainment, In One Act. As Performed by their Majesty's Servants at the Theatre-Royal, Drury-Lane* (1797).

Galt, John, *The New British Theatre; A Selection of original drama, not yet acted; some of which have been offered for representation but not accepted* (1814).

The Gamblers, A new Melo-Drama, in Two Acts, of Peculiar Interest, As Performed for the 1st and 2nd Times November 17 & 18, 1823, Suppressed by Order of the Court of King's Bench, Re-Performed for the 3rd Time, Monday, January 12, 1824, at the New Surrey Theatre (1824).

Garrick, David, *Harlequin's Invasion* (1759).

George Barnwell. The Comic Phiz, &c. Anthony Brown. Fair Young Phoebe (Edinburgh, c.1820).

Gluck, Christoph Willibald, *Il Convitato di Pietra. Grand Ballet...adapted for the Harpsichord, Piano Forte, Violin & Flute, by F. H. Barthélémon* (1785).

Gooch, Mrs Villa-Real, *The Beggar Boy: A Novel...by the Late Mr. Thomas Bellamy. To which are prefixed Biographical Particulars of the Author* (1801).

Greenwood, Thomas, *The Death of Life in London; or Tom & Jerry's Funeral. An Entirely New Satirical, Burlesque, Operative Parody, in One Act...Royal Coburg Theatre, 2 June 1823* (1823).

Greville, Henry Francis, *Mr. Greville's Statement Of Mr. Naldi's Case* (1811).

Grey, Oliver, *An Apology for the Servants...Occasioned by the Representation of the Farce called* High Life Below Stairs, *and by what has been said to their Disadvantage in the* Public Papers (1760).

Hardcastle, Ephraim [pseud. W.H. Pyne], *Wine and Walnuts; or, After Dinner Chit-Chat* (1823).

Harlequin Incendiary: Or, Columbine Cameron. A Musical Pantomime...Theatre-Royal in Drury-Lane (1746).

Harlequin Student: Or, The Fall of Pantomime, with the Restoration of the Drama; An Entertainment as it is now performing...At the late Theatre in Goodman's Fields (1741).

Hazlitt, William, *A View of the English Stage; or A Series of Dramatic Criticisms* (1818).

Hogarth's Works. A Catalogue of the Most Complete Collection of Hogarth's Works, Ever Offered to the Public, the Property of a Gentleman, Well Known as a Collector of that Master's Productions...Which...Will be Sold by Auction by Messrs. Christie, Sharp, And Harper...On Saturday, May 6th, 1797 (1797).

Hogarth's Works. A Catalogue of Prints, Comprising, A Selection of the Scarcest, and Most Valuable Works of Hogarth...Which will be Sold by Auction, by Mr. King...On Saturday, April 21, 1798 (1798).

Holbrook, Ann Catherine *The Dramatist; or, Memoirs of the Stage. With the Life of the Authoress, Prefixed, and Interspersed with, A Variety of Anecdotes, Humourous[sic] and Pathetic* (Birmingham, 1809).

Holcroft, Thomas, *Duplicity: A Comedy...Covent-Garden* (1781).

Holcroft, Thomas, *Seduction: A Comedy...Drury Lane* (1787).

Holcroft, Thomas, *The School for Arrogance: A Comedy...Covent-Garden* (1791).

Holcroft, Thomas, *A Tale of Mystery: A Melodrama, In Two Acts* (1826).

Holman, Joseph George, *Abroad and at Home. A Comic Opera...Covent-Garden* (1796).

Hudson, Thomas, *Hudson's Comic Songs* (c.1830).

Humphreys, R., *The Memoirs Of J. Decastro, Comedian...Accompanied by an Analysis of the Life of the Late Philip Astley, Esq....Also an Accompanying History of the Royal Circus, now the Surrey Theatre* (1824).

Hurly-Burly; or, The Fairy of the Well (1788).

Hutton, Catherine, *The Life of William Hutton, F.A.S.S. Including a Particular Account of the Riots at Birmingham in 1791* (1817).

Ireland, William Henry, *An Anthem on the Lamented Death of her Royal Highness The Princess Charlotte* (1817).

Ireland, William Henry, *Chalcographimania; or, the Portrait-Collector and Print-seller's Chronicle* (1814).

Ireland, William Henry, *The Confessions of William Henry Ireland. Containing the Particulars of his Fabrication of the Shakespeare Manuscripts* (1805).

Ireland, William Henry, *The Cyprian of St. Stephen's, or Princely Protection Illustrated; in a Poetical Flight to the Pierian Spring* (Bath, 1809).

Ireland, William Henry, *Death-Bed Confessions of the Late Countess of Guernsey, to Lady Anne H——; Developing a Series of Mysterious Transactions Connected with the Most Illustrious Personages in the Kingdom; to which are Added The Q——'s last Letter to the K—— ...And Other Authentic Documents Never Before Published* (1821).

Ireland, William Henry, *The Death of Bonaparte, Or, One Pound One. A Poem in Four Cantos* (York, 1812).

Ireland, William Henry, *Gaieté de Paris, by George Cruikshank, or the Rambles of an English Party Through the French Metropolis* (1825).

Ireland, William Henry, *The Hundred Days of Napoleon Bonaparte, Including Memoirs Of Talleyrand, Fouché, and also of Maubreuil* (1827).

Ireland, William Henry, *The Last Will and Testament of Napoleon Bonaparte...As Written with his Own Hand, and Proved in the Prerogative-Court, Doctors'*

Commons : With a Prefatory Address and Copious Notes, Explanatory of Many Interesting Points Adverted to in this Singularly Curious Document (1821).

Ireland, William Henry, *The Life of Napoleon Bonaparte* (1828).

Ireland, William Henry, *The Napoleon Anecdotes: Illustrating the Mental Energies of The Late Emperor of France* (1823).

Ireland, William Henry, *Something Concerning Nobody, Embellished with Fourteen Characteristic Etchings* (1814).

Ireland, William Henry, *Vortigern, an Historical Tragedy, in Five Acts* (1799).

Jackman, Isaac, *Royal and Royalty Theatres. Letter to Phillips Glover, Esq of Wispington, In Lincolnshire; in a Dedication to the Burletta of Hero and Leander, now performing . . . at the Royalty Theatre, in Goodman's Fields* (1787).

Jackson, John, *The History of the Scottish Stage, from its First Establishment to the Present Time; With a Distinct Narrative of Some Recent Theatrical Transactions* (Edinburgh, 1793).

Jenkins, Richard, *Memoirs of the Bristol Stage, from the Period of the Theatre at Jacob's Well, Down to the Present Time; with Notices, Biographical and Critical, of some of the Most Celebrated Comedians who have Appeared on its Boards* (Bristol: 1826).

The Joys of Kilfane. Together with George Barnwell (Dublin, c.1820).

Kenney, James, *The Blind Boy: A Melo-Drama* (1808).

Kenney, James, *A Description of The Blind Boy: A New Grand Historic Melo-Drama* (1807).

Knight, Thomas, *The Turnpike Gate; A Musical Entertainment . . . Covent-Garden Second Edition* (1799).

Laurent, Jean-Baptiste and Mr Male, *British Heroes: Or the Defeat of Junot!* (1808).

Law, James Thomas, *The Poor Man's Garden: Or, A Few Brief Rules for Regulating Allotments of land to the Poor, for Potatoe Gardens, with remarks, addressed to Mr. Malthus, Mr. Sadler, and the Political Economists: And a reference to the opinions of Dr. Adam Smith in 'Wealth of Nations'* (1830).

Lee, Henry, *Caleb Quotem and his Wife! or Paint, Poetry, and Putty!, An Opera, In Three Acts. To which is added a Postscript, including the Scene always play'd in the Review, or Wags of Windsor, but Omitted in the Edition lately published by G. Colman, Esq.* (1809).

Lee, Henry, *The Manager. A Melo-Dramatic Tale* (1822).

Lee, William, *The Plan of the Boxes at the King's Theatre, Haymarket, with an Alphabetical List of the Subscribers, For the Season[s] of 1803[1804, 1805, 1807]* (1803, 1804, 1805, 1807).

A Letter from Timothy Sobersides, Extinguisher-Maker, At Wolverhampton, To Jonathan Blast, Bellows-Maker, At Birmingham (1792).

A Letter to a Member of Parliament on the impropriety of classing Players with Rogues and Vagabonds in the Vagrant Act. By the Author of 'The Vagrant Act in relation to the Liberty of the Subject.' (1824).

Letter To The Right Hon. Robert Peel, Respecting The Proposed Introduction of a Bill . . . To Repeal . . . The act Of 10th Geo.II.Cap.28 . . . Showing that the Consequence of such an Act Would be, to Confirm the Monopoly Claimed by the Proprietors of Drury Lane and Covent Garden, and to Enable Them to Annihilate the Minor Theatres (1829).

Lewis, Mathew Gregory, *The Castle Spectre: A Drama. In Five Acts. First performed at the Theatre Royal, Drury-Lane, on Thursday, December 14, 1797* (1798).

Lewis, Mathew Gregory, *Crazy Jane, a Ballad. Sung by Mrs. Mountain . . . The Words by M. G. Lewis, etc.* (1799).

Lyddal, David, *The Prompter, or Elementary Hints to Young Actors. A Didactic Poem. To which are Prefixed, Strictures on Theatrical Education, and A Prologue* (Dublin, 1810).

Mathews, Anne, *Memoirs of Charles Mathews, Comedian* (1838) 2 Vols.

The London Mathews; Containing An Account of this celebrated Comedian's Trip to America ... To Which are Prefixed, Several Original Comic Songs, Viz. Travellers all ... Mrs. Bradish's Boarding-House. Opossum up a Gum-Tree. Militia Muster Folk. Boston Post-Office. Ode to General Jackson. Illinois Inventory. The American Jester's Song. And the Farewell Finale (1825).

Macarthy, Eugene, *A Letter to the King, on the Question now at Issue Between the 'Major,' and 'Minor' Theatres* (1832).

Macauley, Elizabeth, *Facts Against Falsehood! Being a Brief Statement of Miss Macauley's Engagements at the Winter Theatres; The Subterfuges by Which She has been Driven from the Regular Exercise of her Profession, and Withheld from at Least Two Thirds of the Public of this Metropolis* (1824).

Malcolm, James Peller, *Anecdotes of the Manners and Customs of London During the Eighteenth-Century ... With a Review of the State of Society in 1807* 2 Vols. (1810).

Meadows, Thomas, *Thespian Gleanings, A Collection of Comic Recitals, Songs, Tales, &c.* (1805).

Memoirs of the Life of Madame Vestris ... Illustrated with Numerous Curious Anecdotes (1830).

Mendoza, Daniel, *Memoirs of the life of D. Mendoza. To Which are Added, Observations on the Art of Pugilism* (1816).

Merry, Robert and Charles Bonnor, *Airs, Duetts, and Chorusses, Arrangment of Scenery, and Sketch of the Pantomime Entitled the Picture of Paris. Taken in the Year 1790* (1790).

Merry, Robert, *The Airs, Duets, Glees, Chorusses, &c. in the Comic Opera of the Magician No Conjurer* (1792).

Merry, Robert, *The Wounded Soldier, a Poem* (1795).

Milner, H.M., *Masaniello, The Fisherman of Naples; A Historical Drama, In Three Acts ... Royal Coburg Theatre* (1825).

Milner, H.M., *The Hertfordshire Tragedy; or, The Victims of Gaming. A Serious Drama. In Two Acts. (Founded upon Recent Melancholy Facts) as First Performed at the Royal Coburg Theatre, On Monday, Jan. 12, 1824* (1824).

Milner, H.M., *Songs, Chorusses, Duets, Parodies &c in Giovanni in Paris. An Operatic Burletta Extravaganza; In Two Acts, First Performed at the East London Theatre, Wednesday, November 29th, 1820* (1820).

Mitchell, R., *Mathews's Trip to Paris; or, the Dramatic Tourist; ... and Delivered by him at the English Opera House ... Taken in Short-hand, and Dedicated to Dandy Cockney, Esq* (1819).

Moncrieff, William Thomas, *A Burletta of Fun, – Frolic, – and Flash, in Three Acts, Called Tom & Jerry, or, Life in London. Performed with unbounded applause in London, New York, Philadelphia and Boston* (Boston, 1824).

Moncrieff, William Thomas, *The Spectre Bridegroom; or, A Ghost in Spite of Himself. A Farce* (New York, 1821).

Moncrieff, William Thomas, *Giovanni In London: Or The Libertine Reclaimed, A Grand Moral, Satirical, Comical, Tragical, Melo-Dramatical, Pantomimical, Critical, Infernal, Terrestrial, Celestial, in one word for all, Gallymaufrical-ollapodridacal Operatic Extravaganza, In Two Acts, As Performed at the Theatres Royal Drury Lane And Covent Garden* (1825).

Moncrieff, William Thomas, *Shakespeare's Festival; or, A New Comedy of Errors!* (1830).

Moncrieff, William Thomas, *Songs, Duets, Chorusses, &c. Serious and Comick, as Sung in the Highly Popular . . . Entertainment, in Two Acts, Yclept Giovanni in London* (c.1817).

Moncrieff, William Thomas, *Songs, Duets, and Glees: Sung . . . at the Royal Gardens, Vauxhall* (1827).

Moncrieff, William Thomas, *Songs, Duets, Trios, Chorusses, &c. &c. in Actors al fresco, or, The play in the pleasure grounds (an occasional vaudeville,) first produced at the Royal Gardens, Vauxhall, 4th June, 1827* (1827).

Moncrieff, William Thomas, *Songs of the Gypsies: To which is Prefixed an Historical Introduction on the Origin and Customs of this Singular and Interesting People . . . with music by S. Nelson* (1832).

Moncrieff, William Thomas, *Songs, Duets, Chorusses &c.&c &c. Sung in the New Comic Operatic Melo-Dramatic Pantomimic Moral Satirical Gallymaufrical Parodiacal Salmagundical Olla Podriadacal Extravaganza Bizarro Entertainment . . . Yclept Giovanni in the Country; or, the Rake Husband: as performed at the Royal Coburg Theatre* (1820).

Moncrieff, William Thomas, *An original collection of Songs, sung at the Theatres Royal, etc* (1850).

Moncrieff, William Thomas, *Tom And Jerry: Or, Life In London In 1820. A Drama in Three Acts. From Pierce Egan's Celebrated Work* (1825).

Moncrieff, William Thomas, *Tom and Jerry; Or, Life in London: An Operatic Extravaganza* (1828), promptbook, Harvard Theatre Collection.

Moncrieff, William Thomas, *Van Dieman's Land* (1830).

Morris, James, *Recollections of Ayr Theatricals from 1809* (Ayr, Advertiser Office, 1872).

Murphy, Arthur, *The Apprentice. A farce, in two acts . . . Perform'd at the Theatre-Royal, in Drury-Lane* (1756).

Naval Officer, A, *John Duncombe's Edition. Memoirs of the Life, Public and Private Adventures, of Madame Vestris . . . With Interesting & Curious Anecdotes of Celebrated and Distinguished Characters in the Fashionable World* (1836).

Nott, John, Button Burnisher [psued], *Very Familiar Letters, Addressed to Dr. Priestley, In Answer to his Familiar Letters to the Inhabitants of Birmingham. Earnestly recommended to the serious Attention of my fellow Labourers and fellow Townsmen, the honest, well meaning, and industrious Mechanics and Manufacturers of the Town of Birmingham* (1790).

The number of little Theatres already opened . . . having greatly injured the Theatres Royal . . . (c.1808–10).

O'Hara, Kane, *Midas; An English Burletta* (1764).

O'Keefe, John, *Recollections of the Life of John O'Keefe* (1826) Vol. 1.

O'Keefe, John, *Songs, Duets, &c. in the New Pantomime Called Lord Mayor's Day; Or, A Flight from Lapland. As Performed at the Theatre-Royal, in Covent-Garden* (1783).

Oulton, Walley Chamberlain, *The History of the Theatres of London . . . From the Year 1771 to 1795* (1796) 2 vols.

Oulton, Walley Chamberlain, *Precious Relics; Or The Tragedy of Vortigern Rehearsed. A Dramatic Piece. In Two Acts. Written in Imitation of The Critic . . . Drury-Lane* (1796).

Pack, James, *Some Account of the Life and Experience of James Pack, Late a Celebrated Actor...But Now, By the Grace of God, A Disciple and Follower of the Lord Jesus Christ* (1819).

Parr, Samuel, *A Letter From Irenopolis to the Inhabitants of Eleutheropolis; Or, A Serious Address to the Dissenters of Birmingham* (Birmingham, 1792).

Peake, Richard Brinsley, *Presumption! Or, the Fate of Frankenstein* (1823).

Pegge, Samuel, *Anecdotes of the English Language: Chiefly Regarding the Local Dialect of London and its Environs* (1803).

Percival, John, *A Few Observations in Defence of the Scenic Exhibitions at the Royalty Theatre, and on the Intolerant Censure of the Drama in General; Contained in the 'Solemn Protest' of the Rev. Tho. Thirlwall, M.A.* (1804).

Poole, John, *Hamlet-Travestie* (1810).

Poole, John, *Othello-Travestie: In Three Acts. With Burlesque Notes, In the Manner of the Most Celebrated Commentators; and Other Curious Appendices* (1813).

Powell, James, *The Venetian Outlaw, his Country's Friend. A Drama...Drury-Lane...Altered from the French of A. Pixiricourt* (1805).

Pantomimic Preludio, And...Paris Federation (1790).

Particulars and Conditions of Sale of the Olympic Theatre...13th June, 1820 (1820).

Pretty Peggy of Derby (*c*.1800).

Priestley, Joseph, *Dr. Priestley's Letter to the Inhabitants of Birmingham: Mr. Keri's Vindication of the Revolution Dinner: And Mr. Russell's Account of Proceedings Relating to it, with the Toasts, & c.* (1791).

Proud, J., *A Candid and Impartial Reply to the Rev. Dr. Priestley's Letters, Addressed by him to the Members of the New Jerusalem* (Birmingham, 1791).

Prynne, Peregrine [psued.], *Histriomastix, or, the Untrussing of the Drury Lane Squad* (1819).

Rede, Leman Thomas, *The Road to the Stage; or, the Performer's Preceptor. Containing Clear and Ample Instructions for Obtaining Theatrical Engagements; With a List of all the Provincial Theatres, the Names of the Managers and all Particulars as to Their Circuits, Salaries, &c. With A Description of the Things Necessary on an Outset in the Profession, Where to Obtain them, and a Complete Explanation of all the Technicalities of the Histrionic Art!* (1827, 1836 revised).

Remarks on the Cause of the Dispute Between the Public and Managers of the Theatre Royal, Covent Garden, With a Circumstantial Account of the Week's Performances and the Uproar (1809).

Report of a Case, The Reverend Robert Gilbert versus Sir. M. M. Sykes, Bart, M.P. tried at the York Lent Assizes, 1812...Being an Action brought by the Plaintiff to recover a Sum of Money won on the life of Bonaparte (York, 1812).

Report from the Select Committee on Dramatic Literature: With the Minutes of Evidence...2 August 1832, *Parliamentary Papers* (1831–2) Vol. VII.

The Report of the Trials of the Rioters, At the Assizes Held at Warwick, August 20, 1791 (Birmingham, 1791).

Reeves, William, and William Barrymore, *Songs, Chorusses &c in the New Comic, Melo-Dramatic, Hippodrame Entitled Giovanni in the Country; or, A Gallop to Gretna Green as performed at Astley's Royal Amphitheatre* (1820).

Reynolds, Frederick, *Laugh When You Can: A Comedy...Covent-Garden* (1799).

Reynolds, Frederick, *The Life and Times of Frederick Reynolds* 2nd edition (1827) 2 Vols.

Reynolds, John Hamilton, *One, Two, Three, Four, Five; by Advertisement: a musical entertainment, In One Act* (1829).

Rhodes, William Barnes, *Bombastes Furioso; A Burlesque Tragic Opera...Haymarket, August 7, 1810* (1822).

Robertson, James, *A Collection of comic songs, written, Compil'd, Etch'd and Engrav'd, by J. Robertson; and sung by him At the theatres Nottingham, Derby, Stamford, Halifax, Chesterfield, and Redford* (Peterborough, 1805).

Robinson Crusoe; Or, Harlequin Friday. A Grand Pantomime, in Two Acts, as performed at the Theatre-Royal, Newcastle-upon-Tyne, in 1791 (Newcastle, 1791).

Rules and Regulations for the Lambs Conduit Private Theatre (1799).

Second Edition, Duncombe's Edition...Mr. Mathews's Memorandum-Book, of Peculiarities, Character, and Manners, Collected by him in his various Trips (1825).

Shee, Martin Archer, *Alasco: A Tragedy, in Five Acts...Excluded from the English Stage by the Authority of the Lord Chamberlain, Performed, for the first time, at the New-York Theatre, on Thursday evening, Dec. 16, 1824* (New York: 1824).

Siddons, Henry, *Practical Illustrations of Rhetorical Gesture and Action, Adapted to the English Drama* (1807).

Soane, George, *Masaniello: The Fisherman of Naples, An Historical Play* (1825).

Society for the Suppression of Mendicity, established in London, March 25th, 1818: supported by voluntary contributions (1819).

Somerset, C.A., *Shakespeare's Early Days: An Historical Play, In Two Acts* (1829).

Song's Chorusses, &c. in the Musical Afterpiece, called Garrick's Jubilee...and now Revived...at the Theatre-Royal, Covent-Garden, 23rd of April, 1816 (1816).

The Songs, Parodies, &c. Introduced in the New Pedestrian, Equestrian, Extravaganza, and Operatic Burletta, In Three Acts of Gaiety, Frisk, Lark, and Patter, called, Tom and Jerry; or, Life in London...Monday, April 8, 1822 (1822).

Songs, Trios, Duetts and Chorusses in the Comic Opera of Summer Amusement; or, an Adventure at Margate. As it is performed at the Theatre-Royal, in the Hay-Market (1781).

The Songster's Delight: Being a Choice Collection of Songs. Containing, My Nannie O. Bonny Jean of Aberdeen. The Dutchess of Newcastle's lamentation. The London merchant (1805).

The Sportsman's Companion...a Choice Collection of favorite Songs. Now Singing by all the Gentlemen of the Whip, at Clubs, and Convivial Society's (c.1820).

A Statement of the Differences Subsisting Between the Proprietors and Performers of the Theatre-Royal, Covent-Garden. Given in the Correspondence Which has Passed between them (1800).

Stearns, Samuel, *The Mystery of Animal Magnetism Revealed to the World* (1791).

Stuart, Charles, *The Irishman in Spain. A Farce. In One Act. Taken from the Spanish* (1791).

Stuart, Charles and A.J. Parks, *Variety Stage: A History of the Music Halls from the Earliest Period to the Present Time* (1895).

Thicknesse, Philip, *A Letter To Charles Bonner, Esq...Deputy Comptroller of the Post-Office* (1792).

Thirlwall, Thomas, *Royalty Theatre. A Solemn Protest Against the Revival of Scenic Exhibitions and Interludes, at the Royalty Theatre; Containing Remarks on Pizarro, the Stranger, and John Bull; with a Postscript* (1803).

Timmins, Samuel, *Dr. Priestley's Laboratory, 1791 [reprinted from the 'Birmingham Post,' March, 15, 22, 29, and April 5, 1890]* (Coventry, c.1890).

Tom and Jerry; or Life in London: An entirely new Whimsical, Local, Melo-Dramatic, Pantomimical Equestrian Drama, in Three Acts...as Performed at Davis's Royal Amphitheatre (1822).

Tom and Jerry, Or Life in London; A Musical Extravaganza. With Remarks (Edinburgh, 1824).

Townley, James, *High Life Below Stairs. A farce of two acts. As it is performed at the Theatre-Royal in Drury-Lane* (1759).

Tree of Liberty (1795).

Trials of the Birmingham Rioters (1792).

Truth and Treason! Or a Narrative of the Royal Procession to the House of Peers, October the 29th, 1795. To Which is Added, an Account of the Martial Procession to Covent-Garden Theatre, on the Evening of the 30th (1795).

Tyranny Triumphant! ... Remarks on the Famous Cartel Lately Agreed on by the Masters of the Two Theatres (1743).

Views of the Ruins of the Principal Houses Destroyed During the Riots at Birmingham (1791).

The Virtuous Maid of the Inn; or the Entertaining History of Margaret Sunders[sic], commonly called Pretty Peggy of Derby ... To which is added, a Collection of the Most Choice Songs (1791).

Winston, James, *The Theatric Tourist ... Replete with Useful and Necessary Information to Theatrical Professors, Whereby they may Learn How to Chuse and Regulate their Country Engagements* (1805).

The Wisdom of our Modern Dissenters, Analyzed in the Crucible of Reason, By a Chemical Member of the Church of England (1792).

Index